AMERICAN PLACES

AMERICAN

PLACES

Encounters with History

A Celebration of Sheldon Meyer

Edited by

William E. Leuchtenburg

OXFORD
UNIVERSITY PRESS

2000

OXFORD

UNIVERSITY PRESS

Oxford   New York

Athens   Auckland   Bangkok   Bogotá   Buenos Aires   Calcutta
Cape Town   Chennai   Dar es Salaam   Delhi   Florence   Hong Kong   Istanbul
Karachi   Kuala Lumpur   Madrid   Melbourne   Mexico City   Mumbai
Nairobi   Paris   São Paulo   Shanghai   Singapore   Taipei   Tokyo   Toronto   Warsaw

and associated companies in
Berlin   Ibadan

Copyright © 2000 by Oxford University Press, Inc.

Published by Oxford University Press, Inc.
198 Madison Avenue, New York, New York 10016

Library of Congress Cataloging-in-Publication Data
is available
ISBN 0-19-513026-x

1 3 5 7 9 8 6 4 2

Printed in the United States of America
on acid-free paper

Contents

PREFACE   ix
   William E. Leuchtenburg

TAKING PLACE   xvii
   Peter Ginna

CYBERSPACE, U.S.A.   3
   Edward L. Ayers

PENNSYLVANIA AVENUE   15
   The Avenue of the Presidents
   Paul Boller Jr.

A MONUMENT FOR BARRE   29
   Memory in a Massachusetts Town
   T. H. Breen

GREENSBORO, NORTH CAROLINA   41
   A Window on Race in the American South
   William H. Chafe

WORLD WAR II NORMANDY   53
   American Cemetery and Memorial
   James C. Cobb

THE FRANKLIN D. ROOSEVELT MEMORIAL,
WASHINGTON, D.C.   67
   Robert Dallek

CONTENTS

THE AMERICANIZED MANNHEIM OF 1945–1946   79
David Brion Davis

VASSAR COLLEGE   93
Carl N. Degler

A FAN'S HOMAGE TO FENWAY   105
(Or, Why We Love It When They Always Break Our Hearts)
John Demos

FINDING HISTORY IN WOODSIDE, CALIFORNIA   115
Paula S. Fass

BOSTON COMMON   125
David Hackett Fischer

**CHARLESTON'S BATTERY AND NEW ORLEANS'S
JACKSON SQUARE**   145
William W. Freehling

CLIMBING STONE MOUNTAIN   157
Louis R. Harlan

MEMPHIS, TENNESSEE   169
The Rise and Fall of Main Street
Kenneth T. Jackson

ILLINOIS'S OLD STATE CAPITOL   185
A Tale of Two Speeches
Robert W. Johannsen

"A LITTLE JOURNEY"   201
Elbert Hubbard and the Roycroft Community at
East Aurora, New York
Michael Kammen

CONTENTS

SAN JUAN ISLAND, WASHINGTON   219
The "Pig War" and the Vagaries of Identity and History
David M. Kennedy

1048 FIFTH AVENUE   233
Alice Kessler-Harris

QUEENS   241
William E. Leuchtenburg

GETTYSBURG   261
James M. McPherson

MONTICELLO   269
Merrill D. Peterson

THE MUSSO & FRANK GRILL IN HOLLYWOOD   283
Kevin Starr

THE POLO GROUNDS   295
Jules Tygiel

NASSAU HALL, PRINCETON, NEW JERSEY   311
Sean Wilentz

GRACELAND   325
Joel Williamson

MONTGOMERY   339
C. Vann Woodward

THE GRAND CANYON   353
Donald Worster

SEWANEE—HOW TO MAKE A YANKEE SOUTHERN   365
Memories of the 1940s
Bertram Wyatt-Brown

NOTES   389

Preface

This book has two aims in mind. One is to gather together essays by prominent historians on a fascinating range of American places. The other is to pay tribute to a stellar editor. Of the two purposes, the topic of places is likely to be the one to which the reader will more readily relate. It may be harder to grasp why a book would be motivated by the desire to celebrate an editor. For generations, filmgoers have been tutored to appreciate that beyond the words and images spoken by actors on the silver screen stands a director, and the names of some directors have become legendary—Hitchcock and De Mille, Bergman and Fellini. But it is uncommon for even the best informed reader to be aware of the contribution of an editor to the success of a book. Only rarely does the name of a Maxwell Perkins swim into public consciousness.

It is especially unusual for an editor to be honored with a Festchrift, for "festival writings" have been thought of as a fanfare not for an editor but for a distinguished scholar, a mentor who is tendered on a special occasion, usually his retirement, a volume of essays. *American Places* is very likely a unique enterprise in that it is a testimonial not to a professor but to an editor. Sheldon Meyer, though, invites such an exception. He is, as I said in dedicating my book *The Supreme Court Reborn* to him, "Editor Nonpareil." It is doubtful that any other editor in the long history of publishing in the United States has had so large an impact on a field as has Sheldon Meyer on American studies, or so distinguished an array of authors.

Sheldon Meyer's interest in U.S. history is long-standing. He majored in history and American civilization at Princeton, from which he was graduated in 1949 Phi Beta Kappa and summa cum laude. In the half century and more since then, he has read so widely in history, especially American history, that he has few peers in his familiarity with the literature.

During these same years, he also steeped himself deeply in popular culture—from jazz (on which he is a recognized authority), to the musical theater, to the world of sports on two continents—from the baseball diamond exploits of the Mets at Shea Stadium to the heroics of Leeds United, Bayern München, and Real Madrid in the soccer arenas of Europe.

Before going to Oxford University Press, Sheldon had stints at two publishing houses with names so Dickensian that they have come to seem drolly premodern. He began with Funk and Wagnalls. (Some years later, the TV program *Laugh In* could draw guffaws simply by crying out the inane line, "Look *that* up in your Funk and Wagnalls.") Sheldon then moved on to Grosset and Dunlap, the first publisher's name to catch my attention as a little boy because it appeared to be on the jacket of almost every book I read. Indeed, Sheldon was hired there in 1955 ostensibly to supervise the Tom Swift and Hardy Boys series, although actually to work on a new paperback line: Universal Library. (I should add parenthetically with regard to these early years that our friendship of four decades has survived only because of my largeness of spirit—for Sheldon persists in taking enormous pleasure in the darkest day of my life. He exults in a certain October day in 1951, not because it marked his entry into publishing—which it did—but because it was on that day that Bobby Thomson hit his egregious home run that enabled the Giants to snatch the National League pennant from the more deserving Dodgers.)

In 1956, Sheldon Meyer joined Oxford University Press, and the rest, as sports announcers are fond of saying, is history—in this case, literally so. His new position gave him a desk in what was arguably the most prestigious publishing house in the world—but not one that was a frontrunner in American history. I remember vividly a morning in 1950 in Northampton when my good friend and Smith College colleague Daniel Aaron told me that he was submitting the manuscript of his book *Men of Good Hope* to Oxford University Press, and I expressed bewilderment. Why Oxford? I knew, of course, that Oxford University Press had a luminous heritage going back nearly five centuries and that it was responsible for such landmarks as the *OED*. But in American history, it did not begin to have the éclat of Harper or Knopf. In those years, an aspiring historian hoped not for an invitation to clink glasses and swap yarns at an Oxford party, but to lunch with Alfred Knopf, whose garish shirts semaphored his presence from a great distance away.

Under Sheldon's aegis, Oxford University Press soon assumed a considerably larger presence in the field of American history and after a time became the dominant house. Historians from Orono to San Diego learned to say, as convention time approached, "I'll meet you at the Oxford party." To mark how greatly the stature of Oxford has changed since the 1950s, one needs only turn to a convention program of the Organization of American Historians. At one recent meeting, where Sheldon Meyer was honored, the publication carried an astonishing eight full pages of advertising for OUP books, far beyond the spread of any other publisher; the list comprised no fewer than 138 titles.

The rise to eminence of Oxford University Press in U.S. history closely tracks the career of Sheldon Meyer. He rose from assistant editor to become Executive Editor for Trade Books, then Senior Vice President, Editorial, with his own publishing unit. Though he has recently stepped down from that post, he continues to work with Oxford authors as Consulting Editor.

Sheldon Meyer all but reinvented the calling of editor. He would pop up on a college campus less to sell books, though he did that well, than to inquire of a young professor, "What are you working on?" When he found out that the man or woman was engaged in a topic not regarded as mainstream, he would convey the inspiriting message not only that the project was worthwhile but that there was a renowned firm on Madison Avenue eager to publish it. He did not create new fields, but he did do a great deal to foster communities of scholars—to assure anxious historians venturing into uncharted seas that other explorers had set out on the same sorts of voyages. And when the manuscripts arrived on his desk, he would help shape them into books in which both the author and the press could take pride.

Lewis Bateman, who, as a consequence of thirty years at Princeton University Press, the University of North Carolina Press, and Cambridge University Press, enjoys an enviable reputation as one of the country's foremost history editors, wrote Sheldon in 1998:

You changed the landscape of scholarly publishing in the United States. Most editors at university presses waited until manuscripts arrived over the transom and found them at annual meetings. You actively sought them out on campuses. . . . When I joined Princeton University Press in 1972 . . . everywhere I went you had been there before me or anyone else. A few weeks ago, C. Vann Woodward . . . mentioned to me that you knew what everyone was working on. Few of my colleagues would admit it, but we are merely trying to replicate your efforts in our modest careers. We know what a wide net Oxford has cast as a result of your tenure as editor there.

In short, if any of us accomplishes one-tenth of what you have done in your career, it will be a lot.

Sheldon's performance at OUP has been truly remarkable. He has edited no fewer than six Pulitzer Prize–winning books and seventeen that have won the prestigious Bancroft Prize—a record. Merely reciting the names of the authors of these award winners indicates the extent of his influence: Eric Barnouw, Ray Billington, Charles Capper, Robert Dallek, John Demos, Stanley Elkins, Eric McKitrick, Don Fehrenbacher, Louis Harlan, Kenneth Jackson, Robert Johannsen, David M. Kennedy, Gordon Levin, Leonard Levy, James McPherson, Robert Middlekauff, Samuel Eliot Morison, Mark Neely, James T. Patterson, Merrill Peterson, Joseph Wall, and Donald Worster.

Furthermore, the *kinds* of books he has edited have frequently broken new ground. Consider some of those he shepherded in the single area of African American history:

John Blassingame, *The Slave Community*
Thomas Cripps, *Slow Fade to Black*
George Fredrickson, *White Supremacy* and *Black Liberation*
Louis Harlan, *Booker T. Washington*
A. Leon Higginbotham, *In the Matter of Color*
Nathan Huggins, *Harlem Renaissance*
Lawrence Levine, *Black Culture and Black Consciousness*
August Meier and Elliot Rudwick, *CORE*
Albert Raboteau, *Slave Religion*
Harvard Sitkoff, *A New Deal for Blacks*
Brenda Stevenson, *Life in Black and White*
Sterling Stuckey, *Slave Culture*
Robert Toll, *Blacking Up*
Richard Wade, *Slavery in the Cities*
Joel Williamson, *The Crucible of Race*

Note, too, the impact Sheldon Meyer has had on the publishing of histories of American women, another field shamefully neglected when he began. The books he has edited include:

William H. Chafe, *The American Woman*, revised as *The Paradox of Change*
Allen Davis, *American Heroine: The Life and Legend of Jane Addams*
Carl N. Degler, *At Odds: Women and Family in America*
Mary Kelley, *Private Woman/Public Stage*
Alice Kessler-Harris, *Out of Work*
Gerda Lerner, *The Majority Finds Its Past* and *The Creation of Feminist Consciousness*
Regina Morantz-Sanchez, *Sympathy and Science*
Paul Nagel, *The Adams Women*

Sheldon has been especially innovative in fostering works in popular culture. Just a sampling of the books in this field that he edited embraces Gunther Schuller's *Early Jazz*, called "the most important musicological statement on jazz's infancy"; Martin Williams's *The Jazz Tradition*, cited as "the most distinguished critical work in the field"; Whitney Balliett's *American Musicians*; Gerald Bordman's *American Musical Theatre*; Michael Kammen's *The Lively Arts*; Andrew Sarris's *You Ain't Heard Nothin' Yet*; and Alec Wilder's *American Popular Song*. In 1987, thanks to Sheldon Meyer, Oxford University Press received the Carey-Thomas Award for "creative publishing" for its list in jazz and popular music, and in 1997 it was applauded for having brought out more ASCAP prize books than any other publisher.

Gary Giddins, who has published four books on jazz with Oxford University Press, has written in the *New York Times Book Review*:

Sheldon Meyer merits, at the very least, a flourish of saxophones, a melody by Jerome Kern and a high-kicking chorus-line salute. Over the past 40 years, Meyer turned the world's oldest and most staid publishing house into the leading chronicler of jazz, Broadway musicals, popular-song writers, broadcasting and black cultural history.

Sheldon Meyer's achievements have won international recognition. The Association of American University Presses honored him with its

Constituency Award "in appreciation of outstanding service to the University Press Community," and in 1993 Oxford University bestowed on him an Honorary Master of Arts. The Oxford degree ceremony is an awesome experience because it is carried out entirely in Latin, a language most of us do not readily fathom—although I once read in the *Sydney Morning Herald* that Dan Quayle had been studying Latin so that when he went to Latin America he could converse with the natives. The late C. Vann Woodward, whose essay in this volume is, sad to say, very likely the last he ever wrote, once confessed to me that when he received an honorary degree from Oxford most of the words swam by him. He did piece out, however, that "Jacobus Corvinus" were the two final words of his *The Strange Career of Jim Crow*, yet another book edited by Sheldon Meyer in its later editions. Similarly, Sheldon, wondering what the oration in Latin would do with *jazz*, picked out *"musica vulgaris."* The Oxford ceremony took place at the Sheldonian Theatre, and one chirpy young woman said, "Oh, isn't it nice for Sheldon that they're holding it in his own theater."

Sheldon had yet another tribute in store for him. After he turned in his keys at 198 Madison Avenue and set up advisory editor quarters in his apartment on Riverside Drive, Oxford University Press resolved that proper notice should be taken of his change of status and of his illustrious career. Clearly, neither a gold watch nor a monogrammed briefcase would be adequate. Instead, the press decided to put together a Festschrift, with his most prominent authors as contributors.

When Peter Ginna, OUP's trade editor, first approached me about editing the volume, he already had a well-thought-out conception of it. He sought not a mere "collection of essays" but "a book that will hold together and be of interest in itself to the same kind of general readership that Sheldon's list has reached out to over the years." In the course of a generation, Sheldon had edited manuscripts by so many outstanding historians that it would not be easy to decide whom to invite, but we would collaborate with Sheldon on making the choices, and, to include as many as possible, the total would be unusually large. In the end, there were more than two dozen. Our only regret was that even with so many, there was not room for more numbers of highly esteemed scholars.

Too often, volumes of this sort, no matter how well-intentioned, have wound up as random aggregations of miscellany; at worst, batches of yellowed essays exhumed from file drawers—with no theme and no reader appeal. I recall painfully the opening line of a review by Arthur Schlesinger of a tome in honor of my mentor, Henry Steele Commager, to which I had submitted a piece: "As an art form, the Festschrift is a loser." We agreed that this book must have a theme, and the theme should be "American places."

That topic had more than one feature to recommend it, not least that most of us associate Sheldon Meyer with places: a cavernous hotel room where he reigned benignly at an Oxford party; a dinner table at the leafy Commander's Palace in New Orleans; on a Chicago rooftop overlooking Lake Michigan; a cramped campus office where he appeared in quest of a manuscript; a frigid seat at Giants Stadium in the New Jersey meadows; a sunlit luncheon venue with lobster salad and chilled Chardonnay at his summer home on Fisher's Island off the Connecticut coast.

In our letter of invitation, we told prospective authors that we wanted them to write a short essay on a place that engaged them, and encouraged them to adopt a personal style. We were looking for, we explained, not just a descriptive piece about a particular site, but the interaction of the historian with that place. These were to be personal essays of a sort historians often do not get a chance to write, and the author was to be at the center of his or her essay.

The historians who were invited responded with gusto. All welcomed an opportunity to say thank-you to Sheldon, and almost all found the conception of the book congenial, although, taught from their first days in graduate school to eschew the *I* word, some took a while to adapt to the personal idiom. We made no attempt to impose topics on contributors, and they showed considerable imagination in their choices. James C. Cobb and David Brion Davis defined *American* to encompass the U.S. presence on the European continent; Edward L. Ayers comprehended *Places* to accommodate the virtual sphere of cyberspace. Some other venues were almost as unexpected: Fenway Park and the Polo Grounds, an arts and crafts colony in upstate New York, and a Hollywood bistro. The essays—ranging from coast to coast, with stops at places such as Stone Mountain, Georgia, and Main Street, Memphis, in between—can be no more than suggestive of the range of Sheldon's reach. We present them for the pleasure of our readers, but especially, with abiding affection, for one particular reader: the redoubtable Sheldon Meyer.

WILLIAM E. LEUCHTENBURG

Taking Place

P eople have always had a strong sense of place. The Romans spoke of the *genius loci*, the "spirit of a place," and we can understand their meaning readily today, even if the spirit for us is a feeling rather than a deity. "Place," writes Eudora Welty, "absorbs our earliest notice and attention; it bestows on us our original awareness; and our critical powers spring from the study of it and the growth of experience inside it."

For anyone intrigued by history, the physical traces of the past, especially places, have a particular fascination. Certain sites speak to us because in visiting them we confront the past in a tangible, immediate way. Sometimes we visit historic places as an act of homage. Sometimes we visit them to satisfy simple curiosity—what did Walden Pond look like? Sometimes we discover history in an unexpected locale, like a restaurant or a baseball park. But whatever the occasion for our visiting these places, there is no question that we understand history in a different way when we encounter it "on the ground."

Place stimulates the historical imagination in several ways. These different facets of the historian's sense of place are displayed with sparkling variety in the essays collected in this volume. Perhaps the first way we think of place is as setting—the scene in which the events of history are played out. The battlefield at Gettysburg, so well evoked here by James M. McPherson, was the stage for one of the greatest dramas of the Civil War, while Elvis Presley's Graceland witnessed the less edifying spectacle of the King's demise, recalled in Joel Williamson's wry tour. Yet in either case, we cannot imagine the event without the setting, nor can we visit the place without replaying in our minds what happened there.

Of course, place may be much more than a backdrop for history; it can itself shape people and events. Simple geography can be crucial. As David Kennedy observes, the very remoteness, in 1859, of San Juan Island prevented a spat between U.S. and British troops from becoming an international conflict. Or something harder to define—a *genius loci*—may leave its mark. David Hackett Fischer detects, for example, a spirit in the history of Boston Common that has helped to give that city its unique character. On a more intimate level, Bertram Wyatt-Brown's recollection of growing up in Sewanee tells us about an unusual place (and its unusual inhabitants) that helped to form the writer himself.

Place is also a connector: some sites speak so strongly of individuals who have gone before us that we almost feel we can touch them there. To visit Monticello is, as Merrill Peterson shows, as close as we can come to spending a day with Thomas Jefferson. But we can also feel such a link in places that are not "historic" in the plaque-and-guidebook sense. Paula Fass learned that in a country store in California, where a chance discovery connected her to the past with the jolt of an electric current. And Alice Kessler-Harris writes movingly here of how, in a Fifth Avenue mansion, she heard the voices of Eastern European immigrants.

If places can shape history, it is no less true that they are shaped by it, often indelibly. It is no surprise, then, that many of our contributors "read" places as evidence—a historical record written in three dimensions. To William Freehling, Charleston's Battery and New Orleans's Jackson Square spoke volumes about the varied origins and cultures of the Old South. To William Leuchtenburg, the changing face of a Queens, New York, street corner encapsulates the modern history of his native borough. And Donald Worster, in his elegant essay on the Grand Canyon, finds inscribed there the story of an entire planet.

"One place comprehended can make us understand other places better," Welty went on to say. She might have added that it can make us understand history better, for the unfolding of events is inseparable from their location: that is why we say history "takes place." The writers in this volume have each "taken place," too, and eloquently. They have come together to honor a friend and colleague, but they have given us twenty-eight additional reasons to celebrate.

PETER GINNA

AMERICAN PLACES

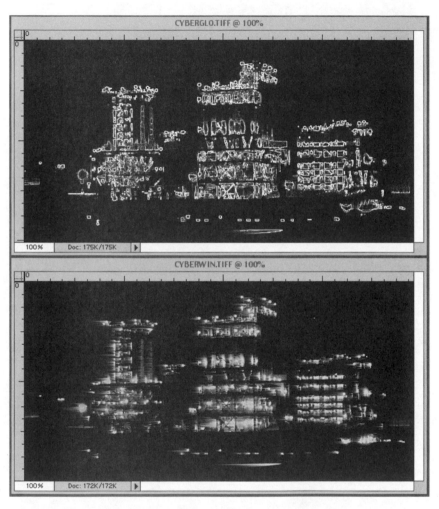

Cyberspace, occupying no actual place, is often imagined with two basic features: grids and glowing lights. Image by Nate Ayers.

Edward L. Ayers

CYBERSPACE, U.S.A.

I write not of Thomas Jefferson's town, where I live, nor of the American South to which I have devoted my working life. Rather, I write of a new American place, one we cannot see but whose effects we increasingly feel: "cyberspace." That place, simultaneously metaphorical and tangible, has touched every part of the United States. Information surges along networks of copper and glass, weaving ever tighter webs across the country and the world. Those networks define a space at once empty and densely populated, desolate and hopeful. By its very nature, cyberspace is the space among other places. It touches them all but is possessed by none.

At one level, cyberspace is merely bits of electronic information, zeroes and ones, stored on computers and networks. At another level, it is more concrete, addresses and linkages whose names people know and can read. And at the sites where people interact with one another, cyberspace becomes physical, filled with color, sound, and image. Even though those places are merely projected on screens, people have fallen in love there, have cooperated, conspired, traded, and raged.

So powerful has this new kind of space become that some observers worry that cyberspace may efface the country it is colonizing with such speed. The portals of cyberspace, critics charge, pull people into basements and bedrooms, encapsulate them in lonely fantasies of sex, greed, and violence, replace real communities with virtual ones. Other commentators hold out the hope that cyberspace will unite people by affinity and passion rather than by the mere accident of physical locale. These optimists believe that the fabric of American society can be strengthened by the new networks. Either way, the stakes are high.

Cyberspace is not a purely American invention; like the railroad, automobile, cinema, radio, and television, cyberspace grew out of international collaboration. But like those innovations, it has been absorbed and dominated by the United States, claimed as an American contribution to the world. The conceit is not baseless, for not only did U.S. military spending and engineering ingenuity undergird the creation of much of the original network, but American business has taken up where defense spending left off. Two-thirds of Web traffic originates in the United States, and two-thirds of Web users speak English, the native language and lingua franca of cyberspace.

This historian came to cyberspace with no intention of staying. I arrived several years after the Internet, the infrastructure of cyberspace, had been constructed by engineers and scientists for their own purposes. When I had first used computers, in the 1970s, they had seemed isolated behemoths, ensconced behind glass, presided over by priestlike figures. Though the first link between computers had been established in 1969, the maturation and spread of the technology had taken years to unfold. When I returned to computing in the early 1980s, everything had changed. Machine and machine connected with hidden protocols, moving information instantly and invisibly, ignoring distance. The networks tied people and machine together in a new kind of intimacy.

No one spoke in the early years of "cyberspace." The descriptive and prosaic "net" served as the term of choice until an influential, if unlikely, book appeared in 1984: *Neuromancer*, by William Gibson. An American living in Canada, Gibson wrote in an American idiom of science fiction and dystopia, of fascination with and dread of the future. Fittingly enough for this pioneering era, he composed his book on a manual typewriter, extrapolating the implications of cyberspace from the merest glimpses of the new technology. Discovering a portable cassette player in a shop a few years earlier, Gibson had slipped the headphones on. "For the first time I was able to move my nervous system through a landscape with my choice of soundtrack," he recalled. Gibson imagined cyberspace when he saw an ad for an early Apple computer and connected it with the experience of the cassette player: "I thought, if there is an imaginary point of convergence where the information this machine handles could be accessed with the under-the-skin intimacy of the Walkman, what would that be like?" Gibson envisioned cyberspace as a "consensual hallucination," people at their computers weaving their imaginations into vast metaphors of information and disembodied energy, power and wealth translating into immaterial but potent form. It did not take long in Gibson's novel for the hallucination to become all too real, for the longing actually to enter cyberspace to become so strong that characters "jacked in" to the network directly with their brains and bodies.

Gibson's vision resonated with those who logged on to the early net. People in the 1980s experienced cyberspace only through words and symbols glowing on a monochromatic screen. No images, no sounds, intruded; imagination confronted limitless space. Across that immense void, mere typed conversation became appealing in a way few would have foreseen. Words, devalued by movies and television, took on a new life. In the absence of ready-made entertainment, people filled the vacuum with role-playing games, dramas of mutual creation. Solitary people sought out compatriots; enthusiasts sought out fellow enthusiasts; people of many sorts sought out titillation of one form or another. The net appeared, paradoxically, both empty and intimate. People rushed to its lists and groups, to its virtual chat rooms, dungeons, and bordellos, and yet the place still felt like a secret sanctuary for the few hundred thousand souls who occupied it.

To most people, even to some of its inhabitants, the world of the net seemed overwhelming and uncertain. Bleak visions of the society that might accompany cyberspace proliferated in the eighties. *Neuromancer* was not alone. The film *Blade Runner* portrayed a postindustrial society awash in its own waste and discarded people, no longer able to keep law and order. A famous Super Bowl advertisement of 1984 evoked a leaden world of robotic clones that only more computers, Apple computers, could supposedly shatter. Neal Stephenson's *Snow Crash* portrayed a world where franchises and viruses attached themselves to weakened hosts in both cyberspace and the material world. Young people in these years imagined themselves as "cyberpunks," marrying a facility with the new networks to the anarchic sensibility of the Sex Pistols. They and their allies waged battles, both legal and illicit, to keep cyberspace beyond the grasp of government and corporate capitalism, to create a libertarian paradise of hackers.

Other people pursued a different vision, one of strengthened community and responsibility. One of the most successful efforts grew from an experiment called the WELL, founded in 1985. The outgrowth of San Francisco–area countercultural leaders, the WELL sought to provide a place for sustained communal conversation. It attracted thousands of participants and for many people stood as the embodiment of what an online community could be. As Howard Rheingold, an active member of the WELL and a pioneering writer on community in cyberspace, later put it, "Hundreds of thousands of people rely on their virtual communities as a real lifeline—people whose illness or disability prevents normal communication, people who are caregivers or who suffer from any one of hundreds of diseases, people who live in isolated areas, the only gay teenager in a small town, people trying to escape abusive relationships." Rheingold had personally taken his "turn sitting by the deathbed of a woman who would have died alone if it were not for the real-life presence of a virtual community."

About this time, in a much more prosaic way, I became entangled in the world of the Internet. I had recently conceived of trying to get at the larger issues surrounding the American Civil War through a linked study of a Northern community and a Southern community, done the old-fashioned way, with notecards and text. Through a series of coincidences and collaborations, however, I ended up in 1991 beginning to build the archive for such a study in a computerized format that could be shared with others. While I had casually used the Internet for years, I could not imagine how to distribute this digital archive in any form other than putting it on a tape and mailing it to the other few institutions that had the considerable hardware necessary to run it. We set to work digitizing newspapers, censuses, diaries, letters, and maps with just this purpose in mind. The Internet let us transfer some files and let us collaborate from our offices, but our project remained isolated.

One day in 1993, however, one of my computer science associates e-mailed me to say that I must come to his office as soon as I could. There, he showed me Mosaic, the key tool for something called the World Wide Web. The Web, an overlay of linked text and image that used the net for its vehicle, redefined the experience of being online. The brainchild of an English physicist working in Switzerland, Mosaic had been designed for scientific collaboration. We confronted Mosaic on a high-end Unix operating system, but versions of this browser software—polished and promoted by Americans—soon appeared for desktop computers. Overnight, cyberspace became a far more literal, and populated, place.

It was immediately apparent that everything had changed, including the Civil War community project. Now we could construct an archive online; our material need not wait for years to be disseminated but could be shared even as we gathered it. The archive could go anywhere in the world people could tie into the network, a network expanding exponentially. We threw ourselves into building a Website devoted to this slice of history. We called it the Valley of the Shadow Project, for our two communities lay in the Great Valley of the eastern United States and had been visited by death and devastation in the war. The archive grew until it contained thousands of sources, detailing, week by week, the fates of a Virginia county and a Pennsylvania county from 1859 to 1869. The archive housed civilians as well as soldiers, women as well as men, enslaved as well as free.

The Web offered a challenge to many of the conventions of the historian's craft. Long, linear prose did not work on the Web, and yet we did not know how to write in any other way. The Web loved images, but we knew words best. The Web depended on instant interactivity, but we were used to laying out our arguments in a fixed form. No one has yet discovered how to write for this new medium, how to tell a historical story in scrolled or interactive text. Some worry, in fact, that the short attention spans and fixation on the future supposedly bred in cyberspace will erode historical thinking. On the other hand, the new medium may be especially well suited to convey the complexity and depth of history. Only trying will tell.

History has traditionally been a solitary craft, the product of one person thinking about something a long time, but the Web demands collaboration. Team-produced history makes some people nervous, as they wonder where authority and accountability lie. As it turned out, however, our collaboration proved a delightful innovation, all the more satisfying for being absolutely necessary. Dozens of students and allies were pulled into the project as the archive steadily grew. We held each other accountable and found our authority in combined effort.

To our surprise, over three million visitors came to the Valley Project

7

on the Web, people of all ages, from all over the world. Some told us that this history on a computer screen, as unlikely as that seemed, touched them more deeply than any other they had ever experienced. Part of the appeal came from the very thing we had worried about: the lack of a visible authority, the absence of a single voice, the empty space where there would normally be an argument or narrative. Instead, we had created a place where visitors in effect collaborated with us to weave stories from the records.

We had stumbled upon what proved to be one of the most appealing metaphors of the Web: community. The historical sources took on meaning because they told of communities of imaginable size undergoing the most dramatic events the people of this nation have ever known. But there was more to the appeal than that, for people using the site seemed to feel themselves a part of a larger community. They knew they were not the only ones thinking about these anonymous people of the past. Messages came virtually every day to the Valley Project, sharing enthusiasm and encouragement. The new technology seemed to be creating new communities, both real and virtual.

Other Web communities were far more self-consciously orchestrated. Businesses quickly sprang up around the metaphor; tens of millions of people "joined communities" by posting Websites reflecting their personalities, interests, and images of themselves. Those virtual communities soon became among the most heavily visited places in cyberspace; twenty million people have created Web pages in one virtual neighborhood or another, and the number of new arrivals continues to expand. The metaphor is pursued with great thoroughness and literal-mindedness. At GeoCities, one of the largest virtual communities, visitors are promised they can "meet people just like you." Websites are divided into neighborhoods, blocks, and houses. Each neighborhood is themed, its denizens united by their fascination with some hobby, celebrity, or cause. The neighborhoods read like an X ray of American obsessions, pastimes, and fantasies. People can choose to live, among many other places, in WallStreet (investing, finance), TimesSquare (games, role-playing), Athens (education, philosophy), Hollywood (film and TV), Pentagon (military), or RainForest (the environment).

As in suburbia, looks can be deceptive; though each house in each block appears the same, behind the surface great variation awaits. Some houses are filled with sophisticated graphics and text, while others bear the marks of residents who lost interest after posting a photo of their cat or listing their favorite television shows. Some communities have active city fathers and mothers who strive for cybercivic pride. In the Heartland community, for example, residents vie for the Heartland Award of Excellence, given to those who do the most to encourage the values of the traditional American community. Special places have been set aside in the Heartland for genealogy, prayer, and other honored practices and values. Sites are decorated with symbols rich in nostalgia and earth tones.

Much of cyberspace, in other words, has become thoroughly domesticated. It would be difficult to imagine places much farther removed from the dark, slick, and sinister spaces of *Neuromancer* than these relentlessly cheerful commercial communities. While early visions of cyberspace envisioned power nakedly displayed in glowing cubes and grids, cyberspace at the turn of the century resembles nothing so much as it does the American suburbia in which it flourishes. Confronted with a blank slate on which to imagine a new kind of space, people on the Web have replicated late twentieth-century America and its car culture of malls, subdivisions, traffic, construction, shopping baskets, and chain stores. People have even begun to buy and sell, at escalating prices, "real estate" in role-playing games. Until proven otherwise, everything on the Web is an advertisement for something else. Eighty-three percent of sites devote themselves to commercial content; 6 percent are devoted to education and science. We have met cyberspace and it is us.

Relentless optimism stands as the official mood of cyberspace. "In this Internet moment—a remarkable convergence of calendar and change—we the people have a chance at last to become our own masters," one booster enthused at the approach of the new millennium. "We are all moguls now, pooh-bahs with our hands on the machinery of vast empires. We are retail lords, media masters, forces on Wall Street and in Hollywood. And we don't even have to put on ties or heels." While critics of the Web complained that over half of all Web traffic was already controlled by a few big companies, optimists pointed out that half remained for everyone else.

The sense of danger, nevertheless, continues to lurk. No sooner had cyberspace been settled than it attracted doomsday cults, pedophiles, and fascist skinheads. Nostalgia immediately developed for the old Internet. "Cyberspace, once thought of as the world's most cozy community," one editorial lamented in the wake of a computer virus, "has quickly become a lonely, infinite expanse of electronic hallways filled with endless queues of on-line shopping malls and shadowy alleys where computer outlaws and their rogue programs lurk." The world of *Neuromancer* has merged with that of Wal-Mart. Faced with this anomie, gated communities have proliferated in cyberspace; some people, presented with an unprecedented possibility, want instead to mingle with people virtually like themselves. Shoppers are automatically guided to the same music and books as other people who bought similar music and books before. The web of "customerization" grows tighter and tighter, hopes of communities based on something other than consumerism dwindle.

It is a familiar pattern: Americans, perpetually optimistic, are also perpetually disappointed. In this way, the accelerated history of cyberspace has recapitulated the history of the country where it has most flourished. Things tend to begin with millennial visions and end in comfort, convenience, commerce, and more than a little regret and guilt. A dominant emotion of cyberspace might be called "anticipointment," a perpetual sense of possibility undercut by the acknowledgment that the reality can never quite live up to the idealized image we have of it.

Echoes of earlier periods in American history run through much of the discussion of cyberspace. Even as they talk about the newest and latest things, commentators reach toward the familiar formulas, standards, and assumptions that have shaped much of American public and private life since the birth of the republic. Confronted with a new medium and a new expressive freedom, Americans have seized on familiar metaphors of prophecy and analysis.

The most obvious analogy of the new information age is the Wild West. Images of gold rushes and gunfights fill stories about otherwise humdrum business Web ventures. The other obvious analogy is that of the robber barons and the Gilded Age. Bill Gates finds himself compared, depending on the purpose of the commentator, to both the rapacious Jay Gould and the generous Andrew Carnegie. Editorials attack the concentration of wealth in the new realm with a spirit the Populists would have applauded: "Five years into the e-commerce revolution," one editorial raged, "the big dogs of mass-market retailing are throwing untold millions into the development of category-dominating megasites." Such people watch with disgust as the democratic possibilities of cyberspace seem to disappear as quickly as they materialize. The Americans with the least access to this new landscape turn out to be the Americans who have the least access to the existing landscape: the poor, the black, the urban, the rural, and the old.

Economic inequality is not the only threat to democracy in cyberspace. Many people worry more about the absence of authority than about its concentration. In the wake of a high-school shooting spree, an editorial in the *New York Times* noted that one of the young killers maintained a Website that contained directions for making a bomb, along with threatening cartoons and lyrics, posted for anyone to see. But no one did see, or if they did, no one attempted to stop the outburst: "Precisely because the Internet is such a neutral, free, open and unregulated technology," the editorialist lamented, "it means that we are all connected, but no one is in charge. The Internet is a democracy, but with no constitution."

Alexis de Tocqueville, of all people, would have understood. Tocqueville, routinely trotted out to explain every facet of American community and character for the last 150 years, did nevertheless seem to speak directly to the world of cyberspace. Indeed, of all the writers on cyberspace, Tocqueville, writing in the 1830s, may have come the closest to capturing its relationship to the United States because cyberspace is a clear projection of core American hopes and anxieties.

Tocqueville's great volumes on democracy in America explored the paradoxes of a place where no one seemed in charge and yet people behaved with remarkable uniformity, where everything seemed possible and yet devoid of the joy one might expect in a land so prosperous and free. One commentator on Tocqueville, writing years before either the net or cyberspace had been imagined, distilled the essence of the French visitor's argument: "The egalitarian principle takes a heavy toll from the human personality, sacrificing depth to busyness, and courtesy to vulgarity, putting easy social relations ahead of meaningful human ones, restlessness ahead of rootedness, independence ahead of authority, private decision ahead of public taste, materialist well-being ahead of the intangibles of the mind, the belief in progress ahead of a sense of complexity in society and history, and the 'indefinite perfectibility of man' ahead of the mystery of the supernatural." These words anticipated, with remarkable thoroughness, the laments of many who worry about the morality fostered in cyberspace. Every clause has been the focus of one critic or another of the new space growing in our midst. Cyberspace seems a distillation of America. Both are quick, shallow, and lonely as well as hopeful, energetic, and sociable.

Like Tocqueville's America, cyberspace America confronts no old order to overthrow, no virtual monarchy, church, or aristocracy to slow its spreading dominion. There is only momentum—of network, of mass communication, of consumerism, of hunger for speed, stimulation, and gratification. As in Tocqueville's America, the government in cyberspace is decentralized, distrusted, and weak, afraid to interfere. As in Tocqueville's America, the denizens of cyberspace are fascinated by any machinery faster and shinier than yesterday's machinery. People flock together to discuss UFOs, politics, or stocks online, just as they flocked to the lodges, reform organizations, and religions they invented on the spot in the America of Andrew Jackson. The impulse is constant; only the medium has changed.

Tocqueville still speaks to us because he refused to speak in mere disdain. No one today reads the European observers who visited only to sneer, and no one takes seriously those who only doled out praise. Tocqueville admired much of what he saw in America, but he worried about the lack of satisfaction he found here: "In America I saw the freest and most enlightened men, placed in the happiest circumstances which the world affords; it seemed to me as if a cloud habitually hung upon their brow, and I thought them serious and almost sad even in their pleasures." Tocqueville ascribed this perpetual longing to the impossibility of ever acquiring true equality; each man thought every other man was getting ahead, leaving him behind with no one else to blame. Americans felt alone, adrift, without a place and without community.

Presented with a clean sheet on which to draw our deepest desires and our best plans, Americans seem to be re-creating much of what Tocqueville saw. In cyberspace, we reconstitute the hustle and anxiety even as we try to build the perfect community to contain both. The Web of today contains virtual versions of earlier monuments to these competing impulses. Without much difficulty, a visitor to the Web can see Main Street and Times Square, Levittown and trailer parks, Brook Farm and Las Vegas, white-steepled churches and storefront ministries, red schoolhouses and night schools. As in Disneyland, we try to re-create our real communities in idealized ones that we can smooth, perfect, and contain. Like many of their predecessors, those places in cyberspace have been put up quickly, often shoddily, because no one expects them to last very long. We build only to tear down for something better, something that may satisfy our hunger for connection and belonging.

The World Wide Web will not long endure in its current state. Today's most sophisticated Websites will seem hopelessly limited in just a few years; the technologies that will permit a new generation of cyberspace are being readied at a feverish pace. Cyberspace may yet grow into the nightmare of *Neuromancer*, the beloved community of the WELL, or something else altogether. Whatever the machinery or the landscape, one thing seems likely: a longing for community, as tangible and as elusive as always, will hover over Cyberspace, U.S.A.

President and Mrs. Kennedy ride in the inaugural parade along Pennsylvania Avenue. *Copyright Corbis Bettmann.*

Paul Boller Jr.

PENNSYLVANIA AVENUE

The Avenue of the Presidents

A s a sport, running (like swimming laps) can be boring at times, at least for an amateur, and a few years after taking it up I began combining it, whenever possible, with sightseeing. It seemed like a bright idea: keeping fit while learning something about cities I visited. I did runs around the Emperor's Palace in Tokyo, down Riverside Drive in Manhattan, along the waterfront in Seattle, on the river walk in San Antonio, near Golden Gate Bridge in San Francisco, and in Rock Creek Park and down Pennsylvania Avenue in Washington, D.C.

Pennsylvania Avenue was a favorite. The sights along the way were impressive: museums, monuments, memorials, statues, imposing government buildings, parks, plazas. The association with presidents, a major interest of mine, was also powerful. Most presidents, I knew, traveled along the "Grand Avenue" from the White House to the Capitol to be sworn into office on Inauguration Day, and then returned to review the Big Parade in their honor that afternoon from a stand erected for that purpose in front of the Executive Mansion. A few went to the Capitol by foot or on horseback; more made the trip in fancy phaetons and barouches and, later on, in automobiles and limousines. At my leisurely pace I made the trip (1.7 miles) in about fifteen minutes. It took the presidents longer because they were usually part of a stately procession witnessed by hundreds, and then thousands, lining the Avenue. Three presidents—Jimmy Carter, George Bush, Bill Clinton—were runners, but none ventured to jog down Pennsylvania Avenue on Inauguration Day, though Carter and Clinton walked part of the way on their return to the White House.

Time gallops on, of course, and in retirement I substituted swimming for running, but I still take walks along America's "Appian Way" (as it used to be called), whenever I am in Washington, admiring the Romanesque Post Office, with its 315-foot clock tower, the East Building of the National Gallery of Art (designed by I. M. Pei), and the Willard Hotel (self-styled "the crown jewel of Pennsylvania Avenue"), the host for American presidents since Franklin Pierce in 1853. As I stroll down the Avenue (at a slower pace than Harry Truman used in his daily walks), I take time out to visit the exhibits in the National Gallery of Art and the National Archives, chat with attendants at the Willard who have witnessed inaugural parades, and examine the sketches, maps, and quotations inscribed on the flagstone surface of the Freedom Plaza between 13th and 14th streets. Two quotes I find especially pertinent. One is an utterance of Samuel C. Busby, president of the Medical Society of Washington, in 1898: "There is not a street in any city in this country entitled to the eminent distinction which crowns the history of Pennsylvania Avenue." The other is from Thomas Jefferson, writing in 1791: "The Grand Avenue connecting both the palace and the federal House will be most significant and most convenient."

Jefferson preferred the dreams of the future to the history of the past, as John Adams put it, but it took a lot of history to transform the Grand Avenue from what it was when he became the first president to be inaugurated in Washington to what it is today. In 1801, Jefferson used New Jersey rather than Pennsylvania Avenue in walking from his boardinghouse to Capitol Hill, because Pennsylvania was still too much of a "Serbonian bog." But after becoming president he saw to it that the Avenue was graded and paved, and he used it when riding in a carriage to the Capitol for his second swearing-in. On both occasions, he received praise for his "Republican simplicity." He avoided fancy garb and insisted on simpler oath-taking ceremonies than those accompanying George Washington's and John Adams's induction into office. And he soon rechristened the "President's Palace" the "President's House."

Jeffersonian simplicity, I found, was short-lived. Soldiers accompanied James Madison to the Capitol in 1809, perhaps because of strained relations with Britain, and became indispensable features of inaugural processions thereafter. Andrew Jackson returned to Jeffersonian austerity in 1829, walking informally with a few Revolutionary veterans along the Avenue, nodding and waving to his fans along the way, as he headed for Capitol Hill. "It is *true* greatness," exclaimed one observer, "which needs not the aid of ornament and pomp." I expected ornament and pomp in William Henry Harrison's inauguration in 1841, and I got plenty of it. The Whigs, I learned, sponsored the first big, colorful parade (reminiscent of their "log cabin and hard cider" campaign), made up of members of Tippecanoe Clubs and log cabin floats, as well as military units and bands. The most striking float (since it showed that the Whigs tried to keep up with the times) was a large platform on wheels, drawn by six white horses, displaying a power loom, with several operators busily weaving pieces of cloth and tossing them out to people lining the Avenue. It was a frigid day, but Harrison joined the procession to and from the Capitol on "Old Whitey," his white charger, and the paraders trooped back and forth for a couple of hours after the inaugural ceremony to entertain the crowds. John Quincy Adams called the procession "showy-shabby," but he meant it as a compliment: elegant but not undemocratic.

Floats became a big thing after 1841. In 1857 two floats demonstrating that Liberty and Union were in good shape (though they weren't) dominated the parade for James Buchanan, and in 1865 three ambitious floats proceeded down the Avenue to celebrate Abraham Lincoln's second oath-taking: a replica of the *Monitor*, from which sailors fired salutes; a structure representing the Temple of Liberty filled with women wearing costumes signifying the different states; and a platform containing a hand-run press, with members of the Typographical Union turning out inaugural programs for the parade-watchers.

Lincoln's first inauguration in 1861 was inevitably unique. With the nation on the brink of civil war on March 4, the inaugural planners realized that the safety of Lincoln and the security of Washington itself were their most urgent tasks. To meet the crisis, General Winfield Scott, the army's general in chief, moved several hundred regular troops into the city and arranged for the presidential carriage to move along Pennsylvania Avenue on inauguration morning between double files of District cavalry, with a company of sappers and miners marching in front of the carriage and the infantry and riflemen of the District following behind. He also stationed soldiers on streets paralleling the parade route and cavalrymen on the side streets crossing Pennsylvania Avenue, and put riflemen on the roofs and at the windows of buildings along the parade route as well.

Fortunately there was no trouble that momentous day, and the inaugural procession, with soldiers, bands, marching clubs, governors, war veterans, congressmen, and Washington officials, went off nicely. The crowds lining the Avenue especially liked the float decorated in red, white, and blue, drawn by four white horses, and carrying thirty-four pretty little girls, one for each state (including the seceded ones), wearing white frocks and waving little flags. The story that Lincoln took time out to kiss each little girl is charming but spurious. So, probably, is the tale told by one of Buchanan's biographers about the exchange Lincoln had with his predecessor en route to the Capitol. "My dear sir," Buchanan supposedly said, "if you are as happy in entering the White House as I shall feel on returning to Wheatland, you are a happy man indeed." "Mr. President," Lincoln is said to have replied, with uncharacteristic stiltedness, "I cannot say that I shall enter it with much pleasure, but I assure you that I shall do what I can to maintain the high standards set by my illustrious predecessors who have occupied it." Later, when General Scott, stationed on a hill nearby, learned that the inauguration had gone off peacefully, he raised his hands and exclaimed: "God be praised! God in His goodness be praised!" I couldn't help liking old "Fuss and Feathers" as I read about his Last Hurrah.

Four years later, at Lincoln's second swearing-in, American blacks marched in the inaugural parade for the first time, both as soldiers wearing the Union Army blue and as members of an Odd Fellows lodge in full regalia. Though some people objected, participation of blacks in their country's quadrennial celebrations continued and increased in importance until the day came when Margaret Truman could boast that at her father's inauguration in 1949 all the activities, including the inaugural ball, were at last fully integrated.

After the Civil War, the military component of inaugural parades increased in importance, and the parades themselves, originally a minor supplement to the task of getting presidents to and from the Capitol, gradually became featured events, were moved to the afternoon, and were scheduled to take place after the inaugural ceremonies at the Capitol. Meanwhile, the morning processions to the Capitol became less significant and, with the arrival of automobiles in the early part of the twentieth century, turned into little motorcades, with the president and the president-elect in the first car, the vice president and his successor in the second car, the presidential wives in the third, and members of Congress, cabinet members, government officials, and Secret Service men in succeeding cars. Crowds continued to gather along the historic thoroughfare on inauguration morning, hoping to get a glimpse of the presidents and their wives as well as to get good seats in the bleachers erected along the way for the afternoon parade. Helen Taft was the first presidential wife to get into the act when she insisted on riding with her husband back to the White House after the inaugural ceremony in 1909.

Automobiles replaced horse-drawn carriages in 1921, when Warren G. Harding succeeded Woodrow Wilson as president. The motorcade from the White House to the Capitol on the morning of Harding's inauguration contained a dozen cars, and the mounted cavalry accompanying the cars came close to galloping in order to stay ahead of them. Cheers greeted the little procession moving down the Avenue, but Wilson purposely ignored them; he assumed they were all for Harding, and he tried to convince himself that he didn't mind a bit. But he was amused by the turn the conversation took soon after they left the White House. Harding began telling Wilson about an elephant he'd heard of whose devotion to his keeper was almost unbelievable. "You know," he said, "I've always wanted to own an elephant some day." Murmured Wilson: "I hope it won't turn out to be a white elephant." History, the *New York Times* observed in 1953, "is an outgoing President riding up Pennsylvania Avenue with his successor, each trying to make pleasant conversation while each hears the loud ticking of the clock that brings noon nearer."

The clock-ticking chats weren't always as amiable as the Harding-Wilson exchange. One of the unpleasantest (and among my favorites) occurred in 1933, when Herbert Hoover and Franklin Roosevelt rode to the Capitol together for the latter's swearing-in. Thousands of people lined the Avenue that morning, waving, shouting, cheering, and singing "Happy Days Are Here Again," and FDR smiled, waved, and raised his silk hat in obvious pleasure as the presidential limousine lumbered along. But Hoover, aghast at his successor's determination to go ahead with his New Deal, stared bleakly straight ahead, utterly unresponsive to FDR's efforts to get a conversation going. FDR prided himself on his skill in engaging people in small talk, but with the ponderously glum Hoover his efforts came to naught. Spying a building under construction on one side of the Avenue, he suddenly exclaimed, almost in desperation: "My dear Mr. President, aren't those the nicest steel girders you ever saw?" There was no response from Hoover, and FDR gave up at this point. As he told Grace Tully, his secretary, later on: "I said to myself, 'Spinach! Protocol or no protocol, somebody had to do something. The two of us simply couldn't sit there on our hands, ignoring each other and everybody else.' So I began to wave my own response with my top hat and kept waving it until I got to the inauguration stand and was sworn in."

Harry Truman's ride to the Capitol with Dwight D. Eisenhower in 1953 was more strained, if anything, than the Hoover-Roosevelt trip. Once on good terms, the two men had come to dislike each other thoroughly during the 1952 campaign, when Truman went out on the stump for Adlai Stevenson, and just before Ike touched base with Truman on inauguration morning, he told aides he wondered "if I can *stand* sitting next to the guy." He refused to meet Truman in the White House, as protocol dictated, forcing the president to go out front to join him in the presidential car. In his diary for January 20, Truman wrote that the conversation en route to the Capitol was at first about "the crowd, the pleasant day, the orderly turnover," and then Eisenhower suddenly remarked that Kenneth Royall (Truman's secretary of war) "tried to order him home" for Truman's inauguration in 1949, "but he wouldn't come because half the people cheering me at that time had told him they were for him." "Ike," Truman retorted, "I didn't ask you to come—or you'd have been here." At that, New Hampshire Senator Styles Bridges, one of the congressional escorts, "gasped," according to Truman, and Massachusetts's Joe Martin, speaker of the House, "changed the subject."

Eisenhower's remark continued to rankle Truman long after Ike became president, and when he came to publish *Mr. Citizen* in 1960, he gave a fuller and more confrontational account of the episode. But both Truman and Eisenhower seem to have had faulty memories. Newspapers covering the 1949 inauguration reported that Ike was actually on hand for the celebration; he appeared in the afternoon parade. The crowds along Pennsylvania Avenue, according to the *New York Times*, applauded enthusiastically "when they spotted Gen. Dwight D. Eisenhower in a car whose placard bore only the name of his host, Secretary of the Army Kenneth Royall." Eisenhower said nothing in his memoirs about the curt exchange with Truman in 1953, but he did recall asking Truman who ordered his son John, a colonel stationed in Korea, to Washington for the inauguration, and when Truman said, "I did," he "thanked him sincerely for his thoughtfulness." Truman remembered it differently; he interpreted Ike's query (which came after they reached the Capitol) hostilely, and in *Mr. Citizen* reported another angry retort on his part. But he said nothing about the friendly letter he received from Ike's son three days after the inauguration, thanking him for enabling him to attend his father's swearing-in. He never forgave Eisenhower for his discourteous behavior in 1953.

The ceremonies of 1933 and 1953 were exceptions to the clock-ticking encounters on inauguration morning. Most journeys of presidents and presidents-elect to Capitol Hill seem to have been polite, if not cordial. The transitional trip of Gerald Ford and Jimmy Carter in 1977 was certainly friendly; Ford reminisced about his days in Congress and explained to Carter that Republicans and Democrats could have their scraps in the House and still remain friends. George Bush and Bill Clinton got along fine, too, in 1993; Clinton was never at a loss for friendly words.

In the twentieth century, the newly installed president usually had lunch with members of Congress in the Capitol after the inaugural address and then returned to the White House to review the parade down Pennsylvania Avenue. Some presidents enjoyed the parades enormously; others simply took them in their stride. But for at least one president, Calvin Coolidge, the parade after the inauguration in 1925 seems to have been an ordeal, though it lasted only an hour and consisted mainly of army, navy, and marine forces. "Silent Cal" was so quiet throughout that some people called it "a review in silence." In an attempt to explain Coolidge's apparent indifference, "Ike" Hoover, the White House's chief usher, mentioned the president's "lack of appreciation for such demonstrations. The people certainly like to be noticed and the President could not or would not warm up to them." The *Emporia Gazette's* William Allen White put it more colorfully: "It takes two to wake up the hurrahs of a crowd, the harrahers and the harrahee. That fine, fair Coolidge day the hurrahee's emotions—never tenacious—were spent by four o'clock." Thoroughly exhausted by the experience, Coolidge returned to the White House afterward for a bite to eat and a good nap.

Theodore Roosevelt was more typical. Like Franklin Roosevelt, John F. Kennedy, and Ronald Reagan after him, he thoroughly enjoyed the afternoon performance, and it was probably the high point of the day for him in 1905. As the inaugural parade passed his reviewing stand in front of the White House, he grinned, smiled, laughed, nodded, waved his hat, clapped his hands, stamped his feet, swayed to the rhythm of the band music, and at times almost danced, as more than thirty thousand men, representing hundreds of military and civilian organizations, passed in review. He liked the band music: the Sousa marches, the ragtime, and tunes like "Maryland, My Maryland," "Marching through Georgia," "America," "Dixie," and especially "There'll Be a Hot Time in the Old Town Tonight." He liked the signs and banners too: THE PRESIDENT'S NEIGHBORS (people from Oyster Bay), ALL I ASK IS A SQUARE DEAL FOR EVERY MAN (a Roosevelt political club), and, in particular, the banner carried by some coal miners in overalls, with lamps on their caps, celebrating his intervention in the anthracite coal walkout in 1902: WE HONOR THE MAN WHO SETTLED OUR STRIKE.

With his affection for things military, Roosevelt was particularly proud of the army and navy units, which saluted as they passed in the parade. "Those are the boys," he exclaimed, as the West Point cadets and the midshipmen from the Naval Academy appeared. "They're superb." When the Seventh Cavalry passed by, its band playing "Garry Owen," TR remarked: "That is a bully fighting tune, and this is Custer's old regiment, one of the finest in the service." As a squadron of the Ninth Regular Cavalry, a black regiment, went by, he cried: "Ah, they were with me at Santiago!" He got a big kick out of the Rough Riders, of course, and joined in the laughter when one of them lassoed a spectator and carried him along with the march. Seeing soldiers from the "Territories" (Puerto Rico and the Philippines) gave him special pleasure, and when a battalion of Puerto Rican militiamen came by, he turned to antiexpansionist Senator Augustus O. Bacon of Georgia and chortled: "They look pretty well for an oppressed people, eh, Senator?" The arrival of some Filipino scouts (with their band playing, for some reason, "The Irish Washerwoman") led him to lean far over the railing and clap his hands vigorously. "The wretched serfs disguise their feelings admirably," he teased Senator Bacon. A little later he remarked to Senator Henry Cabot Lodge in a voice loud enough for the Georgia senator to hear: "You should have seen Bacon hide his face when the Filipinos went by. The 'slaves' were rejoicing in their shackles!" Bacon was too polite to remind the president of how many lives were lost putting down the Filipino insurrection that broke out after the United States took over the Philippines from Spain.

There were civilian groups in the parade that gave Roosevelt a great deal of pleasure too. When fifty or so cowboys, headed by his friend Seth Bullock, came dashing along Pennsylvania Avenue, waving their sombreros and cheering like mad, TR yelled back his greetings and waved his hat frantically. One cowboy, putting spurs on his steed, raced up under TR's very nose at such speed that he almost fell over the railing but, to TR's delight, skillfully spun his bronco around on its haunches and rejoined his companions. Then, as TR watched with a big smile, the entire bunch rolled merrily away, yelling and hollering, and snaring unwary bystanders with their lariats. When it was all over, TR exclaimed: "It was a great success. Bully. And did you note that bunch of cowboys? Oh, they are the boys who can ride! It was all superb. It really touched me to the heart."

Like TR, most other presidents had their favorites in the parades down the grand boulevard. In 1933, FDR's seems to have been the three hundred members of the Electoral College marching in the inaugural parade (at his request) to remind people of the role that electoral as well as popular votes play in American presidential contests. But he admired, too, the model of the War of 1812's famous frigate, the *Constitution*, and exchanged friendly greetings with former New York governor Alfred E. Smith as the latter passed with a contingent from Tammany Hall. (Smith received a thunderous ovation from the people thronging the Avenue, but the cowboy star Tom Mix, in town to promote a new movie, received even more applause.) For John F. Kennedy, the pièce de résistance in 1961 was the reproduction of PT boat 109, carrying members of his wartime crew; as it passed the reviewing stand, he waved vigorously and cried: "Great work!"

Kennedy enjoyed the parade, but he was distressed by the shabby condition Pennsylvania Avenue had fallen into after World War II, and, soon after becoming president, he sponsored a program of renovation that by the early 1980s had produced the majestic boulevard that I was privileged to traverse when I first began jogging in Washington. Unfortunately, JFK didn't live to see any of the redevelopment, and it was the old Avenue that was used for his funeral on November 25, 1963, three days after his assassination in Dallas. Thousands of people crowded the sidewalks that day to watch his casket, placed on a black caisson (the same one that carried FDR's coffin eighteen years before), proceed slowly down Pennsylvania Avenue, followed by a riderless horse carrying empty boots reversed in the stirrups, signifying that the warrior would never mount again.

The transformation of Pennsylvania Avenue was almost completed when Ronald Reagan became president in 1981 and reviewed the customary parade on the afternoon of his inauguration. Reagan's enthusiasm was mainly for the military formations in the parade. He was thrilled as he watched the soldiers and sailors march by the White House reviewing stand and execute an eyes right and a brisk salute as they passed. "Is it appropriate for me to return their salute?" he asked an army general sitting near him in the reviewing stand. "It is appropriate, sir," returned the officer a bit officiously, "if your head is covered." Since he wasn't wearing a hat, Reagan simply nodded, his hand over his heart, when receiving salutes after that, but, as he told his friend Michael Deaver later on: "I really felt uncomfortable not returning those salutes the men gave me, just standing there, motionless." Deaver reassured him. "Mr. President," he said, "you are commander in chief now, you can do whatever you want." Reagan's eyes lit up, Deaver wrote later, and "to this day, he salutes everything that moves." George Bush followed Reagan's practice, and the two of them exchanged spirited salutes as they parted after Bush's oath-taking in 1989, even though Reagan was no longer commander in chief.

What about the twentieth century's last president? In 1993, Bill Clinton omitted the military gesture when the troops marched by on the afternoon of his first inauguration. Reporters covering the parade were condescendingly amused when they saw a high-ranking army officer walk over to Clinton at one point and salute him, while the latter "froze for a few seconds before he realized that his new status as Commander in Chief required him to salute back." In fact, I learned, after a little research, that there is no such requirement. Most presidents, including Eisenhower and Kennedy, refrained from returning military salutes in kind because, as civilian commanders of America's armed forces, they were not in uniform and they symbolized the principle of civil supremacy over the military in the American system. A smile, a wave, nod, or friendly "Hello" sufficed for them and would have been just right for Clinton. But in the end Clinton yielded to reportorial importunities, took up saluting, and then received taunts for not matching President Reagan's panache. It was hard for me to understand why Clinton bothered to go in for saluting since he didn't have to. I had never felt comfortable saluting the quarterdeck when I boarded ships as an ensign during World War II. Snappy salutes by nonprofessionals set my teeth on edge. Even in uniform I was a civilian at heart.

For people lining Pennsylvania Avenue to see the big show every four years, such matters were of little or no account. They were there to see the president in the morning, if they could, and to watch the parade in his honor in the afternoon. The crowds attending inaugurations increased steadily in numbers as Washington's population grew and as the ways of getting to the city—train, bus, automobile, airplane—multiplied. On stormy days, only the hardiest and most determined ventured to take up positions on the Avenue for the morning procession and the afternoon parade, but on pleasant days the Avenue was a hub of activities from dawn until dark. There were decorations everywhere: flags, bunting, banners, flowers. Hundreds of vendors—called "fakirs" in the nineteenth century—swarmed the Avenue throughout the day, hawking soda pop, snacks, and souvenirs. The inaugural trinkets were frequently tailored to the president-elect. For TR there were Rough Rider hats, little brown teddy bears wound up to dance, pieces of wood bound together called "Teddy's Big Stick"; for Wilson, professorial blackboard pointers, yardsticks labeled WILSON'S RULE bearing the words, "A full measure of prosperity for all," songs and ballads announcing "Woody's a jolly good fellow," and even a restaurant on the Avenue with a big sign: WHITE HOUSE LUNCHES LIKE MRS. WILSON WILL COOK THEM, FOR 50 CENTS. With Lyndon B. Johnson came inaugural medals, bracelets, plaques, and ashtrays bearing his likeness; with Jimmy Carter, a former peanut farmer, came scads of inaugural buttons, key chains, scarves, lapels, and tie pins inscribed with the peanut logo; and with Bill Clinton came medallions featuring his face, pens featuring his name, envelopes featuring his hometown postmark (Hope, Arkansas), books featuring his ideas, and license plates emblazoned with a promise "to build a bridge to the future" (one of his favorite fin-de-siècle catchphrases). For rainy days, there were umbrellas for sale, with prices rising as supplies declined. And for any day, rain or shine, there was space inside some of the buildings along the parade route available for rent in front of the windows. On icy days, some groups paid as much as five hundred dollars for comfortable window views of the Pennsylvania Avenue parade.

In the late twentieth century America's inaugural celebrations became so elaborate—lasting several days and featuring hundreds of events on and off Pennsylvania Avenue—that a few people began lamenting the egregious departure from the Jeffersonian simplicities of the early nineteenth century. A few presidents even requested simpler celebrations—Wilson in 1917, Harding in 1921, Coolidge in 1925, and FDR in 1941 and 1945—and from time to time the inaugural planners shortened the afternoon parades or omitted them entirely.

But the opulence persisted. Richard Nixon's first inauguration, in 1969, was the costliest up to that time, and his second, in 1973, was even more expensive. Carter economized in 1977, and then Ronald Reagan threw an "Inauguration Special" that *Time* called "the biggest, most lavish, expensive presidential welcome ever." In 1993, Clinton took a page from Carter's book—he walked some of the way with his family down the Avenue after the inaugural ceremony—but the four-day inaugural festivities on his behalf were Reaganesque in their extravagance. The 1997 inauguration was costly, too, and contained, wrote one reporter, the usual "mismash of patriotism, pride, and silliness." Clinton apparently reveled in the whole mishmash; reading about his boyish glee at the passing parade reminded me of TR's exuberance in 1905. But Library of Congress historian Marvin W. Krinz defended 1997's lavishness. A presidential inauguration, he insisted, was really "a celebration of the American civil religion. It shows the diversity and the oneness of the nation. There's a certain amount of hokiness in it, after all, but so what?"

One participant denied the hokiness: John Pinter, vice president of the Wisconsin Hall of Fame in Milwaukee. When the White House asked him to arrange a polka float for the inaugural parade, he regarded the opportunity for the president to exchange greetings with Frank Yankovic, the King of American Polkadom, during 1997's parade as momentous, not hokey. Crowned the Polka King in 1948, the eighty-one-year-old Yankovic and his wife Ida, an accordion player, arrived in Washington just before Inauguration Day, with a contingent of polka dancers from Milwaukee, ready, willing, and able to take part in the inaugural parade past the White House reviewing stand. "He is an icon; he is a legend," a Hall of Fame spokesman told reporters. "He is to polka what Elvis Presley was to rock-and-roll." In the parade the following day Yankovic sat on a throne attached to the Hall of Fame float, and all around him musicians played and dancers performed the polka, while Barbara Lane, the Polka Queen of Milwaukee, sang "The White House Polka," which she had written for the president:

We're on our way to the White House
Pennsylvania Avenue
We're on our way to the White House
And we're proud of our red, white, and blue.
The polka is our state dance,
A dance that sets the pace.
It's great to play for the President,
But Wisconsin's our home state.

Well, there it was, in a scraggly nutshell: diversity and oneness. Hokey or not, the polka performance seems to have charmed the president. So did the parade as a whole, with its University of Arkansas marching band, the Democratic donkey, Irene, from Alabama, schoolchildren singing "It Takes a Village" (based on Mrs. Clinton's best-selling book), and the Chicago Rope Warrior who jumped rope while in a sitting position (he called it a "tush-up"). From polka to tush-up, Clinton thoroughly enjoyed the lively procession in his honor down Pennsylvania Avenue. It was just as well, I can't help thinking. It was the last bit of serious fun he was to have as he began his second term as president.

Civil War monument, Barre, Massachusetts. Photo by Sam Scarfone. *Copyright Crown Specialty Advertising.*

T. H. Breen

A MONUMENT FOR BARRE

Memory in a Massachusetts Town

T he physical face of Barre betrays uncertainty rather than indifference about more than two centuries of local history. A
maze of highways crisscrosses the Common at the center of
the village, creating curious grass fractals bounded by asphalt. One road
leads to Worcester, some twenty-two miles to the east. Others connect
Barre to small neighboring communities in central Massachusetts, obscure farming towns founded long ago, which now increasingly attract
those who have the resources to sustain a rural retreat.

Prolonged drought has browned the park grass and stressed the maple
trees. Although it is mid-August when I arrive in Barre, the dry scent
of autumn is already in the air. I explore the village park, examining
houses and stores, even open spaces, trying to visualize how this community might have appeared during the American Revolution, for it was
then, one spring morning just as people were setting out their crops,
that an African who had lived here for more than two decades suddenly
decided that he had had enough of slavery. By his own lights, a recently
ratified state constitution proclaiming human equality and political liberty directly affected his own condition. He, too, was free and equal.
Quork Walker's personal logic brought the republican ideology of revolution home to Barre, forcing townspeople to square rhetoric about all
men being created equal with an actual case of bondage in their midst.
Now, more than two centuries later, I am drawn to Barre, seeking to
discover how it has woven that moment of personal rebellion into a

corporate memory, or as a cultural anthropologist might say, into stories that Barre tells itself about itself at the start of a new millennium.

Barre resists my efforts to imagine such a distant past. Unlike classic New England towns that have preserved an eighteenth-century world, this community presents a jumble of different and conflicting pasts, a record of episodes rather than process, so that during my initial walk the buildings circling the Common seem like outcroppings of rock in which each stratum reveals a completely separate moment in a long and complex history. It is clear, however, that the fastidious force of gentrification is nowhere to be seen. From a nineteenth-century bandstand where townspeople once gathered on summer evenings, I survey a cluster of modest stores, a garage, a library, the offices of "Worcester County's Oldest Newspaper," several churches, a modern bank, and the Barre post office. Next to the Historical Society, the home long ago of a leading local family, I see a sadly empty field where until recently a grand old hotel testified to an earlier, more prosperous time when Barre dreamed of overcoming its isolation from a rapidly industrializing society. Destroyed by fire, the structure and the memories it once inspired have given way to weeds. One shop on the Common speaks of more recent change: "The Buddha Place: Meditation Supplies Right Under Your Nose."

The only self-conscious attempt to link contemporary Barre with its Revolutionary origins is the Colonel Isaac Barre Tavern, a small restaurant that like the town itself is named after a member of the British Parliament who during one memorable session in 1765 rose from the back benches of the House of Commons to attack a ministerial plan to tax colonial Americans without representation. He reminded his hostile colleagues that the colonists "fled from your Tyranny to a then uncultivated and unhospitable Country. . . . And yet, actuated by Principles of true english Lyberty, they met all these hardships with pleasure, compared with those they suffered in their own Country, from the hands of those who should have been their Friends." Barre, who had served in North America during the French and Indian War, knew that the colonists would stand firm on principle. In this speech, the colonel coined the phrase "Sons of Liberty." Of course, Americans adored the man who defended their political freedom, toasting his courage even though the Stamp Act passed easily into law. It is not surprising that at the start of revolution a group of Massachusetts farm families who found themselves living in a place then called Hutchinson—an irritating reminder of

Royal Governor Thomas Hutchinson, who sided with the crown against the patriots—voted to change the town's name to Barre.

Albert Clark meets me in front of the Historical Society. A retired local teacher, he brings good humor and welcome enthusiasm to our project. Clark is what is often, and somewhat condescendingly, called a "local historian," as if that designation implied an antiquarian obsession with community genealogy. But like most of the men and women who energize small historical societies throughout the United States, he does not see himself as the hagiographer of Barre's elite families, most of whom have long since moved away. He loves history's less fortunate people, those who had to support families by their own hard labor on this rocky soil. Anyone who has ever lived in Barre, anyone who paid a tax or claimed a few acres of land, merits serious attention, and although Clark's curiosity about the past seldom extends beyond Barre and its immediate neighbors, he reflects carefully on the evidence before us—artifacts as well as written records—always open to new and challenging interpretations of the familiar materials that he has so fiercely sought to preserve.

I have worked with people like Clark in other places—a fisherman in East Hampton, New York, who searched the woods and waters for a forgotten colonial past, and a teamster in North Carolina who mapped the great wagon roads of the eighteenth century as they ran through his own rural county. Like harbor pilots who guide outsiders safely through the back-channels and turbulent waters, these storytellers have helped me link larger narratives of war and nationalism, economic development, and racial tension to the experiences of local figures such as Quork Walker.

Clark and I stroll across the Common, chatting about shared concerns. A section of the park has been set aside for war monuments. The one commemorating Barre soldiers who died during the Civil War commands attention. A tall white spire rising from an ornate four-sided base, it dwarfs the cluster of granite markers listing the men—and more recently the women—who served their country during the wars of the twentieth century. We stand, absorbing the details of the Civil War monument, and perhaps because of an abiding interest in that great conflict, I read through the names of those killed on distant Southern battlefields.

"There is something odd about the monument," I observe.

Clark gives me a look of professional admiration. "You're the first one who noticed," he responds with characteristic excitement.

31

His praise—the kind of reverence that Dr. Watson was always directing at Sherlock Homes—makes me uneasy. What caught my eye was the manner in which the town had chosen to list the score or more names of those who had died in Maryland, North Carolina, and Louisiana. Behind each name appears not only a date and a place but, most peculiarly it seems to me, the cause of death.

I suppose those who construct monuments like the one in Barre generally like to create an impression that local recruits died in actual combat, but, of course, most of those who gave their lives died of less ennobling causes such as camp disease. And so it was for those men from Barre who joined the Union army. They succumbed to sudden fevers and lingering illnesses. The first name on the monument is Edwin L. Howe: died of "disease," Annapolis, Md., November 1861. Somehow the brutal honesty of the Barre Civil War monument undermines the alleged valor of war itself. A good many boys from Barre died not from Confederate fire but in squalor, probably without adequate medical attention, and a very long way from home. I wonder aloud whether more recent generations of young men who had grown up in this town appreciated the antiwar ironies of their beautiful monument. I spare my new friend the possibilities of a deconstructionist interpretation of a beloved Barre artifact, but by my lights I was clearly on a roll.

Clark gives me a look of mild dismay. He is the teacher, and I am the student who has obviously shown himself to be too clever by half. The peculiarity of the Barre Civil War monument, he informs me, is not to be found in the names of dead or in the causes of death. Rather, as Clark now relates, it is the entire stone structure that tells a curious, although arcane, tale. It seems that another, perhaps more affluent, town in eastern Massachusetts had decided sometime during the antebellum period to commemorate the courage and ingenuity of Hannah Duston, a late seventeenth-century Haverhill woman kidnaped from her home in March 1693 by Indians allied with the French in Canada. The Indians had gotten more than they had bargained for. Duston and a neighbor were not about to be dragged off to Montreal without resistance. A local minister recorded what happened:

> The Indians fell upon some part of Haverhill, about 7 in the morning, killed and carried away 39 or 40 persons. Two of these captive women, viz. Duston and Neff, (with another young man,) slew ten of the Indians, and returned home with their scalps.

The Reverend Cotton Mather, among other contemporaries, portrayed the young mother—Hannah had borne a child only five days before the attack—as a model for all God-fearing New Englanders. According to one historian, in 1702 Mather went over the top, depicting this remarkable woman as "an American amazon, a defender of Israel, and an archetypal heroine of the New World frontier." But Duston also had a good eye for the main chance. Even as she was being led ever deeper into the wilderness, she was busy calculating the rewards guaranteed by the government of Massachusetts for killing Indians, and as soon as she got home, she demanded twenty-five pounds sterling for the scalps she carried back to civilization.

Clark had no idea why nineteenth-century New Englanders decided to erect a huge monument in Duston's honor. But they did, purchasing the stone and employing a carver who presumably recorded the statistics of her murderous enterprise. There are hints, however, that the project did not enjoy sufficient local support to pay for its completion. When the Civil War turned popular attention to more pressing matters, the owners of the unfinished monument were only too happy to relegate Duston to oblivion, selling the expertly carved stone work to Barre at a bargain rate. Village laborers removed any mention of the ten dead Indians, and although some town leaders briefly resisted situating such a large monument on the Common they soon gave way to public sentiment. In fact, Barre's good fortune in purchasing the Duston marker meant that it was able to display a finished Civil War monument by 1866, years before most other towns in the region so honored their own Union dead.

Clark tells a good story. As I listen to the Duston tale, however, I cannot help but conclude that I have been set up. After all, how could I possibly know that Barre obtained its monument on the cheap and then erased another town's memories? As much to save face as to enlighten Clark, I ask, "Did you know that Hannah had a notorious sister?" He did not, and he considers carefully what I have to say from other research I had done on colonial Massachusetts about the bizarre history of the Duston family. Hannah's sister—one Elizabeth Emerson—who had experienced a hard, rebellious adolescence, killed her twins soon after childbirth and buried them in a shallow grave in her father's garden. She was easily found out, and the ever intrusive Cotton Mather visited her regularly in prison during the weeks before her execution. Elizabeth apparently did not have much use for Puritan divines.

Mather concluded sourly: "I Question whether ever any Prisoner in this World, enjoy's such mean of Grace as you have done since your Imprisonment, and it may be there never was a Prisoner more Hard-Hearted, and more Untruthful." He apparently never realized that Hannah and Elizabeth were sisters, one the toast of New England and the other hanged by the neck.

I suspect that the Barre Civil War monument has not been the object of such intense scrutiny for a very long time. As we turn to the business at hand, I decide that it is probably just as well that the townspeople of Barre are not burdened with the memory of the Duston sisters. Like the community's soldiers whose names are listed in stone, Hannah was caught up in the violence of war. The difference was that she lived to count the dead. In any case—although I do not say a word to Clark—I still prefer my own interpretation. We agree, however, that from either perspective, the monument is peculiar.

My thoughts return to Quork Walker, who in 1754 came as an infant to America from the east coast of Africa. He was a slave, the son of Dinah and Mingo. So far as anyone knows, Quork—his name sometimes appears in the early records as Quock or Quok—made no trouble for his master James Caldwell. After Caldwell died, however, the slave's life in this rural community, then known as the Rutland District, took a turn for the worse. Caldwell's widow married Nathaniel Jennison, a local man who seems to have possessed few positive virtues. Surviving records depict him as litigious, self-pitying, and occasionally violent. For some years Quork went about his business, probably staying as much as possible out of Jennison's way. Then, quite by chance during the closing months of the American Revolution, the Barre slave got his hands on the newly ratified Massachusetts state constitution. Echoing Thomas Jefferson's bold prose in the Declaration of Independence, the men elected throughout Massachusetts to represent the freeholders at the state convention insisted that "All men are born free and equal."

The proposition owed a lot to John Locke, the famous English philosopher who provided white colonists during the eighteenth century with their basic understanding of human rights. I doubt that Quork had ever read Locke. But he was literate, and however limited his formal education may have been, he recognized common sense when he saw it. The state constitution freed him from slavery; it liberated him from Jennison's tyranny. And with a sense of growing confidence that comes from knowing that one is supported by the force of law, Quork left the

Jennison household, walked a mile or so to a farm owned by John Caldwell, James's brother, and contracted to take a job that paid a real wage. In this society, a salary was the mark of freedom. By some measure Quork's rebellion seems fairly tame. After all, he did not attempt to escape Barre, and he spent his days doing the same kinds of agricultural work for Caldwell that he had for Jennison. But for Quork, the short walk from one local farm to another was the most important journey in his adult life. It proclaimed his insistence on full equality, a standing once enjoyed by Dinah and Mingo long ago in Africa, but lost in the New World.

Jennison rejected such republican nonsense. He went after Quork, confronting the African in one of Caldwell's fields, and when the former slave refused to return to bondage, Jennison became violent. He beat Quork, then carried the poor man back to his own farm and kept him prisoner in a barn. The slaveholder knew his rights. After all, Quork was his property. No state constitution could deprive a man of his lawful estate. He blustered "that the black was his slave, and that the beating, etc., was the necessary restraint and correction of the master."

But Jennison was out of step with the spirit of the times, at least as it expressed itself in republican Massachusetts. Someone in Barre engaged proper legal counsel for Quork—indeed, the services of several of the state's ablest attorneys—and in a complex series of civil and criminal proceedings brought before the Worcester County courts between 1781 and 1783, Quork's lawyers shredded Jennison's arguments. The angry slaveholder whined that if the court upheld Quork's claim to freedom, it would thereby expose other slaves throughout the Commonwealth to needless suffering, "some of them young and helpless, others old and infirm." If a black man was not a slave, Jennison reasoned, who would care for him? Moreover, Jennison insisted the white voters who passed the new state constitution never imagined at the moment of ratification that the language about humans being "free and equal" would lead to the abolition of slavery. And in one final desperate flourish, Jennison warned darkly that the planters in the southern states would not long support a federal system in which the rights of slaveholders were insecure. He could have saved his breath and, no doubt, considerable legal fees as well. The judges of the Massachusetts Supreme Court eventually upheld Quork's freedom suit, and by so doing, they abolished slavery forever in their state. Jennison fled town, desperately searching for another place that still regarded humans as property.

At the conclusion of his long ordeal, Quork elected to remain in Barre. The aging African probably recounted the story of his victory over Jennison to whomever would listen. And if he indulged himself occasionally in expressions of pride, he had the satisfaction of knowing that no one had given him his freedom. He had seized it, suffered for it. His own courage carried him through the crisis, for if Quork had not taken it upon himself to walk off the Jennison farm—not had the strength of character to act upon his deepest convictions—his Barre neighbors and all the lawyers and all the judges in the Commonwealth would probably have turned a blind eye to his bondage.

Clark and I drive off in his monster car that seems a survivor from another age to see the Jennison farm. Several miles outside of the town center we stop at an unprepossessing house. It does not look to be an eighteenth-century structure. It isn't. Clark confesses that Jennison's house as well as the barn where he confined Quork after the beating have long since been torn down. Nothing about what I am looking at marks it as a place where a man and his slave once battled over the meaning of freedom.

Clark must sense my inability to make the Jennison property communicate across a gulf of time about the lost world of Quork. Before my disappointment turns to despair, however, my guide quickly points out an overgrown path barely discernible across the state highway. That, he announces triumphantly, is the actual path that the African took when he left Jennison's farm and sought employment with John Caldwell.

The day has become uncomfortably hot. Although I can easily make out the configuration of an eighteenth-century road, I do not welcome an opportunity to retrace Quork's steps, at least not at this moment. I have a profound fear of ticks, a phobia that Clark finds strangely amusing. I assure him that these dreaded insects are out there, waiting for me in the bramble, each one carrying Lyme disease or worse. When Clark apologizes for not feeling up to the challenge of crashing through the underbrush today, I assume that my silent prayers have been answered.

We decide to look at the opening to the old path from the safety of Clark's car. In the sweltering heat of the day, he tells me that he regularly leads groups on what he calls the "Quork Walk." Starting at Jennison's, these intrepid men and women stumble along the historic route with Clark in the lead. All the time he busily creates an intricate word holograph, so that the threat of ticks and prickers soon fades as the hikers grasp an imagined moment that this skilled raconteur constructs before their very eyes. No matter that Jennison's house was torn down. This, they learn, is Barre's story. It is here—on the very ground upon which they are standing—that a black man made history. It is their history. Insomuch as Quork has been incorporated into the shared memory of this town, it has happened here.

In fact, his "walk" has become a sort of modern pilgrimage. Clark assures me that the number of men and women who follow him all the way to the Caldwell farm—the original barn has not survived—is not small. One Massachusetts judge, a person apparently made of sterner stuff than I, insisted on taking the Quork Walk even though he was dressed in an expensive suit. Clark warned the man about the thorns and burrs, but the visitor insisted that he was prepared to walk the walk. The journey shredded the designer outfit, but the distinguished visitor never complained. He, too, probably fell under Clark's spell. And although Clark takes no credit for Quork's growing importance in Barre, he observes proudly that a local woman has written a full-length play, commissioned specifically for the town's 225th anniversary celebration, which had occurred only a few months earlier. It was apparently an elaborate production, and townspeople competed for parts: a long-suffering Quork, a nasty Jennison, and earnest liberal lawyers. In fact, Clark tells me that a Nigerian man staying at a local Buddhist center took the occasion to correct the spelling of the name of the lead character in the town drama. He immediately recognized an African word. It was definitely Quork, not Quock or Quok, as historians had once insisted.

Clark and I drive down modern gravel roads to reach the other end of the Quork Walk. There are no markers to be seen, and had Clark not pointed out a small opening in the parched woods, I would not have known that Quork had become something of a local hero. But we do not stop. One building from that earlier era has survived, however, and we make our way to what was once the home of James Caldwell, the man who had originally purchased Quork and his parents. The house is located a few miles to the east of the Common, near the banks of the Ware River.

This is an isolated section of Barre, and though I appreciate seeing the eighteenth-century building where Quork and his family lived for so many years, where they labored as Caldwell's slaves, I again experience what might be called a failure of imagination. The difficulty is not simply that the structure has been modified by more recent owners. Rather, it seems so remote, so isolated from other houses, so cut off by an encroaching forest, that I find it hard to visualize what it might have been like for unfree Africans to work here. I have not had this problem on Virginia tobacco plantations or on the old levees of Tidewater Carolina where huge gangs of slaves once produced rice. In those places the Africans made a permanent mark on the landscape. One encounters slave quarters and special rooms in the great mansions reserved for the black men and women who served the masters as house slaves. But here, on a dirt road in Barre, time has effectively erased a slave past, and New Englanders, I suspect, have come to think of their own history as one of sturdy yeoman farmers, independent, somewhat truculent, white Christians who constructed the stone walls celebrated later by the likes of Robert Frost.

Layers of myth separate me from Quork, a process of denial and reinterpretation that began while he was still alive. In 1795, one prominent figure in Massachusetts assured its leading historian that "the state of slavery among us was always, I believe, as easy and as tolerable as can well be imagined, and in very many instances scarcely deserved the name, especially in the country towns, where the negroes were nearly upon an equal footing with the rest of the families in which they lived."

Quork grew up in one of those "country towns," but his experiences around the dinner table, working with an owner in the hay fields, riding in a wagon to church services on Sundays, bred not contentment but dreams of real equality. At the end of the day Quork made distinctions among masters. The Caldwells were not as bad as Jennison. The same self-styled expert on black culture who claimed that slavery in revolutionary New England "scarcely deserved the name" also observed that abolition in Massachusetts whitened the rural inland farm communities, for the newly freed blacks "have generally, as I am informed, left the country towns and resorted to the seaports." They migrated in search of jobs. Quork, however, stayed in Barre.

Clark breaks in on my thoughts. Up the road from the Caldwell house is a stone, marking the very spot where James Caldwell died. He was working in the meadow when lightning knocked down a huge tree, which in turn crushed Quork's master. We drive a half mile up the road to a deserted place surrounded by deep woods. Clark stops the car. He assures me that we can find the Caldwell monument; it is only a few hundred yards away. It is tick time. There is no discussion about the advisability of crashing through the trees. We attack the forest. I follow the indefatigable Clark, convinced that I am a condemned man, wondering if I will one day rate a historic marker. The promised path is not a path at all. Even deer do not seem to have penetrated this place. We thrash through the underbrush, and although both of us stumble over many rocks, none of them record the dramatic details of Caldwell's demise. After ten minutes or so, we give up the search.

We drive back to the Barre Common. We are both tired. The conversation lags, and I reflect on Caldwell's death. The bolt of lightning left a widow who inherited James's estate. And she married Jennison. Along with the furniture and farm tools went Quork. I wonder how he reacted to the news that James had died. Did he sense even then the terrible vulnerability of a man who was property?

Clark understands my frustration. We stand by the car in front of the Historical Society. I am just about to depart Barre when Clark asks whether I want to see the Quork marker. I have no idea what he is talking about. Without fully explaining, Clark leads me up the street to the local playhouse, an old church that now serves as a theater. It was there that the town performed the drama entitled *Quork's Passage*, and although the play closed weeks ago, no one has yet moved a heavy metal monument that dominates the lobby of the little theater.

In boldly painted lettering, the sign proclaims: QUORK WALKER. And under his name appears a short declaration: "Nearby on James Street stood the Home of Quork Walker, former slave, whose lawsuits resulted in the freeing of slaves in the commonwealth in 1783."

"Where's James Street?" I immediately ask Clark.

He points to a road across the Common from the playhouse. There, in a place where later generations constructed a church, once lived Barre's free African. Indeed, he did not die until 1814. I am genuinely pleased. A hot, dry Barre—ticks and all—suddenly looks a lot better to me. Clark and his friends would not allow the town to forget a black citizen who first arrived in 1754. Perhaps this new sign will cause just a few people in Barre to reflect on the powerful words in the state's first constitution that Quork saw as an invitation to freedom and equality. And as Clark and I look at the spot where the marker will soon be installed, I think again of the Civil War monument only a hundred yards away. It somehow makes more sense to me now. Perhaps those local boys who volunteered to fight in Virginia, Louisiana, and North Carolina had heard as children of Quork's brave walk and did not need to be persuaded that slavery has no place in a free society.

Young Greensboro blacks picket the Mayfair Cafeteria, Fall 1962. *Greensboro News and Record.*

William H. Chafe

GREENSBORO, NORTH CAROLINA

A Window on Race in the American South

I first came to Greensboro in the spring of 1972. I had recently completed my first year of teaching history at Duke University, fifty miles to the east. My interest in Greensboro went back to my college years in the late 1950s and early 1960s, when, like so many students of my generation, I was galvanized by the courage of four young men who dared to sit in at a segregated Woolworth's lunch counter to protest against racial discrimination. I wanted to understand how that event had happened.

I remember with warmth how much I looked forward, as a child in Cambridge, Massachusetts, to going to the local Woolworth's with my mother and eating egg salad sandwiches. I also recall my experience growing up in a Baptist church in Central Square. There, I had gleaned the idea that the gospel of Jesus had something to say about social relations in my own time. So at age 15 I dismayed the deacons at my church by asking why we did not have black members, especially in a church that was located within four blocks of thousands of black residents. It was a naive question for many reasons (not the least of which was the strength of the black Baptist church a few thousand yards away), but it led to an abiding personal as well as academic interest in understanding why race has been so pivotal to the way America is organized, socially, economically, and politically. In graduate school, I had focused on another central (and very related) issue—the experience of women— and now, with my book on that subject about to come out, I decided to return to my earlier locus of concern.

As one of a breed of newly trained social historians, I knew that one could not understand the dynamics of social reform just by looking at how powerful national leaders responded to the issue of racial justice. Indeed, the issue came onto their radar screens only after millions of "ordinary" people insisted on its being there through their persistent struggle. I decided that the richness and texture of *that* story could be discovered only by going into a community and exploring the world out of which the sit-inners emerged. Who inspired them? How did they come to their decision? What was the response of white authorities? How did race relations operate in a community where whites and blacks interacted constantly, without ever fully acknowledging the foundational difference that divided them? If racism was, as I had come to believe, democracy's original sin, how could redemption be found?

Those were the questions that led me that spring day into a community that everyone had told me—scholars and lay people alike—embodied the best of North Carolina's tradition of enlightened progressivism. (V. O. Key, the venerated political scientist, had called North Carolina an "inspiring exception" to the South's white racism.) Five colleges and universities dotted the landscape of the bustling small city, giving pride to its boosters, white and black alike (two of the colleges were historically black). Greensboro's Quaker enclave had once served as a stop on the underground railroad; the city had elected a Jewish mayor in the 1940s and a black city councilman in the early 1950s. To be sure, for most of the twentieth century, textile mills headed by Benjamin Cone and J. Spencer Love had dominated the local economy, bringing with them a persistent undercurrent of labor strife. But there was also a burgeoning white-collar economy featuring regional and national insurance giants that projected an image of modernity. Appropriately, the newspaper (the *Greensboro Daily News*) boasted of being one of the most enlightened papers of the South, a training ground for people who went on to editorial and management positions with the *Washington Post* or the *New York Times*. Greensboro was thus a city with some basis for thinking itself distinctive.

My first appointment that day was with two white leaders clearly in positions to speak reliably for the larger white community. I noticed on my drive from the interstate into the downtown area that I was passing through what seemed a totally black community, with numbers of churches and with signs to the two historically black colleges in town. I began my conversation by asking the two white leaders to speak about the history of Greensboro, and especially its reputation for being progressive. They did so with enthusiasm. I then asked who were the leaders of the black community I might talk to. They did not know. I asked who the head of the NAACP was. They did not know. I asked what was the largest black church congregation in town. They did not know. That was the beginning of my journey of discovery into how, and why, a sophisticated and apparently enlightened southern community could also be the site of endemic racism.

Greensboro's twentieth-century racial politics grew out of the same chemistry that helped create the Jim Crow system throughout the entire South. Although racial democracy had never existed, even at the heyday of Reconstruction after the Civil War, there had been at least some recognition by white Democrats of black autonomy, economical and political—in North Carolina as well as elsewhere. Until 1900, blacks made up nearly 50 percent of all the skilled workers in Greensboro; they worked as carpenters, stonemasons, foundry workers, and brickmasons. On seven of nineteen streets in Greensboro in 1880, black and white households existed side by side. Then, in North Carolina, as in the rest of the South, along came the Populists, seeking to forge an alliance based on common *class* interests—the poor (potentially white *and* black) against the rich.

It was at that point that the ruling Bourbon Democrats initiated the "reform" of black disfranchisement. Whites had to stick together, these white Democrats argued, purging the body politic of the corruption represented by blacks voting. Through purifying the electorate, the "reformers" asserted, whites could move forward together.

The "race card" worked for those who played it. Under the guise of reform, virtually all blacks—and eventually most poor whites—lost their rights as citizens. At the same time, virtually every Jim Crow law mandating separation of the races was enacted, forcing separate railroad cars, cemeteries, drinking fountains, and schools—all ostensibly "equal" but in fact never approximating equality. Within such a set of presumptions, upper-class whites would assume the responsibility to treat "their" colored people in a kindly and beneficent way—as long as those colored people "kept their place." It was a new version of the old regime of the days of slavery. As long as none of the blacks questioned, challenged, or rebelled against the presumption that whites automatically deserved to be in control, there would be no problems.

Tragically, North Carolina fully participated in this system. As Tim Tyson and David Cecelski have shown in their recent book *Democracy Betrayed*, white leaders in North Carolina collaborated in a campaign of terror culminating in the Wilmington Race Riot of 1898, when the bodies of black citizens who dared to believe in biracial democracy filled the Cape Fear River. At the same time, other white politicians used the siren call of reform to promulgate segregation and black disfranchisement. Under the "benevolent" leadership of Governor Charles Aycock, a new regime of segregated institutions was put in place, including the first all-black public colleges in the state. Aycock has gone down in the state's history as a "progressive" governor, committed to education, who stabilized race relations and helped provide the infrastructure of a separate educational system for blacks. But the result was a system of arbitrary social control that reversed any gains that had been achieved after the Civil War and put into practice a structure of oppression that offered little room for maneuver or challenge.

In Greensboro, the new regime coincided with the arrival of the "New South" of textile mills that employed thousands of workers, almost all of them white, except for service workers. Blacks were forced out of the skilled occupations they had held years earlier. Whereas in 1870 30 percent of the black population occupied skilled jobs, by 1910 the figure had dropped to 8 percent. By 1910 not a single black was listed as a factory worker, while 80 percent of those gainfully employed served as semiskilled service workers or unskilled laborers. In 1914 a city ordinance proscribed blacks from buying property on any street where a majority of residences were owned by whites, and the same law prohibited building any place of public assembly in an area dominated by the other race. In effect, the social system had been transformed, and while the new system touted a veneer of New South enlightenment, its foundation remained a raw racial caste system that eliminated, step by step, virtually any room for mobilizing collective protest.

Perhaps the most insidious part of this system, born in an era of so-called reform, is what I called in my book on Greensboro (*Civilities and Civil Rights*, published in 1980) the "progressive mystique" of North Carolina politics. At its heart, the "progressive mystique" is a set of rules governing political etiquette and discourse. First, these rules convey an openness to discussion and the free expression of different ideas. Thus, any idea could be considered, at least theoretically, since it would be impolite not to do so. But second, these rules carry a presumption that the current state of things is sufficiently good that only when everyone agrees that change is necessary should change occur. Consensus—unanimity—thus becomes a political prerequisite for reform, automatically ruling out any change that would involve conflict or significant division. Third, there is a conviction that those who are privileged to occupy positions of power and wealth in the society must act with beneficence and paternal responsibility toward those in a lesser position; hence problems of inequality or disadvantage, it is claimed, can be dealt with through charity. And fourth, there is a belief that the entire system is premised on civility in personal and group interactions—a commitment to manners and politeness as the essence of a cultivated society. To belong to such a social system is to agree, from the beginning, on a framework that places as high a premium on how ideas are broached and relationships are conducted as on the content of those ideas or the substance of social relations.

The complexity of the "progressive mystique" is hard to overstate: its ripple effects are almost endless. Why have whites in positions of power insisted that there is no race problem or class problem in their communities? Because these whites "know" their black workers and black associates intimately. They exchange greetings, express condolences when someone dies, joke about the weather, and ask after the family. Surely, if there were a problem, these whites in positions of authority would know about it from those who are part of their extended "family." Daily experiences thus confirm on a repeated and credible basis the degree to which the "progressive mystique" works. It is organic, healthy, and vital.

But beneath this Byzantine complexity, the "progressive mystique" is also devastatingly simple. It operates, in effect, to close off outbursts of protest and stifle expressions of alienation. Instead, all efforts at change are directed into a series of controlled and well-defined channels of communication that remain consistent with, and not threatening to, the overall structure of the status quo.

It is within this structure that the drama of twentieth-century race relations was enacted. Here, Greensboro provides a microcosm of how blacks persisted in their efforts at community-building during the era of Jim Crow and how those struggles, in turn, laid the foundation for breaking out of the "progressive mystique" and challenging its very premises during the 1960s and 1970s. Greensboro also exemplifies the contradictory ways in which whites reacted to black initiatives, especially when the very core of their own control came under assault.

Perhaps the most notable example of black self-assertion within the confines of the "progressive mystique" emerged through the insistence of African Americans on building schools, churches, and institutions of which they could be proud, even if they had to operate within structures that constrained their freedom to achieve all that they wished. John Tarpley came to Greensboro from Texas in 1926 to teach at Bennett College, the segregated (and private) women's school in Greensboro. He soon became superintendent of the black schools in the community. There, he helped build the teaching staff from one where two-thirds of the black faculty had no college degree to a place twenty years later where two-thirds boasted an M.A. Tarpley and his colleagues helped make Dudley High School a synonym for quality and pride, in the same way that Paul Dunbar High School in Washington was for blacks who lived there. Throughout this time, Tarpley played by the rules. When he approached the school board or the superintendent for new equipment or facilities, he always brought two plans—one for all that was necessary to move toward equality, the other for the minimum he needed to move forward. But his skills brought significant change.

Dr. F. D. Bluford, the president of Greensboro Agricultural and Technical College—the public black college in Greensboro—exemplified the same pattern of behavior. Bluford constantly had to appease his white superiors, especially those who appropriated the school's funds in the legislature. More militant students called him "the last of the handkerchief heads" and referred to his house as "Uncle Tom's Cabin." Yet Bluford was guided primarily by his main priority—the college. "If he had to go down to Raleigh and suffer indignities, he would," one faculty member told me. Once in the late 1940s, when Randolph Blackwell, a more radical student and veteran of World War II, was campaigning on campus for election to the state legislature, Bluford stopped him and asked Blackwell to make an appointment to see him. "Here it comes," Blackwell thought. "Now I've had it." But when he entered the president's office, Bluford told him that he was free to use any college facility he wanted during his campaign. The only condition was that he not ask for permission, since if Bluford were called on the carpet, he wanted to be able to deny complicity. Blackwell concluded that, despite Bluford's reputation, he was a "man with a sense of dignity . . . a man [who, although] . . . constantly abused, also had some of the same yearnings as those of us that were out there raising hell."

A final example of this dynamic occurred when blacks in Greensboro in the 1940s sought better recreational facilities for their children and families. They did not go to the City Council, conduct protest rallies, or march on City Hall. Instead, they approached the wealthiest white leaders in the city, stated their case as petitioners seeking assistance, and appealed to the beneficence of their patrons to respond out of a sense of paternal obligation to the needs they had outlined. And, in its inimitable manner, the system worked—in two ways. Separate swimming pools for black citizens suddenly appeared, as did other enhanced "separate but equal facilities," thereby "proving" that if political discourse occurred in a mannerly and civil framework, some change would be forthcoming. But the even deeper and simpler lesson was that *only* when these rules were observed and obeyed could any progress be achieved. So, in effect, the system of civility and the "progressive mystique" perpetuated itself, reinforcing through every exchange the viability and well-being of the status quo.

The deeper problem was that any changes that occurred via this mechanism left intact the *structure* of economic and racial oppression. Refinements, modifications, small improvements might occur, but these simply tweaked a framework of power relationships that not only remained intact but actually became stronger each time the "progressive mystique" came into play. How to challenge that structure thus became the pivotal test.

Ironically—and in some ways not surprisingly—the building stones for challenging that structure emerged directly from the resilience, strength, and courage of the African-American response to Jim Crow. Whatever limits black leaders might accept in order to protect their own institutions, the independence and spirit of the teachers who inhabited the classroom could not be controlled. There was a good reason for the community to have such a sense of pride in those teachers. They were inspiring.

Vance Chavis taught science at Dudley High School. When I talked to him about his experience in Greensboro, he recalled having told students about his membership in the NAACP, encouraging others to follow his example. During his morning homeroom period, Chavis had his students address envelopes urging their parents and others to register to vote. Chavis boasted of his refusal to patronize Jim Crow movie theaters that required him to sit in the "buzzard's roost," and he urged his students not to ride Jim Crow buses or trains. Nell Coley, his colleague at Dudley, taught English, but in a way that carried the message of ennobling literature to a level of personal and immediate challenge to her students. "We were always talking about the issues," Coley told me. "We might read [a poem or a novel] as a kind of pivot," but the words of Shakespeare or John Donne were always linked to the impulse to freedom, self-respect, and dignity of all humans. "I had to tell youngsters," Coley said, "that the way you find things need not happen.... You must not accept; I don't care if they push and shove you, you must not accept that [second-class treatment].... You are who you are."

Many of the students who took classes with Chavis and Coley in the 1950s also attended Shiloh Baptist Church, the largest black church in Greensboro. The pastor, Otis Hairston Jr., had gone to Shaw University, an all-black private university started in North Carolina during Reconstruction. There he participated in civil rights protests, and when he came to the Shiloh congregation, he preached a message that conveyed the imperative need for his parishioners to carry the radical ideas of Jesus into their everyday lives. Many of the young people who went to Shiloh also participated in Greensboro's NAACP youth group—started by the legendary Ella Baker in 1943 when she was an NAACP field representative, and now a gathering place where students could talk about the implications of events like the *Brown* decision in 1954, with its ruling that segregation was inherently unconstitutional, or the Montgomery bus boycott of 1955, with its stirring message of nonviolent protest and mass participation in the refusal to ride Jim Crow buses.

It was these building stones that provided the foundation for the four students who dared to challenge segregation frontally with their sit-in on February 1, 1960. Two of the four had grown up in Greensboro, had been taught by people like Coley and Chavis, and were veterans of the NAACP youth group. As first-year students at Greensboro A&T, the four—coming to maturity in the six years after *Brown*—concluded that it was their responsibility to carry the black struggle to its next stage. "We challenged each other, really," one of them later said. "We constantly heard about all the evils that are occurring and how blacks are mistreated and nobody was doing anything about it." And so they decided to do something bold, something that would highlight—personally and dramatically—the moral absurdity that suffused a system that said you could buy commercial products at one counter and be treated like any other customer but be denied service at a lunch counter because black customers were not supposed to sit next to whites. "The thing that precipitated the sit-ins," one of the four later told me, "was that little bit of incentive and that little bit of courage that each of us instilled within each other."

Understanding the obstructions that had faced their teachers, parents, and friends in trying to create change—and determined that they would not become accomplices in this system of oppression—these four first-year students pondered what *new* steps they might take to break through what I have called the "progressive mystique." Struck by the simple clarity of the lunch-counter example, they determined to act—terrified of what might happen to them and their parents for daring to violate custom, anxious about how their deans would respond, fearful of violence, yet committed to taking history into their own hands. And so they went to Woolworth's in downtown Greensboro on February 1, 1960. They bought toothpaste and notebooks at different counters, holding on to their receipts. And then they went to the lunch counter, sat down, and ordered a cup of coffee. "We don't serve Negroes," they were told. "Well, you served us over there," they said. "Why not here as well?" Opening their books and starting to study, the Greensboro Four remained seated for the duration of the afternoon. The next day, after word of their action had spread around the A&T campus, they returned with twenty-three others. Then the next day with sixty; the day after that with a hundred. And finally, on Saturday, they were joined by a thousand. Within two months, similar sit-ins had spread to fifty-four cities in nine different states. The Greensboro Coffee Party had set off a revolution.

With one simple but courageous act, four young men had broken through the "progressive mystique" and inaugurated a new language of protest, one based on candor and the right to full self-expression—*not* playing by the old rules. "Civilities and Civil Rights" was the headline on the *Greensboro Daily News*'s lead editorial. The paper insisted that civility had to prevail as the critical value that united people in Greensboro and symbolized their devotion to a common good. "NO," the students responded with their sit-in: the substance of civil rights meant far more than the etiquette of civility.

The sit-ins highlighted both the difficulty of aggressively addressing issues of racial injustice and the necessity of finding bold and new mechanisms for doing so. If conventional vehicles of seeking redress had been used—as in the discussions over better school and recreational facilities—the result would, in all likelihood, have been an unsatisfactory and frustrating compromise, such as serving Negroes in a separate seating section of the lunch counter. But new forms of collective self-expression shattered the old rules, reframed the discussion, and altered the stakes and the outcome. Sitting down silently to insist on equal treatment exploded a whole ritual of social control.

At the heart of this dynamic were two realities. First, it was necessary to violate the rules, breaking out of established norms of conduct, daring to define for oneself the terrain on which issues would be engaged, if black Americans were to cut through the multiple layers of control exercised by whites who controlled the "progressive mystique." As long as the social etiquette of paternalism—with change occurring only by unanimous consent—remained in place, no act could penetrate the hegemony of a racially infused and oppressive social structure.

Once the sit-in demonstrators shattered that etiquette, however, the whole landscape of racial discourse changed. Ironically, the silence—and politeness—of the new language chosen by the sit-in protesters spoke more powerfully than any other weapon could have in altering the terms of engagement. How extraordinary that the act of sitting down and studying, dressed in shirts and ties and jackets, with neither a loud word nor impolite gesture expressed, could help turn around and eventually topple more than sixty years of segregation.

But equally important was the second point: this act of insurgency was possible because of, and totally informed by, the ongoing struggle of generations of black Americans who had worked within the prior structure of racial inequality to create the best conditions possible for their families and their descendants. The sit-in protesters could not have done what they did without the John Tarpleys, Vance Chavises, Nell Coleys, and Otis Hairstons in their lives—the people who built Dudley High, shaped it into a bastion of community pride, and taught the young to aspire to better lives and never accept someone else's determination that they were second-class citizens. Their elders did not forge the weapons of transformation created by the young. But they were the ones who planted the ideas, and nurtured the courage, of those who did forge the weapons.

The victories achieved as a result of the sit-ins were not a panacea for America's racial dilemma. To be sure, the explosion of protests triggered by the sit-ins eventually led to the mass-based direct action movement of the early 1960s that made possible the Civil Rights Act of 1964 and the Voting Rights Act of 1965. But in Greensboro, as elsewhere, progress in some areas simply underlined the absence of progress in others. The 1963 March on Washington had been for jobs and freedom, but all too often the "jobs" part of the equation was ignored. Many blacks reacted with impatience to what they perceived as the paternalism of white liberals, leading to the emergence of black power as a political movement of the late 1960s. Greensboro was in many ways a center of black power, fusing an aggressive mobilization of poor people with a heightened determination to have blacks define their own agenda, independent of white-run social agencies. Eventually, those politics led in 1969 to black power activists and their followers taking over A&T University, their forcible expulsion by National Guard troops, and the killing of a black student.

A decade later, violence erupted once again with the Ku Klux Klan murder of Communist Worker Party (CWP) members who rallied in protest against the Klan and its message of hatred. As in the past, themes of race and class were in the forefront. Activists, black and white, sought to unionize textile mill employees while organizing the black community around issues of political representation and poverty. When the CWP mounted a "death to the Klan" march in the black area of Greensboro, Klan members secured their parade route from local police and, on the day of the march, ambushed the participants, killing five of them. The police were not present. Greensboro authorities blamed the murders on "outside" agitators. Yet Greensboro activists and Greensboro textile mills were at the heart of the dispute, and local police had placed an informant in the Klan group who knew in advance of the Klan's intentions and had reported them to local authorities. More to the point, perhaps, was the degree to which the confrontation exposed the raw nerve of how racial and economic issues continued to be a core reality at the heart of the history of Greensboro—and of the nation.

I could not have known, on that first trip to Greensboro in 1972, how rich and textured Greensboro was as an embodiment of our national experience. I could not have known that the gap between my journey through black Greensboro and the white response to my questions about blacks—"I don't know"—would so encapsulate the fundamental flaw in race relations in Greensboro, as well as America. And I could not have known that a place that I had always cherished as a child—a Woolworth's lunch counter—would become, in my history of this community, such a symbol of all that is great about our country. But that is why a sense of place is so important. And why Greensboro is more than just another city in the Triad of central North Carolina.

The graves of American soldiers above Omaha Beach.

James C. Cobb

WORLD WAR II NORMANDY

American Cemetery and Memorial

"The tombs where they rest have made American these
French acres which have become shrines for their countrymen
and for ours."

—*René Coty, president of France, July 18, 1956 (on the
occasion of the dedication of the American Cemetery and
Memorial, Colleville sur-Mer)*

"*What a grand time was the war, my, my!
Did Somebody Die?*"

—*Langston Hughes, "World War II"*

L ike many people who study the American South, I believe that
our attachment to places, especially the places that are familiar
and special only to us, can tell a us a great deal about who we
are. I am also struck, however, by the power of places of universally
recognized importance, places where history actually "happened," to
speak to many people in many ways. Certainly, my connection to one

particularly significant site, the World War II Normandy American Cemetery and Memorial, has shown me that the monumental challenges of history can shape the identities not only of those who faced them but of those who did not as well.

Long a popular attraction for Americans visiting France, the World War II Normandy American Cemetery and Memorial has drawn unprecedented attention since it was featured in the opening and closing scenes of Steven Spielberg's blockbuster World War II film, *Saving Private Ryan*. The cemetery sits on a cliff overlooking Omaha Beach and the English Channel near Colleville sur-Mer, about 170 miles west of Paris. Within its 172 acres lie the remains of 9,836 American soldiers, most of whom died in the D-Day invasion and subsequent fighting. Marking the graves, Latin crosses and Stars of David cut from gleaming white Carrara marble stand out in bold relief against a perfectly manicured carpet of what surely must be the greenest grass on earth. The cemetery is the final resting place for three Medal of Honor winners, three generals (one of whom, Brigadier General Theodore Roosevelt Jr., is also a Medal of Honor recipient), thirty-three sets of brothers, four women, and one father and son. Three hundred and seven of the crosses mark the graves of "unknowns" and simply read: HERE RESTS IN HONORED GLORY A COMRADE IN ARMS KNOWN BUT TO GOD. The cemetery also holds the Garden of the Missing, where 1,557 names of those whose bodies were never recovered are inscribed on a wall.

It is difficult, and perhaps not even desirable, to separate the cemetery from Omaha Beach, where more than two thousand Americans were killed or wounded on June 6, 1944. The peaceful golden sands that stretch for several miles show no sign of the desperate struggle that raged here more than half a century ago. For the Allies, Omaha was the worst possible potential invasion spot, but in practical terms a landing there was unavoidable. It was the only gap in twenty miles of cliffs separating the three British and Canadian beaches (Sword, Gold, and Juno) from the other American beach (Utah) on the west. Unless Omaha could be secured, a German counterattack might split the Allies and foil the invasion entirely.

From the defender's standpoint, Omaha was close to ideal. The beach itself was relatively narrow at high tide, but after traversing it, troops had to fight their way up steep bluffs to reach the plateau where the cemetery now sits. On the orders of Field Marshal Erwin Rommel himself, Omaha had been festooned with waterline obstacles consisting of mined posts and angular steel. Overlooking the beach were eighty-eight- and seventy-five-millimeter guns in eight bunkers, thirty-eight rocket barriers, six mortar pits, and eighty or more machine gun emplacements. The four ravines that provided escapes from the beach were mined, wired, and covered by thirty-five pillboxes filled with riflemen and machine gunners as well as snipers scattered about in concealed locations. To make matters worse for the Allied invasion force, preliminary aerial and naval bombardments proved largely ineffective in weakening the German defenses. This was the setting for the hellish struggle that cost so many lives as American soldiers fought desperately on June 6, 1944, to get onto and then off Omaha Beach.

William Faulkner wrote that "every southern boy" fantasizes repeatedly about reenacting Pickett's Charge and reversing the outcome of the Civil War. Faulkner was referring to white males born between Appomattox and Pearl Harbor, but I came along a little later (1947), and instead of Cemetery Ridge, our backyard doubled as Omaha Beach. (This sort of instantaneous metamorphosis of place happened all the time in the 1950s, an era when parents knew no better than to allow their children to become bored, thereby forcing them to use their imaginations to devise some means of amusing themselves.) In my downsized version of D-Day, taking Omaha Beach was a snap. In fact, I did so repeatedly and singlehandedly, and my assaults were absolutely unstoppable, unless my mama called me in for supper. On literally hundreds of occasions, I boldly abandoned the cover provided by our coal pile and charged up the beach toward our back porch, showing no fear despite the fact that as an only child I had to face death alone. German bullets whizzed all around but never even nicked me, although as I ran zigzag I did occasionally encounter some of the noxious biological agents left on the beach by our chickens.

By age ten I was an undiagnosed World War II junkie, my preadolescent fantasies stoked by innumerable movies (any of which would have been an excellent recruiting film) that I watched over and over on television and by every combat memoir that Miss Lizzie Blackwell would let me check out of our tiny local library. As I grew older, I promoted myself from infantryman to fighter pilot, converting our sofa to the cockpit of a P-47 or P-51 and downing scores of Messerschmitts and Zeroes right there in our living room.

Clearly, at this age I did not understand what was really at stake in World War II. I read about the Holocaust and shuddered at photographic evidence of its horrors, but it never occurred to me that the lone Jewish couple in our entire county was there because they had fled Nazi persecution. Although Daffy Duck's portrayal of Hitler in one of my favorite cartoons was hardly menacing, documentary film footage quickly convinced me that he was one scary dude. He turned up in a few of my nightmares, and somebody was always claiming to have seen him in South America, but in all honesty, it was difficult for me to devote much fear to dead and defeated former enemies when menaced by live ones in the persons of Khrushchev and Mao Tse-tung. Khrushchev, after all, had "the bomb" and was likely to unloose it and charbroil us all at any minute, and both he and Mao were also working to destroy our way of life and subvert our cherished institutions. I even saw a film in high school that demonstrated how easily the Communists could infiltrate an Elks Club.

Ostensibly to stop Communist expansion and aggression, the first American ground combat troops were deployed in Vietnam a few months before I finished high school in 1965. Despite my distinguished childhood military career, by the time I left the University of Georgia in 1969, I had embraced the anti–Vietnam War conviction. My contract to teach U.S. history, world history, geography, and English and coach the debate team at Loganville (Georgia) High School entitled me to a one-year occupational deferment from the draft. At the end of my first year at Loganville, President Nixon announced an end to such deferments, and in the ensuing draft lottery my birthday, April 13, came up at number 120. For me, at age twenty-three and recently reclassified 1A, that would have effectively meant "Get ready to ship out," but because of my background as a ham radio operator, I was able to get into a National Guard unit in need of a communications specialist.

As it turned out, my greatest challenge in uniform was making it through basic training at Fort Dix, New Jersey, during January and February 1971. Save for a nasty case of frostbite, I emerged unscathed to spend the next eight months at Fort Monmouth, New Jersey, just outside New York City. My wife and I lived in Asbury Park on the

Jersey shore and generally behaved like tourists for the duration. When I finally completed my six-year National Guard obligation by marching in the big July 4, 1976, bicentennial parade in Ellicott City, Maryland, the closest I had come to a Purple Heart was a purple buttock, caused by a nasty spider bite inflicted one soggy night in the woods when my unit was activated during a flood.

By this time, miraculously enough, I had made my way through graduate school and, more miraculously still, found employment as a history professor. Although I had been the most ardent of warriors in my youth, as a teacher I deliberately avoided military history and strategy. In the classroom I approached World War II as little more than a prelude to the cold war. I discussed the long-term implications of Stalin's call for a "second front" in Europe versus Churchill's preference for attacking the "underbelly of the Axis" via North Africa and the Mediterranean. Likewise, I stressed the diplomatic implications of both the Russian stand at Stalingrad and Eisenhower's decision to let the Russians participate in the final assault on Berlin. This teaching strategy provided a relatively seamless transition from World War II to the cold war. On the other hand, it made the war itself seem a rather bloodless and sterile affair and offered little sense of the suffering and sacrifice either on the battlefield or the homefront.

I persisted in this tactic for more than twenty years, but my approach to teaching World War II changed abruptly and permanently after my first trip to the Normandy American Cemetery. Since that visit, I have used letters and diaries and anecdotes to dramatize the horrors of combat and tried to humanize the body counts with the first-person accounts of the grief and suffering that comes when loved ones are lost. Beyond that, I share my own very personal impressions and reactions to the cemetery and explain how my visits there have stirred me to think in new ways about both my national and generational identities.

More than any other historical site or monument that I have ever visited—in fact, more than all of them put together—this place overwhelmed me with a teary, tingly, chest-tightening emotional rush. Then, as this feeling gradually subsided, with the whitecapped English Channel churning noisily nearby, I suddenly became contemplative and calm, almost detached. Against a stunning backdrop of lush, ultra-green grass and wind-bent trees, the seemingly endless, perfectly aligned rows of white markers presented an image of peace and order that contrasted starkly with the conflict and chaos that had once raged on the beach below them. The markers bore the names of men from states I had never visited and others that I knew like the back of my hand. As I noted the graves of soldiers from states in the latter category, I found myself wondering whether, until the war came, they had ever been out of Georgia, Alabama, Mississippi, or South Carolina or maybe even beyond a hundred-mile radius of the place where they were born. Yet they came thousands of miles to step off landing crafts into a solid wall of lethal lead or to jump into the night sky uncertain of where they would land but well aware of the perils that awaited them in the darkness below.

After my first visit to this cemetery, I wished fervently that the next time I encountered an arrogant French waiter (which is to say the next time I visited Paris), I could grab him by the scruff of the neck and drag him here, where he would have no choice but to admit that his nation owed mine a great debt. My further reflections on this cemetery, however, have shown me that a single place can speak (or be made to speak) to different people in different ways. When I read the remarks of French president René Coty, offered on the occasion of the cemetery's dedication on July 18, 1956, I learned that the meaning of a place, particularly such a historic one, can be "spun" and effectively politicized. Indeed, the politics of place can be integral to the politics of history, which is, in turn, fundamental to the politics of the present. With the cemetery's dedication at hand, French leaders were still smarting over American refusal to intervene at Dienbienphu in 1954. Moreover, the looming Suez Crisis was being compared to Munich, and Egyptian president Gamal Abdel Nasser (who would nationalize the Suez Canal scarcely a week later) to Hitler. Accordingly, Coty used the dedication ceremonies to offer a lesson on the necessity of resisting aggression as soon and as vigorously as possible. Of the slain Americans, Coty observed, "They are here in such great numbers only because from the very first day of its terrifying ambition, tyranny did not meet the united front of the democratic peoples."

Coty's remarks clearly repudiated the "peace in our time" policies by which England's Neville Chamberlain and France's Eduoard Daladier had sought to placate Hitler. Moreover, by suggesting that had Uncle Sam not been so hesitant, fewer crosses or Stars of David might dot this

Normandy landscape, Coty took a swipe at the United States for allowing the war in Europe to rage for more than two years before becoming
involved. Exhibiting what is by now a familiar determination to assert
French independence and identity in the face of American cultural im-
perialism, Coty hailed those who "gave their lives for our France," but
lest he appear to feel overly indebted to the United States, he noted that
"just as their fathers in the first war, they died primarily for their own
country." For good measure, he also harked back to "a former day" when
the "sons" of France had "also crossed the Atlantic, at the call of American Independence."

On both my visits here I have encountered German tourists at the
cemetery and also at the nearby bunkers and gun emplacements that
were manned by their nation's troops at this vital place where the tide
of war clearly turned for good. As I observed a young German couple,
I wondered what they were feeling. Did they harbor deep within them
something akin to the longing alluded to by Faulkner for a reprise of
Pickett's Charge, an irrepressible impulse that even liberal-minded white
southerners have confessed to feeling when they visited Gettysburg?

In truth, at a very basic level, even my own reactions to this place
were mixed. On one hand, I was filled with admiration for those who
lost their lives in an effort that gave me such security and pride in my
identity as an American. Yet, even as I sought to attach myself to their
accomplishment and glean some vicarious sense of self-assurance from
it, my contemplation of what they did only magnified my doubts about
myself and my contemporaries.

In my mind this cemetery is the most meaningful of all monuments
to the generation of Americans who grew up during the Great Depression and then proceeded to fight and die to save us from Hitler and
Tojo. What is so truly remarkable about this greatest generation, it seems
to me, is their reluctance often even to acknowledge, much less celebrate,
their heroic deeds. I have known men of my parents' age for years before
I discovered that they had served with great courage and distinction in
World War II. Only recently did I learn that Hugh Gray, a friend of
my folks who intrigued me as a child primarily because he sported a
tattoo and raised goats, was one of the elite Army Rangers who landed
at Omaha Beach on D-day. He later told his family of taking cover
behind the stacked corpses of his comrades and of witnessing scenes

more gruesome and horrifying than anything Hollywood could possibly concoct.

If those who are buried in the Normandy American Cemetery seemed to have suffered a terrible misfortune in being of fighting age when mankind's bloodiest conflict began, their place in history is at least secured by the fact that they fought and died in a righteous crusade—and a winning one. In contrast, Vietnam veterans of my generation, who risked and gave their lives in a war whose virtue and wisdom were suspect, have been caught in the whiplash of history. Their service and their sacrifices seemed for many years something better forgotten or hushed up than cherished and praised. The war in which they fought did not unify us in defense of our long-standing ideals. On the contrary, it divided the nation and called those ideals into question. Visitors to this cemetery can leave with the consolation that each cross or Star of David recognizes the heroism of one who gave his or her life in a worthy, necessary, and ultimately victorious cause. On the other hand, many of those who come to contemplate the Vietnam memorial seem largely consumed by a sense of tragedy and waste, skeptical that the lost cause for which these soldiers gave their lives was really worth their sacrifice.

Certainly, Americans do not accord military service the respect it once commanded. I avoided my generation's only war by joining the National Guard. Bill Clinton managed to do the former without even having to do the latter. Yet in each of his presidential races, he soundly defeated two World War II veterans with stellar military records. I remember, as a kid, seeing the local VFW color guard in the Christmas parade. My folks were always quick to warn me about the drinking and gambling that often went on at VFW posts, but I nonetheless saw the organization itself as healthy and dynamic. These days, time and deemphasis on military service is clearly taking its toll. With 60 percent of its membership drawn from the veterans of World War II and the Korean Conflict, the VFW is reportedly losing approximately a thousand members a month to deaths. Others are simply demoralized; some members resigned in a somewhat pyrrhic protest when Clinton was elected in 1992, and membership has fallen steadily since then.

It is the feeling that what is enshrined at this cemetery has all but slipped away that helps to imbue it with such significance for me. Feminist author Susan Faludi is troubled by the "nostalgia of baby boom

men for their World War II fathers," because she believes it is sympto-
matic of a sort of masculinity crisis among those of us in the "fifty-
something" set. Faludi places responsibility for this trauma at the feet of
the returning veterans who excelled as soldiers but, in their rush to come
home and claim "the good life," focused on earning and advancing rather
than parenting and left their sons "devastatingly unfathered and unpre-
pared for manhood." Although it is possible, I suppose, that I am simply
not "man" enough to face the truth, Faludi's sweeping assessment seems
a little too harsh and a lot too complicated for me. My guess is that, by
and large, the men of my generation simply did what men have always
done. They defined manhood in terms of the examples provided by their
fathers, examples in which fighting in World War II often loomed especially large. The challenges that have confronted male baby boomers
appear decidedly less monumental and severe. Even those who fought
in the Vietnam War sometimes express frustration that their service to
their country seems to have won them relatively few points in the courage and patriotism categories.

The feeling of unworthiness relative to one's ancestors is hardly peculiar to me and my contemporaries. For centuries societies have looked
back to a supposed golden age in their past, especially when their present
apparently had little to show for itself. Hence, in what seems to be an
era of moral dysfunction, we are eager to believe that World War II was
a totally righteous crusade in defense of a nation that was far more
idealistic and virtuous than the one we live in today.

In reality, however, this perception requires some suspension of historical memory or realism. For example, despite their participation in a
bloody struggle to defend democracy from a racist, totalitarian onslaught,
African Americans who served in World War II found themselves fighting not just the Germans and the Japanese but the hostility and distrust
of their white comrades and commanders as well. D-Day operations
reflected this reality quite clearly. Although black sailors and Coast
Guard personnel served on ships and transport boats, only one battalion
of black troops actually landed on Omaha Beach on D-Day. Soldiers of
the 320th Barrage Balloon Battalion came in on the third wave and set
up barrage balloons to prevent German pilots from strafing the beach.
Three members of this unit, Corporal Henry Harris of Pennsylvania,
Corporal Brooks Stith of Virginia, and PFC James McLean of North

Carolina, are buried here. Had they survived, they would have returned to essentially the same segregated, discriminatory, and—in the case of Stith and McLean—disfranchised existence they had left behind.

Some black activists and intellectuals had hoped that the war would be what poet Langston Hughes described as "Jim Crow's Last Stand." An exultant Hughes insisted in the wake of Pearl Harbor that the conflict had "put Jim Crow on the run. That Crow can't fight for democracy and be the same old Crow he used to be." Within a few months, however, a disappointed Hughes would be asking, "Jim Crow Army and Navy, too, Is Jim Crow freedom the *best* I can expect from you?" In reality, of course, these contradictions, magnified further by the cold war struggle with Communism that ensued, did help to put "Jim Crow on the run," and many of his most ardent and courageous pursuers were African-American veterans of World War II such as Medgar Evers and Aaron Henry.

There is some irony in the fact that the Normandy American Cemetery provides entrée and closure to the *Saving Private Ryan* saga. No filmmaker is ever going to succeed in conveying the actual horror of combat, but in its unprecedented effort to depict the D-Day landing as a nightmare of bloody, headless, legless, disemboweled carnage and confusion, *Saving Private Ryan* actually seems less connected to this cemetery than do earlier, less graphic, and more reassuring World War II films such as *The Longest Day*. This pristine setting seems far better suited to serve as the final resting place of those who died neatly and apparently painlessly, shot down as they stood just inches from a bulletproof John Wayne or Robert Mitchum. After all, World War II was modern America's "Good War," free of the moral ambiguities that hovered over World War I, Korea, and Vietnam. In our minds, at least, it was a war in which men died bravely and stoically, repeating the Lord's Prayer, or receiving the last rites, or saying the Kaddish, not one where agonized screaming or crying was punctuated by horrible blasphemies alternating with piteous, little-boy whimpers for "Mama."

In the wake of *Saving Private Ryan*, visitation at the Normandy American Cemetery shot up by 30 percent, and pilgrimages by relatives of the dead were up by 50 percent. This new invasion of Normandy by tourists is actually part of a broader boom in World War II tourism. Opportunities abound to pay guided visits to key battlefield, memorial, and museum sites in both Europe and the Pacific. Some of these tourists are veterans themselves, many of whom are approaching the "now or never" years of their lives and are taking the opportunity to reconnect with the war and their wartime experiences while they are physically and mentally able to do so. For many other Americans, however, World War II tourism has clearly become part of a search for the heroes who seem so distressingly absent from the contemporary scene.

If this surging interest in World War II and the accomplishments and contributions of its veterans seems not just appropriate but long overdue, it has its troubling aspects as well. One of these is the all-out effort to commodify and market that threatens to trinketize and trivialize the World War II experience. Websites and catalogues abound, hawking commemorative patches, rings, medallions, and other such items, but the most distasteful example of cashing in on World War II that I have encountered is the twenty-seven-hole Omaha Beach Golf course that caters to visitors to the cemetery and D-Day beaches. I can hardly imagine a combat veteran (or anybody else, for that matter) feeling comfortable as he downs a beer at a nineteenth hole so near the scene of such a bloody struggle.

Interviewed by Walter Cronkite on the twentieth anniversary of D-Day, former Allied commander Dwight D. Eisenhower observed, "It's a wonderful thing to remember what those fellows twenty years ago were fighting for and sacrificing for. . . . Not to conquer any territory, not for any ambitions of our own, but to make sure that Hitler could not destroy freedom in the world. I think it's just overwhelming to think of the lives that were sacrificed for that principle." Surveying the nearly ten thousand crosses and Stars of David above Omaha Beach, one can only marvel that freedom, patriotism, nationalism, honor, duty, or any other mere abstraction could have spurred so many people to sacrifice their lives in a place so far away from their homes and from those they loved. To be sure, most had been informed, incorrectly as it turned out, that bombings and naval bombardment would soften the German defenses so effectively that they could expect only minimal resistance. Beyond that, the majority of those who landed on Omaha Beach on June 6 had never seen combat and thus had no true sense of its horrors. They learned of these horrors quickly enough, however, and yet an astonishingly small number refused to fight.

As a Civil War veteran put it, "The man who does not dread to die or to be mutilated is a lunatic. The man who, dreading these things, still faces them *for the sake of duty or honor* is a hero." James McPherson's impressive research suggests that a great many Civil War soldiers on both sides were in fact fighting and dying for their cause and their country. In World War II, GIs were far less likely to express such sentiments. A set of questionnaires administered to World War II soldiers revealed that "considerations of ideology, patriotism, and politics seem remarkably remote from the concerns of the front-line soldier." In fact, "convictions about the war and its aims" were well down the list of motivations for fighting, and there actually seemed to be "a taboo against any talk of a flag waving variety." One GI put it succinctly, "Ask any dogface. . . . You're fighting for your skin. . . . There's no patriotism on the line."

Differences between the motives of Civil War soldiers and those who fought in World War II may not be as great as they seem, however. In the late nineteenth century it was considered not only proper but laudable for men to speak openly of duty, honor, patriotism, or devotion to one's comrades. Thanks in part to the disillusionment fostered by World War I, by the second quarter of the twentieth century such Victorian rhetoric seemed either naive or phony and, paradoxically enough, even unmasculine. Failure to express such sentiments or even to admit to them need not suggest that they were not held and respected by those buried here. Although the magnitude of their sacrifice almost compels us to reflect on their motivation, in the final analysis, they rest in this honored setting because what they did is far more important than why they did it.

Regardless of what they died for, the event that cost them their lives is what Eric Hobsbawm calls the historical "raw material" from which national identity is constructed and by which it is nurtured and sustained. Even those American visitors who manage to leave this cemetery without a nationalism buzz would surely acknowledge that those who are honored here took extraordinary risks and made extraordinary sacrifices. For many baby boomers, especially those of us who sidestepped service in Vietnam, the Normandy American Cemetery thus poses the question of whether, even when faced with a similar clear and direct threat to our way of life, we would have performed with anything approaching the valor that our parents' generation exhibited. As *Saving Private Ryan* concludes, it returns to the cemetery, where a tearful James Francis Ryan kneels amid the graves of the fallen comrades who saved his life and wonders aloud whether "in your eyes I've earned what all of you have done for me." Though it is merely the product of a screenwriter's imagination, this comment seems wholly appropriate and not the least bit ephemeral, coming in a place that has now been compelling visitors to ask the same question for nearly half a century.

FRANKLIN DELANO ROOSEVELT
PRESIDENT OF THE UNITED STATES
1933 ~ 1945

Landscape architect Lawrence Halprin's plan for the Franklin D. Roosevelt Monument showing the continuous granite wall. Rendering by Lawrence Halprin.

Robert Dallek

THE FRANKLIN D. ROOSEVELT MEMORIAL, WASHINGTON, D.C.

W hen I was asked to contribute an essay on an American place to this well-deserved tribute to Sheldon Meyer, I had no difficulty choosing a subject: the new Franklin D. Roosevelt Memorial commemorating my favorite president. It was an opportunity to grouse about the stinginess of Congress and some recent presidents in taking so long to give our greatest twentieth-century president his proper due. More important, it provided an occasion to say something about the attractions of the memorial and how essential such remembrances are in advancing the national well-being.

The prospect of writing about the memorial reminded me of why I had spent seven years in the 1970s on a book about FDR's foreign policy leadership. As a member of that generation which grew up thinking the presidency was synonymous with Franklin Roosevelt, I had taken special satisfaction in reconstructing and explaining his effectiveness in dealing with the unprecedented international challenges of the 1930s and 1940s. Though his faulty response to the Spanish Civil War of 1936–39, his casualness about civil liberties in agreeing to incarcerate some 110,000 Japanese-American citizens in 1942, and his failure to respond more aggressively to Hitler's destruction of Europe's Jews were forceful demonstrations of his imperfections, I came away from writing that book with a greater appreciation for the man's political judgments and skills than I previously had.

The completion and opening of the memorial to FDR in 1997 was a chance for me and others with direct memories of the man and the heroic struggles of his times to feel good once again about the "greatest generation." More important, though, it meant that Roosevelt's strengths as a leader would be on permanent display as a constant reminder of what has made our democracy so successful.

Since the attractions of having a memorial to FDR seem so obvious, I puzzled over why it took so much hard work to create. Its opening may be described as a minor miracle: not its size or structure or appeal to the millions of visitors who have already visited the 7.5-acre park along Washington, D.C.'s Tidal Basin. I'm thinking instead of its construction and opening fifty-two years after FDR died.

The fact that a Washington memorial to any president is something of a miracle helps explain why FDR's was so slow in coming. Of the forty-one men who have served in the highest office, only four—George Washington, Thomas Jefferson, Abraham Lincoln, and FDR—now have notable memorials in the nation's capital. True, a largely unknown and unvisited Ulysses S. Grant Memorial stands near a James A. Garfield statue on First Street in front of the Capitol. But these remembrances to two undistinguished post–Civil War presidents are minor edifices on the Washington landscape. There are, of course, airports, bridges, buildings, cities, cultural centers, dams, highways, hospitals, islands, libraries, parks, schools, and streets in every part of the country named for many of our presidents, but a substantial Washington memorial has been beyond the reach of thirty-seven of them.

Washington has its share of statues celebrating military heroes, but if the capital is any measure of how we view our presidents, we are content to let almost all of them fall into obscurity. I have little quarrel with consigning forgettable characters like William Henry Harrison, Millard Fillmore, James A. Garfield, Chester A. Arthur, and Benjamin Harrison, to mention just some of the nineteenth-century presidents, to the recesses of our historical memories. But John Adams, James Madison, James Monroe, Andrew Jackson, Theodore Roosevelt, Woodrow Wilson, and Harry Truman? A Madison building is now part of the Library of Congress, but I've searched in vain for any kind of distinctive memorial to Adams or Monroe in the District. Andrew Jackson rides a handsome steed in Lafayette Park across from the White House. Theodore Roosevelt and Woodrow Wilson have done better: each has a memorial bridge across the Potomac named after him. An island in the river commemorates TR's memory; an academic center in the new Ronald Reagan

Building honors Wilson, and his postpresidential home in northwest Washington is now a museum. But Harry Truman, like Adams and Monroe, goes unremembered.

Is it indifference to past politics and presidential history that makes for this sort of amnesia? Or is it continuing political antagonisms that rule out giving the likes of Adams, Monroe, Jackson, TR, Wilson, and HST some greater due? If Truman still provokes political opposition, it's difficult to believe that the other five continue to arouse much partisan ire. I doubt that most people in the country could tell you anything about the policies or party affiliations of these nineteenth- and early twentieth-century presidents.

I'm not sure what explains this ungenerosity toward our presidents. Perhaps it's our egalitarianism at work here. For all our recognition that competition produces distinctions among people, we remain attached to the belief that no one is—or should be—better than anyone else. Reflecting the national unease with celebrities and celebrity, Ralph Waldo Emerson declared, "Every hero becomes a bore at last."

Or maybe it's just an unfortunate feature of a democratic system— the price we pay for free speech. Better the rhetorical wrath visited on presidents than the sort of violent political opposition so common for so long in other parts of the world. Or maybe our verbal excesses are a form of national entertainment at the expense of politicians usually promising more than they can deliver. The bombast is troubling nevertheless. Consider the fierce attacks visited on our three greatest presidents: Washington suffered "censures of the vilest kind"; Lincoln was demonized as a "half-witted usurper" and a "mole-eyed" monster; and FDR was pilloried as a brain-damaged cripple. John Steinbeck remarked: "We give the President more work than a man can do, more responsibility than a man should take, more pressure than a man can bear.... We wear him out, use him up.... He is ours and we exercise the right to destroy him."

National presidential tributes are not only scarce but have also been slow to happen. Consider the struggles to build the Washington Monument and Lincoln and Jefferson memorials. When Washington died in December 1799, Henry Lee eulogized him as "first in war, first in peace, and first in the hearts of his countrymen." But that was not a universal judgment at the end of the eighteenth century. It would take thirty-four years before a citizens' group made plans to build a monument with privately donated monies; Congress showed no interest in appropriating funds for such a project. In 1860, twenty-seven years later, the monument, a "stunted" white marble shaft, as one observer described it, had risen to only one third of its intended height. The post–Civil War passion to heal sectional wounds and the centennial of the country's birth in 1876, however, produced a congressional funding bill that promised to complete the monument in five years. But it wasn't until 1888, eighty-nine years after Washington's death, that the obelisk reached completion.

Constructing Lincoln's memorial was no less a struggle. Although a monument to the martyred president had been proposed as early as 1867, the conflicts over Reconstruction and the incomplete Washington obelisk ruled out any quick action. In 1911, forty-six years after Lincoln's death, a Republican Congress established a memorial commission, which designed the structure and laid the cornerstone for the white marble building in 1915. Seven more years would pass before President Warren G. Harding dedicated the eighty-foot-tall structure on May 31, 1922. The 189-foot-long and 118-foot-wide monument rests on thirty-six columns symbolizing the restored union of the states, which cost 620,000 lives, including Lincoln's, to preserve. The opening of the memorial was emblematic of the national faith in the Union's renewed harmony.

Jefferson's memorial also needed an altered national mood and circumstance to build. The two-hundredth anniversary in 1943 of Jefferson's birth was insufficient to ensure the dedication of the monument, which, like Lincoln's, sits facing the Tidal Basin. Other things had come together to make Jefferson's memorial, 134 years after his presidency and 117 years after his death, a reality. Franklin Roosevelt, a Democratic president, and a Democratic Congress eager for a competing monument with the Republicans' Lincoln Memorial were also necessary prerequisites. But it was principally the "great war for freedom," as FDR declared in his dedication, that made "a shrine to freedom" so timely in 1943. Jefferson, as Roosevelt also said at the opening of the memorial, was our "Apostle of Freedom." He was the perfect symbol for a country at war with Nazism, fascism, and Japanese militarism. Jefferson's words inscribed on the dome of the memorial said it all: "For I have sworn on the altar of God eternal hostility against every form of tyranny over the mind of man." Other declarations of personal freedom adorn the walls of the monument, including the best-known of Jefferson's tenets: "We hold these truths to be self-evident: That all men are created equal; that they are endowed by their Creator with certain unalienable Rights, that among these are life, liberty and the pursuit of happiness."

By 1943, Joseph I. Ellis says, Jefferson had become a prophet of American individualism and freedom, a kind of spokesman for men and women of every political persuasion. "The primal source of Jefferson's modern-day appeal," Ellis writes, "is that he provides the sacred space—not really a common ground but more a midair location floating above all the political battle lines—where all Americans can come together and, at least for the moment, become a chorus instead of a cacophony."

Compared to the difficulties blocking prompt construction of the Washington, Lincoln, and Jefferson memorials, the opening of the FDR site in May 1997 seems relatively quick and easy. But it was not. Roosevelt himself had impeded the building of an imposing shrine by declaring that he wanted nothing more as a commemoration than a plain desk-size block in front of the National Archives with a simple inscription, "In Memory of. . . ." He did not care what it was made of, but he wanted no ornamentation. In response to his wishes, a three-foot by six-foot block of marble noting his dates of birth and death stands in front of the Archives building halfway between the White House and the Capitol.

But anyone with an objective sense of how important FDR had been to the nation in the Great Depression and the country's greatest foreign war was not content to let his memory slip into obscurity. Since his death in 1945, historians have consistently "ranked him with Washington and Lincoln, and the men who succeeded him," William E. Leuchtenburg says, "found one question inescapable: How did they measure up to FDR?"

In 1946, Congress authorized a commission to consider an appropriate monument to the country's longest-serving president, but it did not provide funding for its work until 1955. The commission encountered so many problems that it became "the longest-running single-purpose commission in U.S. history." The search for a site took until 1959, when it acquired twenty-seven acres in West Potomac Park. It also grappled with design questions. In 1962, the Washington Commission of Fine Arts rejected a proposal for an abstract grouping of large stone forms critics derided as "Instant Stonehenge." A 1964 variation on the original design became known as "Son of Instant Stonehenge," and the Roosevelt Commission went in search of a new architect. By 1969, it was still without an acceptable design, and the commission reduced the size of the memorial from twenty-seven acres to twelve. Finally, in 1975, the commission signed off on a plan by San Francisco landscape architect Lawrence

Halprin for "a zigzagging 14-ft. granite wall that would connect a series of fountains, plantings, sculptures and quotes from FDR's speeches."

But the memorial was still a long way from realization. In 1978, the Carter administration rejected the proposed memorial park as too expensive and suggested that future generations of Americans decide whether they wanted such a monument to FDR. In 1981, the memorial remained unfunded. Moreover, as the centennial of Roosevelt's birth in January 1982 approached, Congress showed little interest in any commemoration. But Peter Kovler, a Washington, D.C., philanthropist who was unwilling to let the nation embarrass itself by largely ignoring the occasion, singlehandedly organized a national committee and, in the words of a 1982 *Newsweek* story, "pried $200,000 out of the current Congress to finance a celebration." It was an astonishingly meager amount alongside the seven million dollars a Democratic Congress had appropriated for a Herbert Hoover centennial in 1974. For his troubles, Kovler was denounced as a "lout" for wasting public monies on a commemoration the conservative *National Review* predicted would become "more expensive than before, and perpetual so that our children's children can help pay for it a hundred years from now."

In February 1982, *Time* magazine wondered whether "a Congress besieged by cost cutters will finally vote millions of dollars for a wall and some fountains." But, irony of ironies, Republican President Ronald Reagan, who had voted for FDR four times and saw his predecessor as "one of history's truly monumental figures," signed an authorization bill in July 1982 for the construction of a 7.5-acre memorial park along the Cherry Tree Walk on the Tidal Basin near the National Mall and the other three great presidential monuments. Reagan, however, requested no funds for the project.

It would be another fifteen years before the work could be completed. Congress was unwilling to provide more than $42.5 million of the $48 million cost. Private donors for the other $5.5 million were difficult to find. Almost all of the fifty corporations Michigan Senator Carl Levin, a member of the Roosevelt Commission, solicited for donations turned him down. Only Archer Daniels Midland, International Telephone and Telegraph, and the Kovler Family Foundation were willing to help.

The public response to the memorial has been gratifying to those who labored in its behalf. Thousands of people turned out for its opening. As I looked about me in the brilliant sunshine that morning, I observed lots of folks who had lived through the FDR era and found it appealing to join in another hurrah to FDR and his enduring legacy. But it was not just old New Dealers revisiting earlier triumphs who came. Within one year of its opening, the memorial had become the most heavily visited site in Washington, eclipsing the Vietnam War Memorial and the other three presidential monuments.

The attractions of the memorial are evident to those with even the slightest knowledge of Roosevelt's presidency and his troubled times. The sense of being in a beautiful, expansive park with rushing water and much greenery conveys a feeling of serenity. Compared with Lincoln's brooding presence, Jefferson's philosophical preachments, and the dignified but almost sterile nature of Washington's monument, Roosevelt's memorial elates the visitor. It captures the man's buoyant optimism; his confidence in himself and the country; his refusal to believe that America had seen its best days; his conviction that the nation's future greatness would exceed its past achievements. Like the publisher Henry Luce, an FDR critic, Roosevelt foresaw an American Century in which the United States led the world to a higher ground. As he wrote in a speech that his death on April 12, 1945, left undelivered, "The only limit to our realization of tomorrow will be our doubts of today. Let us move forward with strong and active faith." Small wonder that more than fifty years later, in an America brimming with prosperity and in a world notable more for its attraction to political freedom and free enterprise than the failed twentieth-century totalitarian ideologies, Americans and foreigners alike flock to a Franklin Roosevelt Memorial that speaks to our democratic values.

As with any successful memorial, Roosevelt's not only encourages current hope; it also educates us about the past. The park is divided into four outdoor galleries or rooms, one for each of FDR's terms. The progress of Roosevelt's presidency is recorded in bronze bas-relief, sculptured figures, and quotations from his speeches and messages carved in walls of carnelian granite. Room One begins with the Depression and Roosevelt's messages of hope to a bewildered nation. "In these days of difficulty," he said in a 1932 campaign speech inscribed on one of the memorial's first walls, "we Americans everywhere must and shall choose the path of social justice . . . the path of faith, the path of hope and the path of love toward our fellow men." The president's famous phrase in his First Inaugural counseling us against unreasonable fear also adorns a wall.

The memorial moves on in Room Two, where the sculptor George

Segal depicts brilliantly, but somewhat ahistorically, a bread line (which had disappeared by 1937) of five stark human-size bronze figures dressed in shabby clothes and crumbling shoes. Room Two also presents the social programs—the groundbreaking laws and alphabet agencies comprising the New Deal—that humanized the American industrial system. They are inscribed on five pillars and bas-reliefs that depict the variety of actions taken to relieve suffering. Two of the great early initiatives— the Tennessee Valley Authority (TVA) and the Civilian Conservation Corps (CCC)—to improve the economy and the long-term environment are memorialized in Roosevelt's words proposing those laws. The second room also includes Segal's wonderfully evocative barefoot man hunched over a radio listening to one of FDR's memorable Fireside Chats. It reminds us that Roosevelt was the greatest mass communicator in the country's history and the first to master the airwaves in the service of progressive actions.

Foreign affairs, but chiefly the Second World War that principally occupied Roosevelt during his third and fourth terms, are reflected in Room Three. FDR's pacifist rhetoric in 1936 describes the horrors of World War I and his verbal struggles against unrealistic pre–Pearl Harbor isolationism. His proposal in December 1940 that America become "the great arsenal of Democracy" reminds us of his uphill battle to help Britain combat Nazism. Likewise, his inspiring speech to the White House correspondents in March 1941 calling on "men of goodwill . . . to unite, and produce, and fight to destroy the forces of ignorance, and intolerance, and slavery, and war" underscores his realism about the great challenge faced by democracy in the middle of the twentieth century.

His wartime rhetoric that helped carry the nation through unprecedented battles in the far reaches of the Pacific, the Middle East, and Europe reminds us of the sacrifices and commitment needed to fight an all-out conflict and organize a just peace. His sensible idealism about world affairs remains as relevant today as it was more than fifty years ago: "Unless the peace that follows recognizes that the whole world is one neighborhood and does justice to the whole human race," he declared in February 1943, "the germs of another world war will remain as a constant threat to mankind."

The mural of FDR's Funeral Cortege in Room Four beautifully captures the sense of loss and grief over the premature passing of a much-loved president on whom so many had counted. It put me in mind of the man who, after FDR's death, stopped Mrs. Roosevelt on the street to say: "I miss the way your husband use to speak to me about my government."

But it is the use of water and the statues of Franklin and Eleanor that probably stay with visitors more than the president's words or death. The waterfalls and reflecting pools throughout the park symbolize FDR's love of the sea and the rugged Campobello Island across the Maine border off Canada, where he spent vacations and sailed. It also reminds us of Roosevelt's struggle to repair the damage from polio to his legs by bathing in the waters at Warm Springs, Georgia. And the waters are also there to remind us of the ship voyages to Latin America for the Buenos Aires conference in 1936 and to the wartime meetings in the North Atlantic, the Middle East, and Russia.

The FDR and Eleanor statues are understandably high points in the park. A description of the work of Neil Estren, the creator of the two statues, speaks to the special qualities he brought to the sculptures. His work goes "beyond a mere recording of physical characteristics." It "captures the energy or the repose, the tidiness or the rumple, the wrinkles, the tilts, the gestures and body language—those details that animate a specific personality with a presence as unique as a fingerprint."

Estrin subtly captures the various sides of FDR. Dressed in his familiar cloak and peering confidently ahead, with a kind of sublime confidence in the future, the president impresses himself on us as an imposing larger-than-life figure. The statue conveys not only Roosevelt's aristocratic bearing and dignity but also his humanity, his humaneness. The likeness of Fala, the president's famous purebred Scotch terrier, sitting at Roosevelt's feet provides a marvelous reminder of FDR's mixture of class and common touch.

The statue of Eleanor Roosevelt, the only first lady honored in a presidential memorial, has her standing with hands comfortably folded in front of her before a seal of the United Nations, to which she was the first U.S. delegate. It is a fitting tribute to the woman who gave substantive meaning to a largely ceremonial office and became the compelling model for all future first ladies.

The memorial is not without continuing controversies. Advocates of the fullest possible historical accuracy complain that the president's disability, his paralysis and reliance on steel braces to stand, is barely noticeable in the wheels at the bottom of the chair in which the sculptor has seated him. If it took me a while to detect them (and I was looking), how many less attentive observers will see them? Should not an undisguised replica of his wheelchair have been on display? It is not enough, these critics assert, to have made the memorial the first wheelchair-accessible memorial in the nation's capital. The presence of several people in wheelchairs I saw at the opening of the memorial suggested to me that FDR remains an inspiration to people with disabilities. Do we want to deny them the hope Roosevelt still provides by ignoring his extraordinary courage in achieving so much for the country and the world despite his paralysis?

Defenders of the decision to mute the president's disability argue that it reflects a certain historical accuracy: Roosevelt did all he could to hide his problem from the public. Should we now run counter to his determined efforts to portray himself not as incapacitated but as a robust healthy man able to shoulder the heavy burdens of his office? Moreover, did the public really want to know about his ongoing disability? Most people in the thirties and forties believed that he had fully recovered from his paralysis. That perception gave Roosevelt a special hold on a country trying to overcome the Depression. And what about his declining health that made it questionable for him to run for an unprecedented fourth term in 1944? Should he be portrayed as a frail man dying of arteriosclerosis? When Lord Moran, Winston Churchill's personal physician, saw the president at the Yalta Conference in February 1945, he accurately predicted that he would die in the near future.

Critics also raise questions about the absence of the famous cigarette holder demonstrating that FDR was a heavy smoker. Should current knowledge about the pernicious effects of smoking on the smoker and others around him dictate that a past reality—one that so clearly identified FDR—be the determining influence on what gets included and excluded from a national historical site? Other omissions include any evidence of Eleanor's fox fur. And should there not be something about Roosevelt's prepresidential life and career? Yet another objection came from a Latin American journalist who complained that there is not a word about the Good Neighbor policy, a landmark Roosevelt program, in the entire memorial.

The complaints have received a hearing. The memorial commission is raising money to add a wall depicting Roosevelt's pre-1933 career and a statue clearly showing him in a wheelchair. But in spite of the memorial's success, the three to four million dollars needed for the additions seem to be no easier to come by than the original building costs. Discussions in the House in 1999 of funding the new exhibits have been sharply critical of the "disability lobby" backing the wheelchair display.

The disputes over all the presidential memorials suggest that past political divides never entirely lose their bite. As demonstrated by the national experience with the four Washington presidential monuments, the passage of time—distance from the era in which the president lived and governed—is an essential prerequisite for acceptance of any special commemoration. As important, special circumstances—a centennial (in Jefferson's case, a bicentennial) or a prevailing current crisis or political mood—are necessary to overcome congressional resistance to spending money on historical memory.

But more salient than the very modest sums required to fund enduring recollections of the national past is the reluctance to make controversial leaders into public icons. Peter Kovler and I have been trying for the past three years to convince the Congress to include Lincoln and FDR in Presidents Day, which currently honors only Washington, and to make it the occasion for an annual presidents' history week in the schools. To no avail. Never mind that this promotion of historical memory would be cost-free. Twenty senators have signed on to the initiative, but a current House rule against commemorating anyone bars the introduction of a bill; only a discharge petition signed by a majority of members could put legislation before the House changing the Presidents Day celebration. Such a measure failed to get more than a handful of signatures in the last Congress.

Congressional resistance is at odds with popular eagerness for positive remembrances of past public figures. The four presidential memorials tell us that a democracy devoid of titled aristocrats needs popular heroes. And this need has trumped partisan passions and compelled acceptance of our four greatest presidents into the tiny pantheon of immortal public servants.

The promotion, building, and success of the Franklin Roosevelt Memorial is especially informative about our national political culture. It underscores the fact that a country without heroes is a nation adrift. As the heavy attendance at the FDR Memorial demonstrates, Americans crave leadership, especially when it is as farseeing and wise as that provided by Roosevelt. The current and future Congresses should understand that even if they are reluctant to give great leadership its due, a wiser public will settle for nothing less than a sensible and generous reckoning with the national past.

A small German boy in Mannheim, standing in the ruins of his home, January 1946.

David Brion Davis

THE AMERICANIZED
MANNHEIM OF 1945–1946

I n the past century of wars and disasters, the American occupation of
much of western Germany, reinforced by the Marshall Plan, stands
out as one of the few undeniable examples of historical success. Overcoming more than twelve years of Nazi indoctrination, we helped build
the foundations for a prosperous democracy at the center of Europe, reversing a pattern of instability and conflict that had led to two world wars.
But the early years of American occupation were also a microcosm of the
racial and civil rights struggles that would dominate America in the 1950s
and 1960s and finally succeed in eradicating much of the evil of a Jim
Crow South. Former Nazi youth gazed incredulously at the semifascist
racism of white American officers and enlisted men infuriated when
German girls happily dated African-American troops, who experienced a
racial freedom they had never known at home. This unexpected racial
conflict was one of the ways that cities like Mannheim became "Americanized" in 1945 and 1946, a development I saw with my own eyes.

For several months in late 1945 and early 1946 when I was stationed
in Mannheim, I had an unusual opportunity to view many aspects of
this cultural interaction, though I finally learned more during the early
occupation about America's own racial time bomb and the evils of a
racially segregated army. My memories of a particular "Americanized

Some of this material appeared in a shorter and quite different essay, "World War II
and Memory," *Journal of American History* 77, no. 2 (September 1990): 380–87.

place" draw upon this late-teenage experience backed up by a large collection of yellowing letters to my parents.

Mannheim, located at the confluence of the Rhine and Neckar rivers, ten miles west of Heidelberg, is now a German city of 319,343 people. But when I arrived there as an eighteen-year-old soldier with police duties late in 1945, it was very much an American city, largely reduced to heaps of rubble. I lived in the unbombed central police headquarters, on Bismarckstrasse, across from the castle and Schlossgarten, until the spring of 1946, when I was transferred south to Bad Constatt (a suburb of Stuttgart) and the headquarters of the Third Constabulary Brigade.

My father's classic eleventh edition of *The Encyclopaedia Britannica* (published in 1911), which I still treasure despite its appallingly racist essay on "Negro," notes that Mannheim was "perhaps the most regularly built town in Germany" and that the geometric blocks "are distinguished after the American fashion, by letters and numerals." So even before Americans took over the governing and policing of the city in 1945, Mannheim had something of an "American" appearance. This was partly, at least, because the city had been captured and recaptured five times in the Thirty Years War, burned down in 1689 by the French, largely destroyed in 1794 by the Austrians, and badly damaged in 1803 by the duke of Baden. Thus instead of being rebuilt with winding cobblestone streets, the city became as "regularly built" as Salt Lake City.

My German friends and acquaintances, who continued to live in the underground "bunkers," or air raid shelters, were probably not aware of this repeated history of destruction and reconstruction, but they were very familiar with certain aspects of America. In particular, they looked almost terrified when they heard the name "Chicago," which they associated with Al Capone–like gangsters. As a police officer, all I needed to do to command instant fear and respect was to point to a fellow American and say, "Er kommt aus Chicago!" (He comes from Chicago!)

According to the scores of letters I wrote my parents (telephoning was out of the question for an entire year), the Germans' universal phrase was "Alles ist kaput" (i.e., annihilated). From the Neckar bridge, I wrote, "It is an awful sight—piles of brick and rubble as far as you can see. Amidst all this you can see battered 88s [the famous German 88mm cannon that destroyed countless Allied tanks and planes] and shells of shot down German planes." Former modern apartment buildings were now shards of twisted steel, and three-story houses were sliced in halves and quarters, exposing tiled bathrooms and living rooms with light fixtures still intact. Even the once elegant Wasserturm (water tower) was now a heap of broken rocks. I was deeply shocked when I found an old postcard picturing the beauty of prewar Mannheim and imagined the similar destruction of an American city like Denver, my birthplace. Crowds of begging German kids and old people at the end of our food lines were overjoyed when we scraped our leftover stew into one of their tin cans. Yet "all the people I've run across so far," I reported, "are extremely pleasant and cheerful—they have to be to survive." The Mannheimers also kept reassuring us they had never wanted war and had never supported Hitler, who never came to Mannheim, a leftist or "red city." (I later found a German family photo of Hitler being cheered and saluted in neighboring Ludwigshafen.) In a prediction I made in December 1945 that appeared wholly absurd when I returned to Germany in 1950 on a postgraduate fellowship, I wrote, "I truly believe Germany will never be more than a little agricultural country full of [surviving] historic buildings and beautiful scenery."

At first I was lodged in the city's outskirts and consigned to guard duty, four hours on and eight hours off night and day. I helped protect tarpaulin-covered crates of food and other army supplies; sat shivering at an old rat-infested Luftwaffe airport; and guarded Nazi army prisoners-of-war, who helped me improve my two years of badly taught high school German. As the first and only "replacement" in that spot, living among often drunken veterans of the Normandy landings and the Battle of the Bulge, I felt like the greenhorn of all greenhorns, even though I had been trained as a combat infantryman at the time of the Battle of Okinawa, for that autumn's expected invasion of Japan. McGuire, my first roommate, only a year older than I, had killed several German soldiers in combat and had recovered in an English hospital from a bullet in his chest, the scar from which he made no attempt to hide. In the Mannheim region I saw no trace of the white soldier replacements who had accompanied me from New York to Le Havre on the SS *Argentina*, to say nothing of the hundreds of black troops, segregated in the lowest depths of the ship, whom I was once ordered to guard and "keep from gambling."

Fortunately, it was my smattering of German that soon got me the job as a security policeman in central Mannheim, in the First Armored Division, equipped with a shiny helmet liner, a .45-caliber pistol, an SP armband, and a jeep, as well as a good-natured driver from Texas named Franklin. Because German police were still allowed to do little more than direct traffic, we *Sicherheitspolizei* were charged with enforcing all law and order save for handling unruly U.S. soldiers, who except in emergencies fell under the jurisdiction of the U.S. Military Police. In retrospect, I'm amazed by my total lack of training for the kind of responsibilities I was given. I was officially the assistant or "special investigator" for Sergeant Schultz, who spoke perfect German and who impressed me the first night I was on duty by grilling two young women who were girlfriends of a Nazi lieutenant who had escaped. The second woman finally broke down and guided us to a house across the Neckar where we found our man. "While ascending the stairs," I wrote home, "I began wondering what I was doing there [we could have encountered a squad of armed fugitives], but we had the woman and were well armed."

Sergeant Schultz was obsessed with the idea of neo-Nazi meetings and plans for terrorist acts or guerrilla warfare. We heard repeated rumors, for example, of American jeep drivers being beheaded at night by razorlike wire that young Nazis strung across country roads. Schultz was convinced that Bavaria would be the meeting ground for some kind of Nazi retaliation. At the still functioning Mannheim railway station we searched a train bound for Munich and actually captured a Waffen SS officer who was allegedly heading for some kind of Nazi reunion in Bavaria. Since he was of course dressed in civilian garb, we ordered him to remove his shirt and thus display the SS tattoo under his arm. My teenage letters make it seem that I looked on such events as an exciting game of cops-and-robbers with the unrepentant enemy. I would now conclude that the SS officer was an isolated fugitive.

Still, rumors of Nazi conspiracies continued to circulate. One night, hearing that Nazis were about to blow up the Rhine Bridge, we spent fruitless hours searching the dark foundations with flashlights. On one occasion three of us did discover an underground meeting place, decked out with an enormous Nazi flag on the wall. But it was not until much later, when I twice attended the Nuremberg Trials, that I had the chance to behold the true criminal leadership and especially study the nearby face of Hermann Goering, who occasionally smiled and seemed to be directing the defense side of the trial. His later success in committing suicide in full sight of U.S. guards seemed to say something about the inexperience and unprofessional nature of our occupation.

As I strongly sensed at the time, eighteen- and nineteen-year-old draftees might be competent to fight battles but did not seem equipped to deal with the more complex problems of governing a defeated enemy.

(Actually, the soldiers I was first with, virtually all veterans of the Battle of the Bulge, spoke frequently of freezing their feet and wetting their pants from fear in the previous winter.) Looking now at the letters I wrote fifty-five and fifty-four years ago, I'm struck by the strange mixture of immaturity and growing insight. That said, I'm even more surprised in retrospect by the generally warm and friendly relations between American draftees and the ordinary residents of Mannheim and surrounding towns, people who in 1940 and 1941 had no doubt indulged in fantasies of the Third Reich ruling the world, but who now accepted total defeat, who thanked Providence they were not in the Russian sector, and who looked to Americans for models of all kinds, starting with popular music and consumer goods.

Most of my buddies were very generous in handing out candy, chewing gum, food, and even cigarettes (which became a kind of specie of increasing value); a very few others took joy in conquest, shooting recklessly into the air or even, as I saw myself, shooting a German civilian and a prisoner for no apparent reason. Yet because Germans had heard reports from the east of mass rapes and killings and were terrified of the "Rooskies," they were more than tolerant of American excesses. In fact, in my interviews of 1950, when I was studying the postwar changes, I kept hearing warm nostalgia for the friendly combat troops who had wanted nothing more than to be shipped home and who had mostly left Germany by March 1946.

My letters home express a romantic enchantment over my actually being in *Europe*—the place my mother had longed to see since childhood but did not live long enough to visit. Because of the Great Depression, even my well-traveled father had only been in France as a soldier in World War I and in Portugal, in 1941, as a war correspondent. Trying to imitate the style of Dos Passos and Hemingway, whom I'd read in high school, I kept describing the faces and clothes of the people, the destruction of Mannheim's central buildings, and the trolleys that still ran and clanged on Bismarckstrasse, along with American jeeps and the "put-put-put of the little wood-burning three-wheeled trucks." It never occurred to me to ask Germans to compare the truly lenient American occupation with memories of life under a police state. And though no news in my life had been as shocking as the reports and pictures of Dachau and Bergen-Belsen (it was only later that I became aware of Auschwitz, Treblinka, and the other death camps liberated by the Russians), I don't recall ever questioning Germans about the Holocaust. Yet

I can recall the horror of seeing hundreds of "Displaced Persons" and of later being sent with an armed battalion to protect a convoy of trucks carrying Jewish survivors through the streets of Stuttgart.

I'm also now surprised to realize that my parents had been taken in by much of the American media's pro-Russian propaganda. They were convinced, as my mother put it in a letter of February 1946, that "the Russian zone is the only zone that is operating and taking any steps toward getting on its feet. . . . The Russians had a program worked out and they go ahead with it whether anybody likes it or not. [They] aren't bothered with international cartel arrangements and big business interests the way we are." In actuality, of course, it was the American zone that was laying the foundations for both democracy and prosperity. And regardless of what historians have written about the date when the cold war began, my buddies began predicting early in 1946 that we would be at war with Russia within a year, a nightmare I didn't share. In the previous summer they had experienced a scary confrontation with Soviet troops who tried to block their passage to Potsdam. Referring to Swift's *Gulliver's Travels*, I wrote, "I retain a glimmering of hope that what the whyneemns [sic] said of the yahoos is not entirely true. But it is possible that we are only yahoos, swollen with 'reason.' . . . What disturbs me the most is the bland way people talk of another war, of the way they take it for granted." By March 10, however, my father was urging me to get transferred to France or preferably England, if at all possible, since he thought that a Russian invasion was likely and even talked of Americans being pushed back to another Dunkerque. (The anxiety was understandable. When I later encountered many Russian troops in Nuremberg, they could not have been more hostile.)

Most of the soldiers I knew had German girlfriends who would happily accompany them each evening to a club where they could dance and drink beer. (Officers, of course, had their separate clubs, as did African Americans.) I remember some married men expressing guilt over their infidelity, then stressing the length of time they had been away from what they hoped were faithful spouses. But in 1950 I attended the wedding of a college classmate who had returned after four years to marry his German sweetheart. What astonished me most was the friendliness, even eagerness, of the young German women as they quickly learned or improved their English and became part of the American communities. This was the most obvious expression of the "Americanization" of Mannheim. The women vividly described what it had been like when Mannheim had been bombed, how their hair and eyebrows had been singed by the roaring flames when they climbed out of a bunker too early. Yet, unlike various other conquered groups, such as the Southern Confederate women during the Union occupation following the Civil War, the "fräuleins" seemed to hold no grudges. One young woman who sought police aid against a Czech male who was sexually harassing her proudly showed me photos of the U.S. Puerto Rican troops who had "liberated" her from the war and Nazism. Though venereal disease, especially gonorrhea, was rampant in the Mannheim region, there was virtually no prostitution. Americans joked that there was simply too much nonprofessional competition.

This embrace of the American occupier, which as a historian I still cannot explain, no doubt generated resentment among German men, especially defeated veterans of the Wehrmacht, but I found it amazingly easy to establish close ties with younger German males—teenagers who followed me around, escorted me through noisome bunkers, and above all served as my agents and spies in detecting black market operations. Such "fraternization" meant that I was speaking more German than English each day (though the Mannheim dialect was difficult), and these German youth were at least temporarily fascinated and even transfigured by American power and culture. The war had been so long and terrible, the German defeat so total and complete, that these young men seemed to find a kind of renewal—like their sisters, in a different way—in aiding and identifying with the former enemy. It's also true, of course, that the Americans possessed everything the Germans lacked, from food, soap, and cigarettes to toilet paper. In 1946 I did not consciously witness the beginnings of German democracy. But in retrospect it seems likely that the interest and respect young Germans showed for American abundance and consumer culture, to say nothing of American informality and friendliness, contributed to the kind of democracy that later emerged.

Some American soldiers, I must add, expressed contempt and even hatred for the Germans, though those who had spent time in France and England were often even more negative about those peoples. Some of the warmest feelings I heard about a foreign people pertained to the Czechs, whom the Americans had liberated and then abandoned to the Russians, to the dismay and deep chagrin of the soldiers I knew.

To my parents I kept insisting that only a well-trained *civilian* force of policemen, lawyers, and administrators could handle the kind of problems we faced. My parents agreed, and having been deeply disturbed by my initial letters about my police activities, my mother added, "I hope you will exercise as much caution and discretion as it is possible for a 19-year-old S.P. to have and exercise under the circumstances."

Much of my time as a neophyte policeman involved the rampaging black market that distributed American army goods to the various peoples of Europe. A typical case emerged in mid-February when Sergeant Schultz was ill and I was about to leave for a ten-day vacation on the French Riviera. (No other soldiers signed up for this particular trip, in part because they didn't want to lose a chance to be sent home but also because the GIs I knew had never heard of the Riviera and didn't want to go to "a river someplace.")

Following the tip-off from one of my young German boys who had seen U.S. army trucks delivering army blankets to a civilian apartment, I had Franklin drive me to the suspicious address, where I met a small Belgian man of about fifty-two. He welcomed Franklin and me into his apartment, where he and his female companion denied any wrongdoing and invited us to search the place for U.S. army goods. We had almost given up when I found in the basement a secret door in a wall that led into a room filled with hundreds, perhaps thousands, of GI blankets, which the Belgian was dying dark blue for sale in Belgium and France. There were also, as I wrote my parents, "cases of cigarettes buried in a garden, and suitcases full of bottles of cognac." As I arrested the Belgian, he smiled and admitted, "I am no leetle boy." His girlfriend slipped around a corner and escaped, and it took me more than an hour to track her down. By March 9, after returning from the Riviera, I concluded that "this SP work is largely a joke. A lot of excited people running around chasing nine year old boys and starving people who accepted a little food from a GI for washing his clothes."

In saying this, I seemed to have forgotten what I had written five weeks earlier, when I reported to my parents "my first real triumph" as a policeman. Captain Kelly of the Military Government had called me to his desk and handed me a letter of complaint from the German father of a six-year-old girl who had been raped. "There was very little to go on," I continued. The family lived near a spot where fifty Polish soldiers were on guard duty. Sometimes the Poles had given the children in the neighborhood candy and chewing gum. "Then one day the mother found the girl's bed soiled and at the hospital it was discovered that the child had gonorrhea. That was two weeks ago—the trail was cold." After going to the girl's home, where only her sister was present, "I questioned a Polish guard and found where his company was, how long they stood guard, how long his company had been in that vicinity."

When I next went to the Mannheim hospital to meet the girl, Maria Eisenhower, "I nearly fainted. Maria was truly six, and certainly not large for her age. Just a cute little baby—with VD! At first she was pretty bashful but I talked simple German to her about everything under the sun except what I was after, and I gave her a pack of gum and candy and then got down to business. She told me the man was a Polish soldier with a rifle (on guard); he was dark and had *katzenaugen* [catlike eyes] and was about my size."

My next stop was the Polish guard company. "I talked with the captain, who'd been away from Poland for six years, who'd fought the Russians with Pilsudski [Jozef Klemens Pilsudski, a right-wing general and dictator who ruled Poland in 1926 and 1930]. He called his whole company out and it finally narrowed down to seven men." There was one who fit the description reasonably well, and he had VD. On a chance, I took him to the hospital to see Maria. He laughed and said if he ever got that badly off with regard to females, he'd shoot himself. Maria had never seen him before. "Back to Pilsudski's captain," I wrote. "Six possible men, three away roaming around the country, one there, and two on guard. The guards wouldn't give us their rifles until relieved, so I had to order a relief." I then took several of the Polish soldiers to see Maria. One of the guards did have catlike eyes, and when he entered the hospital room, "Maria's whole face changed. I had my man. He signed a confession an hour later and pleaded he'd been drunk and hadn't known what he was doing. He thought the girl was older—eight or nine! But he knew he had gonorrhöe [German spelling] at the time. I hope he gets shot." Even my mother replied that he should be shot.

I had to appear twice at his trial in the American military court, which was also a symbol of the Americanization of Mannheim. The room was beautiful, I wrote home, "with gold gilded walls and a large oil of Frederick the Great with an American flag hiding all but Frederick's feet. A Major is the [highest-ranking] judge. And you say 'yes sir' instead of 'I do.'" After I testified, the friendly judges dismissed me. I never knew whether the Polish soldier was shot or sentenced to a long prison term.

To my parents I reflected on how in first grade I had felt so lowly when talking with an eighth grader, and then in the eighth grade had felt the same way about high school juniors—much as I was later to feel about the soldiers who had completed the seventeen weeks of basic training, to say nothing of my awe when talking with "the COMBAT MEN." "So it all goes to show that despite growth you don't change much." As I went tearing around in a jeep with a machine gun and SP insignia, "I probably look pretty impressive and fearsome to a kraut kid, but I don't feel much differently than the kraut kid. Well, that just proves Einstein's theory of relativity."

Some time later a high command summoned our police unit to the Mannheim railroad station in order to keep a trainload of African Americans, contemptuously termed "night-fighters" and "jiggaboos," from "acting up" as they passed through on their way back to the United States. This was my first encounter with the segregated, disunited American army that occupied a Germany swarming with uprooted, diverse peoples. In a letter home I described the heterogeneous humanity at the station: "Russians, Slavs, Turks—red boots, black boots, Wehrmacht boots. Feet wrapped in cloth, Asiatic sandals, boots with toes and heels protruding, white in the cold air. Blue velvet Cossack hats, Tyrolian caps, Wehrmacht caps with the swastikas cut off. Faces of all types. Heavy jaw bones, broad cheeks, little beady eyes, long black hair, Hitler mustaches. German giants, straight blond hair, a hollow for an eye, a missing hand, a crutch or a cane. Guys who may have killed a thousand people at Dachau. Guys who'd slit your throat and hang you up if you didn't have a tommy gun and the American army behind you. Ruck sacks, alpine pack sacks, leather packs with the animal fur still on."

While I was watching all this, the black troops arrived. "They arrived," I wrote, "with five [black] captains and a colonel in pinkies [breeches for riding a horse] and fine riding boots. They were very quiet and seemed like a good bunch. One of our southern boys started casting a remark here and there, but all he got back were laughs and shouts of 'What part of Mississippi you from, white boy?' Special Service rolled up with a loudspeaker and tried in vain to play, 'Caledonia, Caledonia, What Makes Your Big Head So Hard?' ... The steam shot out of the little engine and when the train pulled by, I wished the boys the best of luck and they seemed quite genuine when they yelled back, 'Same to you fella, and lots of it.' I'm getting quite bitter on this race question. Perhaps I sound a bit shrill, but it is difficult not to become alarmed when not one or two but dozens of men openly proclaim their hatred of the black race and take every opportunity to shoot or arrest or beat up colored soldiers."

As time went on, I was increasingly struck by the contrast between the Germans, who reputedly believed in Aryan supremacy but who seemed to warmly accept black Americans, and our own white troops, who seemed ready to declare war on "the God-damned black sonsabitches" who dated German girls. The African-American soldiers clearly felt pride in having been part of a triumphant victory over a fascist country that stood for Aryan supremacy. In England, France, and even Germany they experienced a kind of racial freedom unknown in the United States. And they were determined not to accept the Jim Crow society to which their fathers or grandfathers had returned after World War I. Fortunately, they were able to play a large part in the civil rights revolution of the next generation that narrowed the hypocritical gap between democratic rhetoric and social reality.

In a letter of January 17, 1946, I began by describing the bunkers in which most of the Germans of Mannheim lived: "Every evening as the shafts of sunlight break gaping holes through the ruins of their homes, the people file into their caves, long lines disappearing into stinking underground holes. It is a sight which, I think, might convert some of the opponents of international control of the atomic bomb. It was only ordinary bombs that caused this." Then I told about the previous night, when I came as close to "combat" as one could come in the occupation army.

We had just returned from some minor black market raid when the riot alarm rang through the old German police building where we slept. Some officer shouted, "Niggers." In three minutes we were roaring through empty streets in jeeps, wearing steel helmets and carrying submachine guns. "It was very dark," I wrote home, "and we jumped out and spread out along the walls of buildings. Nobody seemed to know what it was all about." I immediately saw a large splash of blood and bullet marks on the building next to me and a trail of blood leading away into the dark. After what seemed like a long wait, "we were ordered to search a house and for a few confusing minutes we groped through dark attics with the bolts of our guns drawn back," ready to shoot. As I entered one bedroom, I stumbled upon a black American soldier in bed with a German girl. They looked alarmed, to put it mildly, but I apologized for my intrusion and quickly left the building.

"Then we were in a typical GI club," I wrote, "dance floor, bar, pictures on walls, orchestra stand. It was smoke filled and a crowd of officers stood in the middle of the floor; there were spots of blood around, a lot of broken glass, and the walls were scarred with bullet holes.

"Outside, a drunken GI was yelling, 'Just like the God-damned MPs and SPs. Come in an hour after it happens with their tommy guns.' 'Shut up,' an officer shouted. 'Why the hell didn't you do something about it?'"

Back in the club the officers argued. In my letter I mention "three Negro lieutenants, one white lieutenant and two captains. The white lieutenant was a West Pointer and seemed to be running things." I am sure, and here memory is essential for interpreting a text, that either a black captain or first lieutenant outranked our extremely racist and Nazilike West Pointer, who began by saying, "'Now as I understand it, these Niggers from your company...'" Glaring eyeball to eyeball, the black officer stood more erect and said, "'Cut out that Niggah stuff, see!'" According to my letter, our commander then said, "Shut up." Even after fifty-four years I will swear that he said, "Shut up, you Nigger!" and ordered us to prepare to fire at the black troops, some of whom were still armed. I wouldn't have written my parents about that.

I did write that "everyone stood tense as the two officers faced each other." Then the cry of "'A-TEN-HUT!' A gray-haired major stomped in, sleepy-eyed, very plainly aroused from sleep a few minutes before. More argument. More waving of arms. The major, unable to find out what had happened, pleaded with the GIs to tell him what it was all about. They didn't know either. The colored lieutenant exclaimed this had been going on ever since his company had moved in, and he was going to move the entire company out. The major screamed." According to later rumor, some armed black troops had entered an all-white GI club. A fight had broken out; the MPs had come; one of them was shot, along with a black man and other soldiers as the battle spilled out into the street before we arrived. But for all I know, white soldiers may have invaded an African-American club. The racist hostility certainly centered on blacks dating or dancing with white German girls. In 1946, twenty-one years before *Loving v. Virginia*, many states still prohibited the intermarriage of whites and blacks. The armed conflict I witnessed was part of the Americanization of Mannheim.

Later on, this racial hatred was outrageously exploited by Major General Ernest Harmon, the commander of the Constabulary who, I later learned, had been trounced by the German Afrika Korps at the Battle of Kasserine Pass. Harmon spoke once at Mannheim, and it was always a big event when he later came to Stuttgart to give us pep talks. "Ernie Harmon came down today," I wrote home, "wearing twenty-one rows of colorful ribbons and a pair of dazzling cavalry boots. Our rooms were spotless, lockers in perfect order, windows invisible, bedsheets immaculate. My boots shone like a pool of oil in the sunlight and my pistol was bone dry.... Pretty soon the planes roared overhead and then the big guns opened up and in drove the long Packard with two stars on the bumper" and sirens blazing.

To my parents I confessed: "I couldn't help but think of similar performances in this same spot [a large army headquarters] only twenty or thirty months ago, when another group of people went mad over the arrival of another god, when the gates and banners and archways were decked with a different, yet basically similar decoration [our logo was a lightning bolt splitting a capital *C* for "Constabulary"], and when great formations of men lined up like they did today, to welcome a leader. I don't believe I'm the only one who noticed this. Among the Germans who work within the kaserne, there were smiles, knowing glances, and I'm sure much talk behind the walls."

"You look swell, men," Harmon said. "The Constabulary is the best organization in the ETO [European Theater of Operations]. I'm not so goddamn sure it's not the best in the whole Army, and I'll lick the son-of-a-bitch who says it isn't. When I broke through at Anzio I told the men exactly what I was going to do. I've always believed in telling the men in the ranks what is going on." The general then told us all about the Soviet menace: "You are going to see that none of these damned Russians cross over into our territory." The only way to treat the Russians, he said, was to smack them hard on the head, the way he had done to Russian officers. But America's stupidest mistake, he then confided, was to send colored soldiers to Europe. He had warned the government not to send any "Niggers" (he showed no hesitation in using the word). Now they were a much bigger problem than the Germans. What I found especially upsetting was the way the American soldiers cheered Harmon on.

In retrospect, I realize that as a late teenager in Mannheim I glimpsed the contours of the United States in which I would mature: a relatively benign, good-natured, and well-intentioned desire to democratize the world, combined with signs of the coming cold war and with conflicts, initiated by African Americans' expressions of freedom, that would begin to heal the cancerous racial division and persecution that has corrupted the core of American society since the founding of the Republic.

I strongly suspect that this experience in Germany influenced my later decision to devote over forty years to the study of slavery and race.

The Swift Hall of History, Vassar College. Photo by Will Faller. *Courtesy Vassar College.*

Carl N. Degler

VASSAR COLLEGE

My first sight of Vassar College on the outskirts of the mid-Hudson river-town of Poughkeepsie, New York, occurred on a dark November night in 1948. The occasion was intended to be a brief—in fact, a very brief—honeymoon from New York City, where Catherine Grady and I had married that afternoon. Since both of us were working at universities and had only a weekend to celebrate, and possessed no car, we looked for a hotel near Princeton University, which was close enough by train from New York for a weekend. There were no rooms, however, since the hotels were overfull because of a big Princeton football game. Looking for another nearby college campus, we thought the short train trip to Poughkeepsie would give us a chance to explore Vassar College, which we had heard of but had never visited. After checking into a small hotel, we walked to the campus.

As we entered the nearest opening onto the grounds of the college, we could see a partly lighted, large brick structure with thick white pillars sustaining a triangular roof front. As we came closer, we could hear some talk and laughter from what seemed to be a large crowd inside. Years later, I found out that it was the Students' Building, the largest auditorium of the college. On that occasion it was being used for a student theatrical performance, and when we entered, it became clear that women were portraying men as well as women. Vassar, of course, was then exclusively a women's college. We watched the performance for a while, then retreated to our hotel and thence to New York and work.

Four years later, when I was seeking a teaching job, I saw Vassar in daylight. This time I entered in the proper way, driving through the large, elaborate gatehouse, which arched over the entry road that stretched a hundred yards, a line of fir trees on each side, before it reached Main Hall, the principal and largest building on the country-style campus. Even today Main appears huge and unusual for an edifice constructed more than a century ago, when it was said to be the largest civilian structure under one roof in the country. Main then encompassed most of the college's activities, including classrooms, offices, and student rooms. It was a lengthy, four-story, dark-red brick building with two large towers at each end and a large cupola over its slate-covered roof. When I arrived, the original front entrance was obscured by a porte cochere, which reached to the second floor. Near Main I could see several buildings, including the President's House, a drama theater, which at the college's inception had been a riding school, a stone Gothic-style chapel, and a similarly styled library. Looking beyond these immediate buildings, I could see extensive lawns, flower beds, and many other buildings behind and beyond Main, including a small observatory. I could easily believe that this was the classic American campus: open, physically attractive, and far removed from New York City College's closely placed buildings devoid of even a patch of grass, where I was then teaching. Even the flowers and the lawns of Columbia University, where I was then completing my Ph.D., could not challenge Vassar's colorful and appealing bucolic country campus, especially now that I had gained a family of two children below the age of two.

That attractive campus easily captured for me what little I knew then about Vassar College. My conception was quite different from my own experience at Upsala College in East Orange, New Jersey. True, Upsala sported an "Old Main" too, although much more recently constructed, and displayed a few stretches of lawn, but its location in a residential part of the city limited its extent to a few blocks; Vassar's campus stretched to a thousand acres with a lake to boot. Like the other so-called Seven Sisters—the leading private women's colleges of the northeastern United States—Vassar was not only physically attractive but also prestigious in reputation, wealthy, and, for prospective students, costly as well, all of which Upsala had not been. And I was not alone in my conception of Vassar. Some years later, after I had joined the Vassar faculty, an indignant critic of a popular article of mine publicly berated me as a "pedagogue of the rich." In fact, the founder of the college, Matthew Vassar, himself told the trustees at the outset that his college was not intended to be a "charity school." Students or parents would be expected to pay for that education, though, in justice to him, he subsequently provided fellowships. As at the beginning, the Vassar College I knew in the 1950s and 1960s was an expensive educational experience. Demography reinforced that judgment. Over 40 percent of the fathers of Vassar students in the 1950s were professionals, and another 45 percent were businessmen. Compare that with the 30 percent of the fathers of students at teachers' colleges who were manual workers.

Matthew Vassar had not intended to invest his money; rather he intended to undertake a minor revolution. His purpose was to educate young women on a level comparable to that of young men at colleges like Yale and Harvard. Vassar himself had been born in England, arriving as a boy in Poughkeepsie. His schooling was meager, and he began work at his father's small brewery. In time, Matthew took over the brewery from his father, then built a new one, moved into local politics for a while, and invested successfully in railroads, whaling, and banking, from which by the 1850s he had accumulated a substantial fortune. Childless and advancing in age, Vassar obtained from a local educator named Milo Jewett the idea of endowing in his lifetime a first-class college for young women. Jewett became the college's first president.

The idea of educating young women was not new. Oberlin College in Ohio had admitted women along with men in 1837, and by the 1850s several colleges for women had been founded in both Georgia and upstate New York; there were also several dozen two-year seminaries for women designed to improve their manners, reading, languages, and aesthetic abilities. The distinction that Vassar intended for his college lay not in being a four-year school, as was Elmira College in upstate New York, but in exceeding in equipment, resources, and size any women's college then in the country—or the world. Women would gain in one stroke that quality of education then available at the country's best private men's colleges. Remember that in 1861, when the first ground was broken at Vassar, Harvard College had been in existence accumulating wealth and prestige for two centuries, and Yale College was not far behind.

With the innovative guidance of Jewett, Matthew Vassar wanted to make sure that his new college would indeed reach the high level he envisioned. Consequently, he put his money where his mouth was by endowing a two-hundred-acre farm outside Poughkeepsie along with four hundred thousand dollars' worth of securities—then considered a rare amount for founding any kind of college, especially from a single donor. Sophia Smith's endowment, for example, ten years later, did not meet Vassar's. In line with his concern for quality, Vassar also enlisted the skills of James Renwick, the architect of the recently constructed St. Patrick's Cathedral on New York's Fifth Avenue. It was Renwick who designed the immense Main building and the elaborate gatehouse.

It may have taken the four years of the Civil War to open the college, but at its opening the staff and their equipment represented a virtual revolution in women's higher education. At the outset, as Vassar had insisted, two of the eight professors were women, and thirty of the thirty-five assistants were women. The facilities for the teaching of a full array of scientific work were present: astronomy, chemistry, physics, botany, zoology, as well as courses in mathematics. The telescope proudly ensconced in the observatory was said to be the second largest in the nation; below, in an apartment on the first floor, lived Maria Mitchell, a nationally known astronomer and outspoken advocate of young women's independence. The teaching of physiology and health was there from the beginning as well, largely because those who expressed doubts about women's higher education feared women's bodies were as fragile as their minds. Matters of physiology and health were not recognized as useful for men until much later in the century.

As observers at the time anticipated, many of the early students chose classes in languages and the arts, as was the usual practice at the female seminaries. The novelty of a Vassar education, however, was strikingly apparent at the outset. Forty percent of the students chose science courses, while 21 percent selected the classics, the long-established measure of a liberal education at the private men's colleges. (Only 7 percent picked the social sciences.) As I learned when I joined the history department in 1952, all those sciences were still operative, with others added. (Indeed, at the time of the discussions about a possible move to Yale in the mid-1960s, proportionately more women majored in some sciences at Vassar than men did at Yale College.)

Behind Jewett's and Vassar's idea for higher education for women stood the fear that not enough young women would take the risk. Numbers turned out to be no problem—almost four hundred women, not all of them young, sought admission—but the preparation needed for admission to a first-class college was another matter. Only 31 percent of the entering students were ready to engage Latin and other fundamental subjects at college level. For almost a decade the college maintained a preparatory department to bring the students up to the required level. The preparatory experience nicely measured how limited education had been for women while revealing, at the same time, how urgent women's drive for higher education had become. Within fifteen years after Matthew Vassar's experiment, Wellesley and Smith had been founded, and by the turn of the century new private universities like Chicago and Stanford opened their doors to women and men.

When I arrived at Vassar in 1952, women's rights, even feminism, were subjects of importance to women faculty members. As I soon learned, however, that importance did not emerge from frank and direct remarks about feminism or women's rights; the time was not yet ripe for that. It came most obviously from the intense interest many of the women faculty members felt in seeing young Vassar alumnae achieving in the outside world. Students, on the other hand, rarely articulated concerns about women's rights, though they usually worked hard to succeed academically and often planned for graduate school. Few of the students knew that there had been a nineteenth-century women's movement begun as early as 1848 at Seneca Falls under the leadership of Susan B. Anthony, Elizabeth Cady Stanton, and Lucretia Mott. Yet as late as the opening of the twentieth century, the third president of the college, James Monroe Taylor, forbade lectures on campus on women's political activities or the suffrage. To Taylor and certainly to the trustees, Matthew Vassar's goal for his college was not to reform society but to educate women under the same standard as men. In line with that kind of thinking, Taylor also resisted to the end of his presidency in 1914 the introduction of any courses or activities at Vassar College that would prepare women for the very likely possibility that most would be wives and mothers.

The new president, Henry Noble MacCracken, acted on a quite different conception of Vassar education. Ironically, just those subjects or courses Taylor had so strongly resisted became the new ideas that MacCracken, the political liberal and ardent proponent of women's suffrage, now introduced into the education of young women at Vassar. Mac-Cracken endorsed a course of study called euthenics that recognized the special needs of Vassar women as homemakers and mothers. Later he expressed the motivation behind his innovation: "Celibate life, independent careers, increase of divorce, limitation of children, were all, or seemed to be, evidence that the American family needed attention." (As early as the turn of the century, some political leaders, especially Theodore Roosevelt, had openly worried about "race suicide" because college women were not marrying and reproducing. And it was true that before the twentieth century more than 40 percent of Vassar women had never married; by 1921, however, the figure had fallen to 25 percent.)

Euthenics did not survive at Vassar, but a more enduring sign of the shift away from Taylor's opposition to courses for women as wives and mothers was the establishment in the 1920s of the Child Study major in connection with the opening of a nursery school. Soon other elite women's colleges added that aspect of women's education to their programs. Of course, no elite men's colleges followed suit. (From my standpoint, the nursery school was a decided plus; both of my children entered it soon after I was appointed.)

My own rising interest in feminism did not develop from any strong expressions of feminism emanating from my women colleagues; only occasionally did they press on me their views on that subject. It emerged instead largely because I was surrounded by lively young women seeking to learn about themselves and their future from the American past. I soon began to make some connections between my professional interest in the American past and the place of women in it. That was especially potent when I wandered through, and then scrutinized, the substantial collection of books and studies in the Vassar library about and by women. Suddenly it became clear that women's history did indeed have a good deal of relevance for the history of African Americans, in which I had become deeply interested since my days at Upsala and later in graduate school. It was while scanning those many books on women at the Vassar library that I read, with engrossing interest, Charlotte Perkins Gilman's 1899 tract *Women and Economics*. I had never heard of the book or its author but soon undertook to read most of her many writings and then published an essay on Gilman's books and her many popular articles. Later, when Betty Friedan came to lecture at Vassar, I sent her a copy of my article on Gilman's ideas, because Gilman had anticipated so many of the ideas that appeared in Friedan's *Feminine Mystique*. Graciously, Friedan acknowledged the similarities, though in the course of her research shc, too, had not come across Gilman's book or name. From that first encounter at Vassar with Friedan emerged my joining with her and a handful of others in Washington, D.C., to found the National Organization for Women.

During most of the sixteen years I taught at Vassar, the president was Sarah Gibson Blanding, who had served as dean of the School of Home Economics at Cornell University before coming to Vassar. She was the college's first woman president, but that did not make her a feminist, though she invariably insisted on using the description "young women" in referring to the students rather than "girls," then a widely used designation. Like her predecessor, Henry MacCracken, Blanding always said that Vassar's principal job was to provide young women with the best education and that education would contribute heavily to their being the primary teachers and supporters of their families.

As a person, Sarah Blanding was open and liberal, full of fun that was often punctuated with bursts of loud, exuberant laughter and with well-disciplined Christmas parties. ("Time to go, Carl," she would interrupt in order to move me out of her living room.) Though she was rather conservative educationally, she was a solid Democrat, for she had been born in Kentucky and still sounded so. Nothing pleased her more than to discover that I was increasingly interested in the history of the South. An important result for me was a steady stream of financial support for my annual visits to the meetings of the Southern Historical Association at various southern cities. Another Vassar colleague, also of southern heritage, Mildred Campbell, supported my southern interests by letting my family and me live in her rural house in East Tennessee. She felt it necessary, if I were to teach southern history at Vassar, that I gain some direct southern experience, especially in the agricultural South, since I had been born and reared in Newark, New Jersey.

Along with fostering my intellectual development, Vassar showed me how young faculty members could soon comfortably ease themselves into a serious and congenial collegial environment. Before joining the Vassar history department, I had taught freshman courses at New York University, Hunter College, Adelphi University, and City College, while pursuing graduate study at Columbia. At all of these institutions, I was little more than a transitory person, barely recognized, except by a few contemporaneous colleagues. As one of them remarked at lunch one day, "We are all, you know, a part of the 'fluid bottom,' " existing, as we were, in truth, on a tide you knew not where to or from.

At Vassar there was no fluid bottom. Virtually from the beginning, as an assistant professor, I felt accepted as a teacher, perhaps as something of a scholar, and certainly as a professional. By my time, Vassar had achieved a democratic governance in which faculty of all ranks met together periodically and in full cognizance that the faculty and the trustees had worked out a written and strictly honored body of agreements. Although I knew about the governance, I was much surprised early on that Charles Griffin, my chairman, actually asked my opinion about a general college issue. No chairman at my earlier posts had included me in any of our infrequent faculty discussions. At Vassar, though, I was soon encouraged to speak out at the full faculty meeting if I thought I had something to add to the discussion. It is true, as I have reflected since at equally democratic faculty senate meetings at Stanford, that a democratically organized faculty with power can also stifle or slow down necessary changes, because coalitions among departments and groups seeking their self-interest can and do do just that. Yet I have always felt that Vassar showed me how a faculty-administration arrangement might or even ought to function.

On a level closer to students, I learned the importance of teaching classes in history, where there were rarely more than twenty-five or thirty students. Indeed, in my department, history was seen as so important that no one was supposed to lecture at all! Class discussions were based on assigned topics, accompanied by reading lists because students had access to an open-stack library. The students were encouraged—prodded, if necessary—to express their thoughts and reactions to the reading. I have never been sure that a class discussion, as opposed to a seminar, was always appropriate in history, even at Vassar, but in learning to lead class discussion, I came to see the limitations of depending upon lectures only, as had been the practice of many of my graduate and undergraduate teachers. In the context of Vassar's belief in the value of published scholarship, the discussion method subsequently provided me with an opportunity to publish my first book. Many universities at the time assumed, as they still do, that a young scholar's Ph.D. dissertation ought to become in time a book, especially if he or she expected to achieve tenure. A number of the senior faculty at Vassar had published scholarly works, but no one pushed me in that direction at the beginning, for which I was grateful. To be candid, I was not sure that my dissertation was something I wanted to work on at all. I still recall the reaction of my chairman when he asked me what my present research project was about. When he heard it, he said he thought the topic seemed too narrow and just plain boring, both of which it was.

Taking that implicit advice, I looked to some other projects. Because I was teaching a general course on U.S. history and chose to emphasize changing interpretations of the past, I thought it would be interesting and even intellectually exciting to do a book organized around that theme. One of the obvious advantages I obtained from Vassar was that I could design my own course and discuss with students in my class changing interpretations of American history. That was something which did not often happen at the places I had taught before. Most of them usually required young instructors to follow a departmental design. What was most valuable to me was another example of Vassar's fine cooperative relation with young instructors: the college's policy of offering competitive faculty fellowships evaluated by a Vassar faculty committee instead of through the traditional sabbatical, which was determined by term of service. As things turned out, I received a full year's fellowship at the end of my fourth year. The result was my first book, *Out of Our Past*, the text of which I had drawn from my course in American social history. Needless to say, no university and few other colleges would have provided such generous support for a young scholar, especially since the book was intended to be a popular and not a scholarly work. (That fellowship policy, I should add, no longer prevails).

From the outset, the college had encouraged young women students to serve society even if it may also have looked to marriage and family as a primary role for post-Vassar women. Teaching or education, medicine, and social work were possibilities, especially as the city and the factory created new needs that socially responsible educated women could fill. During the 1950s and 1960s most Vassar students perceived marriage as an important early step in their lives because a career often appeared to exclude marriage. At one time in my years at Vassar, all my superiors—president, dean of faculty, dean of students, and departmental chair—were single women. Almost all of the male faculty were married. In a student body increasingly determined to marry, a career, as opposed to a job, was difficult to contemplate. As I came to appreciate the implications of Matthew Vassar's mission, I began to recognize that the goal of achieving equal education for women could be personally confusing for many Vassar women given the times and circumstances. That recognition laid the groundwork for my trying to unravel the complexities many Vassar women seemed to face in confronting marriage and work. It later became my book *At Odds: Women and the Family from the Revolution to the Present.*

I became aware of the issue in the early 1960s. Vassar students worked hard—probably harder than students in most of the private men's colleges—and learned as much as or more than the men. Yet given the opportunities available for women's employment at the time and joined with the pressure for marriage, Vassar women approaching graduation found themselves in a dilemma that men had no need to think about. In the 1950s and 1960s young men could strike out directly from college into a career. When marriage and family came, that may have added a new burden, but it did not usually interfere with a man's career. Indeed, it might actually enhance the reason for continuing the career. Vassar women, however, as I learned from them, could indeed pursue a career since they possessed the necessary education. But what would happen when marriage and family arrived? Once, in discussing these issues in class, I told the students about a real-life solution that I heard about. It concerned two loving academic friends in the 1930s, Ada Comstock of Smith College and Wallace Notestein of Yale University. When Comstock was offered the presidency of Radcliffe College, Notestein proposed to her. She refused him, for she knew that as a married woman—that is, with the likelihood of a family—she could not take up the offer from Radcliffe. When she retired at sixty-five, Notestein, who had not married, proposed to her once more. They then married and lived together for more than twenty-five years. To my students that story was romantic, but hardly a solution for them. Indeed, only reliable and easily available contraceptive devices, the loosening of sexual habits, and revised conceptions of marriage and women's careers reduced substantially the sharpness of college women's dilemma, though without entirely resolving it.

It could be said, too, that one evidence of that dilemma was the college's decision in 1968 to become coeducational. The underlying drive, as I perceived it, was the issue of marriage and family versus career. It was a male president, to be sure, Alan Simpson, who initiated, in conjunction with Kingman Brewster, president of Yale, a possible linkage of the two colleges. In the difficult and sometimes acrimonious process of discussing the merger, which, in the end, did not take place, Vassar College decided to become coeducational, as did Yale. That decision clearly broke a tradition among prestigious private colleges that the best education depended upon a separation of the sexes. For a while even Mount Holyoke and Smith seriously contemplated coeducation, but among the men's colleges the change spread rapidly across the nation. Today there are still a number of private women's colleges, but only a handful of men's colleges remain. Even West Point and Annapolis are coeducational.

By the time the decision was made for Vassar to become coeducational and to stay in Poughkeepsie, I had decided to move to Stanford University, after sixteen years of teaching, learning from, and loving Matthew Vassar's college. I was leaving Vassar not because of coeducation; after all, Stanford had been coeducational from the beginning. Rather, I wanted a strikingly different as well as more comfortable location, a larger academic scene, and to be able to work with some colleagues I knew there. As I think about Vassar today, I reflect that once again Vassar was in the forefront of higher education, first at its beginning when it constituted a major shift in women's education, and more recently in helping to expand coeducation across the country. (Not all of Vassar women at the time agreed with that evaluation, I need to admit.) Although I supported coeducation at Vassar and Yale, my feminist outlook appreciates the continuation of single-sex institutions for women. In a still largely male-dominated society, women's colleges provide a needed diversity for young women seeking higher education.

When one leaves a job or an institution after a substantial number of years, those left behind usually entertain one of two general responses. One is that those who remain are glad you have gone, though they may not say that. The other is that those who remain are very sorry you are going and wonder if you did the right thing in deciding to leave. The response I received from my associates at Vassar did not suggest either message to me. They did not feel that I was escaping them, or even that I was injuring them. Instead, as Evalyn Clark, one of the senior Vassar women in the department, said to me: "Carl, this move will be good for you because it will provide a wider and more exciting opportunity for your talents." She knew, of course, as I've been saying, that Vassar had done so much for me that my staying could be easily justified. But that was not the Vassar I had learned about; it sought, rather, to develop its faculty as well as its students.

Fenway Park. *National Baseball Hall of Fame Library, Cooperstown, N.Y.*

John Demos

A Fan's Homage to Fenway

(Or, Why We Love It
When They Always Break Our Hearts)

O *ctober 1, 1978. Final day of the regular season. The Red Sox comfortably ahead, at home. The Yankees losing badly, in New York. If these results hold, there will be a playoff game tomorrow, in Boston. After an entire season of back-and-forth struggle, the two best teams in baseball will be tied—and will play one more to decide it all.*

In the eighth inning I go upstairs to put on sweats. With two out in the ninth, I am poised halfway between the television set and the front door. As soon as it ends, I am out that door and onto the street in full stride. Fans by the thousands, I am sure, are at this moment piling into cars, buses, and subways, in a mad dash to the box office. The best way, the most certain approach, to playoff tickets is to avoid all that—by running.

I am forty-one on the calendar, but fourteen (or seven, or twenty-nine) in my feelings. It doesn't matter; the loyalties here are ageless. I have been a runner for almost as long, and the six-mile trip downtown will be easy, especially with such a powerful incentive. The weather is gray and drizzly, but I hardly notice; there are wings on my feet just now. For the fifth time,

The author wishes to acknowledge, with thanks, helpful suggestions made by various friends and fellow Sox fans in response to earlier drafts of this essay, specifically: Aaron Sachs, E. Anthony Rotundo, Alexander Keyssar, Doron Ben-Atar, Peter Ginna, and William Leuchtenburg.

spanning four decades, I will follow the Sox into postseason play. And for the first time, I will be there. At Fenway.

My route takes me through a varied swatch of Greater Boston terrain. From my home on a quiet suburban street in Watertown. Through the vibrant ethnic neighborhoods just below. Along the sweeping arc of the Charles River, to Cambridge. Past the outer edges of Harvard Square. Close by the stately residential houses of Harvard College. Across a bridge to the Boston side. Back again to the east, beside the river. Then a quick left toward Commonwealth Avenue, with the tall spires of Boston University looming overhead. And on to Kenmore Square, with its trendy bars and boutiques. The last piece, up Brookline Avenue, is one I have been over countless times before: the royal road to the park. Always in a crowd—with much rubbing of shoulders, and mixing of voices, and sharing of motion (and emotion), as onward we go. Joyful march of the fans.

When at length I arrive, there are long lines at the ticket windows; so now I must wait. Never mind: the mood of my fellow-waiters is buoyant, and contagious. We banter like old friends and slowly shuffle toward our goal. In another half hour I am clutching a pair of bleacher tickets and heading home.

Fenway Park opened for baseball in 1912, during the presidency of William Howard Taft and the mayoralty of John "Honey Fitz" Fitzgerald, one of Boston's first Irish chief executives. Its name derived from a nearby expanse of public lands, designed in the late nineteenth century by Frederick Law Olmsted on what had previously been a brackish marsh (the Back Bay "fens"). This location placed it near the epicenter of the still-developing city and within walking distance of other public institutions like the Museum of Fine Arts, Symphony Hall, the New England Conservatory of Music, the Harvard Medical School, and a cluster of leading hospitals.

Now, almost a century later, Fenway is the oldest major-league stadium still in regular use anywhere in the country. And Boston is arguably the oldest of our major cities. Moreover, Boston remains a place where older is frequently seen as better. There are old houses, old churches, old shops, old cemeteries, old hotels, old roadways, an old harbor, old playgrounds and parks. Boston is notoriously a place where "antiques" are much admired (and sought after). And lately, as plans begin to germinate for a new stadium (someday), there is serious talk that Fenway might be left standing—to become itself another antique.

Indeed, the link between Boston and Fenway is worth pondering. For generations now, allegiance to the Red Sox has served to bind Bostonians together: businessmen and factory workers, college professors and students, policemen and firemen, doctors and lawyers, engineers and office clerks, storekeepers, secretaries, salesmen, housewives, and, of course, children of every age and condition. Individuals in all categories travel regularly to Fenway, like pilgrims to a local shrine, filling the place to its somewhat dingy rafters, game after game after game.

To be sure, there were till quite recently certain limits on this pattern of inclusiveness. Black faces hardly appeared among the ranks of the fans—just as they did not appear in the lineup on the field. To their shame, the Red Sox were among the last teams to drop the color bar. But even here, one might well argue, team mirrored city—with its long tradition of rendering its black citizenry invisible.

The link is expressed also in a number of very tangible, very physical, ways. Boston is a notoriously complex and irregular place in its spatial arrangements, with baffling topography, oddly intertwined neighborhoods, and an outrageously labyrinthine street plan. Fenway, for its part, is the most irregular of stadiums. The Green Monster in left, the centerfield triangle, the sharply angled fence in right beyond Pesky's Pole, the bullpens tucked against the bleachers, the box seats that jut toward the diamond past third base, the randomly distributed concession booths: how we prize these oddities—and all the other nooks, and crooks, and crannies! Besides, how very, very Boston!

Taken piece-by-piece, Boston is small-scale and "intimate" (by big-city standards). One may comfortably traverse its leading neighborhoods on foot, and with a limited investment of time. Fenway, too, is relatively small—with its single (not double or triple) grandstand deck, and a footprint half the size of most big-league counterparts. And certainly Fenway is intimate. Players can hear, and respond to, fan comments from almost any distance or direction. Moreover, the seats themselves loom over, and press against, each other, as if to lump their occupants into a single throbbing mass.

But there is more, much more, to this stadium-city connection. Beyond size and space and structural congruence lies the matter of shared culture. This is harder to specify but carries a deeper significance.

Boston's history is, of course, long, and colorful, and compelling. And the cast of its characters is extraordinary. The Puritan founders of four centuries ago, with their vision of "a city on a hill." The preachers who dominated the community for several early generations. The "witches"—a little to the north in Salem—and itinerant Quakers, and other assorted miscreants—who threatened to destroy its spiritual fibre.* The rising merchant aristocracy, which did (by some accounts anyway) do exactly that.

By 1750 Boston had become the largest and most important city in all of North America. Its trade touched the farthest corners of the British Empire. And its political influence was almost as broad. As "patriot" protest mounted against tightening imperial control, Boston consistently took the lead—with its Massacre, and its Tea Party, and its Minutemen, and its "one if by land, and two if by sea."

Through, and after, the Revolution, Boston's preeminence continued. In the opening decades of the nineteenth century its "clipper ships" pioneered the development of a truly worldwide commerce, including the romantic China trade. Meanwhile, too, it served as the organizing center for a host of textile plants, shoe factories, machine shops, and related enterprises in the nearby mill towns—and thus pointed the way toward a new industrial future. Likewise with religion. Boston remained the center of American Protestantism and spawned a variety of sectarian experiments. (The Mother Church of Christian Science occupied a prime location downtown, and Unitarianism was born in the old King's Chapel.) Likewise with movements for social improvement: abolitionism and temperance, peace and prison reform, revivals and foreign missionary effort, radiated out from this same nodal point. Likewise, finally, with educational and cultural development: Boston claimed Harvard and the Massachusetts Institute of Technology (though both were actually across the river in Cambridge), and Transcendentalism (nurtured on West Roxbury's Brook Farm), and a bit later, pragmatism.

With growth and progress came a host of particular adornments. There were landmarks of the built environment, ranging from "colonial" Faneuil Hall, the city's original marketplace, to the elegant Georgian townhouses of Beacon Hill, to the monumental Trinity Church, created

---

* Indeed, in the seventeenth century, witches and Quakers were hanged for their "crimes" on the Common; for further details, see another of the essays in this volume, David Hackett Fischer, "Boston Common." For details almost beyond reason, see John Putnam Demos, *Entertaining Satan: Witchcraft and the Culture of Early New England* (New York: Oxford University Press, 1982), a work produced under the editorial direction of Sheldon Meyer. (Sheldon, alas, is a Giants fan.)

by famed architect Henry Hobson Richardson. There was a steep hierarchy of social privilege topped by a clique of "blueblood" families. ("And
this is good old Boston / The home of the bean and the cod, / Where
the Lowells talk to the Cabots / And the Cabots talk only to God.")
There were salons like the one around "Mrs. Jack" Gardner (whose
magnificent Italianate mansion would later become a special sort of museum). There were culture centers such as the *Atlantic Monthly* and the
Atheneum. There was even a notorious Watch and Ward Society to
enforce local moral standards (whence the moniker "Banned in Boston").
Separately and together, these developments helped shape the profile of
nineteenth-century Boston, parts of which survive to the present day.

They also supported a proud notion of Boston as "the Athens of
America"—or, grander still, "the Hub of the Universe." Even now its
newspaper headlines, and political orators, occasionally invoke the image
of Hub. Distorted though this was (and is), it did describe a feeling
prevalent among many pre-twentieth-century Bostonians. Their city,
they confidently believed, was *first*—in history and social refinement, in
reality and perception, in overall public importance.

Even in professional sports Boston could stake a claim of "first." The
Red Sox, so named in 1907, achieved soon thereafter the prototype baseball "dynasty." The very first game played at Fenway, on April 20, 1912,
produced a stirring win over the New York Highlanders. And the rest
of that season brought both a pennant and a World Series championship.
More pennants and more championships followed: in 1915, 1916, and
1918. The team's lineup featured soon-to-be legends like Cy Young and
Smokey Joe Wood, Tris Speaker and Harry Hooper, and the young Babe
Ruth (then a pitcher). Hub of the *baseball* universe, too.

But it wasn't to last. Not for Boston. Not for the Red Sox either. Most
of the twentieth century was—how else to say it?—a time of descent
and decline. The city steadily shrank, relative both to its own past and
to rival metropoli. Other cities—newer, bigger, stronger—moved past it
in the pecking order of urban supremacy: Chicago, Philadelphia, Detroit,
St. Louis, Los Angeles, Washington, San Francisco, Houston, Dallas.
And one other city, most of all: the despised, envied, feared megalopolis
just down the coast, New York.

In fact, New York had been coming on strong for several generations
(beginning at least as far back as the completion of the Erie Canal in
1825). But for much of that time Boston had managed not to notice.
Well before 1900, New York was assuming the position of national

financial capital; yet as long as Boston's old and respected banks, credit unions, and investment houses remained strong, it didn't seem to matter. Moreover, Boston's nonparticipation in the great industrial expansion of the late nineteenth century (oil, coal, gas, steel, railroads, and, finally, automobiles) was veiled by the continuing viability of its traditional manufactures.

In the twentieth century, however—and especially after about 1950—the disparities became too wide to ignore. Many of the New England textile factories shut down in order to move south, and other, ancillary industries (such as the big General Electric plant in Pittsfield, Massachusetts, and the paper mills of New Hampshire and Maine) followed suit. Boston had always been a regional center for the surrounding states, and now the region itself was in economic eclipse. Tourism still qualified as a growth industry, but this seemed perversely to emphasize New England's out-of-step situation.

Moreover, economic eclipse was compounded by dramatic demographic restructuring. Large numbers of immigrants had begun reaching Boston even before 1850, and in the decades following the Civil War they became a tide of flood proportions. Their ranks included Italians, Greeks, Jews, Chinese, African Americans from the South, and, most numerous by far, the so-called shanty Irish. Soon enough, Irish politicians were vying for city leadership. Their line would eventually run from "Honey Fitz," through James Michael Curley, Thomas "Tip" O'Neill (Speaker of the House, while representing Cambridge), Kevin White, Ray Flynn, and Billy Bulger (brother of "Whitey," an Irish *mafia* don and thus himself something of a Boston original), to the several generations of Kennedys (Ambassador Joseph P., President John F., Senator Edward M., Congressman Joseph P. III, and so on).

In the exclusive "Brahmin" clubrooms of the Back Bay these changes were viewed as the darkest decline. Of course, in other circles they wore a different, more complicated aspect. Irishness, in particular, imparted a new vibrancy to civic life—but it also brought a bittersweet heritage of sorrow and suffering on "the old sod." Thus would some of the newcomers add their own piece to the city's increasingly defensive mood.

Yet all along Boston (and New England as a whole) retained a leading role in cultural life; its museums, its hospitals, its orchestras, its new "high tech" enterprises, and, above all, its universities, were widely acknowledged as being at (or very near) the top. And this allowed Bostonians to reposition themselves vis-à-vis their rivals elsewhere. Though badly outclassed in economic might and political clout (not to mention sheer demographic impact), Boston could yet claim a kind of cultural—or even moral—supremacy. She could still play Athens to New York's Rome.

The result was a strange amalgam of local attitude: what might be called a superiority/inferiority complex. And from this arose a new Bostonism—a distinctive tradition of Noble Defeat. Boston would lose, repeatedly and emphatically lose, but there was grace, even elegance, in her losing. Better to go down nobly than triumph crassly. Better to save one's soul, and prove one's character, than simply to win at all costs. Considered thus, the modern history of Boston could assume the mantle of tragedy.

No other part of Boston would wear this mantle, and carry this tradition, more conspicuously than . . . the Red Sox. A team of tragedy, if ever there was one. And masters, above all else, of the art of Noble Defeat. Actually, it began with a decidedly ignoble moment. In 1920 then-owner Harry Frazee sold the great Babe Ruth outright to the Yankees (a transaction that has been remembered ever since as spawning a retributive "curse of the Bambino"). Other players followed Ruth out a virtual revolving door, and the team plunged precipitously toward the league basement. In fact, during the decade of the twenties, the Red Sox finished dead last no fewer than eight times.

The thirties, however, brought something of a turnaround, with new ownership in the person of Thomas A. Yawkey, a courtly young textile tycoon from South Carolina, whose enormously deep pockets would be opened again and again for the purchase of fresh talent. Yawkey's initial acquisitions included proven stars like slugger Jimmy Foxx, pitcher Lefty Grove, and, appropriately for a growing legion of Irish fans, infielder-manager Joe Cronin. In the forties the team shifted strategy, placing more reliance on home-grown players culled from a much improved farm system. Among the best were Bobby Doerr, Johnny Pesky, Sam Mele, Tex Hughson, and Dave "Boo" Ferris. Plus one more, above all others: the intense, irreverent, incomparable Ted Williams (also variously known as Teddy Ballgame, the Splendid Splinter, the Greatest-Hitter-Who-Ever-Lived, or, simply, the Kid).

For all that, an actual championship eluded them—and has continued to elude them over a span that now covers eight full decades. But they have come close, and they have mostly gone down, well, nobly. Shall we replay some of these lowlights? *1946*: The Sox fall to the Cardinals in the Series' seventh game, as the deciding run scores from first while

"Pesky is holding the ball." *1948*: A summer-long battle is capped by a playoff loss to the Indians. *1949*: Another closely fought pennant chase, this one sacrificed on the final day to the hated Yankees in New York. *1967*: Year of the Impossible Dream, with an utterly surprising run to the pennant, only to go down in seven in another Series with the Cardinals. *1975*: A shining, spectacular season, a pennant, and (by common agreement) "the greatest World Series ever played." So great, in fact, that some say both teams won. Except that the final score will always read: Cincinnati 4, Boston 3. *1978*: Another playoff, as noted above and below. *1986*: Another pennant, another Series—this time against a wretched band of Yankee surrogates, the New York Mets—leading, finally, to the worst, the absolute pits, as Wilson's little grounder skips cruelly through Buckner's bowed legs. As the saying goes around Fenway, they always break your heart.

Running throughout this sorrowful saga, like a wound that will never close, lies a deep fixation on the Yankees. Since the long championship drought began, Sox fans have had to watch their bitterest rivals win an astonishing total of twenty-five World Series. As a result, the atmosphere at Fenway for midsummer Yankee games is like no other. Longing blends uncomfortably with envy and doubt; spasms of hope flutter against a heavy despair that rides on every pitch or swing. To trump the Yankees, to throw off the curse, to *win*: such would truly be Red Sox heaven. New Yorkers, for their part, respond with bemusement verging on contempt. A scene from the men's room at Yankee Stadium, as reported in the august pages of the *New York Times*, precisely captures the view from the other side. "What?" says one man to his neighbor. "You wash your hands after you pee! What are you, a Red Sox fan?" Indeed. (And is this not the story of twentieth-century Boston and New York writ small?)

Tragedy needs heroes, performing their heroics. And the Red Sox have seen plenty of those: Williams's stratospheric averages (including his immortal .406); Carl Yazstremski's triple crown; Roger Clemens fanning twenty; Carlton Fisk's clutch home run to win an unforgettable Game Six (never Seven); the terrible fate of Tony C; Gentleman Jim Lonborg and Lefty Mel Parnell; Rudy York and Buster Stephens; Jim Rice and Freddy Lynn; Jimmy Pearsall of *Fear Strikes Out*; Wade Boggs, the Hit Machine; the Boomer, the Steamer, the Spaceman, and the Little Professor. ("Who is better than his brother Joe? *Dominic* DiMaggio!"

But, of course, we never really believed it.) Heroes, for sure. Bravura performances. And inevitable, noble defeats.

Finally, there was—there still is—Fenway itself: more than just a venue, "a lyric little bandbox of a ballpark" (in John Updike's wonderful phrase), and the visible, venerable token of it all. To pass through its aging portals is to feel the power of this tradition, these soaring dreams and shattering disappointments. Squint a bit, and you can *see* Pesky's hesitation as Slaughter rounds third; you can *see* Ted's gloriously arching homer off Rip Sewell's outlandish blooper pitch; you can *see* Yaz slowly circling the field, touching all those outstretched hands, on his final day in the lineup after twenty-three stalwart years. The old park just keeps on keeping on, deepening its fund of "history" with every passing season. Red Sox history, Boston history, our history. Like us, it is smaller and weaker, but also finer and nobler, than any of the competition.

October 2. Playoff day. The weather has turned unseasonably warm, almost langorous, as we walk the royal road yet again. And Fenway has never looked more beautiful: In the bleachers around us the crowd is excited, expectant, and, yes, more than a trifle apprehensive. The game begins, with the Yanks' great Ron Guidry battling ex–New Yorker Mike Torrez. A Yaz homer puts the Sox up in the second; a Rice double makes it 2-zip in the sixth. Then the ancient karma intervenes. Bucky Dent's lazy fly ball drifts and drifts, right into the net atop the Monster; suddenly the Yankees are ahead. Two more New York runs follow, but in the eighth the Sox close to 5–4. Both game and season come down to the ninth, with the fearsome Goose Gossage on to protect the lead. Burleson gets a one-out walk, and Remy lashes a single to right (on which Piniella slyly fakes a catch, holding the runner at second). Rice flies to left (a ball that might have—could have—would have—scored a man from third). Two on, two out, Yaz at the plate again. The moment is exquisite and unbearable; I can hardly watch from behind my tears. One more blinding pitch from the Goose, one more ferocious swing from Yaz, and then . . . the highest pop-up I have ever seen. Up and up and up it goes, as if to graze the sky. Nettles is camped underneath, waiting for it to come down. But maybe it will stay up there forever, a souvenir for the gods. Maybe.

Later, some will call this "the greatest game ever played." And why not? What a fitting companion, come to think of it, for that other classic, "the greatest World Series" of 1975. The Sox were in both. The Sox lost both. And we fans are left to wonder: which matters more?

Poster found by the author in Woodside, California.

Paula S. Fass

FINDING HISTORY IN
WOODSIDE, CALIFORNIA

I n 1992, California had been my home for seventeen years. During those years, I had raised a family, written extensively about American society, and taught thousands of students about American history. As a good citizen, I always voted in local elections. But in all that time, California had never been for me a historical place. Instead, as an easterner (a New Yorker and European born), I thought of the Golden State as a place without time. East was history. California was nature—a marvel of sea and coastline, breathtaking mountains and valleys. Despite its century and a half of Americanization, and before that its Spanish and native cultures, California remained for me caught in a constant present of visual sensation and on the brink of some unanticipated future, but without the deep institutional clutches of a historical past. There was nothing especially original in my view. California had been perceived in similar terms by many, but it was an embarrassment for a historian. I had fallen for the California myth, and despite my best efforts to grasp its past by visiting "historic" missions, gold country sites, and the Sonoma square where the Bear Flag republic had been proclaimed, California never spoke to me as a place of history. As a result, I thought of California as a region of exile, without connection to my personal past or that of the American people to which I had committed my studies. Then I met Charley.

Charley was the entry to my most personal book of history and an

115

unexpected guide to California. I had begun to work on child kidnapping in the United States, a subject with deep resonances and meanings for me, in 1990. As a mother whose children had been born in the 1980s, a decade marked by hysteria about child abduction, I was emotionally a victim of its pervasive anxiety. And children lost to tragedy had, much earlier, been burned into my consciousness. Since I was a scholar whose interests lay in the psychological crevices of social life, I believed the subject warranted historical investigation. Together with most other Americans, I knew about the Lindbergh baby, of course, but was there an even older story? And how did the present public experience compare with those of earlier times? What about our anxiety? Have parents always worried that their children would be taken by strangers? When did they start thinking this way? Where did the fears come from? Were they justified? These were the questions that underlay my research as I struggled to make a subject that had not been previously studied as "history" take on a past. A little digging brought me to the story of Charles Brewster Ross, the first child widely acknowledged to have been abducted in the United States. The story of his abduction and the history that it created convinced me that child kidnapping was not only worthy of historical study but a significant component of the evolution of modern culture. Pursuing the meaning of that story and its consequences became something of an obsession for me, and one that eventually led me to confront the past in Woodside, California, an environment that seemed to me once part of nature, not of history.

Charles Brewster Ross (known to everyone as Charley) was abducted from the front lawn of his family's home in Germantown, Pennsylvania, on July 1, 1874. He was four years old and one of the seven children of Christian Ross, a Philadelphia shopkeeper, and Sarah Ann Lewis Ross. His family was respectable and middle class. Charley and his older brother, Walter (six at the time), were taken together on a Wednesday afternoon by two men who were not entirely strangers, since they had several times before befriended the boys by offering them candy as they played outside their home. Walter came back on that Wednesday evening after he was found crying in Kensington, another Philadelphia district. Charley would never return.[1]

In its day, and for decades afterwards, the story of Charley's disappearance, his father's negotiations with his abductors, and the long, ago-

nizing search to find him was one of the most widely told tales of kidnapping and one of the best-known stories of childhood in the United
States. It was known even beyond American borders. Indeed, Charley's
story became both a cautionary tale and a kind of template for subsequent ransom abductions, providing, among other things, many of the
basic elements for the elaborate plot that two Chicago adolescents, Nathan Leopold and Richard Loeb, devised in 1924 for the "thrill killing"
of Bobby Franks. Although few today know either his name or his place
in childhood history, Charley's hold on the popular imagination was not
eclipsed until he was replaced by another kidnapped child, the Lindbergh baby, in 1932. As I became acquainted with Charley's story, I was
intensely affected, both as a historian and as a mother; it stimulated my
historical imagination while evoking my own deepest fears. And I came
to understand it as an archetypical story of child loss and parental grief.
I also became convinced that by understanding what had happened to
this child, I could begin to understand why we have ever since been
haunted by fears about child abduction.

In the late nineteenth century, Charley's story became deeply part of
American popular culture, a touchstone for parents who warned their
children to be wary of taking candy from strangers, and a constant
reminder of the new dangers lurking in cities populated by ever larger
numbers of strangers. Since the case helped to transform child disap-
pearances, which had previously been merely insignificant events, into
the new crime of ransom kidnapping, Charley's abduction also became
a model for criminals, and it provided long-term lessons to police and
to parents of what *not* to do in pursuing potential kidnappers. This case
was so broadly familiar that Charley's experience and that of his father,
Christian, who told his story of negotiation, frustration, and emotional
pain in a memoir published in 1876, have influenced how modern childhood has been experienced ever since. Charley, the golden-haired four-
year-old with the sweetly serious face and gentle demeanor, was as much
a part of the mental landscape of the nineteenth century as Harriet
Beecher Stowe's little Eva and Charles Dickens's Oliver Twist. And he
had clearly become a honeypot to the evolving print media. As late as
1927 one experienced newspaperman remarked that "I know that any
kind of an item suggesting the discovery of Charley Ross is always good
copy and will be telegraphed about the country from end to end, and

printed at greater or lesser length. If the thing has the least aura of credibility about it, Sunday features will follow. . . . That sad little boy of Washington Lane long since became a classic to the American press."

Charley never did come home, but the search for him had been furious, and Americans, as a result, came to know about him through all the forms of communications available in 1874: newspapers, broadsides, reward notices, word-of-mouth, traveling circuses. Christian Ross had traveled widely in his search for his son, and information about Charley had been spread by police searches throughout the Pennsylvania–New York–New Jersey area. So intense and well publicized did the search for Charley become that the Western Union company gave Christian free access to a telegraph line so that he could follow up on the more than six hundred leads that he received as sightings of Charley were reported in various parts of the nation and overseas. Christian eventually traveled to three hundred places in his quest.

While Charley's story was extraordinary in every way, similar stories have become ever more familiar to me and millions of other parents in the late twentieth century, and Christian's travails have been repeated many times. Then, as now, these child sightings were the lifeblood of hope in efforts to locate a missing child. Then, as now, the police were usually inadequate to the task. Ross had hired the Pinkerton private detective agency to help find his son; parents today turn to missing children's foundations and other private agencies. By 1876, those searching for Charley had distributed some seven hundred thousand posters of the child, advertising his absence and offering a reward. (All together, three large rewards were offered during the long search.) As the story of Charley's disappearance spread and as people eagerly joined in the effort to find him, so did Charley's name and his fame. Increasingly, missing children began to call themselves Charley or Charley Ross when they were turned in at police stations. As Christian reported, "Whether these children supposed all lost children must be called 'Charley Ross,' or whether they thought that by assuming the name, they would secure kind treatment, I do not know."

Charley also became a subject for various kinds of entrepreneurship, including that of psychics, street hucksters, and local circuses. Eventually, Charley became so widely known that he became irresistible to the great P. T. Barnum, who offered a ten-thousand-dollar reward and help in locating him if Charley were allowed to join his circus if and when he was found. Barnum claimed to know everyone, even crooks and hood-lums, and said that he could assist in distributing the posters advertising Charley's disappearance. Like modern news media and infotainment programs that exploit today's missing children, Barnum knew how to please a crowd and capitalized on instant gut-wrenching news. Once Christian's memoirs were published, the book, too, became a means to spread information about Charley. Like parents today who set out to find their own abducted child and then dedicate their lives to the prob-lem of missing children, Christian devoted the rest of his life to finding his son and in the process found other missing and displaced children. And the other members of the Ross family spent decades thereafter confronted by individuals who claimed to be the lost child. As late as 1938, one man had himself adjudged Charley Ross in an Arizona court.

By the early spring of 1992, convinced of the importance of the story he had to tell modern parents, I had been in hot pursuit of Charley Ross for over a year. I scoured every shred of evidence and document I could find on microfilm, in university libraries, and at the Library of Congress, as well as all the many subsequent retellings of the story (*The Ladies' Home Journal*, for example, ran a story on the fiftieth-anniversary of the abduction), as I tried to piece together what his story meant to Americans at the time and to me and other parents like me whose anxieties about child abduction developed in its long wake. Then I found Charley in Woodside, California.

On Sunday afternoon, February 16, 1992, I had taken my own four-year-old Charlie, his older sister, Bibi, and my husband, Jack, on an expedition to Woodside, a wealthy suburb on the Peninsula, some thirty miles south of San Francisco. We had been spending a wonderful and productive academic year in residence at the Center for Advanced Study in the Behavioral Sciences high on a hillside above the Stanford campus. Looking for local sites of interest, we had been to, among other places, Año Nuevo, where the elephant seals mate and give birth, and other natural preserves along the coast. Woodside, we had been told, was a lovely place, full of horses and a "western" atmosphere that it tried hard to preserve through its laid-back style. Here again was the California I thought I knew so well—natural, tied to a tempo of life and an attitude rather than a past. Then, as we soaked up the local atmosphere, we learned that Woodside, which had been a provisioning outpost for the lumbering industry, had a general store preserved as a kind of historical landmark. It would close shortly. We got there at four-thirty in the afternoon. It was, from the outside, one of those quaint wooden structures you see throughout Northern California as a reminder of gold rush and lumber camp days (many of them looking like Hollywood sets). As I stepped inside, I was literally overwhelmed. On the right side of the doorway was the face of the child I had come to know so well—Charley Ross. Hanging in front of me was one of the thousands of missing child posters distributed to help find him. Here he was, almost three thousand miles from where he had been abducted, here in the midst of California's majestic trees.

At that moment, I recognized that Charley's story, which was so real in every way in my imagination, had been a real experience for the people of Woodside in the 1870s. Like me, they had been informed about the missing child and the parents' grief. They had been connected to an event I had come to know so well, and they had been encouraged to participate in the search for this child. Charley's abduction was alive for them as it had become historically alive and deeply meaningful to me. They had been engaged in the same mystery that had led me to search for the historical traces of a missing child. A special connection had been made, not only between the Ross family and the people of Woodside across three thousand miles but between the people of Woodside (mostly lumberjacks) and me across almost 120 years.

The poster in the Woodside General Store was much more than a fortuitous concretization of a past event that had become almost mythological in my search for the missing child. It began to transform for me the place that had harbored him. If Woodside had sheltered Charley's poster for all these years, then Charley's poster connected Woodside to a past that I knew, a past that I had pursued, a past that was real. The store guide behind the counter knew nothing about the poster or the child, so I told him and others in the store my historical story. Woodside, California, once a tiny lumbering town clinging to the edge of the wilderness and the coast, now a wealthy little California suburb, had a history.

The fabulous treed expanse of the area in which Woodside is located had brought lumbering to the area by 1832. By 1849–50, when California became the frantic site of gold fever, the lumber business was already flourishing; there were fifty sawmills among the redwoods, with lumber being shipped to San Francisco as well as to settlers in the Santa Clara

Valley. There had been some sparse settlement in the region since the mid-1830s, ten years before the American occupation of California, and Woodside was the first home of English-speaking settlers in that area south of San Francisco known today as the Peninsula. Part of the Rancho Cañada du Raymondo, Woodside had been granted to John Coppinger, an English seaman, by the governor of Mexico. By 1875, Henry Huntington, who would grow rich on California railroads as well as timber, and who would leave his name on a famous California museum, botanical garden, and library, had built a mill (and a small rail line) and was avidly harvesting the bounty of the environment.[2] Woodside was neither quaint nor laid-back in those days but a bustling center of an increasingly commercial California securely tied to the main chance.

A provision store was already in place in 1852, and in 1853 it was in the possession of Dr. Robert Orville Tripp, a dentist and lumber dealer, and his sometime partner. Tripp would be identified thereafter with the general store and become famous in the region as a shopkeeper and an honored and much-valued local citizen. It was not a mere coincidence that a store had made California come alive for me as a historical place, since stores were centers of commerce and information, and information had been key to the historical importance of the story that grew around the abduction of Charley Ross. But it was surely a coincidence that Charley's father had also been a shopkeeper at about the same time across the continent. Storekeepers like Christian Ross and Robert Tripp were important members of the community in those days, entrepreneurs with civic connections. Because of Christian's connections in Philadelphia, among them the mayor, Charley had become much more than a missing child.

Before the Ross case, children who disappeared, even if they had been stolen, were not taken seriously by the police, nor did they arouse community concern or provoke publicity. At the time, urban communities were far more worried about abandoned children, who in increasing numbers were just at this time occasioning the creation of innumerable societies for the prevention of cruelty to children. When it became clear that Charley's disappearance was not accidental, the business community of Philadelphia raised a twenty-thousand-dollar subscription—the amount demanded in ransom, and a huge amount in its time (almost half a million in today's dollars). They raised it as a reward in order to find the child *and* his abductors. Charley's family's status, his father's vigorous search for his son, and the ransom note transformed a missing-child event with no public consequences into a new crime, which thereafter redefined the meaning and gravity of child abduction. After the Ross case, child abduction, which was in 1874 merely a misdemeanor in law, became a felony, first in Pennsylvania and then in other states across the nation. The case and its attendant publicity also altered the experience of American parents.

Once Charley's poster had invested Woodside with a history for me, I sought to learn about its past. Eventually, the prosperous Dr. Tripp and the well-connected Christian Ross were bound together in my mind across a continent by their common status as shopkeepers in the 1870s and by their search for a stolen child. Just as Christian Ross's grief had spoken to me over a century of time about a new crime and the tormenting grief of child abduction, now Dr. Tripp, his store, and the people it served, too, became real through his connection to those events. In the guidebook *Historic Spots in California*, the "old Woodside Store" is described as "the first store opened between San Francisco and Santa Clara" and as "the one surviving landmark of pioneer days in Woodside."[3] For me, that one surviving landmark became the anchor of a meaningful California past.

Intersecting with the past with which I was familiar, with an East Coast abduction, with all the millions of missing-children posters of the last twenty years, that historic landmark made me rethink American history. No longer merely a part of nature, Woodside, I now understood, had participated in the historical experiences of the American people. It, too, knew about Charley; it, too, knew the story of the helpless father overcome by the loss of the child; it, too, was part of the search for Charley Ross. Now, when I faced my Berkeley students, I could tell them truthfully that they were deeply connected with history and that they were historical actors, as I had always pretended before but had never really believed. I rethought my courses, adding new lectures on historical issues related to the West Coast, on the gold rush as an occasion for the meeting of peoples from four continents, on Hollywood as a renewal of the American dream. I found that as I did so, I understood American history better once I could position California and the West in that history. As I proceeded with my own history of child kidnapping, I sought out cases that took place where I lived (one of the most arresting concerned the abduction of a Berkeley girl in 1955). California had become a real place in time as well as in geographic space.

When I invested Woodside with history, I also realized that it was anything but quaint. Today, Woodside, California, has become familiar to Americans as a seat of Silicon Valley power, the habitat of millionaires plotting the future of the computer and Internet industries, a meeting place where billions of dollars can be lined up for a new investment in the future. It is a place to which many of my students aspire.[4] The big trees have been edged aside by big estates, the little store overshadowed by small-cap stocks and online commerce. How ironic, then, that I should have found Charley and California's past as a result of much earlier forms of communication than those that keep the Woodside millionaires' dreams alive. How ironic that Woodside had been bound up into the American past by a missing child's poster, distributed before there were airplanes or cars or telephones, let alone the computer and the Internet. But while Woodside would seem to be about the future, I now make sure that my students understand how the future communications to which it is connected are related to its past: with the telegraph, obviously, that linked the two coasts (and the world beyond), but also with the other means that Christian had employed to find his son—the print media that exploded in the nineteenth century, popular entertainments like Barnum's circus, and the sad posters of a little boy. Today's parents still seek to find their children through such posters and rely on word-of-mouth, sightings, and newspaper appeals, while they also use the National Center for Missing and Exploited Children computer as a resource. Woodside may be a kind of missing link—a communications center then as now, a place of prosperity, a part of American history. It certainly was for me as I found that it had a history that joined it to thousands of other places and people, including a historian searching for Charley.

Boston Common, in a sketch by Dobbins, 1804. *Bostonian Society/Old State House.*

David Hackett Fischer

BOSTON COMMON

E very year, in late spring or early fall, Sheldon Meyer was in the habit of visiting his Boston authors. It was an event as regular as the passing of the seasons. He came for several days and stayed at the old Copley Square Hotel or the Ritz Carlton. If it was the Ritz, I would meet him there late in the afternoon, a time of day when the town appears at its best. As the sun begins to set beyond the Fenway, the old brick buildings of the Back Bay are suffused by a special golden light that is unique to Boston.

One afternoon Sheldon and I stood by a window in his hotel and admired the view across Boston Common. The sun was nearly gone, and lights were beginning to appear in the ameythst windows along Beacon Street. People were hurrying home through the Public Garden. We both liked to walk there, and our conversation turned to the history of the Common. Boston authors have written at length about it. One of them has produced a full-scale biography of a single tree on the Common: Joseph Curtis's *Life of Campestris Ulm: The Oldest Inhabitant of Boston Common* (1910). Another published a history of Park Street, which is all of one block long. Many volumes overflow with stories of what happened on the Common.[1]

Even more interesting is the story of the Common itself. For me it has always been one of America's most memorable places. It is also an American idea. Fifteen generations of Bostonians have argued passionately about the Common. It has been attacked and defended, reduced and enlarged, developed and preserved, and redefined in different ways. The result is a living tradition of high importance in this republic.[2]

THE PURITAN COMMON:
ENGLISH MEMORIES, AMERICAN DREAMS

Every history of Boston Common begins with a character named William Blackstone (or Blaxton as he signed himself), an eccentric Anglican clergyman who had a private quarrel with the Church of England and found his way to America. The Puritans found him living alone among his many books on the sunny side of Beacon Hill, which he had purchased from the Indians. According to legend, he wore his canonical coat inside out and rode about his estate on the back of a brindled bull, with floral garlands braided on its horns.[3] The Puritans invited him to join their colony. He refused. "I came from England because I did not like the Lord Bishops," he said, "but I will not join you because I do not like the Lord Brethren." In 1634 Blackstone moved west to another hermitage called Study Hill above the Blackstone River, remote from Bishops and Brethren alike. There he lived happily with his books and an attractive Boston widow until his death a few weeks before King Philip's War began.

Before he left, Blackstone sold his estate to the town of Boston. It was a rough piece of rolling land, covered with rocks and blueberries, but valuable to the town because it did not need clearing. The price was thirty pounds. Every householder was asked to contribute at least six shillings, "none paying less, some considerably more." The town acquired a tract of forty-four acres, which today is Boston Common.[4]

It was called the Common from the start. The word was widely used in England to mean a tract of undivided pasture, meadow, waste, or woodland that belonged to a manorial community or its lord.[5] The idea of the Common was familiar to the founders of Boston, because it was bitterly contested when they left England. Fierce struggles were raging between lords and tenants over the common lands of many an English manor.[6]

In Boston another struggle began over William Blackstone's land only a few weeks after the town had bought it. The question was whether it should be held by the town or divided among the inhabitants. On December 11, 1634, when the town assembled for a regular "lecture day," several men of what John Winthrop called "the inferior sort" proposed to break up the Common. On the spur of the moment, a committee was elected to make the division. The "chief men" of the town were taken by surprise and lost a snap vote by secret ballot.

But they were not without resources. One of them was John Winthrop, who had been elected to the committee, perhaps to give it an air of respectability. He forced a delay by refusing to serve. Then Boston's spiritual leader, John Cotton, put his popularity on the line and preached a sermon against the division of the Common. He persuaded the town "that it was the Lord's order among the Israelites to have all such business committed by the Elders."[7]

The leaders were very clear about their purposes. Winthrop wanted to keep the land intact "for new Commers and for Common," as a way of joining one person to another and one generation to the next. A townsman wrote that it was an idea that John Winthrop "had oft persuaded them unto, as best for the town." Many times he told them, "We must be knit together in this work as one man. . . . We must delight in each other, mourn together, labor and suffer together, always having before our eyes our Commission and Community in the work."[8]

John Cotton stood firmly with Winthrop, and many in Boston believed that "the Lord did not suffer Mr. Cotton to err." On the next lecture day the town reversed its decision. It elected a new committee, consisting of Cotton, Winthrop, and five magistrates, who recommended that the Common should be preserved. The "inferior sort" resisted, but the town responded to the altruism of its leaders. It "voted and agreed" that "henceforth there shall be no land granted either for Houseplott or garden to any person out of the open ground or Common field."[9]

With that decision, Boston Common became something different from the common fields in England. The town began to use the land in many ways. It became a meadow and a pasture. The militia made it a training field. Housewives did their washing at the Frog Pond and beat their carpets in the open fields. It became a burying ground, a stone quarry, and the town dump. From the beginning, the Common was also a place for what the Puritans called "lawful recreation." As early as 1638, traveler John Josselyn described it as "a small but pleasant Common where the

Gallants a little before Sun-set walk with their Marmalet-Madams as we do in Morefields, &c, till the nine a clock Bell rings them home to their respective habitations."[10]

Within a few years, Bostonians took great pride in their Common, but no sooner had the first crisis passed than another threatened it in a different way. Mainly the Common was used as a pasture. A conflict developed between the individual interest of each townsman to graze as many animals as possible and their collective interest to maintain the "herbage" of the Common against overgrazing. In our own time, this issue has become a much debated question of public ethics. One ecological writer has called it the "tragedy of the commons." Others have understood it as a fatal weakness in the idea of the common itself.[11]

It became a serious problem in Boston, but after much discussion the town found a solution. The Puritans were tough-minded that way. "If you tether a beast at night," John Cotton warned, "he knows the length of his tether before morning."[12] He was thinking not of the beast itself but of its owner, and his congregation understood him perfectly. In town meetings, the people of Boston agreed to limit their own use of the Common. In 1646 they voted that "there shall be kept on the Common by the inhabitants of the town but 70 milch kine," and no "dry cattle, young cattle, or horse, but one horse for Elder Oliver." Further, the town agreed that no individual could keep more than one cow on the Common, or four sheep in place of a cow. It enforced the rules by appointing a town keeper, who received a fee for every cow and sheep and lamb. People often tested the limits, but the system worked through eight generations. It succeeded because the town combined the idea of the common with the institution of the town meeting, and because it followed shepherds as wise as John Cotton and John Winthrop. In the end there was nothing of the "tragedy of the commons" on Boston Common.

But other tragedies would follow on Boston Common, and some were very dark. Once the town had agreed to preserve the Common from subdivision and overgrazing, another controversy arose over rights of commonage, which exposed deep divisions in the community. In 1646 a town meeting agreed that "all whom the townsmen had admitted to be inhabitants should thereafter have equal right of commonage, but that those who should thereafter be admitted inhabitants should have no right of commonage unless they hired it." Others were not "inhabitants" but "strangers." They had no rights to commonage at all.[13]

These tensions began to grow in the town, especially after the passing of the founders. Winthrop died in 1649, Cotton in 1652. Something of their large spirit departed with them. The people of Boston felt a deep sense of loss, decline, and danger. Many feared that the Devil himself was abroad in their town, and they turned against one another. A case in point was the sad story of Mistress Anne Hibbens, a difficult woman who quarreled with many in the town and was excommunicated from the Church. In 1656 a jury convicted her of witchcraft. Some of the magistrates tried to save her, but "vox populi went sore against her," and Governor John Endecott ordered that she should "hang until she was dead."[14]

The place of her death is thought to have been the Common, as it was for many others in those difficult years. As many as twelve witches were hanged in Boston. The town also executed others whom it feared. On a single day in 1678, eight Indians were shot by a firing squad on the Common, and a ninth named Old Matoonas was killed in that same bloody year.[15]

The most infamous of these persecutions was the hanging of the Quaker missionary Mary Dyer. She was not a stranger but an inhabitant who had settled in Boston during the Great Migration. John Winthrop described her as "a very proper and fair woman," but "notoriously infected with Mistress Hutchinson's Errors," an allusion to Anne Hutchinson, who had been banished as a heretic. Even her enemies testified to her grace and beauty, but many in Boston feared her spiritual independence, and she was driven out of the town. Mary Dyer went to Rhode Island, where she joined the Society of Friends. In 1659 she returned to Boston as a Quaker evangelist. So successful was her mission that a Puritan magistrate judged her to be a threat to peace and public order and sentenced her to death.[16]

Mary Dyer was offered her life if she would agree to go away. She answered, "Nay I cannot," and the murderous Governor Endecott ordered her execution. Many remembered her appearance on the gallows, "a comely woman and a grave matron" who "shined in the image of God." Then the drums rolled on the Common, and Mary Dyer was hanged. As she was swinging at the end of the rope, a great wind arose and caught her billowing skirts. Boston's brutal Major General Humphrey Atherton made a jest of it. He said, "She hangs there as a flag!" So she did, and does.

The death of Mary Dyer shocked the conscience of the English-speaking world, but the magistrates of Massachusetts remained defiant. Finally, King Charles II felt compelled to intervene. Royal commissioners ordered Massachusetts to stop its persecutions, and imperial officials slowly extended their authority over the colony. A strange twist of fate befell Humphrey Atherton. In 1661 he was riding home from a training day. In the dark, he collided with a wandering cow on the Common, and was killed by a fall from his horse. To a modern sensibility it was merely an accident, but Puritan Boston did not believe in accidents. Here was what Calvinists called a Sign.[17]

Bostonians had need of Signs, and so did Judge Samuel Sewall, one of the judges who condemned the witches. After the victims were in their graves, Sewall had an attack of conscience and did a remarkable thing. In what Perry Miller called "one of the noblest gestures of the period," he stood before his Boston congregation and took the shame of the persecutions upon himself. For the rest of his life he kept an annual day of fasting and prayer, in penance for his sins.[18] Sewall also wrote one of the first tracts against slavery, *The Selling of Joseph*, which argued that "there is no proportion between twenty pieces of silver and liberty." He tried to "prevent Indians and negroes being rated with horses and hogs."[19] He led Boston away from the persecutions that had been enacted on the Common, and toward a new understanding of a community that was more open and tolerant than before.

He combined this mission with a deep concern for the Common. Sewall became its guardian. He rode "in the Coach round the Common," and his diary is a running record of what he saw there. Sewall was one of the first Americans to write of the beauty of nature, and he led his town to a new way of thinking about its environment.

THE COMMON AND THE EMPIRE

On January 1, 1701, Samuel Sewall staged a celebration on the Common. "Just about breakaday," four trumpeters appeared, and awakened the town with a mighty blast. Sewall himself had hired them to greet the dawn of the eighteenth century. He also paid the town's bellman to read a poem of his own composition. "Cost me five pieces of 8/8," he grumbled in his diary.[20]

In Boston a new age had already begun, and Sewall himself had done much to introduce it. The old Puritan town was caught in new currents that were sweeping through the Atlantic world. It rapidly became a seat of the European Enlightenment and a more integral part of the British Empire. Increasingly, the old colonial settlement resembled a provincial English seaport, a process that historian John Murrin calls the Anglicization of early America. But Boston did these things in its old New England way. It held fast to its Congregational churches, preserved its town meetings, and kept up the Common. The result was a complex set of cross-movements, at once Anglicizing and Americanizing.[21]

On the Common itself, many customs remained the same. Cattle and sheep kept grazing there. The militia continued to use it as a training field. Washerwomen still did their laundry at the Frog Pond. A Bostonian remembered that "until the close of the eighteenth century it was customary for women living in the vicinity to wash their clothes beneath the limbs of the old elm. They would light a fire near the base of the tree in order to heat water brought from the Frog Pond, and there do their week's washing."[22]

At the same time, new patterns of use began to appear. Some developed from the growth of poverty and inequality in the town. In 1660 a small almshouse had been built on the east side of the Common at the present corner of Park and Beacon streets. It burned in 1680 and was replaced by a big two-story structure, to which larger additions were later made. For many years the Almshouse served as a hospital for indigent sick. It became an asylum for the insane and a place of confinement for the paupers who were unable to work. One Bostonian remembered it as a set of "old dingy buildings" behind a broken fence. Passersby were greeted by "hands thrust through holes in the almshouse fences, or stretched from beneath the decaying gates, and by the small and forlorn voices of the children of destitute inhabitants entreating for money" and "calling for bread, which oftentimes the town had not to give."[23]

In 1712 the town erected another dreary building on the Common, next to the Almshouse, and called it Bridewell after the London model. It was a place of confinement for petty criminals, disobedient servants, and rebellious slaves who were sent there for a whipping. Next to Bridewell, the town built a Workhouse in 1737, for paupers who were able to earn their keep by picking oakum and spinning yarn. Beside the Workhouse, the town built a Granary, where food was stored for times of need. In the spring of 1713, when the supply of grain was low, a merchant named Andrew Belcher exported a large quantity of corn and made a great profit. The selectmen begged him not to do it, but he defied them. The result was a food riot on the Common by "200 people or more ... mostly poor women." By 1740 the entire east end of the Common was occupied by shabby buildings that dealt with poverty, illness, petty crime, deprivation, and hunger among the poor.[24]

Meanwhile, another part of the Common developed in a different way. The south side, along what is now Tremont Street, became a handsome promenade for people of fashion and fortune. Many improvements were made. As late as 1722 a drawing showed only three trees on the Common. Between 1723 and 1734 the town planted a double row of lime trees, elms, and poplars to create a shaded avenue called the Mall. By 1735 the south side of the Common was enclosed by a new wooden fence, with "posts and rails from Common Street [now Tremont] up to Beacon Street, to prevent carts etc. from spoiling the herbage on the Common." In 1738 a gardener was hired and paid four pounds ten shillings a year. A reward of forty shillings was posted for information about persons injuring trees on the Common.[25]

London was the model for the Mall, as it had been for Bridewell. A visitor to Boston observed in 1740, "Every afternoon, after drinking tea, gentlemen and ladies walk the Mall." He explained, "What they call the Mall is a walk on a fine green common adjoining to the southwest side of the town. It is near half a mile over, with two young rows of young trees planted opposite to each other, with a fine footway in between, in imitation of St. James's Park."[26]

One Boston family took the lead in these improvements. In 1735 Thomas Hancock built a mansion on the brow of Beacon Hill, overlooking the Common. He took a personal interest in the appearance of the Common and paid for improvements out of his own deep pockets. He and his nephew and heir, John Hancock, put up fences on the north side, added a line of ornamental trees to screen the shabby town buildings to the east, cleaned out the Frog Pond, repaired the Granary, planted orchards along Beacon Hill, and badgered the town to make other changes that served the general interest and improved their own view.

The Hancock estate north of the Common and the Mall to the south made a striking contrast with the Almshouse, Bridewell, Workhouse, and Granary. Together they made manifest the growing gap between rich and poor in Boston.[27]

Other parts of the Common were used by Bostonians of middling rank. After 1729 spinners carried their wheels to the Common and competed for a prize of five pounds on annual spinning days. Bricklayers were allowed to make their bricks in a corner of the Common. Individual entrepreneurs were permitted to operate warehouses, a windmill, and other enterprises that were thought to be useful to the town. By the mid-eighteenth century the Common embraced all the people, but in different ways according to their rank. It became a symbol of cross-currents that were stirring in Boston during the eighteenth century.[28]

THE REVOLUTIONARY COMMON

Those trends came to a violent collision in the American Revolution, another drama that was played out on the Common. The Sons of Liberty gathered there to protest the Stamp Act in 1765 and also to celebrate its repeal in 1766. When the Townshend Acts imposed other taxes and new customs commissioners on Boston, the officials' boat was burned on the Common in 1768. After the Tea Party in 1773, Bostonians used the Common for ritual burnings of tea and for brutal tarring and feathering of imperial officers.

In 1774 twelve regiments of regulars were sent to keep order in Boston. They occupied the Common and turned it into an armed camp. The people of Boston were horrified by the events that followed there: the execution of deserters, floggings for minor offenses, acts of violence by drunken British officers. In all of these scenes the town saw the face of tyranny and a grim vision of their future in the British Empire. The behavior of the regulars on the Common deepened their resolve to resist.

After the Revolution, other events on the Common celebrated independence and national union. A great festival was held there for the new Federal Constitution. Other gatherings supported the French Revolution, the fall of the Bastille, and the end of the monarchy in France. President George Washington visited the Common and was received by the town with high ceremony. James Monroe was given a great welcome on the Common in 1817. The grandest of all these celebrations was for Lafayette in 1824. The town put on a huge military review and a dinner for 1,200 people under a vast marquee on the Common.[29]

All of these gatherings celebrated two great principles: liberty and the republic. Together they gave new meaning to the old idea of the Common, but in a way that was very different from our own thinking. We recognize a deep distinction between "public" and "private" interests. The Revolutionary generation combined them, as the development of Boston Common showed. The central figure was Charles Bulfinch (1763–1844), permanent chairman of the board of selectmen for many years, superintendent of police, and Boston's leading planner. He was also the town's most active developer, architect, and builder. His wife wrote, "My husband made architecture his business, as it had been his pleasure." That combination of what we would call public and private roles would be forbidden today, but it was accepted in the early republic, partly because Bulfinch legitimated it. He was the most improbable of politicians and developers. His biographers describe him as "personally unambitious, neurotically self-effacing, and disinclined to engage in controversy." His great love was the physical fabric of the city, and his leading purpose was to bring people together in a collective effort to improve it.[30]

The result was a great rebuilding of Boston. Bulfinch transformed a shabby wood-built colonial town into graceful city of brick and mortar. Much of his effort was directed toward the Common and the streets around it. In John Hancock's garden on Beacon Hill, he built a new State House that still dominates the scene. He also worked with a larger group, called the Mount Vernon Proprietors, to develop Beacon Hill as we know it today. One of his objects was to erect a neighborhood of handsome houses that would define the Common's north boundary.

On the east side of the Common, Bulfinch pulled down the old Almshouse, Bridewell, Workhouse, and Granary. These institutions were abolished or moved to a distant part of town called Boston's Botany Bay, but the land was not returned to the Common. It became Park Street, where Selectman Bulfinch allowed developer Bulfinch to build some of the most handsome private houses in Boston. He constructed a symmetrical border on the east side of the Common, by a process that combined public and private elements in a single act.

A similar pattern appeared in other parts of the Common. In 1784 the town had allowed a lumber and wood market on the south side of the Common "from the granary south to the end of the Common," in part because its timber was a fire hazard in the town.[31] Ten years later, a similar problem arose when the ropewalks burned in downtown Boston. They were vital to the maritime trade of the town, but their combustible stores of hemp and tar were dangerous in a close-built city. To prevent a conflagration, the town made a gift to the owners of tidal flats along the foot of the Common, on two conditions: the owners were forbidden to open a ropewalk elsewhere in town and required to build a seawall along the water's edge. The ropewalk owners were quick to accept the offer. They filled in part of the Back Bay and erected six new ropewalks on the land that had been part of the Common.

Many Bostonians saw no conflict of interest in these acts. Bulfinch himself did much to reconcile them. He was universally praised for his "integrity and purity of character" and realized little gain for himself. With his leadership, public and private interests became one.

THE REPUBLICAN COMMON:
PUBLIC RIGHTS AND PRIVATE INTERESTS

As time passed, new tensions began to grow between public and private interests on the Common. A new problem developed when the ropewalks at the foot of the Common burned in 1819. By that date, the price of Boston real estate had risen so high that the owners could make more money by selling the land to developers than by rebuilding. Ward politicians on the new city council, who were developers themselves, were willing to allow the sale. Others in the town did not agree. The land on the Common had been given to the ropewalk owners for public safety, not for private gain. This issue gave rise to another great controversy and a new crusade for the Common.

Its leader was Josiah Quincy (1772–1864). He was born and raised in a prominent Boston family. When he was three, his father died and left him the collected works of Locke and Sidney, a large estate, and a long tradition of civic responsibility. Josiah Quincy had a career in Congress as a Federalist leader and in 1823 was elected mayor of Boston. He became one of the great urban reformers in American history. Quincy cleaned the streets of the city, some say for the first time since it was built. He constructed its sewers and water supply, broke its unruly mobs by personally leading a posse of draymen against them, and built the handsome market that still bears his name.[32]

Josiah Quincy was of a new generation who thought of "public" and "private" spheres as separate and distinct. One of his most enduring acts was an extended campaign to banish private interests from the Common. As mayor, Quincy persuaded the town to buy back the ropewalks from their owners. A "ropeyard loan" was opened, and $780,000 was raised to restore the land to the Common. A powerful alliance of developers and city councilors fought him tooth and nail, but Quincy defeated them.[33]

No sooner had he recovered title to the lands for the city than politicians on the city council made another attempt to sell it to developers. Once again the mayor appealed to the citizens. They voted that the lands should be called the Public Garden and "forever after kept open and free of buildings of every kind."[34]

Ward politicians and developers kept trying to get the land for many years. Four times they persuaded the city council to sell it to private holders—in 1842, 1843, 1849, and 1850. Four times the city rose against them. Finally they were stopped by a state law. With the help of Governor Nathaniel Banks, the General Court enacted a statute that protected the Public Garden and the Common from the rapacity of Boston's politicians. The people of Boston were asked to ratify the law, and did so by a vote of 6,287 to 99.

Altogether, the Public Garden added twenty-four acres to the Common. The new tract was improved by flower beds, ornamental paths, lakes, fountains, monuments, and handsome bridges and gates. By 1846 promenade concerts, children's dances, and flower shows were held there. The city took pride and delight in it.[35]

Other changes were made in the old Common, with the same purpose of protecting public land from private interests. The right of pasturage ended in 1830, and the cattle disappeared. Washerwomen were ordered to take their laundry elsewhere. Other regulations forbade the dumping of refuse, the quarrying of stone, and the cutting of turf. A controversial bylaw ended carpet-beating and rug-shaking on the Common, an ancient custom that had been kept by many generations. Edward Everett Hale wrote a nostalgic essay called "The Last Shake" to mourn the occasion.[36]

At the same time, public uses were encouraged. The parade ground was opened to "athletic exercises and games." The first organized American football and baseball leagues held their games there on a regular basis; plaques still mark the spot. Fireworks and balloon ascensions drew large crowds to the Common.[37] But public use was regulated by the spirit of what the Puritans had called "lawful recreation." Sabbath laws grew even tighter than before the Revolution. Skating and swimming were allowed six days a week, but never on Sunday. All of this activity defined separate public and private spheres by a process that lawyers call prescription.[38]

While the town wrestled with these questions, a new struggle gave rise to yet another meaning of the Common. People began to think of it increasingly as an aesthetic idea. Always the town had expressed concern about the appearance of the Common, but this was something different—a concept that the community had a "public right" to preserve the beauty of the place.

The first stirrings of that attitude appeared as early as 1784, when private citizens led by apothecary Oliver Smith took it upon themselves to raise money for the Common from three hundred contributors. The rough terrain of the Common was leveled and landscaped by voluntary effort. "Low portions of the common were raised, the holes filled up, the uneven places graded, fences repaired, and a large number of trees planted" in a great labor through many years.[39]

This effort expanded after 1815, both in the breadth of activity and in the depth of its organizing idea. During the War of 1812, the city had raised a large fund for fortifications against an expected British attack. The war ended before the money was spent, so it was applied to the beautification of the Common. Hills were cut down and the earth used to fill marshes and tidal flats. In 1836 a handsome iron fence was erected around the Common, 5,932 feet at a cost of $82,159.85. It purpose was no longer to keep four-legged animals in, but two-legged predators out, which it did with high success.[40]

Much of this work was done by voluntary associations of private citizens who clubbed together to promote the public good, "it being the pride of the committees each year to do something to beautify and adorn this favorite holiday resort of the citizens." The Public Garden became a place for flowers and ornamental shrubs, and the Common was turned into an arboretum. English elms along the Mall were replaced with "new elm-trees of the American species." Other specimens were gathered from around the world. Many of the new trees were planted by Mayor Josiah Quincy with his own hands. He continued to serve his community and the Common until he died in 1864 at the age of ninety-two.[41]

These improvements made the Common more like a city park. A citizen proposed a change of name, from Boston Common to Washington Park. He must have been a stranger and not an inhabitant. The city rose in wrath against him. Boston Common it remained.[42]

Visitors and residents alike delighted in its beauty. Among them were the writers of the American Renaissance, most of whom lived nearby. Sophia Hawthorne, wife of novelist Nathaniel Hawthorne, wrote in her diary about the experience of walking on Beacon Street along the Common: "Could but just keep my feet upon the sidewalk, so bubble-like, balloony were my sensations—the full rich foliage, the hills, the water, inflated me. Oh that Common—that Eden in miniature."

Through the nineteenth century, the people of Boston were quick to act against any intrusion that threatened the beauty of the Common. In 1877 a "Committee of Citizens" argued explicitly that all the people of the city had "public rights" to the preservation of the Common and also to its protection against what diminished its beauty. Their idea of public rights had been long in the making. Americans have fiercely protected their private rights, but they have been less attentive to public rights, a tradition that was fostered on Boston Common.[43]

THE URBAN COMMON:
COMPETING IDEAS OF THE PUBLIC INTEREST

As the city of Boston became a modern metropolis, the Common began to be contested in yet another way. Though nearly everyone agreed that it was a public place, new conflicts arose, not between public and private purposes, but between competing ideas of the public good.

In the late nineteenth century, Bostonians sought to develop the urban services that a modern metropolis required, while preserving the amenities of the Common. One of the leading problems was transportation. By 1880 Boston's white-collar workers were commuting to downtown offices in horse cars that ran along Tremont Street, on the Common's southern edge. To give the cars more space, the city removed the handsome iron fence. So loud was the outcry that the fence was quickly replaced.

By the early 1890s, electric streetcars had replaced horse cars and Tremont Street had become nearly impassable in rush hour. Urban planners proposed to run a line across the Common. The result was a howl of protest. "Save Our Common" became the slogan of the city. Finally the city found a costly solution: America's first subway. In 1895 the electric streetcars were buried in a deep trench beneath the Common. The old trees that bordered the Mall were lost, but others were replanted. After the scars of construction healed, the surface of the Common remained more or less intact.[44]

In the twentieth century, swarms of automobiles required bigger streets in Boston. Some were enlarged by contracting the Common, despite a law that protected it. The most intractable problem was parking. Here another costly solution was adopted in the twentieth century—a large underground parking garage beneath the Common. Bostonians watched in horror as the lower Common was excavated and a concrete garage was buried deep in the ground. The project was dogged by the usual Boston scandals: long delays, surging costs, shoddy construction, and spectacular corruption. No sooner was the garage completed than it began to fall down, even though it was already underground. Major rebuilding was necessary. But when it was done, the Common itself was more or less unscathed. Nothing appeared above ground except four small entry-kiosks, which by the measure of Boston's modern architecture are remarkable for taste and restraint. The only casualty was the "herbage," which has never been quite as green since.

A major menace to the Common continued to be the venality and incompetence of the city's government, which became a corrupt system of outdoor relief for otherwise unemployable Bostonians. Private groups and individuals became defenders of public rights against the depredations of municipal officials. In 1908 a wealthy Bostonian named George Francis Parkman did something serious about protecting the Common. In a codicil to his will, Parkman left five million dollars to the city for the "maintenance and improvement of the Common and Parks now existing," with the specific provision that the Common in particular "shall never be diverted from its present use as a public park."

The tone of the Common changed in the course of the twentieth century, in ways that preserved its ancient purposes and enlarged them with a new generosity of spirit. At the beginning of the century, much of the Common was closed to the public, in the name of the people. During World War I, strict signs read KEEP OFF THE GRASS: IF YOU WANT TO ROAM, JOIN THE NAVY.[45] Gradually a more permissive attitude prevailed. People were allowed to wander freely across the grass. Courting couples were permitted to sit on the lawns in the Public Garden. Children could run where they pleased, at some loss to the "herbage" but a great gain to the pursuit of happiness.

A new spirit also appeared in monuments on the Common. Much heroic statuary had been erected from the eighteenth to the twentieth centuries, beginning with Bulfinch's monument to the Revolution and reaching its climax in a towering memorial to the Union dead. One of the most beautiful and beloved American sculptures is Augustus St. Gaudens's moving memorial to Robert Shaw and the 54th Massachusetts Regiment on the north corner of the Common.

In the Public Garden, Thomas Ball's handsome equestrian monument of George Washington (1869) is still much admired, though Washington's sword is ripped off by undergraduates with such regularity that the city now replaces it with fiberglass. Also in the Public Garden is the Good Samaritan Monument, as tall as a three-story building, which celebrates the first use of ether in an operation at Massachusetts General Hospital in 1846. A local controversy arose over a rival claim by Dr. William T. G. Morton, who used anesthetics in his dental office on Tremont Street and was duly noted. Old Bostonians irreverently call it the Ether-Or Monument.

In the mid-twentieth century, an entirely new style of statuary appeared in the Make Way for Ducklings Monument, which commemorates a classic children's book by Robert McCloskey about a family of ducks that walked from the Charles River to the Public Garden while a burly Boston cop stopped the rushing traffic to let them pass. Today a family of bronze ducklings are permanent residents in the Public Garden. They are large enough for small admirers to sit astride them. One often finds them surrounded by children waiting their turn. The heads of the bronze ducklings have been burnished to bright gold by many affectionate hands. From time to time, a duckling disappears, sometimes to be found in one of Boston's many college dormitories. The disappearance of George Washington's sword is thought to be an amusing act of adolescent larceny, but the theft of Quack or Pack is regarded as a despicable act of treason against the community. Replacements are instantly commissioned at heavy expense.

The new spirit also appears in a reconstruction of the old Frog Pond at the center of the Common. Early in the twentieth century, fences were maintained around the pond to keep "urchins" away from the water. The new spirit of the Common has reversed that attitude. With generous support from Boston philanthropists, landscape architect Lynne Wolff has turned the Frog Pond into a place for children and all the people. From late fall to early spring, her new Frog Pond becomes a skating rink, complete with its own Zamboni. The architect herself is sometimes seen spinning gracefully on the ice. In summer the Zamboni disappears and the Frog Pond becomes a wading pool, filled with swarms of small Bostonians. Teenagers are recruited as lifeguards. They come from Chinatown, Roxbury, Dorchester, South Boston, and the North End and proudly wear tee-shirts that identify them as Frog Pond Staff.

Today the Common serves a highly diverse and fragmented population, and in different ways than ever before. Religious services continue in the open air as they have for many generations, but in a more inclusive spirit. An Episcopal mission holds outdoor services for homeless Bostonians every Sunday morning. Rallies and meetings gather on the Common for every imaginable cause. I was involved in one such event in the 1980s, as chairman of an antinuclear organization. We held a rally on the Common and invited other antinuclear groups to set up booths there. By chance, Jews for Peace were placed next to Palestinians for Peace, and the principles of the movement were severely tested. In the end, peace prevailed. I remember that the spirit of the Common made a major difference.

Other voluntary associations have come together to look after the Common itself. The most important, Friends of the Common, is led by Henry Lee, a civic-minded Bostonian much loved in the city for his grace and good humor and respected for his devotion to the community. He continues a tradition of stewardship that reaches back to Winthrop and Cotton. Henry Lee is active in many civic roles: president of the Massachusetts Historical Society, head of the Boston Arts Commission, and a founder of the History Collaborative. He is fiercely protective of the Common.

Thanks to Henry Lee, the Common keeps improving in the twenty-first century. It does so in a way that calls to mind an old club which instructs its house committee to make "improvement without change." This is the spirit of the new Common, but it is the old Common too. More than ever, it belongs to all the people of the city, as Winthrop and Cotton intended. Today most Bostonians are not descended from the founders. Everyone in town now belongs to an ethnic minority, but we identify ourselves as Bostonians and take pride in the special quality of our city. As we have grown more diverse, we have learned to cherish the things we share. Boston Common is a symbol of that sharing.

These are some of the things that Sheldon Meyer and I talked about when he came to Boston and we strolled in the Public Garden and the Common. As night fell, we would turn west into Commonwealth Avenue and walk to the St. Botolph Club for dinner. Directly in front of the club's door is a monument to a departed member who was another of Sheldon's Boston authors, Samuel Eliot Morison. He sits on a rock of pink granite in the middle of Commonwealth Avenue and gazes pensively toward the Common. We would pause for a minute beneath his bronze feet. Then we would take our meal in the old dining room beside a portrait of the club's first president, Francis Parkman.

In that setting, the conversation turned from history to historians. Morison thought of himself as a follower of Parkman, and Sheldon Meyer encouraged me to work in the same tradition, which I have tried to do. It is a special way of writing history, with deep roots in Boston and a strong kinship with the values of the Common. It is very far removed from the academic scholarship that is fashionable today. This Boston School does not "do history," in the academic phrase; it writes history. Its writings center on history itself, not historiography. It addresses a large public in a serious way on spacious subjects of general interest. Always it has rigorous standards of primary scholarship and works closely from archival materials. It also has a strong sense of place. The first rule of Parkman and Morison was to visit the scene. I have tried to do all these things in books I have written for Sheldon.

The Boston School constructs its books as this essay is constructed, as a story which becomes a sequence of stories, with highly articulated actors. The stories are about people who make choices, and choices that make a difference. It writes with a large spirit and a sense of humor. Always it avoids the dark idols of the academic cave: determinism, relativism, alienation, and cynicism. It rests on a belief that history actually happened, and it has a strong sense of continuity with the past. Here is a way of thinking that fits the condition of Boston. It comes naturally to mind when one strolls across the Common, late on a sunny afternoon, and that special Boston light illuminates the landscape.

Charleston, 1880. *Division of Prints and Photographs, Library of Congress, Washington, D.C.*

Jackson Square, New Orleans. Photograph by Leon Trice Photography. *From the Municipal Government Photograph Collection, City Archives, New Orleans Public Library.*

William W. Freehling

CHARLESTON'S BATTERY
AND NEW ORLEANS'S
JACKSON SQUARE

I first came to do what I love partly because of what I could not do. Physical infirmities helped make the life of the mind my passion, and an intellectual weakness helped make the Old South my professional preoccupation. First coming to consciousness in the horrendous Hitler years, I was appalled to learn that an advanced Western democracy had *elected* the assassin—that something in democracy, at least in German democracy, had snapped. What could be so vulnerable in my favorite system of government?

Answering that question, at least in the German context, was not within my powers. Intense research into the failings of the post–World War I German republic required fluency in German. Foreign languages are my intellectual Achilles heel. I could limp through high school and college classes in French, if I worked especially hard. But no way did I have the talent to develop a scholar's ease with that language—much less with German.

So I had to turn to an English-speaking culture to investigate why democracies fall apart. I came to think that a failure in our own history might throw light on democracy's German failure in the 1920s. I became increasingly absorbed with American democracy's inability to resolve internal conflicts peaceably in the pre–Civil War period. Of the two sections that drove our national republic toward implosion, I found the southern side more fascinating—more exotic, more quirky, more mysterious, more full of dark passion and rich irony. In the Old South and the causes of the American Civil War, I had found my subject— the match between my talents and my curiosity.

True, I hear now and then southern murmurs that my capacity to understand the South is necessarily defective too. The irredeemable defects this time are alleged to be not peculiar to my talents but common to all northerners. Supposedly, only southerners have the special experience and instincts, the exquisitely honed antennae, to achieve peak empathy with their own diverse, complicated culture.

I consider that position infested with a rat's nest of problems. A contemporary southerner, after all, has experienced only some of past southerners' travails and joys. That partiality of an insider's experience yields as many biases as the partiality of an outsider's experience. Insiders and outsiders equally need the artifacts that the past has left behind to strip off the blinkers that limited experience in the present has fastened on us all.

I concede that my southern friends sometimes know in their bones some truths that I must find the right relics to understand. But I also think that my upbringing in Chicago actually aided my understanding of crucial aspects of the Old South. A splendid high school anthropology course with Jack Ellison sent me deep into the Chicago housing projects, where I experienced the full horror of American (not just southern) racism. Some acquaintance with the northern upper class also led to experience with American (not just southern slaveholders') paternalism. A great book will someday be written on the similarities between American paternalisms.

No, my experience for understanding the South was limited less because Chicago happened to be in the North than because Chicago was a huge city. The Old South was a profoundly rural civilization, and life on the farm has other problems and joys than home in a skyscraper. I not only had to comprehend nonurban experience but also had to explain this alien life to my predominantly urban readers. I believe, with Sheldon Meyer, that academic explanations must be clothed in concrete portraits of people and places to attract nonacademic readers. But how could this city resident visualize, much less colorfully portray, the Old South's rural squires?

The New South preserves scant agrarian relics to enrich the imagination. Much as I cherish Middleton Place near Charleston, Rosedown near Baton Rouge, and several dozen other Old South plantation sites that still more or less endure, they display less rather than more of the world we have lost. Almost all slave cabins and even many Big Houses have vanished, as have ice houses and spring houses and whipping posts and overseers' huts. My overly urban imagination needed help.

Charleston and New Orleans came to the rescue. In both cases, surrounding rural societies molded the urban culture. Both well-preserved cities are colorful, arresting, perfect for breathing vibrant life into a past civilization. Both, taken together, show that the Old South as well as America was a house divided. Both offer public spaces, Charleston's Battery and New Orleans's Jackson Square, that reveal their colliding essences in a glance.

I glimpsed Charleston first, in the early 1960s. This Atlantic Coast tourist mecca is home to the South Carolina Historical Society, where many documents furthered my first book on the South Carolina Nullification Controversy of 1832. In that attempt to nullify U.S. laws, South Carolina took on not only the North but also the rest of the South, especially that southern U.S. president Andrew Jackson. I called my study of the controversy *Prelude to Civil War*, for this early confrontation between South Carolina and the nation presaged the secession crisis of 1860–61. In 1832 and 1860, South Carolina's extremists outdistanced mainstream southerners, and especially Andrew Jackson, in rage at the North. Why?

Charleston's overpowering private houses drew me out of the archives to find the best answers. Having relished the street life of Boston, San Francisco, and Chicago, I had never imagined that houses could overwhelm streets—that a city could be largely its homes. The surprise intrigued me all the more because Charleston's consuming mansions exuded paradoxes: such gorgeous upper-class dwellings and yet (in the early 1960s) so obscurely shabby, the homes packed so tightly together and yet so severed, homes so close to the street and yet so guarded against the streets. And where amidst all these obscurely troubled mansions were all those other defining elements of almost any other city: the slums, the gangs, the coffee houses, the bars, the restaurants, the roaring trades, the parks, the symphony halls, the opera halls, the rubbing together of humanity?

The strangeness all started, I slowly began to see, with the city's odd geography. This urban gem occupies a narrow spit of land, shaped like a tongue stuck out at the world. The tip of the tongue licks the Atlantic Ocean. Across the ocean rises the only non-Carolina world nineteenth-century Charlestonians could speak about without a sneer: Old England. Along the two edges of the tongue course the Ashley and the Cooper rivers, serving the only American civilization that nineteenth-century Charlestonians found up to snuff: the Carolina coastal world. Other early American cities served rivers that originate deep in the continent. In contrast, colonial Charleston had been marketing center for only the lush, dank swamps that extended westward less than fifty miles from the ocean.

In the eighteenth century, the Carolina swamps spawned a grain golden in every way, rice; and the cash from its export made lowcountry aristocrats America's richest pre–Revolutionary War gentlemen. The swamps also sent enriched gentlemen scurrying to find second homes. Because of malarial and other fevers, whites fled their plantations from spring's first flowering to fall's first frost. When squires departed, they left behind huge slave gangs to coax golden grains from the flooded fields (and to sicken in the miasmatic semijungle). Healthy absentees gathered in Charleston. Here they commissioned their elegant houses. Once their mansions had been built, they had little to do but enjoy ultra-exclusive drawing rooms.

The domestic architecture of exclusion, no less than a city shaped as if sticking its tongue out at the world, hints at the essence of these first Charleston dandies. The old dwellings sit almost on the streets, almost atop each other, with almost all scarce vacant land tucked behind garden walls. Apparent street doors to houses are often but entrances to gardens. To reach the drawing room, one must penetrate the door in the wall, cross the private garden, enter the real house door, and climb a flight of stairs to the drawing room, full of signs of an English country gentleman's parlor. No brooking familiarity with American streets, this elevated bit of Old England.

Though neither Charleston's drawing rooms nor its houses nor its gardens are remotely up to English lavishness—nothing in colonial or mid-nineteenth-century America was—these houses are no sorry imitations of European sophistication. Carolina's gentlemen, while often newly rich New World tycoons, profoundly experienced the Old World, whether by London visits or English educations or reading the classics. From their architects and builders, squires demanded magnificently wrought iron gates, external walls stuccoed every conceivable color, curved stairways seemingly nowhere supported, and so-called piazzas or porches, on one, two, three levels. What tourist can tire of strolling by these glorious homes?

Not this city lover, who had to struggle to find the other usual urban pleasures (and terrors). When I first visited Charleston, slums abounded. But they remained largely concentrated on the Charleston neck, the gateway to the city proper from the upcountry and nowhere near the riot of mansions. Some retail stores flourished, but they were largely concentrated on a few thoroughfares such as King Street (for the most part devoid of mansions) and the open air market (often devoid of white retailers). A few wholesale establishments, where rice had been marketed, survived, but they usually remained segregated along the Cooper River's East Bay Street. A lovely antique theater and art museum endured, each the oldest of its species in America. But both were cramped treasures, and where were expansive concert halls and opera houses?

In the early 1960s, only a relatively few hotels and restaurants flourished, and no antebellum coffee houses or dram shops. The only Charleston restaurant of distinction and musty charm was the esteemed (and now extinct) Perdita's, which served up an exquisite version of she-crab soup (actually made with he-crabs!) and shrimp over hominy. The only venerable and sizeable hotel (I except the then decrepit, now refurbished Francis Marion) was the Fort Sumter, glaring at that fort from the tip of the tongue. (Now that old pile is, sadly for nostalgic tourists, given over to residents' apartments.) The Mills House had not yet been restored to its antebellum glory. Nor had a dozen mansions yet been turned into charming inns.

But for a historian in the 1960s, the dearth of hotels and eating spots had an advantage: the Charleston of the 1960s remained much like the city a century earlier. The upper crust had apparently always preferred to lavish its leisure time exclusively on entertaining in secluded drawing rooms. Its passion for private encounters had evidently left a dearth of Charlestonians to patronize public establishments and a paucity of spots for outsiders to sleep and to dine in an insiders' city.

Insiders' houses also hinted at too much disdain for other Americans' materialism. When I first saw these hoary structures, too many houses needed painting. Too many piazzas sagged. Too much lacy wrought-iron decoration rusted. It was as if the relics of the ancient gentry had paid a permanent price for their founders' determination to soar far above the vulgar crowd, far from their unhealthy swamps.

In their Battery, part of it called White Point Gardens, early nineteenth-century gentlemen apparently conceded that contempt for commonplace crowds had gone a trifle far. They filled in the sea a bit at the tip of the tongue. Here they created a public green space beyond their private houses. Here they could gaze at the ocean and imagine England across the way. Surely that imagined utopia was on gentlemen's minds, for their city constantly recalled England. Charleston's streets were named King and Queen. Its finest churches were titled St. Phillip's and St. Michaels'. Its best drawing room decorations were copycat English, even down (or rather up!) to the papier-mâché on the ceilings. These would-be English country gentlemen's favorite mid-nineteenth-century sneer had been that "the greatest absurdity in the world was a 'Liverpool Gentleman.'"

Nothing seems like Liverpool in the Battery. The green space has paths for walking but few benches, no picnic tables, no tradesmen, no concession stands, no restaurants, no coffee houses, no residences except towering mansions behind the park. Gentlemen apparently wanted to be seen strolling but never sitting, never pausing, never mixing promiscuously; just take in the ocean air, perhaps tut-tut at a few vulgar types, and then back up to the drawing room. In Charleston, so much an anticity for antientrepreneurs routed from the farm, the Battery seems the ultimate antipark.

In this unconventional American park with its back turned to the American West, nothing hints of inland America. Some trees are palmettos, as alien beyond the coastal swamps as the rice that had financed city sumptuousness. All the Battery's historic monuments are Confederate cannon. The Battery artillery that had once blasted Union "invaders" looks no less capable of whirling to fire shots at the ghost of Carolina's earlier nemesis, Andrew Jackson and his progressive (for white men) Southwest.

Only documents back in the libraries could tell me whether Charleston was similar in the nineteenth century and whether the city scene caught the mood of an absentee planter class. The documents gave reassuring answers. Charleston and its Battery had barely changed. Eighteenth-century gentlemen had been fabulously rich. Their nineteenth-century fortunes had turned sour. Declining squires had been chary about commoners and worshipful of aristocracy and disdainful of materialism and in love with everything English. Because they had loathed nineteenth-century American egalitarianism, they had only slightly updated their eighteenth-century elitist state constitution. They had given the mob (alias poor white men) the vote, but only to elect propertied gentlemen to the state legislature. Wealthy legislators elected everyone else.

Absentee planters had clung to their declining plantations, when they could. Often they could not, a phenomenon especially mortifying when their ex-overseers bought their estates. They had been scared of swamp illnesses and, a little, of the huge black population that supported their city idleness. They had known that unless they could force slaves to risk swamp fevers, they would lose their remaining plantations, lose the lowcountry, maybe even lose Charleston.

And then in the mid-nineteenth century, Yankees beyond the Slave South had told these antiques that their labor institution was a sin, their city an anachronism, their beloved Battery worth dumping back into the sea. Almost as insufferably, the *southern* world west of the coast had considered these gentlemen outmoded, their rice swamps no economic match for the Cotton Kingdom, their eighteenth-century elitist regime no political match for Andrew Jackson's white men's egalitarianism. Nouveau southwesterners made all (white) men eligible for all offices and all voters the electors for all positions. In his famed spoils system pronouncements, Andrew Jackson called for annihilation of Carolina's ideal, government by the richest and best. Any (white) Tom, Dick, or Harry, pronounced Andrew Jackson, could handle any office. More insufferably, the roaring new Southwest had drained away Carolina's ebbing energy, importing many Carolina blacks and whites to populate the supposed new southern paradise.

To all that, Carolina gentlemen screamed *No*—No to Yankee holier-than-thous, No to the South's new Andrew Jacksons, No to American mobocracy, No to the American Union. From Charleston's federal customs house in 1832, they defied President Andrew Jackson to enforce King Numbers's tariff law. From the Battery in 1861, gentlemen fired those cannons at Fort Sumter, thus beginning the Civil War and their final road to obliteration. What else but a fossil's defiance could one expect after seeing grand old Charleston?

New Orleans aroused different expectations. I first saw this second

151

southern urban jewel in the late 1960s while working on my second book, a history of the South's *Road to Disunion*. I early became convinced that no SOUTH existed, for the most northern South, the so-called Border South, differed profoundly from the most southern Deep South. But I had not yet fully appreciated differences within the Deep South. New Orleans, and particularly Jackson Square, opened my eyes, especially in contrast with Charleston and its Battery.

One word, enormous, captures the difference. Everything about New Orleans is huge compared to Charleston. New Orleans has always contained at least four times as many people. It occupies a wide plain at least five times more sprawling than the Charleston tongue. It commands the Mississippi, America's mightiest river, a broad highway of water that makes Charleston's Ashley and Cooper streams look like needles. Where Charleston has only that one neighborhood of imposing houses ending at the Battery, New Orleans is a riot of impressive neighborhoods: the Garden District, the French Quarter, the Faubourg Marigny, the Canal Street business district, and more. Where Charleston venerates its cramped old Dock Street Theatre, New Orleans exudes concert halls, opera houses, sports palaces, convention halls, gambling dens. Where Charleston now offers a few dainty inns, New Orleans still offers endless raucous hotels.

Perhaps most enticing to a traveling gourmand, where Charleston in the early 1960s offered pretty much only Perdita's, New Orleans displayed a rich spread of eating palaces. My New Orleans favorites include Galatoire's, where reservations are taboo and rich and poor happily wait together for tables in a line snaking along Bourbon Street; Antoine's, where plebeian waiters command their wealthy customers (you used to beg your table from your waiter; mine was Little Willie—what a Cajun character!); and Brennan's, where poor folks used to be able to afford a splendid Sunday brunch in an exquisite aristocratic mansion that Andrew Jackson loved.

These establishments and more remain largely as they were before the Civil War. They all serve the New Orleans palate's special mix of French, Creole, and Cajun, especially lavished on shrimp and crayfish, pompano and trout. If you prefer a gargantuan soup, the loaded gumbo makes Charleston's she-crab soup seem almost effete.

Nothing is effete about another New Orleans tribute to gluttony, the raw oyster bars. At a dozen and more of these culinary extravaganzas, the oysters are huge and the beer plentiful. I remember the night I devoured three dozen oysters, slathered with horseradish-loaded red sauce, and was still weeping for more. The bartender, who knew that liquor was not the only threat to moderation in his house, saved my life (or at least my evening) by responding that enough was enough.

When I sadly departed, the noise on the street seemed as over-powering as the oysters. In Charleston, one quietly strolls hushed residential streets. In New Orleans, crowds sweep down avenues roaring with sound. The din is of car horns screeching, of jazz blaring, of street merchants advertising their wares, of hawkers trumpeting their strip shows, of prostitutes offering to show still more skin.

No walls in New Orleans guard against these loud streets. In Charleston, doors blockade private gardens. In New Orleans, many street doors are flung open to reveal patios full of flowers and drawing rooms beyond. In Charleston, exquisite ironwork decorates closed gates. In New Orleans, equally lacy ironwork enhances balconies above the streets, where residents come out to share the revelry below. In Charleston, parties remain in second-floor drawing rooms. In New Orleans, balls erupt into the open air, turn into parades. New Orleans fanciers will not wait for Mardi Gras to dance and prance down the avenues.

The street life spills into Jackson Square, New Orleans's antiequivalent of Charleston's Battery. The open end of Jackson Square faces not east, toward the Atlantic and England, but south, toward the Mississippi River, the Gulf of Mexico, and the Caribbean. Along Jackson Square's back edge loom not mute private houses but three busy public buildings, two originally devoted to governmental affairs (the Cabildo and the Presbytere) and one to Jesus Christ (the St. Louis Cathedral). In the church, a discordance of dialects, Creole and Arcadian and French and Spanish and northern and black, and old southern white too, chant praise of Jesus Christ. Along the two sides of Jackson Square, long brick three-floored buildings (Madame Pontalba's Apartments) face each other. The Madame's buildings, erected in the 1850s, combine residences (on their upper floors) with businesses (on their ground floors). In front of the retail stores, painters display their creations and concessionaires laud their treats.

The Jackson Square scene seems a continent removed from the Battery. Here, churches, governmental officials, apartment dwellers, store-keepers, artists, restaurants, bars pack together. There, only grass and trees and cannon could be found. Here, all is buying, selling, celebrating. There, nothing but strolls beckoned. Here, crowds fill the air with shrieks. There, only murmurs could be heard.

In the center of Jackson Square's celebration of city exaltation, Clark Mills's statue of Andrew Jackson dominates. South Carolina's enemy is portrayed astride his excited horse, who paws the air with two front feet. Jackson, somehow in no danger of falling off, faces west while he tips his hat to the future. His favorite defiance of South Carolina Nullifiers, THE UNION, IT MUST BE PRESERVED, decorates two sides of his platform. The sculpture is antitype to the monuments of the Battery: those cannon aimed at Fort Sumter and the Union.

Jackson, with his anti-Charlestonian invitation to Americans to keep moving west, seems to impel the Jackson Square crowd to keep exploring the city. Past the open end of Charleston's Battery, no land remains. Past the open end of Jackson Square, celebrants stride toward the Mississippi River. Most folks stop at a coffee house, with mirrors on all four sides, doubling and doubling again the sense of packed-in humanity. Here the late (and early!) crowds feast on America's best doughnuts (the French-style delicacies called beignets) and chicory-laced coffee. Past the coffee houses looms the river edge. Here, having finally reached land akin to the watery edge of the Battery, New Orleans's sojourners can peer toward that anti-England, the Caribbean cultures.

Few pleasure seekers stop to peer. There is always another non-English adventure awaiting back in the old French city, the Vieux Carré, for all who have cash left to spend. There remains pleasure to buy, whether gambling or imbibing or feasting or dancing or stomping feet to the endless beat of the jazz. Only dawn's first light quiets the din and sends lingering revelers to sleep off their spree. With that contagion of public spending for pleasure, New Orleans establishes its last difference from those silent Charleston dwellings, with their air of brooding over gentlemen's declining fortunes.

Once again, only sources in the library could tell me if the urban streets mimicked nineteenth-century agrarian planters' mood. Once again, I was in luck. Mid-nineteenth-century New Orleans was much like the city's latter-day self. Gentlemen came to Sin City not for six months, to flee from malaria, but for a week or so of decadent pleasure and resourceful business, before returning to healthy Mississippi River plantations. Their wallets were as stuffed as Charleston gentlemen's were thin; southwestern entrepreneurs constantly bought the slaves that Charlestonians begrudgingly shipped west. In the 1850s, southwestern plantations yielded fabulous profits, whether from cotton or sugar. The boom made every extravagant vision seem reachable, whether adding more Caribbean land to the Union or escaping the federal ban against importing more Africans.

Carolina rice aristocrats shuddered at the new West and the hero of New Orleans, Andrew Jackson. Louisiana's cotton and sugar planters embraced everything modern and new. Decaying Carolinians wished out of the old Union and nervously voiced qualms about new Latin acquisitions. Booming southwesterners had their doubts about disunion and a passion for extending the Union to the Amazon. With that difference so perfectly reflected in the two gentries' urban spaces, maybe a city boy could yet recapture the differences between agrarian Deep South gentlemen—even if he did come from the North.

Stone Mountain, with the sculptor Gutzon Borglum's scaffolding in the foreground. *Borglum Historical Center.*

Louis R. Harlan

CLIMBING STONE MOUNTAIN

Stone Mountain, about sixteen miles northeast of Atlanta, is in the middle range of natural wonders, though some provincials call it the eighth wonder of the world. Compared with other mountains, Stone Mountain is but a foothill, rising 780 feet above its surroundings. Even so, as an entirely *stone* mountain it is unique, an impressive mass of solid granite, denuded of soil or vegetation except for a small grove of stunted cedars high up, known as Buzzards' Roost. The granite was formed some two hundred million years ago when a volcano extruded a mound of magma upward without breaking the earth's crust. As the magma cooled, it crystallized into a light gray stone flecked with mica. The softer stone and soil around it eroded, leaving the granite mound exposed above the red clay countryside of north Georgia. Its isolated prominence on the skyline made it a landmark over the centuries. Native Americans used it as a signal station. In 1790 the Creek chief Alexander McGillivray chose it as a meeting place for the regional tribal leaders who accompanied him to treat with U.S. government officials on questions of Indian land policy. By 1825 white settlers had made it a stagecoach stop and built a resort hotel at the base, and by 1842 Cloud's Tower, 165 feet high, had been constructed on the summit to afford visitors an even broader view of the countryside.

History is usually more concerned with human subjects and with change than with enduring, inanimate objects, and yet place is intimately linked with time and human events as one of history's dimensions. Places no less than events punctuate our lives and cast shadows over remembrance. Stone Mountain is one such memorable place. For me—and particularly my brother—the mountain played a melodramatic role in our growing up during the Great Depression. Though we knew nothing of its history, and the abandoned carvings on its north face were to us as timeless as an ancient ruin, the mountain's looming presence cast a large shadow over our adolescence.

Decatur, our hometown, was Atlanta's streetcar suburb, about six miles from the heart of the city. Not yet the teeming metropolis of today, Atlanta was a medium-size city of about three hundred thousand people, many of them on their uppers during the hard times of the 1930s. But it was a city "with attitude." When the South rose again, Atlanta would be its commercial and cultural capital. The Great Depression had not ended but only deferred that dream. Atlanta's suburban sprawl encompassed Decatur, the county seat of adjacent DeKalb County, but did not extend as far as Stone Mountain. The mountain and its village were in another, rural world of overall-wearing farmers, dirt roads, and chewing tobacco. Stone Mountain granite, on the other hand, was very much a part of my suburban life. I grew up in a house made of Stone Mountain granite, with walls two feet thick. It was wonderfully cool in the daytime, when the stone walls insulated the interior from the heat of the sun, but shirtless hell at night, when the walls radiated their stored heat inward.

The town of Stone Mountain, as a railroad terminal, had played a minor role in the history of the South, as the scene of two minor skirmishes in the Union campaign to capture Atlanta in the Civil War. The chief significance of Stone Mountain, however, was a symbolic one, as the birthplace of a revived Ku Klux Klan in 1915, and as the site of a half-completed and abandoned monument to the Lost Cause dear to unreconstructed southern whites. The idea of a Stone Mountain monument to the Confederacy was also born in the year 1915, a time when extreme white racism was reaching a crescendo in the South and spreading rapidly in the North. In January of that year, Mrs. Helen C. Plane, president of the Atlanta chapter of the United Daughters of the Confederacy (UDC), wrote to Gutzon Borglum, an Idaho-born sculptor living in Connecticut, inviting him to look at Stone Mountain as a possible site of a monumental sculpture depicting the Confederate army and its leaders. Borglum came and liked what he saw, a *tabula rasa* on which to sculpt on a large scale—with dynamite! It would be by far his most ambitious sculpture up to that time.

Later in the same year, D. W. Griffith, also a northerner, completed his magnum opus, *The Birth of a Nation*, the first full-length motion picture. Griffith's melodrama had a racist message: that black people were inferior and that the Ku Klux Klan of the Reconstruction era was a band of knights errant who righted wrongs and restored the racial hierarchy after the end of slavery. The film played to large crowds in northern cities and then opened with much fanfare in Atlanta in December 1915.

A few days before the Atlanta showing of the film, on the cold, windy, pitch-dark Thanksgiving eve of 1915, fifteen white men led by "Colonel" William J. Simmons gathered at the foot of Stone Mountain. They ascended its sloping western side in the silence suited to a solemn occasion. Reaching the top, they donned the white bedsheet robes and the pointed caps provided by Simmons and formed a semicircle around a crude stone altar on which lay an open Bible and an unsheathed sword. Simmons led the men in prayer and then lit a huge cross drenched in kerosene that must have been visible for miles. The men pressed close to the fire's heat and light as Nate Forrest, grandson of the Confederate general who had founded the Klan during Reconstruction, administered the Ku Klux Klan oath. The ceremony anointed Simmons as the Grand Dragon, and the word went out that the Ku Klux Klan, outlawed for forty years, was back in the saddle. From this symbolic beginning, the modern Klan grew slowly in its first few years, then rapidly in the early 1920s throughout the South and into the North. Among the founders of the hooded order were Sam Venable, the principal owner of Stone Mountain, and Robert Ramspeck, deputy U.S. marshal for the northern district of Georgia and later my congressman. A few weeks afterward, Mrs. Plane wrote to Borglum, who had returned to New York to address his other commitments, urging him somehow to include the Klan in the design of his monument. "Why not represent a small group of them in their nightly uniform approaching in the distance?" she asked. Obligingly, Borglum included a KKK altar in his design. World War I intervened, however, to put his Stone Mountain project in abeyance for the next five years.

In 1920, when Borglum turned his attention once more to the Stone Mountain project, it was clear that a sum of several million dollars would be needed to sustain the work and that the UDC was too narrow a base for the fund-raising. Accordingly, a group of Atlanta business and civic leaders, including some Klansmen, incorporated the Stone Mountain Confederate Monument Association. The association had two main purposes: to receive ownership of the north face of the mountain from Sam Venable and other members of his family, and to raise funds from the Ku Klux Klan, from the state of Georgia, and from the sale of a memorial half-dollar at more than its face value

Borglum set to work in earnest on what he expected to be the greatest of his many sculptural projects. He created a plaster model of his proposed bas-relief that promised an impressive representation of the Confederate cause. It showed General Robert E. Lee on his horse Traveler as the central figure of a trio that also included President Jefferson Davis and General T. J. "Stonewall" Jackson. It was never explained why Davis, who had spent the war years in his presidential office in Richmond, was portrayed on horseback. A shadowy gray army of lesser figures on foot brought up the rear. Borglum and a crew of stonemasons erected an elaborate scaffolding, brought the plaster cast to the mountain to guide the work, and began blasting and chiseling on the north face. By 1924 he had completed the head of Lee and the outline of his horse and had begun to outline the figures of Jackson and Davis. Borglum joined the Ku Klux Klan in the early 1920s, perhaps initially as an effort to keep the Venables happy, but he found the Klan in tune also with his own social biases, his conspiracy theories about Jewish bankers, and his vague dreams of national political influence. For the moment at least, this mercurial man agreed with most of the Klan's purposes. During the Klan's peak years in the mid-twenties, Borglum was a member of its executive committee. He saw the Klan as a potential source of millions of dollars needed for his monument project. But the Klan, despite its symbolic use of Stone Mountain as the capital of Klandom, made only token contributions to the Confederate monument, and its close connection alienated some other potential donors. By 1925 the Klan bubble had burst.

As years passed and Borglum went unpaid even for his expenses, he became discontented with the promotional efforts for the Stone Mountain monument. The poor showing of the monument association in both fund-raising and administration created dark suspicions and charges that were never proven. The Venable family became as disenchanted as Borglum and threatened to revoke their deed to the carving site. In the end, public funds from the state and DeKalb County accounted for most of the inadequate resources for the monument carving. The U.S. Treasury minted 1.3 million Stone Mountain half-dollars to be sold for two dollars each to raise funds for the monument, but the government withheld them for years, and fewer than half of them were sold by the feckless monument association All together, the sums raised were far from sufficient to realize Borglum's grandiose vision, and too much of the money raised went into further fund-raising and office expenses.

Borglum in 1924 refused to continue work unless he was paid, and at about the same time he received a better offer from South Dakota for a grander, more national monument at Mount Rushmore. Borglum wanted to do both projects, but when the Stone Mountain association read in the newspapers about his other big project, the executive committee in secret session voted to fire him. According to his biographers, Howard and Audrey Shaff, in their fascinating book, *Six Wars at a Time* (1985), Borglum was at the Stone Mountain carving site when word came of his dismissal. He immediately ordered his work crew to break up his plaster model and drop it over the mountainside. Later he maintained that the contours of the mountain made so many adjustments necessary that the model would have been of no use to a successor. Furthermore, he claimed sole ownership of his creative product. The association did not share his viewpoint. While Borglum was at the Venable home making plans to move north until the furor died down, the boss of his stonemasons burst in to tell him the sheriff was right behind him with intent to arrest. The two men fled, with the law in hot pursuit until they crossed the state line.

The monument association reorganized and began anew with the New York sculptor Augustus Lukeman, who blasted away Borglum's work and began on his own, less ambitious design. It envisioned the same three central figures of Lee, Davis, and Jackson in higher relief, but no army. Lukeman, too, produced a head of Lee and little more. Money shortages continued until the Great Depression brought an end to the carving. Sam Venable sued to get his mountain back and forced an audit that revealed that only 27 percent of the expenditures had gone for actual construction. Stone Mountain remained a wreck for decades, a pathetic monument to the continued failure of the Lost Cause. My own view is that all such carvings-up of nature desecrate scenes of natural beauty that would better be left in their pristine state. Such expressions of human egotism are distinct only in size and degree of artistry from the warnings that THE END IS COMING painted on rocks all over America, examples of a tackiness that seems to be an element of the American character.

My brother and I, as a sixteen- and a fifteen-year-old off on a lark, knew little and cared less about this history when we made our climb on a Saturday afternoon in the early fall of 1936 or 1937. We climbed Stone Mountain "because it was there." My friend Charley and I were sophomores in Decatur Boys' High School. With the weekend before us, we thought a small adventure was called for. We had seen the mountain only from the top floor of the Hurt Building in downtown Atlanta or from the highway that passed close by on the way to Athens. It was easy to enlist my brother George, known as "Buddy." He was the daredevil of the high school who had fought every bully there and even a couple of teachers. He squinted through thick eyeglasses made necessary by an unfortunate experiment with gunpowder. My elder by a year, he was a year ahead in high school. Buddy was generally acknowledged to be a genius and a polymath, and IQ tests bore this out. I was in awe of my older brother but could not hope to emulate him. I was content simply to tag along on some of his adventures. Formal schooling at the pace of the slowest, however, was unbearably boring to Buddy, who found relief in pranks and general mischief. Climbing Stone Mountain was made to order for him.

Off we went to the northeast, crossing Decatur on foot and then hitchhiking the eight or ten miles to our destination, a matter of several rides. In the thirties, hitchhiking was more widely tolerated than now. The mountain gradually came into full view, a single, massive gray stone, with a slightly greenish cast from moss and lichens, and marked also by weathered streaks of a darker gray that looked from a distance like the thin hair on top of a bald head. We arrived at the foot in the dust of midafternoon.

Our ascent of Stone Mountain on its western slope was gradual at first, past the abandoned rock quarry, along a trail well marked by empty Coke bottles and paper bags that had held the snack food of earlier hikers. The surface of the mountain, which had looked cold when viewed at a distance, felt quite warm, having absorbed the heat of the sun. Buzzards glided above on the thermals. The going became more arduous as we climbed, and by the time we reached the broad, rounded summit, Charley and I had had enough of the strenuous life for one day. Our sense of achievement was somewhat diminished by the discovery of an entire Sunday school that had already reached the summit for their annual picnic, climaxed by a bonfire of their trash and some wood they had brought with them.

Buddy went in search of a bigger thrill, however. He clambered down from the top onto the sheer north face where the carvings were. A KEEP OFF! sign, posted just above the half-completed carving and abandoned scaffolding, was less a warning than a dare to a person of Buddy's temperament. He hurried back to us, his mood having changed from laconic to one of suppressed excitement. Buddy was at his most dangerous when he spoke quietly, as he did then. Pointing below, he invited us to climb down with him past the carvings to the bottom of the mountain. "The short cut," he called it.

I agreed to take a look. Inching by short steps and handholds down to the sign and the barbed wire fence behind it, I was suddenly torn between the urge to be at one with the landscape below and the recoil against that urge. My panic took the form of paralysis. Though my brain was awhirl, my body was pressed against the stone. I clung to it for dear life. I was afraid to move a muscle lest the move become a leap. This was my first experience of acrophobia, and as yet I had no name for what ailed me. I thought that it meant that I was capable of suicide. After what seemed an eternity, I made myself inch upward, and nothing could have made me look downward again, not even to see the tantalizing head of Lee or the reassuring sight of the scaffolding anchored by steel pilings driven into holes bored in the stone.

I crawled up until I could stand in safety. Seeing my white face, Charley wouldn't even venture as far down as I had gone. We urged Buddy to give up his mad scheme and spoke darkly of death and dismemberment. Buddy simply thrust his lower jaw out further and held fast to his decision. "I'm going," he said. After thinking for a moment, however, he did need our help in one respect. In order to get good toeholds in the rock, he would have to take off his shoes. He asked us to carry them down and meet him around the bottom of the north face.

We watched Buddy disappear over the edge and made our own descent, much easier than the ascent, of course. Then we walked around to the rendezvous in good time, debating whether Buddy would really beat us down by way of his shortcut. I had forgotten my acrophobia by

then, or at least had suppressed the memory. In later life, whether viewing the Grand Canyon or Mount Rushmore, or driving mountain roads,
I have always tried to keep a railing, a stone wall, or, best of all, some
people between me and the gaping void. Not panicky anymore, just
playing it safe! No cliff-hanging for me.

Charley and I waited perhaps half an hour for Buddy. Maybe, we
thought, he had made such good time that he was ahead of us on the
way home. It now being late afternoon, Charley and I headed home to
supper. We were lucky enough to get a single ride all the way to Decatur.
Sharing our adventure with the driver, we had a few good laughs at the
mental image of Buddy barefooted on the side of the road, trying to
hitch a ride. We hardly gave a thought to the possibility that he might
have had a mishap. Buddy had had many other close calls and usually
landed on his feet.

When I reached home, I found that my parents had invited friends
to dinner. Buddy was hardly missed until after the cocktail hour. I easily
explained his absence by saying he had taken a shortcut. That got a good
laugh. All present were acquainted with Buddy's shortcuts. Then, in the
midst of dinner, a call came from the county courthouse. The county
police were bringing Buddy under arrest from the Stone Mountain jail
to the county police headquarters! There, as a juvenile, he could be
released into my father's custody pending trial. It was not yet clear, at
least to me, what the charge was or even whether it was a criminal one.

My father and his male guest hastily made plans to arrive at the
courthouse in force, calling a lawyer friend to meet them there. My
mother stayed behind, in woman's sphere. Dealing with the law was
considered men's work. After asking me a few stern questions, my father
decided I should go along to bear witness, if witness were needed. Soon
after our arrival at a little room on the ground floor of the courthouse,
Buddy came in under guard, along with a young man who had also
been arrested at the foot of the mountain. Buddy stood barefoot with a
defiant air, his dirty-blond hair askew, a habitual, squinting frown creas-
ing his brow. He had the look of a captured wild animal.

Somewhat taken aback by Buddy's well-dressed rescue party, all of
them wearing shoes, the chief of police explained in a mild, deferential
manner that some of the scaffolding on the face of the mountain had
been destroyed by fire and that these two suspects had been arrested as
they descended the rubble at the foot of the carvings. The other alleged

perpetrator turned out to be a news photographer for one of the Atlanta newspapers. He had climbed up to the carvings to take pictures, and there had met Buddy climbing down.

The police said that they guessed that one or both of the suspects had caused the fire while lighting a cigarette. "But the boy doesn't smoke," my father said. At my first opportunity, I plucked Daddy's sleeve and whispered, "But Buddy *does* smoke sometimes!" "Hush! Keep out of this!" my father whispered back, with a certain sternness of tone. I spoke not another word, silenced not only by my father's manner but by the fact that I had never before known my father to shade or evade the truth.

While I quietly absorbed this lesson in worldliness, Daddy and his friends arranged bail for Buddy. The photographer lacked the wherewithal for bail and had to languish in jail. Though a wife and children depended on his paltry salary at the newspaper, his editor refused to go his bail on the ground that he had been photographing the mountain on his own time and not on assignment.

On Monday morning, Buddy was back at school, regaling a small crowd in the smoking corner of the athletic field with a heroic version of his exploit: his risky climb, his close acquaintance with General Lee's nostril, his incarceration in the Stone Mountain jail. The jail in this hick town, he said, resembled an animal cage. It was a single room with bars on one side, opened to the public. A Saturday crowd had gathered to gawk at Buddy pacing back and forth in his bare feet like a wild beast at the zoo. Though Buddy could now return to his everyday life awaiting trial, the photographer spent several months in jail and lost his job at the newspaper because of his inability to report for work. Those were hard times. Sometime in the late winter or early spring, news of the Sunday school bonfire on top of the mountain became public, and witnesses were even found to say that the picknickers had tossed the flaming brands over the side of the mountain. This information cast such reasonable doubt on the appropriateness of the arrests that the owners of the Confederate monument dropped the suit. They probably realized they could never convict a white Protestant Sunday school in a Georgia court.

Buddy's daring climb down the face of the mountain turned out to be not as unique as we believed at the time. As David Freeman reports in his well-researched book *Carved in Stone* (1997), the climb became a regular pastime of local unemployed young people in the Depression years, somewhat like the dance marathons of the period. The real local hero was Elias Nour, the son of a restaurateur in Stone Mountain, who between 1927 and 1963 saved thirty-six people and six dogs stranded on the mountain and received a Carnegie Hero Medal for one of his rescues. Nour also was the winner of at least two "Suicide Derbies," in which a number of climbers would race down the north face of the mountain, over the carvings to the rubble below. Buddy's only distinction among the daredevils, it would seem, was that he did not have to be rescued by Elias Nour.

Our Stone Mountain climb, however, was a harbinger of Buddy's and my diverging career paths. Buddy was kicked out of two high schools and never graduated. After gaining admission to the state university through an entrance examination, however, he scored not only the highest grade on the placement examination of the university's freshman class but one of the three highest in the country that year. He later became a pioneer electronics engineer, the inventor in the 1960s of a multiple satellite tracking device adopted by the U.S. Air Force. We remained temperamental opposites. Buddy was more experimental with life, which resulted in creativity but also in early death. He died in an auto crash at the age of fifty. As on Stone Mountain, my approach was more cautious and reflective. I took away from my afternoon on Stone Mountain a kernel of skepticism about the Lost Cause, heightened by my later discovery that my southern ancestors were Unionists. The only one involved in the Civil War was a Union Army surgeon. It was only much later that I learned of the cozy relations between the Confederate memorialists and the Ku Klux Klan, but I despised the Klan's racial terrorism from an early age. The Klan was no distant bugaboo to me. The local klavern regularly paraded, in full regalia except for the hood, around the county courthouse, casting a menacing late afternoon shadow over commuters getting off the trolley at the square. Perhaps my later participation in the civil rights movement and my lifelong study of African American history derived in some part from a mentality stirred into life by these experiences at Stone Mountain and Decatur.

Stone Mountain's monumental failure must have haunted many southerners during the decades of depression and war, particularly those around Atlanta who still dreamed the ancient dream of southern triumphalism. After World War II, in a time of greater prosperity, talk of completing the monument renewed. The state government through the State Park Authority undertook a fresh start in 1958. Lively debates broke out over the choice of architect, over high versus low relief, and over whether to complete Lukeman's work or begin a third time from scratch. It was finally decided that another sculptor, Walker K. Hancock of Massachusetts, would simply round out the Lukeman trio. The renewal of carving proceeded in tandem with development of a sort of theme park at the foot of the mountain, including a scaled-down Tara plantation of eighteen acres, a Stone Mountain Scenic Railroad that encircled the mountain, and other real and imaginary mementos of the Old South. The United Daughters of the Confederacy still had a minority voice in plans for the monument. The Ku Klux Klan, which had already indelibly tainted the history of Stone Mountain, was on the rise again in the 1950s and 1960s, but its principal business in those years was threats and attacks on the rising black freedom movement in Atlanta and elsewhere.

In the fullness of time, on May 9, 1970, Governor Lester "Ax Handle" Maddox dedicated the completed monument to the entire nation on behalf of the people of Georgia. Vice President Spiro T. Agnew gave the principal address of the occasion, somehow reconciling the Confederacy and the Union as one grand, patriotic enterprise. At the Atlanta Olympic Games in 1996, the state park at Stone Mountain was designated as an Olympic venue. The author Tony Horwitz ironically noted in *Confederates in the Attic* (1998) that the Stone Mountain museum exhibit removed all mention of the Ku Klux Klan, in a hasty cleaning up of its image before the world. As Horwitz succinctly commented, "The Invisible Empire became, well, invisible." By this time, Stone Mountain was no longer a country village but a suburb of the Atlanta megalopolis, a playground of yuppies.

In retrospect, the chief problem of carving the Stone Mountain monument was not that it was too large a feat but that the scale was too small to make a big impression. Gutzon Borglum once remarked that the chief lesson he took from Stone Mountain to Mount Rushmore was that, to achieve grandeur, he would have to double the scale. That lesson was lost on his successors down south. Today, the three Confederate leaders on horseback, seen from the distance below, appear too small for a grand effect, about the size of a postage stamp or the Stone Mountain commemorative half-dollar. The men do not match the mountain.

Goldsmith's department store, Main Street, Memphis. *Goldsmith Collection, Memphis & Shelby County Room, Memphis/Shelby County Public Library & Information Center.*

Kenneth T. Jackson

MEMPHIS, TENNESSEE

The Rise and Fall of Main Street

A half century and more ago, every American town and city had a main street. Sometimes it was known by another name— Chestnut in Philadelphia, State in Chicago, Market in San Francisco, Canal in New Orleans, Broadway in St. Louis, Hennepin in Minneapolis, or Peachtree in Atlanta, for example—but often it was called what it was: Main Street. It was the thoroughfare with the highest land values, the biggest department stores, the heaviest traffic, and the most crowded sidewalks. It was the focus of business, entertainment, and retailing; the hub of the streetcar and bus system; and the visible expression of economic success and community pride. It was even the title of Sinclair Lewis's merciless 1920 satire of life in a midwestern small town.

Main Street was a place of wonder and excitement when I was growing up in Memphis in the 1950s. It showed me at an early age what a city could be; it taught me the value of what Jane Jacobs would later describe as mixed ages, mixed uses, and eyes on the street; and it gave me a glimpse of a larger world. To be sure, my hometown was not itself a large world, and its Main Street would never have been confused with Fifth Avenue in New York. But Memphis had 396,000 people in 1950. It was Tennessee's largest city and the eighteenth largest in the United States, and it had most of the characteristics of a major metropolis. And

Main Street in Memphis was the most important road for hundreds of miles in any direction. It was surely big enough to impress me.

Founded in 1819 by Andrew Jackson, Marcus Winchester, and John Overton on a bluff overlooking the Mississippi River, Memphis is located near the point where the Spanish explorer Hernando de Soto had crossed the Mississippi centuries earlier. My own ancestor William Little Vance, for whom Vance Street was named, played an important role in the early growth of the fledgling community. By 1860, it had become a leading livestock, cotton, and slave market and was the largest city between St. Louis and New Orleans. In fact, it was something of a melting pot, and 37 percent of its population was foreign born.

The Civil War changed Memphis. On June 6, 1862, it was the site of a major naval battle, which disappointed thousands of spectators on the bluffs when it turned into a Confederate defeat. The city was in Union hands for the remainder of the war and was at one time the headquarters of General Ulysses S. Grant. Meantime, as the federal government gained control of the entire region, recently emancipated slaves poured into Memphis, so that the black population, only 3,882 in 1860, had exploded to 15,471 in 1870. After the Confederate surrender at Appomatox, racial antagonism increased, culminating in a riot in 1866, when a white mob went on a two-day orgy of rioting and killed forty-four African Americans.

Reconstruction did not change the structure of Memphis, but epidemic disease did. In 1873 and again in 1878–79, yellow fever decimated the city. Families with sufficient wealth left the area, and many thousands of them, especially Germans, decided that the risk of future pestilence was reason enough to move away permanently. So they decamped to St. Louis, never to return. Unfortunately, the Irish were too poor to flee, and so they died by the thousands. The disaster was so great that in 1879 Memphis actually surrendered its charter to the state, the only time a major city has done so in all of American history. It was not restored until 1891. Meanwhile, the loss of the Irish and German population meant that Memphis would later be deprived of the ethnic diversity that might have reduced racial tensions or given the city more cultural balance.

In the next half century, Memphis became the wholesale distribution center of the midsouth region and a center of the lumber business, a function of the city's location in the heart of the still untouched hardwood forests of the Mississippi Valley. Logs were floated down the river to Memphis in immense rafts. By 1900, there were an estimated five hundred mills within a hundred-mile radius of the Bluff City, producing over one billion feet of lumber annually. And all through these decades, black and white sharecroppers and farmers from the adjacent lowlands of Mississippi and Arkansas poured into Memphis's expanding neighborhoods. Along the way, the city became the unofficial capital of both the cotton economy and the black belt, and proportionately the home of the largest African-American population in the United States. As historian David Cohn wrote in 1935, "The Mississippi Delta begins in the lobby of the Peabody Hotel and ends on Catfish Row in Vicksburg."

Meanwhile, Memphis was ruled by E. H. "Boss" Crump, whose Democratic political machine was, along with those of Frank Hague in Jersey City and Tom Pendergast in Kansas City, one of the three strongest in the United States. A rural immigrant himself, Crump was born in 1875 on a farm near Holly Springs, Mississippi, about forty-five miles south of Memphis. Like many others at the time, he concluded at an early age that life on the land offered permanent misery and little else. So he made his way to Memphis at age seventeen, worked as a bookkeeper for carriage manufacturers and harness dealers, married a prominent local woman, and won city-wide elective office in 1907, when he was thirty-two. As mayor for two terms, he won a reputation as a progressive and a reformer, he attacked the liquor interests, and he ended Memphis's reputation as the nation's murder capital. Although he officially left office in 1924, he personally chose Memphis's mayors and congressmen and most of Tennessee's governors and senators for the next three decades. Along the way, he made Memphis clean, quiet, safe, and prosperous, at least for the white majority.

None of that rich history was apparent to me in 1950. All I knew was that the focus of the entire region was Main Street and that just getting there could be an adventure. My first public transportation experience was on the Number 2 Fairgrounds streetcar, one of sixteen routes in Memphis and the only one that ran every five minutes and operated twenty-four hours a day. A typical "trolley," it resembled a railroad car, with metal wheels underneath, open platforms front and rear, and large windows all around. With a constantly humming motor controlled by a driver in a glassed-in cubicle, it was about half the size of a modern bus. It swayed and clanged down small railroad tracks that were specially designed for its use as it connected the central business district with the Memphis version of Brooklyn's Coney Island. Mostly operating along Madison Avenue, the streetcar brightened my eyes as it passed Baptist Hospital, the Forest Hill Dairy, and Russwood Park, the minor league home of the Class AA Memphis Chicks of the Southern league.

Unfortunately, a rubber-tire mentality had seized the nation in the 1920s, as the price of a Model T fell below three hundred dollars, and as an affordable car for the multitudes became a reality. Thereafter, politicians and businessmen convinced themselves that the automobile and the bus represented the future of civilization and that the streetcar was simply an old-fashioned obstacle to progress. General Motors helped the process along by buying up trolley systems across the United States and then substituting buses for their rail cars. As federal and state governments allocated huge sums for road construction, streetcar patronage declined precipitously. After peaking at 73,000 in 1917, the number of streetcars in the United States fell to 17,911 in 1948. Memphis was part of this larger trend; it removed its last trolley from service on June 15, 1947.

I did not at the time know this larger story. But I did know that a nearby bus operated to downtown Memphis along an established route, at a set schedule, and for a single fare—seven cents. Thus, it was convenient, safe, and cheap, and from the time I was ten years old I was allowed to go to town alone. My typical journey began on High Point Terrace, two blocks from the FHA-financed, three-bedroom brick tract house to which my family moved in 1948. The total trip took about an hour, but what an hour it was. There were a dozen neighborhoods—new and old, rich and poor, black and white—and scores of businesses between Aurora Circle and Main Street, and the window of a bus revealed them all in panoramic fashion. Together, they were a microcosm of America at mid-century. Some in fact were as foreign to me as another land. Along Walnut Grove Road, for example, were elegant homes with pseudo-Gothic towers, cupolas, and mansard roofs surrounded by enormous lawns thick with trees and shrubbery behind iron or wooden fences. Then came the innovative Poplar Plaza Shopping Center (1948), Memphis's first major commercial development outside the downtown area. Then came my favorite neighborhood, Chickasaw Gardens. Laid out as a rambling English romantic garden around a small lake, this expensive subdivision was created in 1926–27 on the former estate of Clarence Saunders, the founder of the modern supermarket through his chain of Piggly-Wiggly stores.

Moving slower as the streets became busier and the neighborhoods denser along Poplar Avenue, the bus passed the public golf course and shallow lake of Overton Park, itself the creation of Kansas City landscape architect George Kessler. That the Jewish population in Memphis was large became apparent as I traveled past the great Byzantine hulk and strong twin towers of Temple Israel. Closer to downtown there were apartment buildings and then public housing projects where poor people lived, especially Dixie Homes and Lauderdale Courts. The latter development was then the residence of the yet unknown Elvis Presley.

When the bus reached the Poplar Tunes record store at Lauderdale and then the First Methodist Church at Second Street, I knew I was getting close to the promised land. At Main Street the bus turned south, past the giant Italian Renaissance barn known to adults as Ellis Auditorium and to children as the home of the Ringling Brothers Circus and the Holiday on Ice skating show, and then on by the Fortas and Rhodes-Jennings furniture stores and various county office buildings. Only the jail was remotely interesting to me, and even then I never saw a prisoner. I would exit near the north end of Main Street at Court Square, one of four public squares marked off in the original city plan of 1819 and the only one which survived into the twentieth century. Small, lively, and befouled by hundreds of annoying pigeons, the square was dominated by the biggest and most impressive bronze fountain I had ever seen, as well as by an octagonal bandstand.

What was it about Main Street that was so intoxicating to me? It was certainly not the courthouse, post office, or city hall. Neither did I give any thought to the downtown hotels—the Claridge, Chisca, Gayoso, William Len, Tennessee, and Adler, even though radio disc jockey Dewey Phillips, who was already famous with every teenager in Memphis, broadcast daily from WHBQ at the Gayosa. I never even took an interest in the South's grand hotel, the Peabody, where the famous ducks had been daily parading back and forth on a red carpet between the elevator and the travertine fountain in the Spanish-Moorish lobby since 1932. And of course I gave a wide berth to the many medical, dental, and law firms that occupied the big office structures, like the Columbian Mutual Tower and the Commerce Title Building. But there was something about the lights and the possibilities of Main Street that mesmerized me. And I was not alone. For example, in 1956 Robert Johnson of the *Memphis Press-Scimitar* wrote in the first official fan biography of Elvis Presley: "He saw the street late, with the signs glowing, and to this day it holds a spell over him. . . . Sometimes with friends, sometimes alone, Elvis would head to Main Street, where the windows, the bustle of moving traffic, the hurrying crowd gave him something to watch and to wonder about."

I felt the same wonder. When I hopped off the bus, I would usually visit one of the four grand department stores which defined Main Street. Brys was the cheapest of the emporiums, and I still recall that when my mother indicated that an item looked like it came from the Brys basement she was not being flattering. The John Gerber Company was the most elegant and expensive of the Big Four, but because it sold only clothes, I regarded it as a waste of time. B. Lowenstein and Brothers was one of the great commercial structures of nineteenth-century Memphis, and it carried its grandeur well from its prominent location. I not only frequented its lunchroom but even worked an entire summer in its basement shoe department. Finally, Goldsmith's was the largest retailing operation in the region, and more than anyplace else it anchored and defined the entire downtown business district.

Realistically, however, the grand department stores, like the boutique dress and shoe shops and most of the other businesses on Main Street, were all female territory. From my perspective the stores and restaurants all seemed to cater to women. This feminization of downtown actually began in the second half of the nineteenth century, and by the time I noticed the pattern in Memphis, the dominance of women in the culture of retailing was an established fact. To them, an excursion to Main Street meant dressing up, often replete with hats, gloves, heels, and stockings, and it followed well-established rituals. Whether window-shopping, strolling through store aisles, chatting with friends, assessing the look and price of various items, making purchases, or lunching at the fashionable Gerber's Tea Room, women made department stores the signature institutions of the metropolis. As Gunther Barth has noted: "With its far-ranging utility, the department store reflected the culture of the modern city. It constantly assessed people's hopes for a better life and responded to their dreams. As a creative social force, the department store sustained the shared experience of shopping, produced a new form of communal life, and provided links among heterogeneous people."*

But not for me. I was not a girl, and my downtown interests tended to focus on four pursuits unrelated to department stores: (1) toy soldiers, (2) reference books, (3) sex (which unfortunately was limited to explicit photographs), and (4) popular entertainment. My love of miniature armies derived partly from a lifelong interest in military history and partly from the fact that both my father and godfather were lieutenant colonels in the field artillery during World War II. Initially, I played with bottle caps and would stop at bars and restaurants to collect their discards. I then translated brand names into nationalities, defining Coca-Cola caps as the Americans, Budweiser beer as the Wehrmacht, Stag beer as the Red Army, and on through the French, Belgians, Italians, and Dutch. As I grew older, I shifted to more realistic troops. But, unable to afford the hand-painted lead figures that later became expensive collectibles, I still went for quantity over quality and used my allowance and meager earnings as a paperboy to buy mass-produced plastic figures for ten cents apiece, or less. Ultimately, I owned hundreds of such soldiers, along with a variety of plastic and metal tanks, airplanes, ships, and guns. My closest friends also had their own armies, and we would occasionally array our forces at some outdoor location, imagine that we were all powerful generals, and proceed to have a mock war. When you knocked over a tank or a soldier that piece would be of no more use. On other occasions I would play alone in my room and take command of both sides. In any case, the only places in Memphis to buy military reinforcements were in the basement toy departments of the four Main Street dime stores—Silver's, Woolworth's, Kress, and Grant's. I usually made a beeline for those stores, all the while wondering why their entire selling floors were not given over to toys, the only items there in which I had the slightest interest.

Reading was another passion which could best be indulged downtown. Memphis had several colleges and a number of branch public libraries, but in the 1950s no other book depository in the city was as well stocked and as grand as the Cossitt Library. Located on the bluff overlooking the spot where Union gunboats had outdueled the Confed-

* *City People: The Rise of Modern City Culture in Nineteenth-Century America* (New York: Oxford University Press, 1980), 145.

erate navy in 1862, the library was actually a red sandstone mansion that had been given to the city in 1893 by the daughters of a man who had lived briefly in Memphis before moving on to New York to amass a great fortune. The very grandeur of that Romanesque structure suggested to me, and presumably to passersby, that learning and knowledge were as important to society as the visual work of classing cotton, which was the central business of Memphis and which took place in less impressive buildings along Front Street's adjacent Cotton Row. Magnificent in its riches, the Cossitt Library offered an apparently endless array of books, atlases, and photographs. My favorite was an account of the 1862 Battle of Fredericksburg, where well-entrenched Confederate forces decimated the attacking Union Army under General Ambrose Burnside. If only Gettysburg had turned out so well for the South.

Information on the Civil War was abundant compared to information about sex, an adolescent concern that seemed to become more important with each passing year. Unfortunately, Memphis was a poor place to learn about females, and especially female body parts, if only because it had the strictest censorship in the United States in the 1950s. Allegedly, the public library did not buy anything about Peter Rabbit because such books had pictures of black and white rabbits playing together. Compared to Memphis, Boston was wide open. Loyd T. Binford, the official arbiter of morality in my hometown, routinely banned movies about Charlie Chaplin, train robberies, or sex. For example, two of Jane Russell's most famous movies, *The Outlaw* and *The French Line*, were banned in Memphis because Binford thought too much of her ample bosom was on display. In my view, nothing worth seeing could be seen because of Binford.

Fortunately, downtown Memphis offered respite for the sexually curious. Just off Main Street on Linden Avenue was the Fun Shop, a little place that specialized in games, gadgets, and "wolf cards." This last item consisted of fifty-two playing cards that were ordinary on one side and featured topless women on the other. It was thin gruel, but we took what we could get.

One day in 1954, a close friend and I skipped school at East High and took the bus to town for a day of adventure. Before noon we made our way to the Fun Shop and bought a deck of wolf cards. We then repaired to the snooty and pretentious Britlings Cafeteria to have lunch. The cafeteria offered wonderful food at reasonable prices—haddock for thirty-five cents was a treat I will never forget—and so the two of us went through the cafeteria line. After we received our bill, a waitress carried our respective trays to a table on the second-floor balcony, over-looking the large main dining area. Before eating anything, however, my friend, Benjamin Houston Graham, who died of stomach cancer in 1994, unwrapped his cards for a quick review. Then disaster. Ben accidentally fumbled the deck, which then spilled over his lap, through the openings in the railing, and over the edge. To our horror, shameful pictures were fluttering down onto the hats, plates, and tables of dozens of imposing women on the main level. My instinct was to flee. Unfortunately, you paid your bill at Britlings as you were leaving, so flight would have meant running out without payment. With escape impossible, we sheep-ishly and hurriedly ran down the stairs, walked among the shocked patrons, and retrieved our wolf cards.

Undeterred, we did not give up our search for more explicit photo-graphs. Soon enough, we discovered that an otherwise nondescript mag-azine store on Main Street, just south of Court Square, actually sold nudist magazines. This was important, because in 1954 ordinary adult publications, including *Playboy*, either airbrushed their models or dis-creetly draped them so that only their breasts were exposed. But not the "naturalist" publications in this dive. Unfortunately, the tiny store was presided over by an obese white woman who was also mean. She sat imperiously behind an elevated cash register facing the door, and she refused to sell us the material we sought. Our strategy was to enter the establishment while "Brunhilda" was busy with other customers. With luck, we might have ninety seconds to turn page after page before she discovered our duplicity and ordered us off the premises. It was embar-rassing, but we felt we had no choice.

As the years passed, such photographs lost allure as I discovered that real women had important advantages over pictures of women. I bought my first car, a 1948 Studebaker, for ninety dollars when I was sixteen. A year later, I moved up to a 1951 Pontiac convertible for $475. Along the way, I abandoned the buses that had earlier given me a measure of freedom. But downtown remained an attraction and a draw because of such spectacles as the Cotton Carnival and Christmas parades, the many fireworks events over the river, and the opportunity on weekend eve-nings to "drag Main Street," which essentially meant to ride up and down the city's grandest street along with hundreds of other teenagers to see and be seen.

Main Street was also the location of choice for a "hot date," if only because the city's four grand movie theaters were all downtown. The Loews State was particularly impressive, with its broad marble staircase, ornate lobby, twinkling chandeliers, huge mezzanine, and cavernous auditorium, replete with elaborate carvings and loges elevated along the side walls. The Malco (now known as the Orpheum) was also grandiose and had an organ which could rise from the floor below. The Loews Palace and Warner Brothers movie houses had velvet curtains and carved woodwork of the type that would never have been installed in the 1980s or 1990s. And by my teenage years, young men as well as young women were dressing for the occasion. There was no such thing as taking a date downtown without being in a coat and tie.

In the late 1950s, I also became more aware of Beale Street, which ran into Main Street at right angles near the southern edge of the central business district. It was another world. Earlier in the century, W. C. Handy, father of the blues, had made his headquarters at Pee Wee's Saloon at 317 Beale, and thereafter it became the most famous street in black America. The Palace Theater, like the Apollo in Harlem, became a major venue for aspiring African-American performers, and the neighborhood itself attracted such great musicians and vocalists as Ike Turner, A. D. "Gatemouth" Brown, Muddy Waters, Al Green, Isaac Hayes, Otis Redding, Aretha Franklin, and B. B. King—whose name today graces a restaurant on Beale. One-man band Joe Hill Louis was often playing in Handy Park. By the mid-1950s white youngsters occasionally ventured into that mysterious place, sometimes to get a barbecue at Johnny Mills's at Fourth and Beale, sometimes to browse at Lansky Brothers, where Elvis bought his clothes, and sometimes just to listen to the music coming from the various beer joints. "Boss" Crump, it was said, allowed anything to happen on Beale Street as long as it did not threaten the safety of whites. I particularly remember a performance by Little Richard on a steamy summer evening at the Daisy. And of course, not far from Beale Steet was Sam Phillips and his Sun Record Company, from whose modest recording studio were launched the careers of, among others, Johnny Cash, Roy Orbison, Jerry Lee Lewis, and Charlie Rich, as well as Elvis himself.

Forty years have passed since I moved away from Memphis in 1961. Beale Street, which essentially was torn down and left for dead in the late 1960s, has since been reborn and is now an important tourist attraction, especially on weekends when a half dozen blues palaces light it up for several blocks. And the Peabody is once again touted as the South's finest hotel. But most of downtown Memphis has become a dispiriting collection of burned-out buildings, grimy warehouses, and vacant lots. Main Street is quiet. And nearby office structures, including even the twenty-nine-story Sterrick Building, long the tallest tower in Tennessee, are totally empty. The Union Planters Bank has moved its headquarters to Germantown, fifteen miles from Main Street. Tony's Fruit Stand, King's Furs, the Black and White Store, Brodnax Jewelry, Walkover Shoes, Mosely-Robinson Drug Store, Haverty's Furniture, York Arms Sporting Goods, Oak Hall Men's Store, Rhodes-Jennings Furniture, Three Sisters, Britlings Cafeteria, and the Pantaze Drug Store have disappeared, as have all five movie theaters, all four department stores, and all four dime stores. The quietest time now on Main Street is on a weekend afternoon, when once it was busiest. There are almost no pedestrians, no cars, no buses, no life. Boarded-up storefronts outnumber the forlorn discount outlets. New streetcars glide by every ten minutes or so, but the only passengers are lonely tourists wondering what happened to the city. If you want to know what is happening in Memphis in the twenty-first century, you need to travel to spacious areas like White Station, Cordova, Germantown, Lakeland, and Collierville, where prosperous white families live. Even sin seems to have moved elsewhere.

What happened? Conventional wisdom holds that Main Street and its businesses were victims of the black violence that accompanied the 1968 assassination of the Reverend Martin Luther King at the Lorraine Motel in Memphis. Certainly there was rioting and a growing racial divide. And just as certainly, white customers stopped going downtown to shop in the 1970s.

In actuality, the decline of Main Street began before World War II, and racism was less important in the transformation than the automobile. Quite simply, the extraordinary prosperity and vitality of America's urban cores between 1890 and 1950 were dependent upon rail transit systems. Their tracks radiated out from the city centers like spokes on a wheel, tying residents from all over the region to Main Street. After all, the routes almost invariably led downtown, with only an occasional crosstown or lateral line, and the practical effect was to force almost anyone using public transit to go to the central business district.

The rise of the downtown department store was the natural result of this pattern. Alexander T. Stewart in New York and John Wanamaker in Philadelphia, the two pioneers of nineteenth-century retailing, were the first to see this, but other merchandising kings, like Gimbel, Rich, Marcus, Hudson, Goldsmith, Woodward, and Lothrop, soon followed. None could have succeeded without an efficient public transit system. The streetcars delivered the hordes of shoppers to the huge selling spaces, and the streetcars took them home again. In Memphis, John Gerber, B. Lowenstein, and Jack Goldsmith were following economic logic when they located their department stores on Main Street. Because it had the densest concentration of streetcar traffic, it offered the highest pedestrian accessibility. That led to high land values. The example of Chicago is apposite. In 1910, the one-half square mile of the Loop in downtown Chicago represented almost 40 percent of the total assessed land value of the entire two-hundred-square-mile city. The accessibility of State Street, made possible by good mass transit, accounted for the rise in value.

The automobile changed all this. Unlike public transportation, the private motorcar did not require its passengers to go to Main Street. Indeed, it actually discouraged motorists from going downtown where they might be stuck in traffic or have to pay for parking. So Americans began creating a drive-in culture of work, residence, and shopping that almost required wide roads, big yards, and acres of free parking, the very things that older cities could not provide. The outward exodus was mightily aided by Washington policies that made the suburbs desirable and affordable, such as income tax writeoffs for mortgage interest and property taxes, FHA and VA subsidies to home ownership, public housing programs that concentrated minorities and poor people in the urban cores, and a national tradition of weak land-use controls. The vast interstate highway program that began in 1956 provided the final push. These multilane ribbons of concrete encouraged factories, offices, and stores to relocate to the urban edges. As automobile ownership in the United States soared by 200 percent between 1950 and 1980, millions of families moved farther and farther out on the exurban fringe. And in the space of a few decades central business districts across the land became marginal to daily life.

The retailing embodiment of the shift was the shopping center. The first of the modern genus was Baltimore's Roland Park in 1896, but other early prototypes included Country Club Plaza in Kansas City (1923), Upper Darby Center in West Philadelphia (1927), Suburban Square in Ardmore, Pennsylvania (1928), River Oaks in Houston (1937), and Hampton Village in St. Louis (1941). Meanwhile, the enclosed, climate-controlled indoor mall was introduced by Victor Gruen, an Austrian refugee from the Nazis, at the Southdale Shopping Center near Minneapolis in 1956. It included two department stores, 139 shops, parking for 5,200 cars, and a two-story, skylit pedestrian walkway. Ironically, Gruen hoped that his innovation would stop suburban sprawl. Because Minneapolis was so often cold, he advertised that "In Southdale Center every day is a perfect shopping day." The concept proved wildly popular, and indoor malls proliferated. By 1980, anything that was not enclosed was considered second rate.

A few of the indoor behemoths, such as Midtown Plaza in Rochester and Chapel Square Mall in New Haven (both unsuccessful as of 2000), were located downtown, but the best place to be was at the intersection of controlled-access highways. As Memphis's central core deteriorated, developers put up the Raleigh Springs Mall, Wolfchase Galleria, Hickory Ridge Mall, Oak Court Mall, and Southhaven Mall, all of which attracted shoppers from trading areas of a hundred square miles or more. New shopping patterns changed the entire city. As David Guterson wrote in *Harper's*, "In our collective discourse, the shopping mall appears with the tract house, the freeway, and the backyard barbecue as a product of the American postwar years, a testament to contemporary necessities and desires and an invention not only peculiarly American but peculiarly of our own era too."

Memphis has hardly been unique. Thus far, the most famous victim of America's drive-in culture has been downtown Detroit, and especially the stately J. L. Hudson Company. For generations, all roads in the Motor City led to Hudson's. Featuring tall chandeliers, wood-paneled corridors, and brass-buttoned doormen, the twenty-five-story, full-square-block emporium at its height ranked with Macy's in New York as the world's largest store. After 1950, however, the once-grand structure was choked by its own branches, all of them in outlying shopping centers. As soon as Hudson's opened Northland, its sales downtown began to fall from a peak of $153 million in 1953 to $45 million in 1981, when the landmark department store closed its doors for good. The same sad pattern repeated itself in other cities as their great downtown department stores left the Main Streets and moved to malls: Rike's in Dayton, Rich's in Atlanta, Woodward and Lothrop in Washington, G. Fox in Hartford.

The pattern is evident in small towns as well as in large. Across the United States, whether on the open plains of Nebraska or the winding rivers of West Virginia, small towns have seen their downtown shopping districts wither and die. Old businesses and buildings are boarded up and abandoned; other structures, poorly maintained, have only marginal firms as tenants. Meanwhile, several miles away, often adjacent to an interstate highway, a Wal-Mart, a Kmart, or some other big-box retailer rests in the midst of a large parking lot. Such is the physical shape of America's modern consumer culture.

So what? Why does it matter whether one buys a suit on Main Street or at the local mall? Indeed, many Americans argue that the modern shopping mall—clean, safe, convenient, and cheerful—is superior to any downtown alternative and is in fact the reincarnation of the Main Street culture within a suburban setting. The mall is now the place where senior citizens walk in comfort and security, where singles of both sexes court each other, where teenagers socialize, and where everybody consumes. Indeed, a new term, "mall rats," has been coined to describe the legions of young people who spend their free time cruising indoor corridors. This expansion of uses and customers has reinforced the notion that regional malls are the new downtowns, the centers of informal social interaction, the successors to the traditional marketplace.

In my view, shopping malls are poor substitutes for the Main Street of my youth. The traditional central business district was an unpredictable and unexpected amalgam of old and new buildings, parks, strange characters, public spectacles, high- and low-end shopping, and locally owned stores which worked together to create a whole that was far greater than the sum of its parts. It was open to all people at all hours. It gave each city a unique character and sense of place. In contrast, a mall looks like it came out of a box. There is not ten cents worth of difference between a mall in Spokane and a mall in Tallahassee. As Russell Baker wrote many years ago, "Either America is a shopping center or the one shopping center in existence is moving around the country at the speed of light."

More to the point of this essay, the mall is private property, owned and operated by a single corporation, and thus subject to coercive, centralized authority. The theme of mall design is enclosure, protection, and control. Litter, panhandlers, vagrants, suspicious characters, protesters, and cold winds are not tolerated. Such fake and artificial environments are sterile and boring and rarely offer the serendipitous experiences of the old central cities.

To be sure, the past in Memphis was likely not as stimulating and pleasant as I remember it. For half the population, the city was a racist hell, and downtown was the nerve center of oppressive policies. Blacks knew only separate and inferior schools, as well as segregated hospitals, parks, swimming pools, theaters, restaurants, and cemeteries. Watercoolers and restrooms were conspicuously marked either WHITE or COLORED. Blacks rode only at the back of the bus, and they were typically denied even the possibility of economic opportunity. Indeed, several Memphis State College professors lost their jobs in 1956 after they publicly protested the fact that Negroes could not use the main public library. Obviously the city of African-American memory would be very different from the Main Street that I remember so fondly.

But the central business district was the one place in Memphis where the races came together without conflict and in an atmosphere of at least superficial equality. In 1955, where else but downtown could blacks and whites intermingle on the sidewalks, browse together in department store aisles, or stand in the same line at shopping counters? In fact, Main Street by the 1960s had come to be so associated in the white mind with black patrons that middle-class consumers began to avoid downtown altogether.

In recent years, many once sleepy downtown areas around the United States have begun to wake up, attracting single people, young couples, and empty nesters no longer worried about deteriorated schools. Together, they are turning old Main Streets into thriving entertainment and business centers. And at Disney World's new planned community of Celebration, the business district, quaint and old-fashioned, went in before the houses.

In most places, however, Americans have come to realize almost too late that without a central business district, a city has no soul. For that reason, the loss of Main Street—whether in Cotton Plant, Arkansas; Newburgh, New York; Detroit, Michigan; or Memphis, Tennessee—is a national tragedy. I have lost a memory, but Americans in the twenty-first century will have lost much more.

The Illinois State Capitol as it appeared in 1858. *Illinois State Historical Library.*

Robert W. Johannsen

ILLINOIS'S OLD STATE CAPITOL

A Tale of Two Speeches

I n the heart of downtown Springfield, Illinois, flanked by modern office buildings, stands the Old State Capitol. I cannot now recall my sensations when I first noted the incongruity of the scene—the small, stately building amid all the noise and movement of a modern city—but in subsequent years, whenever I mounted the steps into the cool, quiet interior, insulated from the bustle, it was like stepping back in time.

Constructed in the 1830s and 1840s of a warm yellowish-brown dolomite limestone cut from a nearby quarry, the building became known beyond the state's borders as a distinctive example of early nineteenth-century Greek Revival architecture. The Greek style was popular in the United States at the time, especially in the construction of public buildings such as museums and state houses, but, as Talbot Hamlin observed more than half a century ago, in Illinois it "dominated the architectural scene."

The northern and southern entrances of the capitol, which is located in Springfield's public square, were balanced by pedimented Greek porticos, each supported by imposing Doric columns. The sturdy simplicity of the style, accented by pilasters on all sides of a heavy stone exterior, suggested the authority and permanence of the state government while reflecting the freedom and democracy of classical Greece. Surmounting the Greek colonnaded building and supported by ornate Corinthian columns was a Roman-style dome—a unique combination.

More was intended by the building's planners, however, than a tribute to the origins of democratic government in classical Greece and republican Rome, if indeed that was even a conscious decision. The state's capitol would also embody the romantic aspirations of a society in transition. It was an age of movement, of population growth and the building of new towns, of innovation and invention, of reverence for the past and faith in the future, no less in Illinois than in other parts of the country. Uniting both utilitarian and aesthetic functions, the capitol, so said its planners, would reflect the spirit of the age by revealing "our steady progress to the high destiny every where predicted for us." It would be "permanent, strong, convenient, imposing in appearance, and ample in dimension; a building which should stand as an evidence to posterity that the State, even in its infancy, cultivated a fine taste, and practiced a wise economy."

Politics was in a state of flux when the legislature voted on the last day of February 1837 to make Springfield, then a town of fewer than two thousand inhabitants, the permanent capital. The departure of Old Hickory, Andrew Jackson, from the national political scene after two tumultuous terms as president and the succession of the Little Magician, New York's Martin Van Buren, to the office unleashed new and unfamiliar political forces. As the state's population increased with the settlement of the central and northern counties, the older political leadership was challenged by the newcomers. In a move spearheaded by the young, dynamic, Vermont-born Stephen A. Douglas, fresh from a sojourn in upstate New York, the personal politics of the past gave way to a new politics based on issues and principles. Douglas brought with him notions of party organization that transformed the loose, amorphous Democratic party of Jackson into a disciplined organization, in turn propelling the youthful twenty-four-year-old into a position of party leadership he would never lose.

The anti-Jackson men were not immune to the Democrats' success. Following the lead of the popular Kentuckian Henry Clay, they called themselves Whigs (after the British antimonarchical party) while decrying the organizational techniques of the Democrats as robbing the voters of their individuality. Victory at the polls, however, depended upon organization and discipline, as the ambitious two-term legislator Abraham Lincoln quickly recognized. With the presidential election of 1840 looming on the political horizon, the Whigs in Illinois, persuaded by Lincoln, gradually followed the Democratic example.

Construction of the new state capitol began in the spring of 1837 in an atmosphere of urgency, for the relocation of the capital to Springfield had become a controversial political issue. Undaunted by an earlier statewide referendum in which Springfield had come in third, the Sangamon County delegation in the legislature, led by Lincoln and known as the Long Nine because their height averaged six feet, had cleverly linked the capital relocation issue to a mammoth internal improvements bill. The measure provided for a vast system of state-financed railroad and canal construction that would facilitate population movement and hasten the state's burgeoning economic development, though it later carried the state to the brink of bankruptcy. With some skillful log-rolling (one Springfield citizen called it "judicious management") the Long Nine promised to back all of the bill's projects (including an appropriation for those counties unfortunately bypassed by the proposed schemes) in return for support for Springfield's claim to be the state's permanent capital. The plan worked, and Springfield won. For Lincoln, the result was a personal triumph.

Douglas, like Lincoln, was a member of the legislature that approved the relocation of the capital, although as a resident of the older and larger town of Jacksonville, he had strongly opposed the Springfield site. Both men, however, recognized the political and economic benefits of living in the state capital. Within weeks of the legislature's action, Lincoln had moved from his home in New Salem to Springfield, where he joined the law office of John Todd Stuart. At about the same time, Douglas arrived from Jacksonville with a commission in his pocket, signed by President Van Buren, to assume the post of register of the Springfield Land Office. Both men were residents of Springfield by April 1837.

By the terms of the capital relocation bill, Springfield provided the site for the new capitol building and pledged fifty thousand dollars toward the costs of construction. Three commissioners were appointed to superintend the erection of the building, headed by Dr. Anson G. Henry, who soon would become Lincoln's personal physician. The town's public square, on which a county courthouse had been built, was hastily deeded to the state, and the courthouse was demolished. On April 8, the Whig-leaning *Sangamo Journal*, Springfield's principal newspaper, carried an advertisement "To Architects," announcing that a premium of three hundred dollars would be paid for the "best plans and estimates of a Building for a State House." Newspapers in Missouri, Kentucky, Ohio, and Pennsylvania were asked to copy the advertisement.

In spite of the wide net cast for an architect, the prize was won by a Springfield resident. John Francis Rague, the town baker, had lived in New York City, where he had studied in the office of Minard Lefever, one of the country's foremost champions of Greek Revival architecture. Finding little demand for an architect in Springfield following his arrival in 1831, Rague operated the town's bakery, while at the same time taking part in a number of civic enterprises. With the acceptance of his design for the state capitol, he was appointed the supervising architect of the project, with a salary of a thousand dollars per year.

The beginning of construction was celebrated on July 4, 1837, when with "unusual éclat" the building's cornerstone was laid. The town's military companies were out early, performing their maneuvers and firing their salutes, and at midday a sumptuous dinner was served the citizenry "in the Grove." Led by members of the Mechanics' Institute, of which Rague was president, a procession marched to the public square for the dedication ceremony. A short but "animated" address was delivered by Whig leader and member of the state legislature (and close friend of Lincoln) Edward Dickinson Baker, standing atop the cornerstone. In the language of the local newspaper, Baker "glanced at the history of our State and Nation; anticipated the brilliant destiny of Illinois under the controlling influence of virtue and intelligence; and sought to impress on the People that under this influence, they might expect all they could desire for our country in the years yet to come."

For all the enthusiasm, however, the following months were bleak, as the Panic of 1837 tightened its grip on the state. Construction proceeded slowly as money became scarce, amid charges that the building commissioners were squandering their funds and that the building's costs were exceeding the original estimates. Springfield was only able to meet its last installment of the promised fifty thousand dollars when 101 of its citizens, including Lincoln, pledged their own personal resources. It was not until late in 1839 that some of the state offices moved into the building and not until December 1840 that the state legislature began holding its sessions in the new Hall of Representatives.

Lincoln, more than any other single individual, was responsible for the removal of the capital to Springfield and, as an influential member of the state legislature, he continued to promote and defend the construction of the capitol building. Indeed, he felt such a strong stake in its completion that one recent writer has dubbed the building "The House That Lincoln Built." It is not that he recognized the capitol as an architectural gem; there is no record that he ever discussed architecture in general or Greek Revival architecture in particular, or that he was even familiar with the term. Rather, the statehouse became an important site for both his legal and political careers.

Within easy walking distance of his home and his various law offices, the state capitol became "practically a second home." There is scarcely a spot in the building that does not conjure up the figure and spirit of Abraham Lincoln. Aside from sitting in the first legislative session to occupy the Hall of Representatives, Lincoln monitored election returns in the secretary of state's office, researched his speeches in the state library, studied in the law library, argued more than two hundred cases before the state's highest court in the supreme court chamber, and used the governor's office to receive well-wishers following his election as president.

As Lincoln's career as a party leader developed, the statehouse became his forum. He had delivered one of the first speeches in the capitol, a defense of the Second United States Bank, even before the building was completed. His eulogy of Henry Clay—in which, describing Clay's politics, he said so much about his own—was given from its platform; and it was in the Hall of Representatives that he launched his first major attack on the expansion of slavery.

A common denominator in Lincoln's platform appearances was Stephen A. Douglas, the Little Giant, four years Lincoln's junior and exactly twelve inches shorter. Ever since they had sat together in the legislature that selected Springfield as the state's permanent capital, they had been sparring with one another in what would become one of the great political rivalries in American history. Douglas likewise was no stranger to the corridors of the statehouse. When Lincoln had business with the secretary of state, he dealt with Douglas, who was the first to occupy that office in the new capitol. When Lincoln argued his cases before the supreme court, it was Douglas who sat on the bench, the youngest supreme court justice before or since. When Lincoln first spoke from the platform in the as yet unfinished Hall of Representatives, he was answering a speech Douglas had made from the same platform the night before. Where Lincoln's spirit is felt so also is that of Douglas. The Old State Capitol truly belongs to both.

The two men represented divergent tracks in the political culture of nineteenth-century America: Lincoln, the Henry Clay Whig, espousing the latitudinarian (as it was called) concept of national centralization and authority, wary of human nature, and distrustful of mass democracy; Douglas, the Andrew Jackson Democrat, standing for a strict construction of the Constitution, local self-government, and states' rights, with an almost transcendent faith in the popular will. Theirs was not exactly a friendly rivalry, but then it was not an angry one either. Each had good things to say about the other, even if their tributes were frequently barbed. "Mr. Lincoln," Douglas remarked, "is a kind-hearted, amiable, good-natured gentleman, . . . a fine lawyer, possesses high ability, and there is no objection to him, except the monstrous revolutionary doctrines . . . which he conscientiously entertains." Lincoln spoke of Douglas's "great hardihood, pertinacity, and magnetic power" but added that of all the men he had known, Douglas had the "most audacity in maintaining an untenable position." Although Lincoln was wrong when, in a burst of humility, he moaned that his career had been a "flat failure" when compared to Douglas's "splendid success," he did concede that he found it impossible to speak of politics "without associating Judge Douglas with it."

The Lincoln-Douglas rivalry assumed a new level of importance on June 16, 1858, when the state capitol's Hall of Representatives became the scene of one of Lincoln's most eloquent efforts, his House Divided Speech. Alongside the Emancipation Proclamation, the Gettysburg Address, and the Second Inaugural Address, the speech occupies an exalted position in the Lincoln canon, widely regarded as one of the great statements in the history of American oratory.

Earlier on that day, a convention of wildly enthusiastic Republicans nominated Lincoln as their candidate to capture Douglas's seat in the U.S. Senate, an unusual course considering that U.S. senators were elected by state legislatures, not the people. That evening, Lincoln accepted the nomination and opened his campaign against Douglas before a cheering throng of Republican faithful. It had been a hot day, and the atmosphere in the Hall of Representatives was stifling, yet hardly daunting to those who crowded the chamber and gallery "almost to suffocation."

For weeks Lincoln had labored over the themes of the speech in the state library, and as the day drew near he wrote it all out word for word so that it could more easily and quickly be put into print. It was to be, he told his friends, the most important speech of his career, and he hoped it would have an impact beyond the borders of Illinois. Lincoln's purpose was political—to demonstrate that a widening moral gulf existed between the Republicans and Douglas that would prevent his party from ever supporting the Little Giant, as some eastern Republicans were urging. He grounded his stand against the extension of slavery more firmly than he had done before on a foundation of moral principle. By identifying Douglas with the southern slave power and by portraying him as a conspirator bent on expanding slavery throughout the United States, Lincoln was able to frame his campaign for Douglas's Senate seat as part of a larger struggle between right and wrong. He exhorted Illinois Republicans to remain united in opposition to Douglas. He "is not now with us," nor does he "promise to ever be."

It was not Lincoln's barrage of charges against Douglas or his forceful appeal for moral responsibility, though, that gave the speech its significance in the sectional conflict. Rather, it was the first several lines with which he opened the speech that eventually caught the nation's attention. The agitation over slavery, he began, had increased rather than abated, despite Douglas's assurances. The agitation, Lincoln predicted, would continue to grow "until a crisis shall have been reached and passed." To emphasize the inevitability of the conflict, he made use of a well-known biblical metaphor:

"A house divided against itself cannot stand." I believe this government cannot endure permanently half slave and half free. I do not expect the Union to be dissolved—I do not expect the house to fall— but I do expect it will cease to be divided. It will become all one thing, or all the other. Either the opponents of slavery will arrest the further spread of it, and place it where the public mind shall rest in the belief that it is in the course of ultimate extinction; or its advocates will push it forward, till it shall become alike lawful in all the States, old as well as new—North as well as South.

With these opening lines, Lincoln not only proclaimed his belief in the "ultimate" abolition of slavery, but he also expressed his belief in an inevitable conflict between freedom and slavery, North and South, that would eventually result in slavery's abolition. Some of his Republican friends were disconcerted. The statement, they feared, was too radical for the Illinois party, "too far in advance of the times," and would result in Lincoln's defeat.

The editor of the Republican *Chicago Tribune* feared that Lincoln's speech would be construed as "an implied pledge on behalf of the Republican party to make war upon the institution [of slavery] in the States where it now exists." Modern scholars have agreed that the speech played an important part in heating up the sectional conflict between North and South. It was, according to Lincoln's most recent biographer, "the most extreme statement made by any responsible leader of the Republican party."

Although Lincoln was not persuaded by the fears of his Republican friends, he was mindful of their concerns. During the campaign that followed—the campaign that featured the celebrated Lincoln-Douglas debates—he devoted much of his time to explaining what he meant in those opening lines, in response to Douglas's relentless questioning. Douglas was alarmed at Lincoln's predictions, which he feared would be interpreted as a call for a sectional war. By the end of the contest, Lincoln became aware of the construction some might put on his words. "To the best of my judgment," he explained in his last campaign speech, "I have labored *for*, and not *against* the Union."

In spite of his disclaimer, many people, especially in the South, soon thought otherwise. Southerners had paid little attention to Lincoln's statements in 1858, so long as they were uttered by what they regarded as an obscure frontier lawyer who was little more than a wisecracking "cross road-politician." But while those words may not have won Lincoln a seat in the U.S. Senate, they did win him recognition and prestige among the leaders of the Republican party beyond the borders of his state. And when the "obscure" lawyer of 1858 was nominated for the presidency two years later, his statements suddenly assumed new and ominous meanings to those who read them for the first time.

Newspaper editors from Richmond to New Orleans concluded that Lincoln's nomination was a deliberate act of hostility by the Republicans against the South. Clergymen, politicians, and pundits issued the same grim warning: the ultimate extinction of slavery would mean the ultimate extinction of the South. Lincoln was seen as a "thorough radical Abolitionist, without exemption or qualification," who really meant that "slavery must be abolished in the slave states, or the government and the Union must be overthrown." The rail-splitter would become the Union-splitter.

To Douglas, the growing chorus of charges hurled by the South against Lincoln put the Union in jeopardy, even though many of them echoed his own attacks on the doctrines of the House Divided Speech. As the presidential candidate of the northern Democracy, he urged Lincoln to take the southern threats seriously, while at the same time he carried his campaign for the Union into the heart of the slaveholding states, in a futile effort to dissuade southerners from disunion. Convinced that he knew Lincoln better than they did, Douglas assured them that they had nothing to fear from Lincoln, should he be elected. Lincoln would be "utterly powerless for evil" even if he should be disposed "to do wrong," an object of pity rather than of foreboding.

Douglas's worst fears for the Union were realized following Lincoln's election as president, when South Carolina voted to secede from the Union. Among the causes cited to justify the state's action was the House Divided Speech. A sectional party had elected a man "to the high office of President of the United States whose opinions and purposes are hostile to slavery," who had declared that the " 'Government cannot endure permanently half slave and half free,' and that the public mind must rest in the belief that Slavery is in the course of ultimate extinction." What Lincoln had proclaimed in an abstract opinion in 1858 had become an argument for disunion two years later.

By the time Lincoln was inaugurated, seven southern states had seceded and a new nation, the Confederate States of America, had been born. From his seat in the U.S. Senate, Douglas had worked with mounting desperation to find a compromise that would check the secession movement and restore the Union. He had pleaded with northerners and southerners alike to put their differences aside in the interest of saving the nation and averting armed conflict. "Are we prepared IN OUR HEARTS," he asked, "for war with our own brethren and kindred?"

When Lincoln arrived in Washington, Douglas was one of the first to call on him. He implored the president-elect to do everything in his power to prevent dissolution of the Union, urging him "in God's name, to act the patriot, and to save our children a country to live in." Lincoln replied that the crisis had been on his mind, and he thanked Douglas for his concern.

Crestfallen, Douglas looked to Lincoln's inaugural message as a last resort. The inaugural ceremony recalled the moment twenty-four years before when the cornerstone of Illinois's new capitol had been dedicated. Edward Dickinson Baker, now a U.S. senator, who had delivered the dedicatory address in 1837, introduced Lincoln, while Douglas, who had been in the audience at the dedication, sat close by, holding Lincoln's hat. The conciliatory tone of Lincoln's inaugural address offered Douglas a glimmer of hope for the Union, but that too quickly faded. The bombardment and surrender of Fort Sumter ended all possibility that the nation could be restored peaceably.

On the day the newspapers screamed of the surrender of Fort Sumter, Douglas hastened to the White House to offer Lincoln his full support. Though he was "unalterably opposed to the administration on all its political issues," he told Lincoln, "he was prepared to sustain the President in the exercise of all his constitutional functions to preserve the Union, and maintain the government."

The outbreak of hostilities opened a new arena for Douglas's leadership, as he turned his energy to molding the northern Democracy into a responsible loyal opposition party. His place at this critical moment, he decided, must be with his constituents. The Illinois legislature, summoned by the governor to meet in special session, offered the opportunity. Douglas's supporters urged him to be on hand when the legislators gathered in Springfield.

When Douglas and his wife boarded the train for what would be their final trip west, the city that had been his home for the last eighteen years bore all the earmarks of a city under siege. Confederate flags flew on the opposite bank of the Potomac, and there were rumors that southern soldiers were preparing an assault on Washington. The first troops to answer Lincoln's call had arrived and were quartered in the House chamber of the capitol. A local militia force composed of Washington's citizens had been hastily organized to defend the city.

After being detained in Harpers Ferry by Virginia militia who boarded the train and threatened to take Douglas prisoner, Douglas arrived in Springfield early on the morning of April 25, 1861. Hearing of his arrival, the legislature quickly passed a joint resolution inviting him to address the members "upon the existing crisis" that very evening in the Hall of Representatives.

It was immediately apparent that the pressures of the previous months had taken their toll on the Little Giant. His desperate but futile effort in Congress to halt the breakup of the Union had left him deeply depressed and physically exhausted. All he had sought to accomplish during his eighteen years in Congress—the extension of democratic self-rule, the progress in technology and the arts, the achievement of the republic's manifest destiny—seemed at an end.

The night of April 25, predicted Springfield's Republican press, would "long be remembered." At an early hour, the candlelit Hall of Representatives and the corridors of the statehouse were crowded with ladies and gentlemen "anxious to hear our distinguished Senator." Hundreds were turned away, unable even to get within hearing distance. When Douglas entered the hall, he was greeted by "tremendous and long continued applause." Following his introduction by the speaker of the lower house, the hall erupted in "deafening and unanimous cheering."

Douglas had spoken from the capitol's platform many times before, but no previous occasion had been so momentous. Although he had had little opportunity for rest since his arrival that morning, his words, at times personal and emotional, had retained their power. There were frequent interruptions, as the audience burst into shouts of approbation and enthusiasm, and prolonged cheering. Some men, it was reported, were moved to tears.

Douglas opened on a melancholy note, "with a heart filled with sadness and grief," as he contemplated the issues faced by the country. "For the first time since the adoption of the Federal Constitution," he observed, "a wide-spread conspiracy exists to destroy the best Government the sun of heaven ever shed its rays upon." He portrayed the threat in dire terms. A hostile army was marching on the nation's capital, a "piratical flag" had been unfurled against the country's commerce, and the navigation "of our great river" had been obstructed by hostile batteries on its banks. A "war of aggression and extermination" was being waged against the "government established by our fathers." Not only would constitutional freedom be subverted, dashing the "hopes of the friends of freedom throughout the wide world," but the "very foundations of social order" were to be undermined. No person who had been in Washington the past week, he maintained, would consider his picture to be "overwrought."

For what cause, Douglas asked, had the authority of the government of the United States been invaded? The institutions of the southern states, it had been alleged, were no longer safe under the federal government, yet all the evidence pointed to the contrary. The rights of the slaveholders were never more secure. For the first time in history, there was no congressional restriction upon slavery in any of the nation's territories, and the Fugitive Slave Act had never been enforced more faithfully. It was argued that the success of the Republican party in the presidential election justified disunion. If defeat in a presidential election can justify the minority "in raising the traitorous hand of rebellion," Douglas declared, then is constitutional government at an end. "The first duty of an American citizen, or a citizen of any constitutional government," he insisted, "is obedience to the constitution and laws of his country."

As long as there was hope for a peaceful solution of "all these troubles," Douglas noted, he had "prayed and implored for compromise." He had spared no effort, missed no opportunity, to restore "peace, happiness, and fraternity" to the country. To no avail. When all else failed, and a war of aggression had been proclaimed, but one course was left to the patriot: "to rally under that flag which has waved over the Capitol from the days of Washington."

As Douglas recalled his career and his lifelong devotion to the Union, his words became sadly reminiscent. "It has been my daily avocation, six months in the year, for eighteen years, to walk into that marble building, and from its portico to survey a prosperous, happy and united country on both sides of the Potomac," he reflected. He had been, he believed, as "thoroughly national" in his opinions and actions as any other man. If there had been error in his course, it was in leaning too far to the southern section of the country against his own. He had never pandered to the prejudices of his section against the interests of the South, and, he declared, he would not now sanction any warfare upon the constitutional rights or domestic institutions of the southern people.

In the crisis, Douglas maintained, party creeds and platforms must be set aside, party organizations and partisanship must be dispensed with—

surely a remarkable concession for one whose career had been based on party discipline and fidelity. Republicans, he warned, would not be true to their country if they made political capital out of the country's misfortunes, as he suspected some were doing. For those Democrats who seemed to be wavering in their support of the president's war measures, he had a special message: "Do not allow the mortifications growing out of defeat in a partisan struggle, and the elevation of a party to power that we firmly believed to be dangerous to the country—do not let that convert you from patriots to traitors to your native land." The shortest way to peace, he held, "is the most stupendous and unanimous preparation for war. The greater the unanimity, the less blood will be shed. The more prompt and energetic the movement, and the more imposing in numbers, the shorter will be the struggle."

No one, he hoped, would misunderstand his motives. "So far as any of the partisan questions are concerned," he assured his audience, "I stand in equal, irreconcilable, and undying opposition both to the Republicans and Secessionists." But not until the country had been rescued from its assailants would it be proper "for each of us to resume our respective political positions, according to our convictions of public duty." Once the Union had been restored, "then we will have a theatre for our party organizations to operate upon."

In conclusion, Douglas revealed the heavy impact the events of the previous months had had upon him:

> I have struggled almost against hope to avert the calamities of war, and to effect a re-union and reconciliation with our brethren of the South. I yet hope it may be done. . . .
>
> I see no path of ambition open in a bloody struggle for triumph over my own countrymen. There is no path of ambition open for me in a divided country, after having so long served a united and glorious country. Hence, whatever we may do must be the result of conviction of patriotic duty—the duty we owe to ourselves, to our posterity, and to the friends of constitutional liberty and self-government throughout the world.
>
> My friends, I can say no more. To discuss these topics is the most painful duty of my life. It is with a sad heart—with a grief that I have never before experienced, that I have to contemplate this fearful

struggle; but I believe in my conscience that it is a duty we owe ourselves, and our children, and our God, to protect this government and that flag from every assailant, be he who he may.

The speech was a valedictory for both Douglas and his country.

Not long after Douglas delivered his address, on June 3, 1861, worn out and exhausted, he was dead. His death brought to a close the rivalry that had informed so much of the nation's political life during the critical midcentury years. It was fitting that Douglas's last address was delivered in the building that had helped to shape that rivalry, in commemoration of which Leonard Volks's exquisite life-size statue of the Little Giant now stands at the entrance to the second-floor Hall of Representatives.

In the spring of 1865, having brought the ship to port, "anchor'd safe and sound, its voyage closed and done," Lincoln returned to the state capitol, not in life but in death. Felled by the assassin's bullet at his moment of triumph, Lincoln lay in state in the Hall of Representatives before his burial in Oak Ridge Cemetery. His spirit lived on to haunt the scene that was so closely linked to his career, as Springfield's Vachel Lindsay will always remind us:

> It is portentous, and a thing of state,
> That here at midnight, in our little town
> A mourning figure walks, and will not rest,
> Near the old court-house pacing up and down.

Both Douglas and Lincoln were casualties of the Civil War as surely as if they had died on the field of battle.

The Old State Capitol, in providing the principal forum for the state's two most distinguished citizens, not only served their political careers but also framed the sectional conflict itself. The House Divided Speech thrust Lincoln onto the national stage and placed the presidency within his grasp, while Douglas's anguished appeal for national unity marked the end of a long and celebrated career. Lincoln's statement, however well intentioned, became in the mouths of southern leaders an argument for revolution and disunion; Douglas's message aroused the citizenry to restore the Union, to rally under the flag, and to save "the best Government the sun of heaven ever shed its rays upon."

It is important, I have always believed, for the historian to *feel* the past as well as to *know* it. To stand in the Hall of Representatives, impressed by its aura of simple dignity, is to feel the presence of the two great rivals, to share the enthusiasm that attended Lincoln's address and the solemnity that marked Douglas's valedictory. In short, I feel that I am a witness to the crisis that threatened to destroy the republic, and that by itself is always a humbling experience.

For thirty-six years the building served the state as its capitol, until 1876 when the state offices outgrew its quarters and moved into the imposing structure Illinoisans know today. Sold to Sangamon County, the building became a county courthouse for the next eighty-five years, until space again became a problem. In the meantime, its interior had been renovated and its exterior altered. In 1961, the building was sold back to the state, and a vast project to restore the building to its original appearance began. It was dismantled stone by stone; each stone was numbered and stored. Excavations were carried out at the site to provide a two-story underground parking garage and quarters for the Illinois State Historical Library. The building was then reconstructed, both in its interior and exterior, according to its original appearance in the 1830s. The reconstruction completed, the building was rededicated and opened to the public in 1969.

Groups of schoolchildren and tourists now tour the building, seeking to connect with their past, while researchers from around the nation and the world are attracted by the rich collection of books, manuscripts, and other materials that among other things document the era of Lincoln and Douglas. The Old State Capitol, a striking witness to the past, is today a monument to the moment when the nation was itself on trial, and to the towering figures whose fortune it was to save the republic and all for which it stood.

A group of women gathered outside a Roycroft shop, East Aurora, New York, 1900. Cyanotype print by Frances Benjamin Johnston. *Division of Prints and Photographs, Library of Congress, Washington, D.C.*

Seven women working in a Roycroft shop, East Aurora, New York, 1900. Cyanotype print by Frances Benjamin Johnston. *Division of Prints and Photographs, Library of Congress, Washington, D.C.*

Michael Kammen

"A Little Journey"

Elbert Hubbard and the Roycroft
Community at East Aurora, New York

E ast Aurora is nestled near the far western edge of New York, well over one hundred miles west of the village of Aurora, New York, which makes for just one of the more amusing place-name paradoxes in a state well salted with quite a few. Because I teach American cultural history, primarily from the 1870s to the present, the Arts and Crafts movement that flourished at the turn of the century figures prominently in the episodic narrative that I need to relate, directly following the story of American utopianism and coinciding with the meteoric rise of electrified popular culture.

Although the Arts and Crafts movement had important roots in diverse locations ranging from Boston to Syracuse to Pasadena, East Aurora is the only site that still remains distinctively steeped in it—the only one where structures and artifacts and mementos not only remain intact but also where many are still made. These new products include both reproductions of those styled a century ago and newly designed ceramics and prints that perpetuate the tradition. The movement remains as more than just a memory in East Aurora. It's a vital presence, and that is why I like to take members of my class there on a field trip in mid-October, when the fall foliage upstate happens to be spectacularly at its peak.

During the last decade of the twentieth century, a strong revival of interest in the Arts and Crafts movement occurred, characterized by special museum exhibitions, serious publications, historic preservation activity at several significant sites, and escalating prices for objects that were produced by prominent craftspersons a century ago. Though it is appealing to see these objects so handsomely displayed on shelves and in glass-covered cases, there really is no adequate substitute for seeing them as an ensemble in the very buildings where they were made, with devoted guides explaining their provenance and telling the enchanting personal stories that illuminate them. From the perspective of someone who teaches American history, East Aurora offers a kind of scriptural opportunity that can transport students from genesis to revelation.

There is yet another reason why this town is notably attractive to the historian in me. Millard Fillmore, the only American president born and raised in central New York, relocated from Locke and Moravia (villages quite close to my own) out to East Aurora in 1826 to practice law, and there he built a charming, small home that remains (recently restored) to this day. When the house became a target for historic preservation a few years ago, it was moved from Main Street to a more bucolic side street. In 1999, when C-SPAN devoted a weekly, multihour series to each of the American presidents, the channel chose to situate its June 11 program at the Fillmore home in East Aurora, conducting informative interviews there and calling to our attention Fillmore's love of books. He gathered an impressive personal collection; and when he settled into the White House in 1850, he created the first permanent library that the presidential home ever had. All of his predecessors took their books away with them. Millard Fillmore today has come to be a synonym for a political nonentity, one of those obscure nineteenth-century presidents we conveniently forget. Nevertheless, he was a man with a passion for books.

Because of Fillmore's important connection to the town and because of its significance to the Arts and Crafts movement, East Aurora is an especially meaningful site for the historian of American culture. That is why I love to introduce students, friends, and visitors to the town. It's a charmer.

Ralph Waldo Emerson once remarked that "an institution is the lengthened shadow of one man." That is certainly true of the unusual artisan community created at East Aurora, New York, between 1895 and its demise as an enterprise during the 1930s. Although Elbert Hubbard's name is no longer a household word, he became an American celebrity at the end of the nineteenth century, attracting admirers by the millions along with detractors in more modest numbers who would have preferred the word *notoriety* to the word *celebrity*. Be that as it may, the prominent guests who gathered at his Roycroft community comprised quite a notable array of Americans, including Henry Ford, Clara Barton, Eugene Debs, the naturalist John Burroughs, Margaret Sanger, Booker T. Washington, Clarence Darrow, Harry Lauder (because Hubbard spent 1909–10 in vaudeville on the Orpheum Circuit), Scott Nearing (because Hubbard was a pacifist), the actress Ellen Terry, Judge Ben Lindsey, Horace Fletcher (the diet and fabled mastication fanatic), the poet Edwin Markham, the sculptor Gutzon Borglum (Mount Rushmore), Frederic C. Howe, and many others.

East Aurora, sixteen miles southeast of Buffalo, emerged in 1805 as a very rustic village within Erie County, part of the Holland Land Purchase, which corresponded to the whole western end of New York State, bounded on the north by Lake Ontario, on the south by the Allegheny River and the Pennsylvania border, on the east by the Genesee River, and on the west by Lake Erie. Situated approximately in the center of that large tract within the township of Aurora, East Aurora is not a "one-horse town," historically speaking; but it is surely safe to say that it would barely be known today and attract no tourists had Elbert Hubbard not decided to settle there in 1884 and then develop, little more than a decade later, a large cohort of workers eventually numbering around five hundred who figured prominently in the Arts and Crafts movement that flourished for about a quarter of a century beginning at the close of the nineteenth.

The topography of Aurora township is gently rolling in the north and hilly in the south. The declivities of the hills are mainly gradual slopes, and their summits range between 150 and 300 feet above the valleys. The soil in this agricultural region is gravelly loam in the valleys and more clayey among the hills. The principal streams are Cazenovia Creek and its tributaries, essential for Dorr Spooner's smelly tannery that flourished in East Aurora for almost six decades starting in 1839. In 1855, more than twenty years after Elbert Hubbard's father came to study at the Aurora Manual Labor Seminary (called the Aurora Academy after 1838), East Aurora had 360 residents, two churches, a large sawmill, and a lumber yard. Future president Fillmore owned a small home and practiced law on Main Street, but he later moved to Buffalo. Land sold for two to five dollars an acre during the 1830s, which was more than most of the newcomers could really afford.

By 1875, the latest state census prior to Elbert Hubbard's arrival, Aurora township had a population of 2,557, the greatest number of them descended from emigrants coming from Cattaraugus and Cayuga counties in central New York. There were 588 families, 568 inhabited houses, 19,000 improved acres, 3,877 acres of unimproved woodland, and an equal number of unimprovable acres. The entire township had just one African-American inhabitant. The population, therefore, was white and pious, most of them attending Congregational and Presbyterian churches, though Baptist, Lutheran, and Catholic churches soon appeared, necessitated by a residential building boom, of sorts, that took place between the 1880s and the eve of World War I.

Hubbard's parents, a doctor and a homemaker, had migrated from Buffalo to Bloomington, Illinois, where Elbert was born in 1856. Following a carefree youth in nearby Hudson, Illinois, young Hubbard sold soap as a "drummer," or traveling salesman, from 1872 until 1875. When his brother-in-law's partnership in the soap business split up in 1875, Elbert went with him to set up a new plant in Buffalo, with rights to all of the sales territory east of Detroit. Their enterprise achieved immense success, much of it due to Elbert's ingenuity in developing promotional schemes, such as premiums, so that people would purchase Larkin soaps in bulk. Meanwhile, in 1881, the energetic Hubbard married Bertha Crawford of Normal, Illinois, and they moved to Buffalo, where they promptly began to produce a family.

In 1884, however, the prospering Hubbard bought a large house (called Monticello) with an acre of land on Grove Street in East Aurora. The village had a convenient train link to Buffalo; but besides being an agricultural entrepôt, East Aurora had developed a reputation as a center for the breeding and training of trotting horses. Elbert had always loved horses and rode whenever he could throughout his life. Although the Knox Stables enjoyed considerable prestige, an extravagantly ambitious attempt to construct a glass-enclosed racetrack at East Aurora resulted in complete failure, a million-dollar loss for the Knox operation. Hubbard's commercial success a decade later in a very different line would more than compensate the local economy.

By 1891–92, having made a modest fortune in soap, Hubbard yearned for success as some sort of writer, and he soon tried his hand at writing novels. The first two turned out to be utter failures; but the indefatigable Hubbard decided that he simply needed more education, especially in the history of English literature. So late in 1892 he boldly sold his interest in J. D. Larkin & Co. and began to study Latin and Greek with an Episcopal minister in East Aurora. His goal? Admission to Harvard College, where he did become a "special student" in 1893 at the age of thirty-six. His course work there did not go well, however, which left him with a lifelong antipathy toward academic pedants.

Yet his time spent in the Boston area turned out to be fruitful and positive for his long-term liberation and outlook. First, it provided him with opportunities to spend time with his true love, Alice Moore, a bright and independent-minded New Woman he had met in 1889 when she taught at East Aurora High School. In 1894, just a few weeks after his wife gave birth to a daughter, their fourth child, Alice also produced a daughter. She and Elbert named the girl Miriam. Hubbard's word-concept for his relationship with Alice, "affinity," echoed the exact notion that Henry Ward Beecher had used to rationalize his adulterous affair with Elizabeth Tilton twenty-five years before.

The second benefit of his time spent in Cambridge emerged from a pilgrimage that Hubbard made to nearby Concord in order to visit the homes of Emerson, Thoreau, and other notable writers of the American renaissance. (Emerson always remained Hubbard's favorite author. Had he not written in "Self Reliance," "Whoso would be a man must be a nonconformist"? One of Hubbard's many epigrams would later be "Conformists die but heretics live on forever.") Genuinely inspired by his initial visits to the homes of these famous authors, Hubbard wrote the first of his *Little Journey* booklets, accounts of the places where great men and women lived—and the inspirational thoughts that filled his mind while present at these special sites. It is not surprising that he included women, for he was a feminist, of sorts, and ardently supported woman suffrage.

At first, however, he found no publisher who saw any future in such a project. Undaunted, he went to England and Ireland in 1894 in order to see the homes of more famous writers and extend what would eventually become a remarkable series of *Little Journeys*. In England he visited Hammersmith, the home and workplace of William Morris, the innovative leader of the Arts and Crafts movement there, a Socialist who rebelled against industrialization by reviving medieval and early modern handicrafts, ranging from papermaking and bookbinding to handmade textiles and wall coverings. Hubbard returned to East Aurora imbued with nostalgia for Olde England, fascinated by the prospect of printing elegant hand-set books, and filled with notions about the prospect for benevolent paternalism in the revival of traditional arts in America.

He also brought back numerous topics for his booklets, because he had traveled indefatigably to the homes of Wordsworth, Coleridge, De Quincey, Scott, George Eliot, Ruskin, Turner, Carlyle, Dickens, Gladstone, and many others. G. P. Putnam's Sons decided to take a chance on the *Little Journeys*, and they began to appear promptly in the autumn of 1894 and caught on immediately. Hubbard customarily brought out one each month and ultimately published 170 of them. Eventually he would write about European artists, scientists, and musicians whose homes he had never seen, often improvising or even inventing information that simply sounded attractive. When I lead my students to East Aurora every autumn, we feel as though we are making our own "little journey," in the spirit of a Hubbard pilgrimage but with a little less hokum.

By 1908 Hubbard had reached "Great Teachers," which translated into *Little Journeys* to Moses, Confucius, Pythagoras, Plato, King Alfred, Friedrich Froebel (a great favorite of the well-read Alice Moore), Booker T. Washington, Thomas Arnold, Erasmus, St. Benedict, and Mary Baker Eddy. In 1909 he undertook the last "serious" series, *Little Journeys* to the homes of great businessmen, all treated as heroic figures: Robert Owen, Stephen Girard, M. A. Rothschild, Philip Armour, John Jacob Astor, Peter Cooper, Andrew Carnegie, A. T. Stewart, James T. Hill, and others.

Except for one more journey devoted to Thomas A. Edison, Hubbard then turned the project into a totally commercial undertaking because he had long since drifted far from William Morris's Socialism in favor of enthusiastic support for big business. What resulted were commissions for "A Little Journey to the Home of Pebeco Tooth Paste" and the like. Hubbard had no shame and had long since been called both a charlatan and a plagiarist. In 1908, when William Morris's daughter, May, gave a public lecture in Buffalo, Hubbard dispatched a disciple to hand her a warm letter of invitation. When she opened it, her eyes flashed in fury and she declared: "I most certainly will not go to East Aurora, nor do I have any desire to see that obnoxious imitator of my dear father." In

1910, when Hubbard received a commission to write "A Little Journey to the Standard Oil Company," his chief designer rendered an art deco octopus on the cover so skillfully that no one at Standard Oil even noticed. John D. Rockefeller, who greatly admired Hubbard, invited him to come to Cleveland to play golf on the monopolist's private course. Hubbard loved it.

All of which completes the astonishing success story of Hubbard's *Little Journeys*—a mix of sentimental moralism and nostalgia at a time when the Chautauqua experience had aroused hunger for knowledge that might uplift the spirit—but carries us fifteen years ahead of our narrative and the *other* elements of Hubbard's success that made East Aurora a highly notable place-name in American culture. To succeed as a self-made man, Hubbard combined driving ambition with vision, which in his case meant shifting the rewards of fame from politicians to people with creative minds whose ideas had made a difference. As Hubbard wrote to his mother early in 1893, just before leaving for Harvard: "As to the History . . . what we call History . . . concerns itself with the nobility who manage the affairs of state, not the common people—when the real fact is the people are the state, not the nobles; so I am writing a record of the events that have influenced the popular mind. In our day Vincent [a founder of the Chautauqua movement nearby in western New York] has moved the people more than Cleveland—Edison more than Blaine—Frances Willard more than Harrison. So you see, it is the *thinkers*, not the politicians, who change mankind."

In June of 1895 the local Pendennis Press published the first issue of a monthly magazine edited and mainly written by Hubbard. He called it the *Philistine: A Periodical of Protest* because he eagerly wanted to thumb his nose at all of the custodians of polite culture in late Victorian America, ranging from Richard Watson Gilder, prissy editor of *The Century* magazine, to Barrett Wendell, the proper professor of English and American literature at Harvard who had given Hubbard such a hard time. Filled with antielitist essays, irreverent epigrams, and stories, the *Philistine* swiftly caught on and attracted subscription requests faster than Hubbard's primitive print shop in East Aurora could satisfy them. So Hubbard bought a series of more elaborate and modern presses in addition to a hand press on which to produce distinctively elegant editions of books, starting with Solomon's *Song of Songs* in January 1896.

Meanwhile, in November 1895 Hubbard decided to inaugurate a

Roycroft tradition: an annual dinner of the Society of Philistines, for reporters and any subscriber to the new monthly who cared to attend. The first guest of honor would be young Stephen Crane, still relatively unknown as a novelist and poet, who had been spending time that autumn as Hubbard's guest, despite his belief that Hubbard was an affected bohemian, a "clever looking duck." Following the banquet at a hotel in Buffalo, the Genesee House—an event that degenerated into a farce—Crane wrote to his bemused host: "When I think of you I rejoice that there is one man in the world who can keep up a small independent monthly howler without either dying, going broke, or becoming an ass."

By 1896, when Hubbard began publishing books as art objects and proudly bringing them to the attention of the American public, he decided to call his growing community of artisans Roycrofters in honor of two very eminent bookbinders from seventeenth-century England. It was a clever choice because the French source of the word meant "king's craftsmen." Quite soon Hubbard and his principal assistants began to train young men and women from the area in an array of artisanal skills, ranging from papermaking to fine binding. By the end of the century, aspiring craftsmen were arriving from great distances, and curious visitors who had read the *Little Journeys* and the *Philistine* appeared in order to see how things were done.

Meanwhile, during the summer of 1896 Hubbard made yet another trip to Europe to collect still more material for his widely read *Little Journeys*, this time gleaning ideas and inspiration in Scotland, the English Lake District, Liverpool, London, Antwerp, Brussels, and other choice spots. During the following year he found that the demand for his printing and binding operations still kept outgrowing his production facilities. So he built a large stone and half-timber building—a pseudo-English structure—and that provided adequate space at last. In 1899 Hubbard's workers completed the Roycroft Library using the fieldstone so abundant in rural Erie County to add yet another Anglophile design to the rapidly growing "campus," as it came to be called. In 1900 the new fieldstone shop close by enhanced the opportunity for commercial sales to the steadily increasing number of tourists and curiosity seekers.

The March 1899 issue of the *Philistine* included a brief untitled homily soon known as "A Message to Garcia" that Hubbard had dashed off in little more than an hour. He wrote it in response to the tale of a heroic feat achieved by an officer named Rowan the year before during the Spanish-American War. President McKinley needed to learn just how strong the anti-Spanish insurgents were in the mountains of Cuba. So he sent Rowan, disguised as an English gentleman, to find Garcia, interview him at his hilly hideaway, and bring back the necessary information. Hubbard viewed this achievement as the perfect parable for many of his strongly held views, and he packed his narrative in a resounding message of his own about the virtues of rugged individualism, gritty determination, self-reliance (in the context of a quick diatribe against Socialism), the success ethos in a Darwinian world ("it is the survival of the fittest"), and above all the need for employees to carry out orders in a deferential manner, no questions asked. He lavishly praised the man who "quietly takes the missive without asking any idiotic questions," such as "Where is he at?"

Obedience and subordination combined with reliability and initiative—that was the message preached. It had immense appeal to those who ran large-scale organizations in that era of American industrialization. So orders streamed in for reprints of "A Message to Garcia," starting with the New York Central Railroad. Generals ordered copies distributed among their troops. Government officials handed them out to civil servants. Judges read the piece aloud from the bench. With the exception of labor unions and their members, it seemed to be exactly the right lesson for turn-of-the-century America. Consequently, many millions of copies were printed, foreign language translations proliferated, and Hubbard swiftly became a national celebrity. Henceforth, he would feel justified in calling East Aurora "the Land of Immortality" and holding chauvinistic (yet self-serving) Fourth of July Conventions there.

Meanwhile, encouraged by the growing appeal of the Arts and Crafts movement in Boston, Syracuse, Pasadena, and other places, Hubbard began to train young workers in the production of pottery, hammered copper products (such as wall sconces), wrought-iron andirons, lamps and hinges, tooled leather goods, rugs, baskets, mission-style furniture, stained glass lampshades and windows, paintings, preserves, and maple sugar candy. These products were featured in ads that appeared in the *Philistine* and sold extremely well as subscriptions exceeded one hundred thousand. Structures to house all of the small "manufactories" sprang up along Grove and Walnut streets, with tidy homes for the workers rising

AMERICAN PLACES

swiftly on the aptly named Oakwood and Prospect avenues. Emerson Hall was built as a gathering place and dormitory opposite some of the Roycroft cottages on Prospect.

And in 1903–04, Hubbard displaced the big home he had bought almost two decades earlier in order to make room on Grove, just off Main Street, for the Roycroft Inn, a huge fieldstone and wood building with an elaborately raftered superstructure—a blend of English and Arts movement architecture for the Niagara Frontier countryside. Each bedroom, named in honor of a famous historic figure, had a Roycroft calendar bearing daily mottoes (Hubbard loved mottoes and epigrams), but with a blank space beneath so that guests could inscribe their own. The walls in the first-floor salon were covered by Alex Fournier's murals depicting great cities of the world. (These paintings have now been meticulously restored and remain a memorable moment on our contemporary tour.) They add yet another curiosity for this small and rustic American town: glorification of urbanization and urban culture on a global scale. If the contrast seemed ironic or oddly juxtaposed, no one seemed to notice.

Hubbard's decision in 1903 to erect the handsome inn came in response to the growing fame of his village, but also amidst his greatest personal crisis. Despite the decade-long deterioration of his marriage to Bertha, he had managed to keep his "affinity" life (and his alternative "wife") a well-guarded secret, aided in several ways by his extensive travels. In 1902, however, Alice's brother brought suit against Hubbard for nonsupport of Miriam, the daughter born out of wedlock. It is quite possible that Alice actually conspired in the suit in order to precipitate a crisis, and Hubbard himself may even have encouraged the litigation. In any case, predictably, many people in East Aurora were scandalized. Bertha obtained a divorce in 1903, leaving the two older sons with Elbert but taking the two younger children.

That left Elbert and Alice free to marry on January 20, 1904, a highly successful match of complementary temperaments. Alice soon gained acceptance among the Roycroft community, though not so readily among other, more traditional, residents of East Aurora. She had excellent organizational and supervisory skills, which Hubbard did not; so she became, in effect, the chief executive officer of these rapidly expanding and immensely successful Roycroft operations. Her talents could not have been more vital, since her husband soon became the most sought-after public speaker in the United States. According to some accounts, from 1905 until 1915 he was also the most highly paid. Because his lecturing junkets frequently kept him away from East Aurora, Alice's considerable managerial abilities as well as her own essays for the *Philistine* were essential.

Hubbard, meanwhile, increasingly referred to as the Sage of East Aurora because of his whimsical punditry and the evident commercial success of his diverse enterprises, wrote a daily column for the Hearst newspaper syndicate, an undertaking that earned him the then huge sum of thirty thousand dollars a year. He was also retained as a business adviser by numerous concerns and by 1909 supplemented his considerable income by doing advertising copy for others—a skill that he had honed as a youngster promoting Larkin soap with fanciful premiums during the 1870s and 1880s. In 1910, when Hubbard made two appearances daily on the Orpheum vaudeville circuit, he received $2,500 per week and added even more to his notoriety with arty costumes and elaborate schemes for achieving success against all odds and in defiance of conventional orthodoxies.

Whenever Hubbard was in residence at East Aurora, he kept busy in countless ways. On one hand, as a highly successful businessman, he continually developed clever innovations in the realm of direct-mail advertising. On the other hand, as paterfamilias of a very considerable workforce, he raised benevolent paternalism to the level of benign authoritarianism. He defined *cooperation* in the *Roycroft Dictionary* as "Doing what I tell you to do and doing it quick." A broad range of locals as well as pilgrims to East Aurora accepted or tolerated that dictum and were placed on the payroll. Some were classic "seekers" in the mode of communal utopianism, while others apparently had wanderlust and wanted to try the novelties of life at East Aurora at the very peak of the Arts and Crafts movement's appeal in the United States. Still others were simply young people in need of employment and some sort of meaningful personal development.

A carefully recruited few and some who simply arrived by serendipity gave the Roycroft products their attractively distinctive appearance. Artist W. W. Denslow, who did a great many illustrations for the *Philistine* and for promotional purposes, later achieved fame as illustrator for the Oz books written by Frank Baum. Dard Hunter, a creative craftsperson, designed and made all of the handsome leaded glass windows for the

Roycroft Inn. After six months' work in 1903, he felt anxiously dissatisfied with the garish colors. On a very cold November morning, before anyone had come to breakfast, he smashed them all out with a hammer. After he explained why and promised to make new ones, Hubbard simply said: "Dard, if you feel inclined to smash your next set of windows, please wait until summertime."

Life among the Roycrofters was quasi-communal. Everyone was welcome, everyone would somehow be fed and sheltered, but everyone was expected to work hard for very modest pay. They generated their own language and legends and developed a nominal orientation to the medievalism of William Morris—as explained to them by Elbert Hubbard, who claimed more familiarity with Morris's establishment at Hammersmith, near London, than he actually had. Because of a certain masquerade monasticism, Hubbard came to be called Fra Elbertus, let his hair grow to shoulder length, and wore odd combinations of "arty" clothes along with a very wide-brim western-style hat. His buildings turned out to be a bastardized Gothic-Tudor-Jacobean, which at least meant that the Roycroft campus had the coherent appearance of a planned community within the village.

There were all sorts of communal programs for recreation—softball and medicine balls for fitness being particular favorites—and when Hubbard was at home in East Aurora, he would lecture every Sunday evening at the Roycroft Chapel before the assembled workers as well as any guests staying at the Roycroft Inn. He sat or stood on a dais with mission style furniture made *in situ*—furnishings on a platform that conveyed the impression of a medieval baron, perhaps even a king, in full command of his flock.

Hubbard's high-handed manner and strong opinions did attract disciples but also cost him many friends and well-wishers. East Aurora had a fair number of saloons, for example, and Hubbard was a teetotaler. When he decided to diminish the saloons, he insisted that every Roycrofter must march in a "dry parade," under threat of dismissal. So his legion marched to the music of the Roycroft brass band, almost four hundred strong. A few libertarian members who did not drink but believed in personal liberty for all refused to march; they incurred the Fra's wrath but were not fired.

Some of the residents of East Aurora who were not Roycrofters resented Hubbard for an array of reasons, and he responded with satirical essays in the *Philistine*. In 1908 Hubbard and a feminist friend, both freethinkers, offered to give the village library a complete set of the works of the controversial Robert G. Ingersoll. The local board of education, which had responsibility for the library, declined to accept these "atheistical" writings on the ground that it had a duty to protect the young against subversion of "the religious faith of the American nation." Hubbard then offered to give the library a deluxe set of *his* collected works (then in progress, forty volumes handsomely bound selling for ten dollars each). He called attention to his position in East Aurora: the largest taxpayer in town, the only major employer, the principal post-office customer, the bulwark of village prosperity and morals! While acknowledging that his own writings were just as subversive as Ingersoll's, he cited the constitutional separation of church and state and invited the board to consider whether there was nothing in the Bible to "bring the blush of shame to the cheek of innocence."

The board responded with a long and dignified letter in which it still rejected Ingersoll but accepted Hubbard's works with a proviso that to safeguard the village children it would establish a restricted "department of objectionable literature" into which some of Hubbard's ten-dollar deluxe books might be placed. Hubbard promptly withdrew his offer, mocked the board in print, and declared that the man chiefly responsible for all this rigidity "has been appointed Commissioner of Lunacy."

Hubbard had, early on, developed a thick skin from necessity. In 1902 one of his own staff, Michael Monahan, denounced Hubbard's adultery from the East Aurora Opera House—every small town in the United States seemed to have one as an all-purpose place of performance—and urged the Roycrofters to repudiate their leader. Hubbard promptly left for a western lecture trip and weathered the storm. He eventually became a target for earnest clergymen across the country, an indication of the ubiquitous reach of Hubbard's writings. As one minister implored a YMCA meeting: "When some of these little, narrow-minded, East Aurora type of vaudeville artists try to tell you that the Bible amounts to nothing and that Christ was the illegitimate child of a peasant girl, you'd better take their 'Little Journeys' and chuck them into Hell through the sewer and put such men down as unprincipled asses." Hubbard invariably managed to turn these attacks upside down and to his own advantage by mocking them in the *Philistine*.

Having attacked revival meetings, however, he felt obliged to print a rebuttal from Billy Sunday, the most popular evangelist in America during the early twentieth century: "I do not care whether a man lives in East Aurora, East Paradise, or East Gehenna, if he despises the word of God he has got something coming that will make him stutter at the Last Great Day. The *Philistine* is doing more to blight faith than any other publication in America. I have no use for self-appointed sissified long-haired prophets."

Hubbard's prolific but often slapdash writing prompted quite an array of responses, ranging from angry accusations to wicked spoofs and satires. Particularly alarming and problematic for Hubbard were the numerous charges of plagiarism brought against him, most of which he simply shrugged off. More flattering though equally disturbing were the parodies that started to appear as early as 1901, indicating the prominence that Hubbard's publications had achieved and showing that printing inspired by the Arts and Crafts movement could take many derivative and imitative forms. In 1901, for instance, *A Little Spasm at the Home of Wolfgang Mozart*, purportedly published by the Rakeoffers at Rising Sun, New York, appeared as part of a series devoted to "Great Organ Grinders."

Even more wickedly amusing was *The Billioustine: A Periodical of Knock*, a parody of the *Philistine* created by William S. Lord in Evanston, Illinois. It appeared on brown butcher paper (like its prototype), "whenever we need the money, by the Boy Grafters," under the direction of Fra McGinnis, "very long in hair, and . . . the original goo-goo eye man." Its place of production was referred to as the Philandery. As a person who enjoyed wealth, celebrity, and power, Hubbard simply laughed at all of these spoofs. In the June 1912 issue of the *Fra*, an oversized library-table magazine that he launched in 1908, Hubbard observed that "Satire is a giant wasp playing in and out of the mouth of a sleeping clown." Not a bad riposte, and typical of Hubbard's epigrammatic skills, except that the clown in question seemed to sleep very rarely. His energy level was quite remarkable.

East Aurora enjoyed its peak productivity (and notoriety) between 1908 and 1915. By 1906 the *Philistine* was attracting advertising from nationally known, name-brand products. The *Fra*, which never achieved the wide circulation of *Little Journeys* and the *Philistine*, was created as an oversized magazine in order to maximize space for large ads. But above all, an extraordinary array of Arts and Crafts products, quite variable in quality and price, were in high demand because the movement was at its apogee and Hubbard's unwarranted reputation as the leading American disciple of William Morris made Roycroft products widely recognized as desirable household objects. Summer gatherings called Roycroft Conventions attracted large numbers of visitors to attend three programs daily on the East Aurora campus, mainly for speeches, song-fests, recitations, and product exhibitions.

In April 1915, in the first year of World War I, Elbert and Alice Moore Hubbard decided to go to Europe to learn more about the devastating war at first hand. Ever curious and ever intrepid, they had the misfortune to sail on the *Lusitania*, which took several torpedoes from a German U-boat and went down in May near the Irish coast with tremendous loss of life, including both Hubbards.

Because Hubbard had visited so many communities as a public speaker and performer, memorial services were held for him in numerous cities; the public services held in his honor at East Aurora were impressive and eloquent. More than forty thousand letters of condolence poured in to the community; they serve as testimony to the way he had put his town on the map. Always an astute promoter of himself and his many products, Hubbard's ego, imagination, and versatility had nevertheless altered a village and provided it with an enduring identity. As one loyal disciple has phrased it, with perhaps unintended irony, Hubbard's principal legacy "is the *idea* of Roycroft, the creation of the community and the transformation of the village of East Aurora into a center, however brief its existence, of real intellectual ferment—a place where things were going on that don't often occur in most American towns."

Clearly, Hubbard's reputation has had its ups and downs. In 1929, for example, a figure with vivid memories of Hubbard's heyday, Claude Bragdon, recalled the *Philistine* as

the speaking-trumpet, so to speak, of Elbert Hubbard ... pungent, abusive, witty, knowing, vulgar. Hubbard apparently dramatized himself as a sort of composite of Ralph Waldo Emerson and William Morris, but his chief claim to fame is that of being the Father of Modern Advertising. He had a perfect genius for publicity, smoking up other people's talents and throwing them away like a daily newspaper, accomplishing a considerable amount of good in the process, for to his vast clientele he sustained something of the relation of

Chautauqua, disseminating about as rich a brand of "culturine" as the middle-class American stomach was able to stand.

Contrast that with the response of Terence V. Powderly, the tough-minded founder and leader of the Knights of Labor, an important organization for workingmen toward the close of the nineteenth century. After attending a Roycroft Conference one summer, he felt moved to write *A Little Journey to the Home of Elbert Hubbard*, published by the Roycrofters in 1905. Not known as a sentimental man, Powderly nonetheless noticed that "On going to East Aurora you go to a place where more people who love inanimate nature go than most places. At home you do not meet such people, and you are richer for your visit." At the end of his booklet, however, Powderly concluded that Hubbard "detests cant, hates hypocrisy, and despises sham." Those are just the attributes that students of the Arts and Crafts movement have been debating about Hubbard for almost a century now.

Burton Rascoe, a prominent literary editor, perhaps struck a judicious balance between Hubbard's ardent admirers and his hostile detractors. He wrote this assessment in 1937:

> Frowned upon and sneered at by these "intellectual leaders" was Elbert Hubbard of East Aurora, who, whatever may have been his limitations (he was a superb showman, and all showmen have a degree of charlatanry in their make-up) *did* have a deep sense of the essential values of a living literature and was committing (in their eyes) the vulgarism of interesting the masses in the arts of literature, music, sculpture, painting, architecture and in the handicrafts of printing, typographical design, furniture making and tannery.

Following Hubbard's death at sea, his eldest son, Bert, held the Roycroft community together, and it remained productive for almost two decades. Recycling the diverse writings of Fra Elbertus kept the publications going, and the products of skilled artisans enjoyed a reasonable vogue into the 1920s. Soon, however, national enthusiasm for the Arts and Crafts movement waned, supplanted by modernism on one hand and a neo-colonial revival on the other. The Great Depression caused the whole enterprise to become unviable, and in 1939 the Roycroft facilities were sold. The village population at that time was 5,239. During the 1980s and 1990s, however, quite a few of the buildings were restored, most notably the inn in 1995–96. Visitors tour the Roycroft campus once again today, just as I do with my Cornell students.

Meanwhile, four enterprising residents of East Aurora launched a totally new undertaking in 1930. Fisher-Price, born in what had been the Roycroft copper shop, chose to specialize in educational playthings and offered age-appropriate toys designed and approved by experts in the field of child development. The Fisher-Price motto, "Good toys never die!," seems to have been an unintended echo of Hubbard's epigram concerning heretics. Fisher-Price continued for decades to feature Snooper Sniffers (a pull-along dog) and Busy Bees (with revolving wings). Herman Fisher insisted for years that any toy that lasted from "one child to another" would guarantee a loyal market of parents. And he was right.

Fisher-Price was taken over by Mattel in 1993, but its proud legacy over six decades actually meant that toy manufacturing turned out to be even more enduring than arts and crafts in East Aurora. It was the latter, however, that gave the village its peculiar prominence on the national map. Elbert Hubbard's persona, and perhaps his vision, remain alive and well as a new millennium begins. It would delight him, I feel certain, that we have made our own "little journey" to East Aurora, New York.

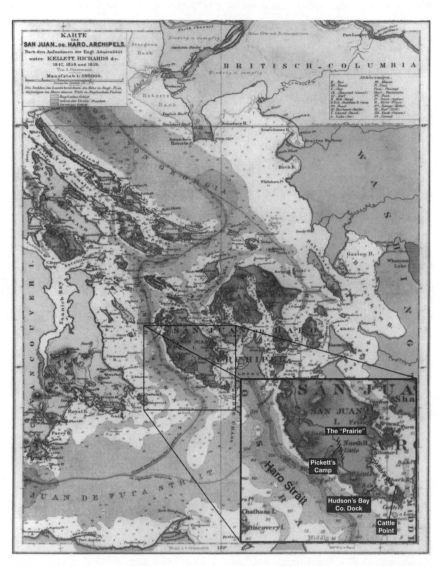

Map of the San Juan Islands drawn by the German arbitration commission in 1873. The dotted line around the island indicates the British and U.S. boundaries. "H.B. Co. Farm" and "Griffin Bay" are both marked on the southern tip of San Juan Island. *The Bancroft Library, University of California.*

David M. Kennedy

San Juan Island, Washington

The "Pig War" and the Vagaries of Identity and History

No place is a place until things that have happened in it are remembered in history.

———Wallace Stegner

My first awareness that I might be living in a distinctive historical place came at age thirteen or so—and with a shock. I was sitting in my neighborhood Carnegie Library in Seattle reading Edward Everett Hale's short story "The Man without a Country."

Originally published in the *Atlantic Monthly* in December 1863, Hale's celebrated yarn relates the bizarre fate of one Philip Nolan. As a gullible young army officer in the early nineteenth century, Nolan is seduced by Aaron Burr's promises of adventure, somehow finds himself implicated in Burr's shadowy conspiracy aimed at the lower Mississippi Valley, is arrested, tried for treason, and found guilty. Asked at his court-martial if he wishes to make a statement, a bamboozled Nolan blurts out, "D – – n the United States! I wish I may never hear of the United States again!" That outcry quite literally determines Nolan's sentence: "that you never hear the name of the United States again." That faintly gothic opening scene arrested my attention, and I read eagerly on.

Nolan is made a prisoner aboard a succession of U.S. naval vessels whose officers and crews are under strict orders never to mention the United States in his presence. They scissor maps of America from his atlas, clip all references to his homeland from his newspapers, allow him reading materials of any kind only if they are not published in the United States and make no allusion to it. This young reader saw Nolan as a sympathetic figure who serves out his sentence with stoic dignity. The prisoner even heroically mans a gun during a naval battle in the War of 1812. And he is revealed at the end to have turned his shipboard cabin into a little shrine of patriotic devotion, to have "loved his country as no other man has loved her." Yet his sentence is never commuted. Nolan neither sees nor hears of the United States for the remaining half century of his life, excepting only a highly selective history (conspicuously omitting any mention of the then-raging "infernal Rebellion") recounted at his deathbed by a sympathetic shipmate. He becomes "the man without a country." In one especially poignant scene, Nolan serves as a translator for a group of Africans liberated from a slave trader. He reports their plea: "Take us home, take us to our own country, take us to our own homes, take us to our own pickaninnies and our own women"—a touching reminder of the cruelty of slavery and of Nolan's predicament alike.

Hale's story, however, was only incidentally about the injustice of slavery. It was chiefly a paean to the idea of Union, a parable about the compelling power of national loyalty, an allegory that breathed life into Abraham Lincoln's invocation of the "mystic chords of memory" that bound the nation together and bound citizen to nation. It was also a morality play about the high crime of secession. Writing in the weeks just after Gettysburg, Hale meant to issue a "warning" to the "Vallandighams . . . of today of what it is to throw away a country" and to rebuke "every Bragg and Beauregard who broke a soldier's oath two years ago." But beyond its specifically historical context, many of whose details then meant little to me (including those now-familiar Copperhead and Confederate names), "The Man without a Country" was also a searching rumination on the timeless psychology of belonging, on the essential link between physical place and personal and national identity.

Above all, Hale's little fable was intended to make readers feel the precious value of their identity as Americans. That point even my barely pubescent sensibility could grasp, especially in the reflexively patriotic 1950s. But the story seized my callow imagination with particular force, and has held on there for all these years, principally because one phrase in it stung: Hale's casual reference to "that distant Mississippi Valley, *which was farther from us than Puget's Sound is today*." Reading that line as I sat on the very shores of Puget Sound (the possessive having disappeared in the intervening century), I was viscerally, grievously affronted—that *my* native ground should be made to serve as a metaphor for the ends of the earth, or at least for the remotest, apparently most inconsequential corner of the United States.

My boyhood brooding about that galling offense to regional pride is now regularly reawakened when I make my annual summer remove from California to San Juan Island in Washington State. I go there, of course, for the express purpose of "getting away from it all." Ironically enough, remoteness, the very item that had provoked my youthful irritation, has become the island's main attraction for me.

Now, remoteness is a relative concept. It connotes the distance between the crush of civilization and the serenity of nature, to be sure, but it also measures the space between center and periphery, between someplace and someplace else. So with reference to what center is San Juan Island peripheral? From what other place is its "someplace elseness" calibrated? And has that imaginative and geographic calculus changed over time? Can a place be moved, either in the mind or on the map? Can its very location have a history? To those questions the case of San Juan Island suggests some interesting answers.

San Juan is the westernmost island in the eponymous archipelago that lies at the head of Washington State's Puget Sound—or at the foot of British Columbia's Strait of Georgia, depending on one's perspective. (The matter of perspective, it turns out, has had telling implications for the islands' fate.) On a map, the San Juans are tucked into the little crinkle in the northwest corner of the "lower forty-eight" United States. There the straight-running forty-ninth parallel along which the U.S.-Canadian boundary tracks westward from the Lake of the Woods meets what water-wise Pacific Northwesterners call the saltchuck, in the Strait of Georgia. From that point the international frontier angles its aqueous way around the south end of Vancouver Island and out the Strait of

Juan de Fuca to the open sea. That snaking line traces a bit of history that resonates hauntingly with Hale's story.

The cartographic crinkle originated in the Oregon Treaty of 1846. Britain and America had jointly occupied the sparsely settled Oregon country without serious incident for nearly three decades after the Anglo–American Convention of 1818. But "Oregon Fever" brought a rush of American homesteaders into the region in the 1840s and compelled a more precise definition of just who owned what. Britain insisted that the Columbia River, lying approximately along the forty-fifth parallel, should define the frontier between the two countries. Expansionist Americans demanded that the boundary be fixed far to the north, at the line of 54°40'. Between the two claims lay most of present-day Washington State and a good chunk of British Columbia. The treaty of 1846 compromised on the line of the forty-ninth parallel. But it contained a proviso that the boundary should leave in British hands all of Vancouver Island (a large piece of which lies below 49° North) by proceeding along the parallel to "the middle of the channel which separates the continent from Vancouver's Island; and thence southerly through the middle of said channel, and of [Juan de] Fuca's Straits to the Pacific Ocean."

Despite the availability of detailed charts made in the preceding half century by the English sailor George Vancouver (and his aide, Peter Puget) and the American navigator Charles Wilkes (later famous for removing Confederate commissioners James Mason and John Slidell from the British mail steamer *Trent*), the framers of the Oregon Treaty inexplicably left undefined precisely which of several possible channels might be deemed to form the southern outlet of the Strait of Georgia— and thus to define the body of water that "separates the continent from Vancouver's Island" below the forty-ninth parallel. There were two principal candidates: Rosario Strait to the east, and the Canal de Haro (now Haro Strait) to the west. Between them lay the San Juan archipelago. Like the Oregon country as a whole before the treaty, the islands remained open after 1846 to both British and American settlers with scant certainty under whose sovereignty they might be taking up residence.

The most important of the group was San Juan Island itself. It was situated at a strategically valuable juncture that overlooked Admiralty

Inlet (the entrance to Puget Sound) and commanded the inland exit from Juan de Fuca Strait—as well as the approaches to the British military outpost at Fort Victoria and to the "inside passage" up the British Columbia coast in the lee of Vancouver Island to Russian Alaska.

James Douglas had founded Fort Victoria in 1843. Born in British Guyana in 1803 to a Scots father and an Afro-Caribbean mother, Douglas was a child of the British Empire and devoted to aggrandizing its domains. He had long served as the Hudson's Bay Company agent at Fort Vancouver near the mouth of the Columbia. By the 1850s Douglas was installed at Fort Victoria as the governor of Vancouver Island. He felt aggrieved that his government had ceded the area between Juan de Fuca Strait and the Columbia to the United States. He watched with alarm as the last vestige of disputed territory in the San Juans began to fill with American "squatters." With the example of Oregon's loss fresh in his mind, Douglas determined to emulate American tactics by preemptively establishing a strong British presence on San Juan Island, thereby blocking the grasping Yankees from seizing yet another piece of Pacific Coast real estate. On December 15, 1853, he dispatched Charles Griffin and several Kanaka (Hawaiian) herdsmen, along with 1,350 sheep, to set up a Hudson's Bay Company outpost on the naked, rocky "prairie" that sloped out of the dense fir forest down to the driftwood-clogged shingle beach at the island's southern tip.

For their part, the Americans in the first session of the Washington territorial legislature in 1854 included the San Juan Islands in the new county of Whatcom (whose earliest days were later vividly re-created in Annie Dillard's splendid novel *The Living*). Local British and American officials alike fitfully tried to assert their jurisdiction over the islands. Douglas high-handedly confiscated a load of lumber from an "unauthorized" American logger on Lopez Island. The Whatcom County sheriff attempted to kidnap several of Griffin's sheep for payment of taxes—a venture that foundered when a sheep-bearing canoe swamped and the rams that should have been revenue swam ashore and escaped into the woods.

Committed to peaceful resolution of the boundary question, and awaiting the report of a binational commission charged with defining the appropriate channel, neither London nor Washington took much note of these shenanigans. But at Griffin's sheep station on June 15, 1859, a Kentuckian named Lyman Cutler fired a single rifle shot that heralded the onset of what came to be known as the "Pig War." For a short but troubled season, the improbably remote and otherwise irrelevant speck of San Juan Island threatened to become the site of a nasty military confrontation between the United States and Great Britain.

Cutler was one of a handful of Americans who had drifted down to San Juan from British Columbia's Fraser River gold-rush diggings. He awoke on the morning of June 15 to the derisive laughter of a Kanakan shepherd ("a colard man," Cutler later called him in a sworn affidavit). The Hawaiian was amused at the sight of a Hudson's Bay Company hog rooting in the American's potato patch. Cutler was not amused. He grabbed his firearm and shot the trespassing pig. He soon repented the impulse and offered to pay compensation to Griffin. But when Griffin responded with threats to remove Cutler and the other Americans from the island, tensions quickly escalated. Cutler complained to General William S. Harney, commander of the U.S. Army's Department of Oregon. Griffin complained to Douglas. Harney ordered troops from Fort Bellingham to bivouac on San Juan to protect American settlers. Douglas ordered two Royal Navy vessels to proceed to "Griffin's Bay" on the leeward side of San Juan Island.

On the morning of July 26, 1859, Griffin awoke to the sound of an approaching steamer, its "great cylinders panting and clanking over the flat, gray inland seas," as National Park Service historian Michael Vouri describes it. The racket came from the U.S. propeller *Massachusetts*, a steamer-sailor mounting eight thirty-two-pound cannon. She could wheeze out three knots an hour under steam and under ideal conditions do somewhat better under sail, though then and later canvas was a dubious means of propulsion on the wind-fickle and current-riven inland waters. On lease from the navy to the army, the *Massachusetts* was a venerable vessel, having served more than a decade earlier as General Winfield Scott's headquarters during the siege of Veracruz in the Mexican War.

As Griffin looked on with mounting apprehension, the *Massachusetts* dropped anchor and swung lighters down from its davits to ferry a company of fifty-seven soldiers ashore. Forty of them were Irish immigrants. Their commander was a wispy thirty-four-year-old Virginian, Captain George Edward Pickett.

Fey and impetuous, Pickett had placed last in his West Point class but had fought with bravado in the Mexican War, notably in the assault on Chapultepec Castle. In the intervening years he had soldiered against Indians in Texas and in the Puget Sound country and fathered a son with a Northwest Indian woman who died shortly after childbirth. Just a few months hence Pickett would abandon the child, resign his U.S. Army commission, leave Washington Territory forever, travel incognito to the East Coast, join the Confederate army, and set out on the road that eventually brought him up to the cannon's mouth in the swale below Cemetery Ridge at Gettysburg. Pickett thus took his conspicuous place alongside the turncoat Braggs and Beauregards whom Edward Everett Hale sought to vilify.

On this summer morning on San Juan Island, Pickett with characteristic abandon ordered his troops to pitch their conical Sibley tents on the barren hillside just above Griffin's dock, where they would be plainly exposed to naval gunfire. He neither fortified nor entrenched his position.* No less irresponsibly, moments after splashing ashore Pickett posted a proclamation that began "this being United States territory"—a claim that his own government had not made and that the British government, especially in the person of James Douglas, was not about to honor.

As they set about the familiar military routine of making camp, Pickett's soldiers may well have stopped to wonder where fate and their feckless commander had brought them. A majority of them had transited the Atlantic from Ireland's vales and lochs only to find themselves posted to North America's far Pacific shore and deposited on a stony beach thousands of miles from nowhere. As Hale was shortly to muse, this barely peopled bit of forest and rock at the edge of Puget Sound must have struck them as the farthest back of beyond, as distant a place as could be imagined from whatever they had dreamed of as their immigrant destination, not to mention its distance from the defining terrain of their old-country youth.

---

* Within weeks, an engineering unit arrived to begin the construction of earthen fortifications. Its commander was Second Lieutenant Henry Martyn Robert. His work is still visible today, its precise, methodical layout typifying the peculiar genius of the author of *Robert's Rules of Order.*

The south end of San Juan Island, then and now, combined formidable weather with awesome vistas. Pickett's campsite lay in the figurative cross-hairs of the Strait of Juan de Fuca, a seventy-mile-long meteorological gun barrel that Nature loaded and cocked in the open Pacific and aimed directly at the island's southern tip. The Gulf of Alaska brewed up immense tempests that shot roiling, moisture-freighted storms down the strait. Their drenching rains and scouring winds had long since scrubbed the ridge above Griffin's dock clean of all vegetation save a patchy carpet of bunch-grass. Yet on a clear summer day, far down the sleeve of Puget Sound to their south, Pickett's troops could spy the topmost part of Mt. Rainier's towering cone—the earth's curvature having swallowed the lower twelve thousand feet or so. With no more than a swivel of his head a man standing above Griffin's landing could sweep his gaze over two soaring, serrated mountain ranges, their crests ever-snowy in this far northern latitude. The Olympics rose across Admiralty Inlet to the southwest, a long shoulder of peaks crowning steep hillsides black with dense Douglas fir and cedar forests. The Cascade range loomed beyond the other islands of the San Juan archipelago to the east, its rugged summit-line punctuated by the glaciated mass of 10,700-foot-high Mt. Baker. Minke whales, harbor seals, Dall's porpoises, enormous schools of spawning salmon, and great pods of orca whales frequently broke the gray surface of the surrounding sea, while noisy gaggles of pelagic birds—gulls, diving ducks, cormorants, and guillemots—wheeled overhead in the brine-scented marine air.

But if Pickett's soldiers did in fact pause to take in the scenery, their reverie was soon broken. On the evening of June 29, the HMS *Tribune*, a thirty-one-gun steam frigate and the first of the two warships Douglas had ordered to San Juan, hove into Griffin's Bay. In the lingering evening light, Captain Geoffrey Hornby anchored the *Tribune* to present a fifteen-gun broadside to Pickett's exposed position. Hornby then came onto the beach and confronted the American commander with the prospect of putting a large British military force ashore. Pickett reportedly replied that if Hornby did so the outnumbered but defiant Americans would "make a Bunker Hill of it." Hornby prudently decided to await further orders.

Some writers have seen more than rash bravura in Pickett's threat, as well as in Harney's orders that had brought Pickett to San Juan in the first place. In this view, Pickett and Harney deliberately set out to provoke a fight with Britain in the distant Northwest in order to preoccupy the American armed forces while the Confederacy struck for its independence in the South. The cast of characters on San Juan, as well as the coincidence of events there and elsewhere in 1859, lend superficial plausibility to that theory. Pickett was a Virginian, after all, and Harney a Tennessean. Harney in particular had a reputation for insubordination. During the Mexican War he had several times violated his orders and launched unauthorized attacks on Mexican positions. He was also notoriously bloodthirsty. During the siege of Chapultepec, he had lined up several Irish-American deserters on a gallows facing the castle, melodramatically dropping the traps beneath them just as the U.S. flag was raised over the captured battlement—raised, as legend has it, by First Lieutenant George Pickett. And just weeks after Hornby and Pickett faced off on Griffin Bay, three thousand miles to the east John Brown descended on the federal arsenal at Harpers Ferry, Virginia, in his futile crusade to ignite a slave insurrection—a dramatic signal that sectional tension over the slavery issue might not be reconcilable by political means.

Yet the fact remains that in 1859 the Confederacy had not yet formed, and not a scintilla of reliable evidence has ever emerged to support the extravagant notion that the Pig War was the product of a secessionist cabal. Moreover, it was yet another southerner, Pickett's fellow Virginian and U.S. Army General in Chief Winfield Scott, who made sure that the dust-up at Griffin's Bay did not explode into a full-scale British-American war.

Scott, a stickler for formality and a man of unbending principle, popularly known as "Old Fuss and Feathers," had a nose for cabals. As a young officer he had briefly left the army after accusing General James Wilkinson of complicity in the same Burr conspiracy that had ensnared the fictional Philip Nolan. Scott also had a history with Harney, whom he had tried unsuccessfully to restrain on several occasions during the Mexican War. Now it fell to the seventy-three-year-old Scott to play the sober senior statesmen to his headlong young subordinates shooting craps with their nation's security on the isolated northwestern frontier.

Distance itself shaped the course of events—for Scott, and for others. The very isolation of the Puget Sound country, beyond the easy reach of either Washington or London, had given Harney and Pickett, and Douglas too, wide scope for discretion as well as mischief. Scott's role in the Pig War drama now unfolded according to the deliberate cadences of mid-nineteenth-century technologies of communication and transport. On July 19, Harney drafted a message informing Scott about the situation on San Juan. The dispatch went first by ship to Panama, then by railroad across the isthmus, then by ship again to New York, where Scott got to read it only on September 3. Scott then departed for Puget Sound, passing down the American Atlantic coast, across the Gulf of Mexico, through Panama, and up the Pacific coastline of Central America, Mexico, and Baja California. He arrived at San Francisco in the same week that John Brown, unbeknownst to Scott or anyone else west of the last telegraph station in Fort Leavenworth, Kansas, attacked Harpers Ferry. On October 24, Scott entered Puget Sound, boarded his old command ship, the *Massachusetts*, and proceeded to parley with local officials, American as well as British. He swiftly concluded that Harney and Pickett were surely guilty of poor judgment, but almost certainly not of treasonous conspiracy.

On November 7, Scott's ship arrived off Pickett's camp on San Juan Island. There the tense atmosphere of the summer's confrontation between Hornby and Pickett had given way to a desultory standoff. British ships and troops remained offshore. On the land, the British and American whiskey-sellers and Haida and Salish Indian prostitutes who swarmed about the bedraggled troops in their sorry, rain-drenched billets could not have made for an inspiring sight. Small wonder that Scott chose not to go ashore.

But he did order Harney to back off, and Pickett to stand down. The Pig War thus ended with Lyman Cutler's single cartridge the only ordnance expended, and Charles Griffin's foraging hog the sole casualty. Scott renewed his government's commitment to peaceful arbitration of the boundary dispute. Until a settlement was reached, he agreed to joint military occupation of San Juan Island. A detachment of British troops therefore established itself at newly named Garrison Bay, a pleasantly sheltered inlet on the island's forested northwest coast. About a dozen miles from Pickett's camp, Garrison Bay was immeasurably more hospitable in terrain and climate. Today it forms the decidedly more picturesque half of the National Historic Site that embraces the old American and British camps. It has become the customary venue for the periodic ceremonies that commemorate the Pig War as a monument to British–American harmony.

As for Pickett, he was in command on San Juan Island when the Civil War broke out in the spring of 1861—though it took six weeks for news of the rebellion to reach him. He was still wearing his U.S. Army uniform when the first battle of Bull Run was fought, but shortly thereafter resigned his commission and made his fateful way eastward.

On the island, meanwhile, the British and American occupation forces fraternized without incident for more than a dozen years. Then in 1873 a three-man panel of geographers and lawyers appointed by the designated mediator, Kaiser Wilhelm, voted two-to-one that Haro Strait was the channel that separated Vancouver Island from the mainland, placing the San Juan Islands in the United States. The arbitrators' decision thus "moved" the islands to their permanent location, so far as political jurisdiction was concerned. Their action also ended the last dispute between major powers over territorial sovereignty in North America, and thereby drew in the final lines on the now-familiar map of the lower forty-eight states. For more than a century, the San Juans have been part of America's Pacific Northwest, rather than Canada's Pacific Southwest. Washington, D.C., not Ottawa, defines the political center on whose periphery they lie.

The story of the Pig War suggests the aptness of Hale's simile of 1863, despite my youthful resentment. "Puget's Sound" was then indeed almost inconceivably removed, in space, time, and imagination, from the settled parts of the United States, not to mention Canada. But its very remoteness, and the quite literal *arbitrariness* of the San Juan Islands' eventual disposition, make one wonder what the issue of their ownership could have meant to someone like George Pickett, or William Harney, or for that matter Lyman Cutler. The America they knew was made up of ancestral places and familiar terrain, places long lived in and with dense histories accumulated over generations. By what measure of psychological attachment, blood-tie, or memory could they have cared whether this remote island, with its tiny but astonishingly diverse clutch of freshly arrived Kentuckians, Kanakas, Englishmen, Irishmen, Haidas, and Salish, was or was not part of the United States—attachment to which Edward Everett Hale considered so emotionally indispensable and so politically sacred? What could the idea of America have meant to them? How difficult was it for Pickett to give up his connection to it? How would they have reacted to Hale's patriotic tale?

I frequently think of such questions as I sit on the deck of my house on the west side of San Juan Island, looking out over Haro Strait. On summer evenings I often see Japan-bound colliers, loaded to their Plimsoll lines with Canadian coal, make their way down the international boundary line that divides the strait. The muffled wump of their distant diesels evokes the long-faded clatter of the *Massachusetts* that brought Pickett and Scott to the island a century and a half ago. And when I reflect that I sit here watching in affluent, sun-warmed security, while their cargoes come from the Crows' Nest Pass mines in British Columbia, where my Irish immigrant grandfather descended daily into the bowels of the Canadian Rockies to pick-axe a coal face; that unlike Philip Nolan, I have a country—which happens to be America thanks only to the adventitious events that brought my family in four successive generations from Ireland to England to Canada to the United States; that I have made a career out of trying to understand the history of that last place; that I am sitting on a part of that place that but for a single vote of a long-forgotten German arbitrator would have been Canada; that had James Douglas and Charles Griffin been more bold, George Pickett and William Harney still more rash, or Geoffrey Hornby less restrained, the Pig War might just have escalated sufficiently to affect the outcome of the American Civil War, changing all the contours of the subsequent American story—when I think of all these things, I cannot help but be struck by the capriciousness and contingency of history.

Perhaps in no country is that lesson more apparent than in the United States, a wondrously complex society so recently wrought out of a near-vacant continent. No other American place drives the point home more emphatically for me than the San Juan Islands, a site at the outermost edge of America whose fate was decreed by arbitration, a word whose Latin root connotes "uncertainty."

It's also true that age (mine) and history (America's, Britain's, and Canada's) have made these islands into a different place from what they were in the 1850s, or even the 1950s, for that matter. The remoteness that led Edward Everett Hale to equate distance with irrelevancy has now become an asset, not a liability, as Americans who once sought to bring civilization to the wilderness now seek haven in these islands from the hubbub of modern life. And of course the question of sovereignty over the islands, the fundamental question of their color on the map, controversy over which generated the little swatch of history they can claim, has long since been settled—as have the much larger historical questions of Union and slavery that so moved Hale. However immodest the comparison might seem, the San Juans, like America itself, are not simply a place. They are what we, and time, have made of them.

1048 Fifth Avenue. *Museum of the City of New York Print Archives.*

Alice Kessler-Harris

1048 FIFTH AVENUE

A s such things go it is certainly one of the lesser mansions on Fifth Avenue. Number 1048 sits unobtrusively on the southeast corner of 86th Street, its gray brick stones tucked into the surrounding neighborhood. It boasts no sweeping circular driveway; no generous portico flanked by brass or iron balustrades; no defenses against the pedestrian traffic on the sidewalk it directly abuts. This was once the home of a banker who earned his riches in the Gilded Age and who passed it on to a Vanderbilt family widow. Its quiet elegance, its clean lines, its understated solidity, testify to the wealth that once flowed through its rooms. And yet, for many years, these lines concealed a quintessentially American institution that literally captured the efforts of immigrants to meld their New and Old World roots. For nearly forty years, 1048 Fifth Avenue did not function as a mansion at all: it housed the collections of the Yidisher Visnshaftlekher Institut, now officially known as YIVO Institute for Jewish Research. That's the guise in which I encountered it in the fall of 1965.

YIVO specializes in the history of diasporic Jewry. Its mission is to preserve and study the history and culture of a group of the displaced to whom the United States for so long served as a beacon. In pursuit, it collects documents and books that reveal something of a vanished past and makes them available to students and scholars eager to reconstruct

Grateful thanks to Marek Web and Jung Pak.

and interpret it. Created in the city of Vilna in 1925, YIVO focused at first on Yiddish-speaking Eastern European Jewry. Too quickly it found itself in the position not merely of housing past records but of salvaging them from the threat of imminent destruction by the Nazi occupiers of Lithuania. Forced to sort them so that the most valuable could be shipped to Germany, some of YIVO's collectors managed to hide significant portions of the collections within the Vilna ghetto, though much was destroyed or scattered. After the war, survivors gathered what remained of the hidden documents, and whatever they could find of the dispersed materials, and transported them to a branch that had already been set up in the United States. The American center quickly expanded to include the records of Jews who had emigrated to the United States, some before the turn of the century.

In 1955, YIVO brought these tattered records of a destroyed lifestyle into the marbled quarters of 1048 Fifth Avenue. With a generation of refugees and their children in charge of materials that they had sometimes helped to rescue by dint of will and cunning, YIVO became a center where memory lived in many forms. Its halls echoed with argument and debate about what could and should be salvaged; disagreements rooted in prewar politics bounced off every wall. Neither the written not the oral voices would be quiet. By 1965, the archives constituted a treasure trove: account books of immigrant *landsmanshaftn*; the manuscripts of lost poets; handwritten autobiographies of immigrants; the detailed records of institutions constructed to help Jews survive in unfamiliar and sometimes unfriendly worlds. Simultaneously, the library became a repository for the history and culture of these refugees. Books in Yiddish, English, Polish, German, and many other languages lined the shelves. Maps, photographs, memoirs, and an eclectic array of documentary materials appeared in every niche.

The twenty-eight rooms of the Vanderbilt mansion (as everyone then called it) silently embraced their tiny piece of Jewish history. From the street, only a small brass plate announced the building's new role. Inside, the transformation seemed curiously minimal as well. The main dining room served as a magnificently paneled conference room, the downstairs parlors as spacious classrooms. An elegant center hall boasted a subtly carved staircase that led upstairs to a sunbathed library. Though it still looked like the ballroom it had once been, the space with its huge windows and high ceilings, seemed perfectly designed to open the way to the ethereal heights of knowledge. Chandeliers illuminated the cluttered tables of researchers; cloakrooms and anterooms stored books and records. Further upstairs and down the hall, fireplaced sitting rooms and master bedrooms became large, carton-filled offices where survivors of the Nazi holocaust sorted and preserved and made tortured acquisitions decisions on a daily basis.

Filing cabinets, folio boxes, and overstuffed cartons announced the archives and manuscripts collection. These seemed appropriately tucked into the bowels of the house in basement rooms that must surely have fed and housed servants. I imagined the butler and housemaids sitting here over their interrupted meals. Researchers piled their materials on what looked like a large old kitchen table. Here the light was poor, intensifying the sometimes mysterious trajectory of the documents themselves. And here the chief archivist, himself the savior of much of the collection, vigilantly supervised access to it.

At the time I started my research at YIVO, I was one of the displaced. A fairly recent immigrant, product of a refugee family, I was committed to searching the historical record for a past that had seemed irretrievably lost in the destruction of my family and its culture. My parents were Czech citizens, Hungarian by birth and language, and living in Prague when the Germans invaded in March 1939. By dint of well-planned escape routes, they landed safely in England just in time to watch the war begin. They lived out the war there, hoping to return to their childhood homes. When that proved impossible, they dealt with their despair by immersing themselves in British culture. They subordinated language, tradition, and family history to a deep desire to have their children belong somewhere. I came of age in postwar Britain, ignorant of everything Jewish, of my Central European heritage, even of the family past. Graduate school provided an opportunity to discover the breadth of the heritage my family had discarded. YIVO was its medium, a role made all the more evident by its location in the midst of alien walls.

When I first encountered the gentle clutter at YIVO, I neither saw nor felt any contradiction between the space and its contents. For me, the house held other mysteries. Eager to explore a past I could only dimly comprehend, and convinced that revelation lay in the Yiddish words I had by then painstakingly mastered, YIVO seemed a treasure trove waiting to be tapped. Surely its possessions rivaled the valuables once held there by the families of the newly rich.

My first lesson in how precious these objects were came from the archivist who had salvaged many of YIVO's documents and subsequently used them to write classic histories of Eastern European Jewry. Zosa Szajkowski, eminent historian and emigré, guarded his collection as Mrs. Vanderbilt must once have guarded her silver and jewels. Daily, I sat in the basement as a junior archivist slowly brought me one folder, then another. Never two at a time. Between folders, during the long waits, I had plenty of time to contemplate the tensions between the building and the purpose to which it had fallen, but I can't say that I appreciated the ironies of exploring the history of refugees in the home of robber barons. I was too focused on outcomes. Several weeks into the process and frustrated by its slow pace, I approached the guardian of the treasures to ask whether it might not be possible to speed the distribution of manuscripts just a little. He hesitated, stingy as any Midas guarding his wealth, and said he'd think about what I needed. The documents continued their uneven dribble. Not until weeks later did he relent. "Meydele," he said to me as if I had passed some threshold of loyalty to the house, "you have *zitsfleysh*"—literally, the capacity to sit. And he placed the treasures on my table.

Would such hoarding have gone on among the occupants for whom the house was built? At the time, I was hardly conscious of a tension between the mansion's early purpose, to house the rich and privileged, and its present use, to house the records of the unwanted and the displaced. I like to think now that the poignant irony of its double function might have been anticipated by the building's architects. Carrère and Hastings had produced more than one public building. Among the city's most prestigious architectural firms, they had designed and built residences for famous figures such as Elihu Root and several Vanderbilts as well as a handful of churches in and outside New York. But by all odds, their most distinguished work is the main building of the New York Public Library, opened in 1897 at 42nd Street and Fifth Avenue, just two miles from 1048, and not coincidentally the other major site of my research. Like the NYPL, the house at 1048 Fifth Avenue, which they designed in 1912 and whose first occupant took possession in 1914, avoids the appearance of internal as well as external austerity with touches of warmth and welcome. The one seems almost a scaled-down version of the other, its spaces capacious and accommodating rather than overwhelming or grandiose. At 1048 Fifth Avenue, the simple, symmetrical exterior lines are softened by Louis XIII details; the interior spaces, humanized with wood and light.

In my imagination, Carrère and Hastings designed those rooms to signal the public function to which they would soon be put: to mark the transition that was even then turning the lower reaches of Fifth Avenue into the commercial zone that would soon extend northwards. This house could not be compared with Andrew Carnegie's formidable mansion, which stood just a few blocks north on 90th Street. Nor did it reach for the grandeur of the Henry Clay Frick house just half a mile to the south. In size and appearance, it dimly reflected the opulence of Fifth Avenue's Gilded Age, prefiguring instead the more measured display of wealth that accompanied the Depression of the 1930s and the war that followed. The understated elegance of the house encapsulated the declining phases of a historical moment and might well account for its survival. Perhaps its modesty served as a protective cloak. By the 1920s, some of the great palaces on the lower part of the avenue had already been torn down to make way for apartment buildings and office towers. Others had been converted to museums and galleries. 1048 survived intact.

Capacious as it was, 1048 was designed for a more subdued lifestyle than either of its two private owners had once lived. We know very little about William Starr Miller, who commissioned it and lived there until he died in 1943. The *New York Times* described him as a "retired capitalist" when he moved there in 1914 from a much grander place at Fifth Avenue and 11th Street.

Grace Wilson Vanderbilt, the widow of Cornelius Vanderbilt III, bought the house in 1944 after Miller died. For her, too, it was something of a comedown. As the legend goes, Grace Wilson had been born poor and become a showgirl, dancing bit parts on the thriving vaudeville circuit. After her fortuitous and fortunate marriage to an heir to one of the world's great fortunes led his parents to disinherit him, she determined to make her place in society. She was successful beyond her wildest imaginings, forging her way to the heart of New York society by parlaying the family seat at 640 Fifth Avenue (inherited by Cornelius from a forgiving uncle) into a symbolic throne. This fifty-eight-room mansion with its huge ballroom designed to reproduce the one at Versailles became the site of Grace Vanderbilt's famous parties and infamously lavish dinners. Her invited guests included presidents and politicians, diplomats and royalty, celebrities of every sort, all of them magnets for New York's society families. The death of her husband in

1942 left Mrs. Vanderbilt not quite destitute. She gave up the big house and moved to the far more modest twenty-eight rooms at 1048 Fifth Avenue. Half the size of her former home, the new mansion forcibly curbed her extravagant style. She is said to have lived a bitter and lonely life there until she died in 1953. The huge house at 640 soon met the wrecker's ball. 1048 lived on.

When I started to work at YIVO in 1965, I lived in the Bronx in an area peopled by the aging turn-of-the-century Jewish immigrants whose early lives I was trying to recapture and whose memorabilia YIVO was even then collecting. I did not then imagine myself part of this human archive. Yet I could not escape the contrasts and continuities between that neighborhood and the one in which YIVO thrived. The classic postwar red brick row houses of the northeast Bronx, two families to a house and often a third in an illegally converted basement, lined the streets. The ethnically mixed neighborhood boasted all the trappings of escape from poverty: parents lived above or below grown children just starting families of their own; garden ornaments highlighted neat lawns; thriving commercial streets smelled of familiar old-country foods and resonated with its languages. Italian and Yiddish were everywhere. Some days, I wandered the benches on Pelham Parkway to find the oldest and sharpest memories or arranged an interview in a neighborhood settlement house; then I rode the train downtown.

The hour-long subway ride from Pelham Parkway to 86th Street let me out in a different world. Had I walked east from the subway stop I would have been on familiar turf. From Lexington Avenue to the river, Irish working-class houses marked the side streets to the north; Hungarians, Germans, and Czechs still occupied many of those to the south. In the thirties, brown-shirted Nazi sympathizers had paraded along 86th Street's triple-width roadway. I walked west toward the park following an 86th Street that defined the boundaries of Carnegie Hill. Echoes of the neighborhood's former grandeur infused every step. To be sure, by the 1960s, familiar twelve-story apartment buildings defined its face; but from Park Avenue to Fifth, these were (and are) announced by protective canopies and policed by uniformed doormen.

Around the corner on Fifth, new apartment buildings competed with smaller yet still stately houses, each of which once housed a family of some wealth. Some of these had already been transformed into consulates and missions, institutes and libraries. Many of them had recently been restored, their shiny brass knockers reflecting the glory of the surrounding streets. Most of the great mansions had become museums. They housed galleries displaying photography, sculpture, artifacts of industrial design, and the memorabilia of history. To the north, the circular galleries of the Guggenheim broke the plane of the perpendicular buildings. To the south and west, the Metropolitan Museum dominated the vista, overwhelming even the huge adjacent park. The bustle of New York City scarcely invaded the quiet preserves of 1048 Fifth Avenue. Only the traffic that entered and exited Central Park's transverse roads a block or two to the south reminded YIVO's visitors that the world stretched beyond its four walls. On the corner of 86th and Fifth, the peace was disrupted by an occasional dog-walker or a nanny pushing a baby carriage. Their entry into the park lay just across the street through a narrow walkway lined with myrtle and ivy that opened up as if to admit the mansion's occupants to the beauty of their own personal estate.

A couple of years after I had completed my stint at YIVO, my family moved into what I still think of as its neighborhood. For several years, almost daily, I walked my toddler past the closed doors of 1048 Fifth Avenue, admiring the capacity of the building to hide the flurry of activity within. No longer among the displaced, I couldn't bring myself at first to cross the threshold. The doors that had opened to the Old World now felt like barriers to fend off the New. I wondered how the place would appear in my new persona as a successful, and by now thoroughly American, academic. Would it still be an outpost of the displaced in an island of affluence? At last I went back, first for a lecture, then to meet a friend, pick up a student, talk to the new archivist, listen to the voices, and watch the boxes spread as the life of the institute seeped into the building's pores. For all its silence, the building continued still to protect its occupants. Like it, they would survive.

YIVO lived in the Vanderbilt mansion for forty years, making the building a library for about the same length of time it had been a private residence. The organization sold the building in the fall of 1993 in preparation for its move into a new, modern facility that a consortium of libraries and archives would build in lower Manhattan. 1048 is now surrounded by scaffolding. As I pass by, I can still glimpse the marble floors, the wonderful staircase to the library haven. Curiously I watch as the house takes on yet another incarnation: only the fourth in its eighty-five-year history. I am relieved, but not surprised, that it will appear from the outside to be exactly what it has always been: a quiet cloak for the history inside.

Nineteenth-century Elmhurst, then known as Newtown Village. Photo by Vincent Seyfried.

Under the Number 7 Line: Roosevelt Avenue, Jackson Heights–Elmhurst Border, June 30, 1999. Here 83rd Street is also named in honor of Manuel de Dios Unanue. Photo by Jean Anne Leuchtenburg.

William E. Leuchtenburg

QUEENS

I grew up in a place now closing in on a population of two million which does not get a line in the history texts—unlike much less populous communities such as Boston, Charleston, and San Francisco. A land where Late Woodland people roamed and both the Dutch flag and the Union Jack unfurled, an area settled nearly two centuries before Chicago was much more than an outpost, home to two Signers of the Declaration of Independence, it has rarely been regarded as "historic." In the more than seventy years that I have known it, few have thought of it, if they have thought of it at all, as an "American place."

Queens, a county of New York State and since 1898 one of the five boroughs of New York City, occupies the northwestern sector of Long Island above Brooklyn. It is bounded on the southeast by the Atlantic Ocean, on the north by Long Island Sound and the East River, a strait that does a right-angle turn to divide Queens from Manhattan Island to the west. To the east, two other Long Island counties (the first of them Nassau, for centuries part of Queens) meander all the way to Montauk

I am very grateful for literature on Queens thoughtfully sent me by the folklorist Ilana Harlow of the Queens Council on the Arts, author of *The International Express*, an excellent brochure on the Number Seven line; Jon Peterson, co-editor with the prolific Vincent Seyfried of an indispensable guide to research sources on the borough; and Roger Sanjek, who has written extensively and brilliantly on ethnicity in Queens.

Point. Queens comprises more than a third of New York City. With 120 square miles, it is almost as big as Manhattan, the Bronx, and Staten Island put together.

Despite its impressive size, no tourist to New York City thinks of putting Queens on any "must see" list. In the 432-page *Eyewitness Travel Guide to New York City*, Queens rates less than a page and a half. Outsiders have chosen Queens as a destination only if they had a plane to catch at La Guardia or Kennedy airports or were going to a sporting event—to see Tom Seaver and the Miracle Mets at Shea Stadium or tennis matches at Forest Hills or Flushing Meadows, perhaps to bet on the horses at Aqueduct (where Man o' War won a storied victory in 1920)—and even then they were unlikely to be conscious of being in Queens.

Only once in *belles lettres* does Queens emerge, and it is as the nightmare world of "spasms of bleak dust" presided over by the faceless Doctor T. J. Eckleburg with his "blue and gigantic eyes," their irises a yard high, peering out of "enormous yellow spectacles which pass over a nonexistent nose." Jay Gatsby, recalling the "desolate" sight he encounters on a journey from West Egg to Manhattan, ruminates:

> This is a valley of ashes—a fantastic farm where ashes grow like wheat into ridges and hills and grotesque gardens; where ashes take the forms of houses and chimneys and rising smoke and, finally, with a transcendent effort, of ash-gray men who move dimly and already crumbling through the powdery air. Occasionally a line of gray cars crawls along an invisible track, gives out a ghastly creak, and comes to rest, and immediately the ash-gray men swarm up with leaden spades and stir up an impenetrable cloud.

Those who identify with Gatsby's circle at the Plaza have long viewed Queens as a vast dumping ground, as well as a catch basin for sundry vices. You may spend your life in Manhattan, but you spend eternity in Queens—in huge metropolises of the dead, acre upon acre. Of ugly Ravenswood, a WPA guide wrote in the 1930s, "There is hardly a sprout of vegetation, and the drab cobblestone streets stretch sordidly to the river front." Queens has been depicted as the quintessential locale of twentieth-century *anomie* and of virulent racism. It was in Queens in 1964 that Kitty Genovese was murdered, and, though thirty-eight people acknowledged that they had heard her cries, none came to her aid. It was in Queens, at Howard Beach, that a white gang beat three blacks, chasing one to his death under the wheels of a car on Shore Parkway. And on a dreary street in Queens that irascible icon of bigotry, Archie Bunker, dwelt.

Like F. Scott Fitzgerald's protagonist, more recent wayfarers have perceived Queens to be something to be gotten through, eyes averted. A decade after Gatsby's journey, the noisome Corona Dumps were leveled to create the 1939 World's Fair, but traversing Queens remained an ordeal. Travelers regarded it as a purgatory to be survived as, breathing in exhaust fumes on the tortoise-paced Long Island Expressway, they inched toward Sag Harbor and the Hamptons or, bound for Europe, were trapped in a motionless taxi, the meter running, on the Van Wyck—a name to send chills through any tourist—as the minutes ticked by toward takeoff at JFK for Air France to Orly. It was understandably hard for them to imagine that there is a great deal more to Queens than a soulless concrete wasteland of strip malls and convenience stores, and that, not so long ago, Queens was a green and appealing countryside and has reason to command attention now.

I spent most of the first twenty-one years of my life in Queens, and, though I was never a habitué of the Plaza (save for a brief stint, at nineteen, as a bellhop), I shared much of the disdain others felt for where I lived. Born in Ridgewood, just over the Queens line in Brooklyn, I was raised in a number of Queens communities—Woodhaven, Astoria, Winfield, and especially, through all my high school days, in Elmhurst. The names, I can now see, are redolent of the past. Astoria came from the fur merchant John Jacob Astor; Winfield from "Old Fuss and Feathers," the Mexican War hero Winfield Scott; while Currier and Ives chose Woodhaven as a locale for one of their engravings. But I knew nothing of any of that as a teenager when I would stare out of the darkness of the Jackson Theater at the movie screen showing the young hero returning home to the bluegrass of Kentucky or the valley of the Wabash and wish that I came from a real place.

No one could have asked for finer history teachers, but never did any of them suggest that Queens had a history. Instead, in the halcyon days of FDR's New Deal, they focused my attention on the national government. At the age of twelve, I earned enough money tutoring neighborhood kids to take the Number Seven el into Manhattan, board a Greyhound bus, and ride for nine hours to Washington, D.C., where, altogether on my own, I spent three days, wide-eyed, visiting the White House, Congress, and the brand-new marble palace of the U.S. Supreme Court. In later times, I would venture into national political history, especially that of the Roosevelt administration, not into urban history. It has only been in the past year, as I contemplated an appropriate subject for an essay to honor my friend of four decades, Sheldon Meyer, that I gave any serious consideration as a historian to Queens.

Not historic? The very name "Queens," I have learned, derives from the consort of the Stuart monarch, Charles II. That designation came only after a period when Queens was part of the colony of New Netherland. In 1614, a Dutchman, Adriaen Block, was the first European to lay eyes on Queens as he navigated treacherous Hell Gate (a maelstrom that scared me as a child), and another Dutchman, Governor William Kieft, purchased Queens from the Indians. A few years ago, when I lectured at a medieval abbey in the Netherlands, I stayed in Middelburg, what Elmhurst was originally called, and I made a point of visiting windswept Vlissingen, whose namesake, rendered into English, endures today as the bustling Queens community of Flushing.

The Queens Vlissingen provided the venue for one of the earliest chapters in the long struggle for religious liberty in the Western Hemisphere. A zealous Calvinist, the governor of New Netherland, Peter Stuyvesant, imposed a heavy fine on any colonist who permitted a Quaker to enter his home; half of the levy went to informers. In the Flushing Remonstrance of 1657, a town meeting reminded Stuyvesant that citizens were guaranteed liberty of conscience. Infuriated, Stuyvesant retaliated by arresting and imprisoning John Bowne for turning his kitchen over to Quakers for services, though he himself was not a Friend. In Amsterdam, Bowne, banished from the colony, won vindication. The Council of the West India Company ordered the hot-tempered governor to "shut his eyes" to nonconformist worship so long as it did not disturb the peace. As a boy, I only dimly grasped the significance of "Bowne House," and I never troubled to visit it on my many rides on the Number Seven train from Elmhurst to Flushing. Only subsequently did I find out that nine generations of Bowne's descendants lived in that house, which still stands.

In 1652, five years before the Flushing Remonstrance, New England Congregationalists crossed over to Long Island and, in the locale of later-day Elmhurst, founded what the Dutch called Middelburgh but the Yankees thought of as a "New Town," to distinguish it from a settlement that had been wiped out nine years earlier in an Indian uprising that in Westchester County took the life of Anne Hutchinson. (The school I attended in the 1930s, Newtown High, drew its name from that designation.) They built cottages of thatch and stone; laid out farms; raised cattle; trapped wolf and fox; planted cherry orchards, lilacs, hollyhocks, and sweet william; cultivated "Newtown Pippin" apples; picked wild strawberries; went off on "clamming frolics"; dug a pond on which skaters glided on moonlit winter nights; and erected a gristmill in a terrain of massive nut trees and fresh and salt meadows that called to mind Cambridgeshire. Before long, Newtown's growers were marketing flour and meat in the wealthy Caribbean colonies, but in the eighteenth century, quarrels with the British (who in 1664 had succeeded the Dutch as rulers) cast a somber cloud over the flourishing economy.

When in my history classes in Queens schools I studied the American Revolution, I learned of the Boston Tea Party and Bunker Hill, but not that in 1774 Newtown freeholders had created a committee of correspondence which adopted resolves protesting that the late acts of Parliament were "absolutely intended to deprive His Majesty's most dutiful and loyal subjects ... of their most inestimable rights and privileges." Nor did I know that, after defeating George Washington at the Battle of Long Island to the south, the British occupied Newtown, as well as Jamaica and what the redcoats were pleased to call "the famous and plentiful town of Flushing." In 1782, the British forces there were honored by a visit from His Royal Highness William Henry, Duke of Clarence, subsequently King William IV.

The occupying army did not depart until 1783, seven grim years later. In Newtown, where ten thousand plundering redcoats bivouacked, General Sir William Howe resided in a house still there when I was a boy. The octagonal Dutch Reformed Church served as a powder magazine. For firewood, they devastated all that was left of the primeval forest, tore out the pews of the First Presbyterian Church, and even sawed off its steeple; the pulpit they used for a hitching post. With the surrender of Cornwallis, large numbers of George III's followers abandoned Queens to rebuild their lives in the Maritime Provinces. Loyalists from Queens founded the city of St. John in New Brunswick; its first mayor had tilled a farm in Flushing.

Just as I had been unaware that there had been redcoats where I lived, I would have been shocked to have been told that by the end of the seventeenth century, Newtown's 1,100 residents included one hundred black slaves. With the smugness of other northerners, I looked down on southerners for nurturing so barbaric a system. Not until recently did I discover that in 1708 an Indian slave and a black woman, denied the traditional Sabbath off, had murdered their owner and his family—and had been tortured and executed in Jamaica, the woman burned to death. As late as 1820, slaves drove the carriage of a prominent Queens landowner. In 1862, the Colored Citizens of Queens County issued a manifesto informing President Lincoln that they wanted no part of his scheme to resettle African Americans on a small island off Haiti, and even after the Civil War Newtown still had a Jim Crow school.

The Civil War, though, little changed the leisurely pace of life in Queens. In the mid-nineteenth century, Newtown was, according to one account, "a pleasant farming country of orchards and meadows, many of which were divided by hedgerows after the English fashion." Here lived both Clement Clarke Moore, author of "A Visit from St. Nicholas," better known as " 'Twas the Night before Christmas," and the merchant Samuel Lord, proprietor of a clothing store that later became Manhattan's upscale Lord & Taylor. My father, born in 1894 on a farm in Astoria, often regaled me with stories of how his father had ferried produce across the East River to Harlem, with its substantial German community.

Queens maintained much of its small-town character well into the twentieth century. When I entered Newtown High School in 1935, one concentration offered was farming, a course of studies available as late as the 1960s. The Elmhurst (formerly Newtown) I knew as a teenager in the 1930s was a place of innumerable grassy lots on which we played baseball and football; on Saturdays, we built campfires in the woodlands of Alley Pond Park by Little Neck Bay. Communities self-consciously modeled themselves on tony London suburbs, as their very names suggest: Richmond Hill, St. Albans, Kew Gardens. I visited one of my high school classmates in Forest Hills Gardens, designed by Frederick Law Olmsted Jr. in the fashion of an English village with an inn, a green, Georgian houses, garden apartments, curvilinear streets, arched passageways, and a tree-shaded square by the railroad depot.

The Industrial Revolution trod only lightly on Queens. For Corona, "industry" meant the manufacture of Tiffany glass; for Woodside, Schirmer Music scores and Bulova watches. In 1853, the German piano maker Henry Steinweg moved to America; two decades later, his son William Steinway, as the family now called itself, developed a large piano factory in Astoria—together with a company town that included a kindergarten and a library. The 1939 World's Fair—to which I was drawn, as to a magnet, day after day at sixteen—highlighted not the heavy industry that begrimed Gary and Birmingham but the consumer culture. It introduced me to television (the RCA exhibit), color film (Kodak), nylon stockings (duPont), and air conditioning (Carrier's igloo pavilion), while the most remarked-upon novelty of the 1964 World's Fair on the same grounds was the Belgian waffle. Each morning on my way to classes at Newtown High, I would see, with a glance to my left, the Durkee spice plant, but that structure bore no resemblance to Blake's dark Satanic mill. In all of Queens, only Long Island City, facing Manhattan, could have been said to be industrial; yet its conspicuous wares were Chiclets, Sunshine Biscuits, and the Silvercup Bread whose tantalizing fragrance sweetened the air as the Number Seven subway I rode home from trips to Manhattan surfaced to become an elevated train on its way to Flushing.

If Queens had a characteristic industry, it was not steel or rubber but entertainment. An indefatigable hiker as a teenager, I often walked from Elmhurst to Astoria, which, I did not begin to comprehend, had been a motion picture capital. My favorite destination was "Bareass Beach," more properly North Beach, where there was a modest landing field alongside Bowery Bay. Those sands on which I skylarked as a boy have long since been tarmac; in 1939, my senior year in high school, the spot became, thanks to the New Deal, La Guardia Airport. On my way to the beach, I would pass the massive Paramount Studios but, fixated like the rest of America on Hollywood, never realized that here, during the silent era, films had been turned out starring Rudolph Valentino, Gloria Swanson, W. C. Fields, Clara Bow, and Dorothy Gish. When sound arrived in 1929, the Marx Brothers made both *The Cocoanuts* and *Animal Crackers* in Queens, and in 1930 a celluloid romance with Maurice Chevalier in love with a chewing-gum heiress, Claudette Colbert, took advantage of the proximity of the Chiclets factory. Edward G. Robinson and Noel Coward appeared in the first talkies made in Queens, and full-length films and short subjects featured Ginger Rogers, Gary Cooper, Jimmy Durante, Bob Hope, and Cary Grant. Starting in 1975, the

Astoria studio enjoyed a renascence with movies such as Woody Allen's *Radio Days*, Paul Newman's *The Glass Menagerie*, and *The Exorcist*. More recently, it has housed two television series, *Sesame Street* and *Cosby*, and has shared quarters with the Museum of the Moving Image. In neighboring Long Island City, Silvercup Bread has become Silvercup Studios, which turns out television productions such as HBO's raunchy series *Sex and the City*.

Quite apart from the impact of Queens on motion pictures and television, it has made an impression on twentieth-century America to an extent that I now find surprising, though this period has long been my specialty as a historian. At Grover Cleveland High, one of Newtown's rivals, a New Deal mural project gave young Jackson Pollock the opportunity to mount a scaffold and experiment with painting on a large scale. In Corona, the very next town to Elmhurst, resided Louis Armstrong ("Satchmo") from 1929 until his death in 1971. Flushing Meadows–Corona Park, on the site where Jay Gatsby first encountered Daisy Buchanan, served as temporary headquarters of the United Nations after World War II. Queens was home to two Italian-American boys destined to rise high: Mario Cuomo of Ozone Park, who would become a memorable governor of New York State, and an Elmhurst lad called Nino who lived across the street from Newtown High School and would one day be more formally addressed as Justice Antonin Scalia of the U.S. Supreme Court. The first woman to be placed on a national ticket by a major party, Geraldine Ferraro, represented Queens in Congress. In Freedom Summer of 1964, a Queens College senior, Andrew Goodman, volunteered to register black voters in Mississippi, where, together with James Chaney and Michael Schwerner, he would be brutally murdered, a martyr of the civil rights movement.

Why, then, with so rich a past, has Queens failed to make it into the textbooks, rarely been regarded as an "American place"? I once put that question to Mario Cuomo in the course of a rambling afternoon's amiable conversation in the governor's office in Albany, and he replied, "It is a transition place. That's why. It has no permanence." People buy their first houses there, then move on, he said. "So it doesn't have a history because it doesn't have continuity." I thought of my mother, born Lauretta Cecilia McNamara in County Limerick, who arrived in America from Ireland as an infant; grew up in Hell's Kitchen on the west side of Manhattan; came to Queens from New Jersey, but later returned to

New Jersey, where she died; and I surmised that Cuomo had one part of the answer—but maybe not the whole answer.

The distinguished urban historian Kenneth T. Jackson has suggested to me a different solution: that Brooklyn, which seems similar to Queens but has a much more sharply defined identity, was a single community—Brooklyn Heights—that expanded into the surrounding area, whereas Queens was a congeries of villages and towns. Today, he points out, Queens has six separate post offices, unlike Brooklyn, which has only one. There is, in fact, no such postal address as "Queens."

The Queens College historian Jon Peterson, one of the foremost authorities on the borough, has amplified Jackson's perception with his own insights. The incorporation of Queens into the greater city in 1898, he maintains, was a traumatizing event. "Queens was a fabrication from on high," he has written me. "All institutional structures that sustain local identity (town governments, voluntary fire departments, local police and schools) stopped. The sense of localism perished." As befitted a fabrication, the city renamed almost all of the streets in the most mechanistic way, so that, even today, they march across the landscape number by number. Unlike the Bronx, with its Grand Concourse, Queens, he observes, never developed a center. Furthermore, he remarks, the sheer size of Queens militates against a holistic sense. Certainly that has been my own experience. When I am birdwatching in the marshes of the wildlife refuge at Jamaica Bay, which empties into the Atlantic Ocean, I feel light-years removed from Long Island City, which, many miles to the northwest, stares across the water at the United Nations.

Yet another response to the question is that Queens has had an underdeveloped sense of its own history. Writing in the late nineteenth century, an amateur chronicler, impressed by a roadside commemorative marker he had seen on the Boston Post Road near Groton, Connecticut, commented:

> The history of Newtown [in Queens] goes back to a date antecedent to that of many of the New England towns. One would suppose that the historic sites ... would be as interesting to the descendants of the Newtown settlers as to those of the settlers of New England, and yet while memorials of one kind or another are common throughout the latter region, where is there anything of the kind in Newtown?

Indeed, Newtown had so little pride in its past that in the 1890s it obliged the whim of a real estate developer, Cord Meyer, by surrendering its seventeenth-century name and taking on a new designation: Elmhurst. (Little wonder that when I was appointed to the De Witt Clinton chair at Columbia University, I had not the foggiest notion that Governor Clinton had sketched the plans for the Erie Canal at his summer home in Maspeth, bordering on Elmhurst.)

One explanation, however, looms larger than any other: that Queens has seemed so insignificant because it is dwarfed by the towers across the East River, though that consideration also applies to the other outerboroughs. Even when a new cocktail was created in Queens, it was named a "Manhattan." Though we all understood in the 1930s that, by statute, Queens was every bit as much a part of New York City as any other borough, when one of us said, "I'm going into the city," everyone understood that to mean, "I'm going into Manhattan," for only there did one find the real city: Jascha Heifetz at Carnegie Hall, Carl Hubbell and Mel Ott at the Polo Grounds, Santa Claus at Macy's. I felt deep affection toward much about Elmhurst and Jackson Heights—streets lined with Norway and silver maple, sycamore and rose of Sharon; classes, clubs, and pals at school; the airy, inviting branch libraries; countless baseball and football games on vacant lots—but Manhattan was where one found the action.

Decades later, that continued to be true. The answer to a recent crossword puzzle query, "Suburb of Manhattan," turned out to be "Queens." Though it plays at Shea Stadium, the National League baseball club is not called the Queens Mets (unlike the former Brooklyn Dodgers, proudly named for their borough) but the New York Mets; even the team's logo is the Manhattan skyline. In that sense, "Queens" is both a specific locale and a metaphor for all those places across America whose identity is devoured by megalopolises—like Irving, Texas, where the "Dallas" Cowboys hold forth.

While I was growing up, bridges and trains were tying Queens ever more closely to Manhattan. From the nearby el platform, 82nd Street Jackson Heights, you could see all the way to the Empire State and Chrysler buildings some six miles distant, as you can today, despite the intervening years of construction, and the Number Seven sped you to Grand Central Station in only twenty-one minutes. In the 1930s, there were new ligaments: the Independent subway line, which my father took to work at the huge post office across from Pennsylvania Station, and a magisterial three-borough bridge bonding Queens with both Manhattan and the Bronx. On a sultry July day in 1936 when it opened, I was, at age thirteen, the first person ever to walk all the way across the Triborough Bridge and then all the way back to Queens. (I make that claim confidently, because no one else could have been so daft as to attempt such a feat.)

Every summer when I was a teenager in the Great Depression a night would be so stultifying and Manhattan so enticing that, with only two nickels rubbing together in my pocket, I would leave my claustrophobic apartment in Elmhurst and start walking. I would tramp block after block, mile after mile, through Jackson Heights, Winfield, Woodside, Sunnyside, Long Island City, until I reached the Queensboro Bridge, where, in a dark recess, I would find an unreliable staircase and climb until I reached a parapet walkway that would take me west, over the black, worrisome waters of the East River 135 feet below, toward the lights of Manhattan. On the far side, I would descend, then doggedly resume my walk until I reached brightly lit Grand Central Terminal, where, after mingling with the bustling crowds and soaking up some of the spirit of the big city, I would part with one of my nickels for a Coke at a drugstore soda fountain in the station. Reluctantly, knowing that only the lassitude of nighttime in Queens lay ahead, I would cough up the remaining nickel for a subway-el trip on the Number Seven Flushing line that took me home.

Manhattan gave me the feeling, as Queens never did, that I was making my place in a larger world. When Newtown High School played in citywide basketball tournaments, I would take my seat at the press table in the old Madison Square Garden pretending, at age fifteen, that I was not in the least awed by the alignment: the *New York Times*, the *Trib*, the *World-Telegram*, the *Journal*, the *Sun*, the *Post*, and *me*. On other occasions, proudly flourishing credentials I had coaxed from the weekly *Jackson Heights Journal*, I posed questions to Burgess Meredith and other Broadway actors at Manhattan press conferences. For my school magazine, I wrote a review essay of a Julien Duvivier film I saw at a 42nd Street movie palace that had lately been a burlesque house, and by boarding a transatlantic liner at the Hudson River docks before departure time I got Duvivier's autograph—as, one fabulous summer day, I obtained those of a promising track star ("Good Luck, Jesse Owens, Ohio State") and the 1936 Olympics team about to cross the ocean to Berlin.

Manhattan had exotic Harlem and Chinatown, but Elmhurst was as white as Silvercup Bread. There was, to be sure, ethnic diversity, but wholly within a European matrix. Though some of my friends had English names (Bill Westley), most were Irish (Kay Kelly) or German (Charlie Preusch) or Italian (Al Spano); at a time when anti-Semitism was endemic (the cornetist across the dumbwaiter shaft in the adjacent apartment belonged to the Christian Front), my inseparable chum was Ralph Kisch, who had escaped Hitler in 1933. That composition largely characterized the rest of Queens too. In the nineteenth century, College Point, it has been said, "might well have been transplanted from Germany's Ruhr," and Astoria, a refuge from the Irish potato famine, named streets "Shamrock" and "Emerald." For years, my McCann and McNamara relatives lived there. To this day, bars in Woodside divide their clientele not along ethnic cleavages but on Irish county lines; Kerry men go to one pub for their Guinness, Dubliners to another. Among the many thousands of students who went to Newtown High School with me, I cannot recall a single black, Hispanic, or Asian face. As late as 1960, Elmhurst-Corona was 98 percent white.

I did not get the first hint that the universe of my teenage years was changing until 1977, when I returned to Elmhurst to be inducted into the Newtown Hall of Fame. Each year the high school adds one name to a plaque in the foyer; the roster includes appellate court judges, star athletes, a president of the New York Stock Exchange (Richard Grasso '64), and a Metropolitan Opera diva (Risë Stevens '32). At lunch after the ceremony, where I had spoken in an auditorium of more than a thousand seats that I had not seen since I was a sixteen-year-old, I mentioned that I had studied Latin at Newtown—only to be told that Latin had just been dropped "because of the changing ethnic character of the neighborhood." In its place: Mandarin Chinese. There was also, I heard, an enhanced Hispanic presence blending with the Asian, and that afternoon, in the shadow of the Roosevelt Avenue Number Seven el tracks, I spotted a café with the improbable name "Casa Wong." For the most part, though, Elmhurst seemed much as I had remembered it. I should have been more observant. In 1972, a Geeta Hindu Temple had opened near the high school, and by 1976 Newtown High was only 38 percent white.

Nothing about that preview prepared me for what I would find on a late June day in 1999 when I went back to Queens to show my wife, born on an Indiana farm, my childhood haunts. As I had done countless times in the 1930s, I led us down level by level at Grand Central until we reached the very lowest subway platform, where we caught the Number Seven Flushing line. When, minutes later, the train rose above ground to the din of squealing brakes, Queens emerged as an unprepossessing, gritty industrial backyard. With Silvercup taken over by the media, I missed the wonderful aroma of freshly baked bread at Long Island City, where the Sunshine Biscuit and Adams Chewing Gum plants have been absorbed by an International Design Center. The most conspicuous aspect of the landscape as the train rattled on was a plague of scabrous graffiti. They disfigured mile after mile of stores and apartment houses; they were even scratched into the glass of the train doors, so that it required an effort to see out. Still, change, no matter how unwelcome, is to be expected. What truly jolted me was the vista I encountered when we got off at my old station stop, 82nd Street Jackson Heights.

The block I once knew so well looked like a movie set devised by Cecil B. DeMille in one of his more extravagant moments to represent a town somewhere south of the border. Almost all the familiar landmarks—the ice cream parlor, the florist, the deli where my father sent me for hot pastrami on rye—were gone. In their place was an array of enterprises with signs such as COMIDA RAPIDA (fast food), ABOGADO (an immigration lawyer), CARNICERIA (a butcher shop featuring *fiesta* specials), and, in a storefront window, CONSULTAS ESPIRITUALES and ARTICULOS RELIGIOSOS. A small travel office advertised airfares to popular destinations: Bogotá $529, Lima $349, Guayaquil $349. A moneychanger published currency rates: Brazil .49, Costa Rica .59, Chile .29. Casa Wong had disappeared, but another restaurant, La Nueva Chinita, plugged COMIDAS CHINA Y LATINA.

A walk through my old neighborhood deepened the sense of disjuncture. Developers had long since devoured the diamonds and gridirons on empty lots, and when I reached my old apartment house, its number sign askew, I found that the schoolyard across the street, on which for years I had played basketball and stickball, had been consumed by an elementary school bursting at the seams. On the bridge across the Long Island Rail Road tracks, I could espy the towers of Newtown High School in the distance, as I had on many a frosty day in the late thirties, but in every other respect the setting was unrecognizable. On the avenue where once there had been an old-fashioned ice cream parlor now stood the Grace Chinese Lutheran Church, Seventh Day Adventist Chinese Church, Chinese Church of the United Brethren in Christ in Queens, and the Centro Civico Colombiano. A food store offered ECUATORIANA COMIDA, while a mail service promised delivery of parcels to CENTRO Y SUD-AMERICA PUERTA A PUERTA.

The zip code for Elmhurst, so Rinso white only one generation before, is, I learned, now the most ethnically diverse in all the United States. From 1990 to 1994 alone, legal immigrants from 123 nations—China and Guatemala, Ghana and Bangladesh, and more than a hundred others—crowded into this space of little more than two square miles. At Newtown High School, the impressive principal, John Ficalora, told me that students hear at home forty separate languages. The Newtown Centennial Committee's cookbook with which I was presented starts off with a recipe for *bandeja paisa*, a beans-and-plantains dish contributed by a man from Medellín, Colombia. The pamphlet was typed by Gee Kay Cheung and Chi Yao Chen. Two white congregations in Elmhurst—Methodist and Christian Science—have folded and have sold their buildings to Korean churches. St. Bartholomew's in Elmhurst, where my mother was a sometime parishioner, celebrates masses not only in Spanish but also in French—for devout Haitians—and the rebuilt First Presbyterian Church, a bastion of the Patriot cause in the American Revolution, welcomes congregants from Nigeria and Togo. In the "Baxter-Roosevelt" tract where I was raised, whites in 1990 numbered only 4,757, in contrast to 1,029 blacks (almost all Haitian), 11,710 Asians, and 17,125 Latin Americans. Near the Clement Moore Homestead Park, close to an apartment house where I spent my final grade school years, one of the last Irish pubs in Elmhurst, shamrocks in the window, has hired a Mexican disk jockey—in a neighborhood that now includes a Dominican hair salon, an Indian pizza parlor, and Malaysian, Thai, and Vietnamese restaurants. The Elmhurst Branch Library, from which I had borrowed Ibsen's dramas and Galsworthy's *Forsyte Saga*, makes materials available in Urdu, Gujarati, and Hindi, and across from the Elmhurst Hospital, where my father died, Chinese men perform graceful *tai ch'i* exercises.

We reboarded the el and at the end of the line came upon a scene in some ways even more exotic than that on 82nd Street. Flushing, where President George Washington had once paid a visit to America's first commercial nursery, looked like downtown Taipei and Seoul conflated. Stores identified themselves in Chinese or the blockier Korean lettering; a few made no concession at all to English. On Main Street, a Chinese baby dozed in a carriage, and at one stand an elderly man with a Fu Manchu beard looked like someone you might see in Nanking. Not many blocks from the Bowne House, the dormer-windowed saltbox shrine of the seventeenth-century Quaker remonstrance where William Penn had once stayed, a Hindu temple with carved elephant heads enables the devout to offer coconut milk to their deity.

Our experience in Queens reflects a little-noted phenomenon: more foreign-born are living in the United States today than at any time since the barriers against immigrants were raised in the 1920s, and, with nine hundred thousand legal newcomers each year, we are witnessing the biggest wave of immigration since the first decade of the twentieth century. A 1965 act ended Asian quotas, while, by the hundreds of thousands, Latin Americans have headed north. In the mid-1970s, *every* engineering graduate in the Dominican Republic relocated to the United States.

Many from overseas wound up in Queens, whose population, one scholar has said, "may be the most racially diverse in the world." Iranian Jews fleeing the despotism of Khomeini settled in Kew Gardens; Turks clustered in Sunnyside; Forest Hills Gardens, once the enclave of white-shoe Wasps, made room for people from India, Russia, and Israel; and in bourgeois Richmond Hill 40 percent of arrivals from abroad came from Guyana, a country that also furnished numbers of cricketers for matches near Shea Stadium. Within twenty years after enactment of the 1965 law, Flushing had seventy thousand Asian inhabitants.

Some sought to adapt speedily to the U.S. consumer society. At the foot of the 82nd Street el steps, I was accosted by women handing out leaflets with the message "Aprenda inglés ahora," pledging that classes would be taught by "instructores Americanos con experiencia," and on a train platform I glimpsed a young Hispanic woman in a top with the legend TUFTS, while a young man speaking Chinese sported a J. Crew sweatshirt. As we ascended the moving stairway from the Grand Central stop, I overheard a Chinese boy in a BALTIMORE shirt lecturing his mother again and again, "The word is *escalator*, not elevator, *escalator!*" In Christmas season, Asian and Latino children sing "Frosty the Snowman."

More striking, though, is how many are determined to preserve their indigenous cultures and to identify not with the US of A but with their homelands. In Jackson Heights, women in brilliant saris buy boxes of red and yellow mangos; an emporium hawks books in Punjabi and Bengali, as well as holy water from the Ganges; and you can wolf down a Peruvian breakfast or move to the beat of the flamenco or the salsa. Flushing Meadows–Corona Park hosts both Colombian fêtes at which people in Cartagena and Cali T-shirts munch on *chorizo* beneath yellow, blue, and red balloons (marking Colombia's tricolor) and Korean harvest celebrations organized by greengrocers. In tavernas and pastry shops in Astoria, home to the largest Greek Orthodox community outside of Athens, nary a word of English is heard. Afghans, Thais, and Uruguayans send their children off for instruction in their native tongue, and at St. Sebastian's in Woodside, Filipinos worship Santo Niño de Cebu, their island nation's patron saint. On the border of Corona, a concentration of Argentine restaurants calls itself "Esquina Diego Maradona" in honor of the soccer superstar. When a Colombian team defeated a Paraguayan squad, five thousand deliriously happy fans poured out into Roosevelt Avenue, but when, not long after, the United States overcame Colombia in a World Cup match, only one celebrant, a Puerto Rican, turned up, and police escorted him away for his safety.

As the hours went by, I felt increasingly rattled, and at the same time perplexed by why I was so discomfited. Anyone raised in metropolitan New York learns early in life to be at ease in a multiethnic society. Shortly after leaving Queens, I worked for an early civil rights lobby in Washington; at twenty-three, I was the only white on the field staff. When the fair employment bill was filibustered to death, I hitchhiked to the Spanish Southwest, where I lived in an Albuquerque *barrio* for several weeks before taking off for Mexico. In Cuernavaca, where there was almost no other *yanqui*, I bargained in college Spanish each morning in the marketplace for that day's vegetables and fruit.

My uneasiness derived not from ethnocentrism but rather from the sensation that I was a stranger in my own land. When at an 82nd Street luncheonette mainstream enough to be recommended by *Zagat's* I asked the Hispanic waitress what was meant on the menu by "Mix Soup," she did not understand a word I was saying. In the entrance hall of my old high school, a female guard who knew scant English barred my way until I pointed to my name on the Hall of Fame plaque behind her. Newtown students in the 1930s came from diverse backgrounds, but we took for granted a common English tongue and a common culture that had made the transit from the British isles. Almost all of the young people my wife and I came upon as we headed toward Newtown High on that June day in 1999 were speaking Spanish. Beyond any of these impressions was the simple melancholy reality that so much that was familiar had been obliterated.

On the train back from Flushing to Manhattan, as I looked about me and ruminated about what I had seen and heard, the sense of alienation deepened. The man next to me was reading a book with vertical columns of Oriental characters, while across the way a young fellow perused South American *futbol* results in *El Diario*. No wonder, I thought, the Number Seven line is called "the International Express." Not even the street names had been left alone, I grumbled. The corner of 83rd Street and Roosevelt Avenue, where I had often roller-skated as a teenager, had been renamed for Manuel de Dios Unanue, whosoever he might be. I had been dismayed, too, to hear that thousands of students at Newtown High School never hear a word of English at home. What possibly could the future hold for them? And what could the Americans about whom I had been taught—Roger Williams and Thomas Hooker, George Rogers Clark and Kit Carson, Jane Addams and Lillian Wald—possibly mean to them? That afternoon, the last lingering hope that Queens would ever be regarded as historic, as an "American place," evaporated.

But early the very next morning, as I leafed through the *New York Times* on our way north to summer in Maine, I came upon a stunning article. The White House, it reported, had just released a list of sixteen "National Millennium Trails." Most of the selections were predictable— the Lewis and Clark route, the underground railroad, the Mississippi valley from Minneapolis to New Orleans, even the Iditarod dogsled run in Alaska. In this distinguished company, one choice stood out as altogether unanticipated: the Number Seven line from Times Square to Flushing—"that packed, red-bodied snake crawling noisily above Roosevelt Avenue in Queens." It was, the *Times* noted, "the only trail on the list to commemorate social history," for it was the route of a new generation of pioneers—men, women, and children who migrated not to St. Joe or Spokane but, thanks to Number Seven, were "flying above the Irish pubs of Woodside and the Colombian night clubs of Jackson Heights to the jumble of Chinese herb shops and all-night Korean barbecue houses of Flushing."

So Queens has come to be "historic" after all—though not in a way any of us could have imagined in 1938, when in Mrs. Hayes's class we learned about Bunker Hill and Shiloh, John Greenleaf Whittier and Emily Dickinson. Some of the celebration of cultural pluralism implied in the award strikes me as too sanguine. As the new sense of Queens as historic evolves, more than a few legacies of the past centuries that are worth treasuring, paleface though they may be, are bound to be lost.

Still, it did not take many days of reflection to realize that there was a new generation every bit as deserving of a place in the sun as those who had lived centuries earlier, or who had come to Queens in my parents' generation. A bit of sleuthing revealed that Manuel de Dios Unanue was an extraordinarily courageous journalist (the former editor of the leading Spanish-language newspaper) who had exposed drug dealers in Queens and had been cold-bloodedly murdered in an Elmhurst restaurant on orders of a notorious narcotics lord in Cali, Colombia. The editor's name on the signpost gives a distinction to that street corner it never had in my day. But what about those Newtown students whose prospects troubled me? In 1996, Qi Qi Cheng debouched in Elmhurst from Shanghai with hardly a word of English. Less than three years later, she was one of six students in all the city to win a *New York Times* College Scholarship. The twelve thousand dollars bestowed on her (she will get the same sum in each of the ensuing three years) is nearly twice as much as her mother, a victim of the Cultural Revolution, earns in an entire year as a waitress in Chinatown, to which she commutes daily on the Number Seven train. In June, the month of my return visit, Qi Qi was Newtown High School's valedictorian.

Anyway, I have come to recognize, it does not matter what I think about how Elmhurst has changed since my childhood. What I saw on that June day is the way it is going to be. Noting that blacks had adopted the slogan "We shall overcome," the founding editor of the magazine

Latina declared, "Ours is going to be 'We shall overwhelm.'" By the time a white infant born in America in 2000 reaches the age of thirty-five, it will be a member of a minority race. Queens, which once seemed so nonhistoric, prefigures the history of the United States in the twenty-first century. Queens, to borrow the title of the Queens College anthropologist Roger Sanjek's superb book, is *The Future of Us All*.

Battle of Gettysburg. From a drawing by A. R. Wand, 1863.

James M. McPherson

GETTYSBURG

I have lost count of the number of times I have visited Gettysburg. Over the past forty years I have walked, bicycled, and driven around the battlefield and town by myself, with a few friends, and with groups as large as a hundred. I honestly believe that if I were blindfolded and winched down to any spot on the battlefield from a helicopter on a cloudy night, I could remove the blindfold and identify my surroundings within seconds. Gettysburg has come to have a special place in my consciousness, just as it has acquired an unequaled place in the American historical consciousness.

When Congress created Gettysburg National Military Park in the 1890s, the Gettysburg Electric Railway Company owned part of the land on which the battle had been fought. The GERC had begun moving earth to build a trolley line to carry tourists over the battlefield. The company refused to sell its land to the government, which began proceedings to seize it under the power of eminent domain. The case went to the Supreme Court, where the government argued that "the ground whereon great conflicts have taken place, especially those where great interests or principles were at stake, becomes at once of so much public interest that its preservation is essentially a matter of public concern." Nowhere were such great principles at stake more than at Gettysburg, which embodied "the national idea and the principle of the indissolubility of the Union." The Supreme Court agreed, ruling unanimously in 1896 that Gettysburg was vested with such importance for the fate of the United States that the government had the right to "take possession of the field of battle, in the name and for the benefit of all the citizens of the country.... Such a use seems ... so closely connected with the welfare of the republic itself as to be within the powers granted Congress by the Constitution for the purpose of protecting and preserving the whole country."

This ruling established a precedent that made possible the preservation of many other Civil War battlefields where the fate of "the whole country" was determined. Millions of people visit these battlefields every year. Not all of the visitors are Americans, for the Civil War has a striking resonance elsewhere in the world. More people go to Gettysburg than to any other battlefield. They find something moving and powerful in the fields and woods where 165,000 men fought in the largest and most important battle of the Civil War. They find inspiration in the national cemetery that is the final resting place of more than four thousand Union soldiers who gave "the last full measure of devotion" so that "government of the people, by the people, for the people, shall not perish from the earth."

Even the adversaries of the United States in the cold war considered Gettysburg a special place. In 1976 a group of historians from the Soviet Union came to this country to take part in events commemorating the bicentennial of the American Revolution. Their host, a historian of the Revolution and the early republic, asked them which sites they wished to visit. He assumed they would want to go first to Independence Hall, or perhaps Lexington and Concord, or Williamsburg and Yorktown. Their answer was: None of the above. They wanted to start with Gettysburg. Why? asked their astonished host. Because, these Russians replied, Gettysburg was the American Stalingrad—the hallowed ground in America's "Great Patriotic War" that turned the tide toward ultimate victory.

My own serious engagement with Gettysburg began that same bicentennial year, for though I had visited the battlefield twice before, it had been only as a casual tourist. On our way from Minnesota to Baltimore, where I began graduate study at Johns Hopkins University in September 1958, my wife and I had stopped at Gettysburg. We were driving an old Chevrolet, borrowed from my father, and pulling a U-Haul trailer filled with our worldly goods. Like many tourists, we spent only an hour or two at Gettysburg and saw little more of the battlefield than the "high-water mark" where Union forces stopped the Pickett-Pettigrew assault. I had not yet focused on the Civil War era as my field of study. In graduate school I wrote a Ph.D. dissertation on the abolitionists during and after the Civil War, but I considered myself a historian of race relations and civil rights movements rather than a Civil War historian.

My next visit to Gettysburg occurred in 1966, when I again went as a nonexpert with my parents-in-law, who were returning to Minnesota from a visit with us in Princeton, where I had been teaching since 1962. This time we ventured beyond the high-water mark, south along Cemetery Ridge to Little Round Top, stopping halfway to admire that imposing monument to the 1st Minnesota Infantry, which suffered 80 percent casualties in a solo charge to break up an attack by a whole Alabama brigade on July 2. But I still knew little more about the battle than anyone can learn by watching the electric map show at the Visitor Center—which we did on that occasion. Not until my next visit, in 1976, did I really know what I was doing.

By that time I had become something resembling a genuine "Civil War historian." I was teaching the bread-and-butter Civil War/Reconstruction course at Princeton. I had signed a contract with Knopf to write a Civil War/Reconstruction textbook (which became *Ordeal by Fire*, first published in 1982). Perforce, therefore, I had to bone up on the military history of the war. The bias in the halls of academe against military history as a legitimate scholarly enterprise had perhaps subtly influenced me to avoid doing so earlier. I quickly changed my mind. After all, this was a *war*—the biggest war this country ever fought (the 620,000 military deaths in the Civil War almost equal the number of American deaths in all the other wars this country has fought *combined*). Victory or defeat on the battlefield shaped the social and political dimensions of the conflict. Lincoln got the last clause of his sentence right when he said at Gettysburg: "The world will little note, nor long remember, what we say here, but it can never forget what they did here." In his Second Inaugural Address, he got it all right when he said that "all else chiefly depends" on "the progress of our arms."

"All else" included those developments that academic historians *do* consider important: the fate of slavery, the structure of American society, the direction of American economic development, the destiny of competing nationalisms in North and South, the definition of freedom, the very survival of the United States as one nation, indivisible—all rested on the shoulders of those three million men in blue and gray who fought it out during four years of fury unmatched in the Western world between the Napoleonic Wars and World War I. If some of the battles—above all, Gettysburg—had come out differently, the war might have ended with Confederate independence, whose consequences not only for this continent but also for the whole world are incalculable.

The best way to understand those battles is to walk the ground where they happened. If I had not previously realized this, I did so the first time I took students in my Civil War course to Gettysburg in 1976. Most of them had not been there before, and hence had not been able to visualize how geography and topography—the pattern of fields and woods, hills and valleys, roads and fencelines and rock outcroppings and rivers and streams—influenced the tactics and outcome of the battle. Most of the students had read something about Gettysburg before we went there. But not until they saw the ground did real understanding dawn. Not until we saw how the high ground at the Peach Orchard commanded the terrain did they comprehend why General Dan Sickles moved his corps there on July 2. Not until we climbed Little Round Top did they see how its retention by Union forces after desperate fighting shaped the course of the battle. And most of all, not until they first viewed and then walked the three quarters of a mile of fields over which the Pickett-Pettigrew assault took place did they fully grasp why the attack failed. One can read millions of words about the battle of Gettysburg, but only by going there can one really begin to understand it.

This understanding is not only a matter of grasping the topographical and tactical details. Of greater importance, perhaps, is a kind of emotional empathy that one experiences with the men who fought and suffered and died there. "In all great deeds, something abides," wrote Colonel Joshua Lawrence Chamberlain of the 20th Maine Volunteer Infantry. More than anywhere else, the greatness of deeds abides at Gettysburg. One need not be a mystic to sense the presence of ghosts on the battlefield. One needs only a little imagination to hear the hoarse yells of the exhausted survivors of Chamberlain's regiment as they launch their bayonet counterattack at Little Round Top. Few who look east from Seminary Ridge toward the scene of Confederate carnage in front of Union lines at the bloody angle and copse of trees on Cemetery Ridge can fail to see Pickett's broken men come limping back or fail to empathize as they hear Robert E. Lee shoulder the blame with the words "It is all my fault." I know, because I have been there and have felt and heard these ghosts. And so have many of the hundreds of students, parents, alumni, friends, colleagues, and neighbors I have taken to Gettysburg in the quarter century since that first tour in 1976. Powerful emotions have profoundly moved some of these people as they walked this hallowed ground.

Two incidents in particular stand out in my memory. One of the "preceptors" (Princetonese for section leader) in my undergraduate Civil War/Reconstruction course several years ago was a native of South Africa. He had seen bloodshed and tragedy in his own country. He joined our trip to Gettysburg that spring, driving his car with a full load of students. Halfway through the tour he told me that he could not go on; he must return to Princeton. Are you ill? I asked. Not physically, he replied, but the palpable presence of death surrounding us as we trod the battlefield and looked at the regimental monuments listing their casualties was too much for him. He couldn't take it anymore. I had to let him go, for he was in real distress, even though his passengers had to crowd into other vehicles for our return trip hours later.

On another occasion, one of the students on our tour had written her senior thesis under my direction. She had just completed the thesis, a study of Joshua Lawrence Chamberlain, who commanded the 20th Maine in its desperate defense of Little Round Top, where he won a congressional medal of honor. We retraced the attack route of the Confederate brigade that assaulted Little Round Top. When we reached the place where the 20th Maine fought, marked with a monument that Chamberlain himself had dedicated a quarter century after the battle, my student could no longer hold back the tears. Neither could others in the group, who had all read about Chamberlain in Michael Shaara's novel *The Killer Angels*, which I assign in my course. My own voice choked up as I tried to describe the action that took place there during that fateful late afternoon of July 2. Emotions too powerful to explain overtook us; ghosts were unquestionably present.

The site where the 20th Maine fought has become the most heavily visited spot on the battlefield, according to the National Park Service. It was not always so. During my first two trips to the battlefield, in 1958 and 1966, I knew nothing of the 20th Maine's heroics, and no marker existed to inform me. By my third visit, I had read *The Killer Angels*, published the previous year, and I was eager to locate the 20th Maine position. I had to bushwhack my way through the woods to find it. By my next visit, the Park Service, in response to many queries by tourists, had put up a small sign and cut a dirt path to the 20th Maine Monument. By the 1990s, after Ken Burns had vividly dramatized the 20th Maine's fight in the video documentary *The Civil War* (Burns had first learned about Chamberlain from Shaara's novel) and *The Killer Angels* had become the TV miniseries *Gettysburg*, the Park Service had paved the path, lined it with full-color interpretive markers, and put in an overflow parking lot. Those ghosts on Little Round Top now have plenty of live company.

My tours of Gettysburg and other Civil War battlefields developed a symbiotic relationship with my scholarship. Like many others who have stood on the spot where Lincoln delivered the Gettysburg Address, looking out over the graves of soldiers who fought there, I have taken inspiration from his words and their deeds. This experience has enabled me to write of the tragedy and triumph of the Civil War with greater insight and empathy. Touring the battlefield with students had a direct causal relationship with one of my books, *For Cause and Comrades: Why Men Fought in the Civil War*. We always finish our tour by walking the ground over which the Pickett-Pettigrew charge swept forward on the afternoon of July 3. The first time we strolled peacefully across the open fields, knowing that those thirteen thousand Confederate soldiers had come under artillery and then rifle fire almost every step of the way, students asked in awe: What enabled these men to do it? What caused them to go forward despite the high odds of coming out safely? The same question came up again and again, at Gettysburg and other Civil War battlefields, about Union as well as Confederate soldiers. The first few times I could not answer the question—at least to my own satisfaction. I determined to plunge into the writings of the soldiers themselves to look for answers. *For Cause and Comrades* was the result.

That book and my other principal books about the Civil War have been published by Oxford University Press. Sheldon Meyer was my editor for all of them. He has always encouraged me to write with a sense of immediacy and specificity, to turn words into visual images that help the reader to see through the words to the reality. For a historian, there is no substitute for going to the actual *place* where occurred the events one writes about to help one describe them in that concrete, vivid manner. And of all places a Civil War historian can go, none can match Gettysburg, where the pervasive presence of death helps to bring that most crucial event of our past to life.

Monticello. *Copyright 1993 by Robert C. Lautman/Monticello, Thomas Jefferson Memorial Foundation, Inc.*

Merrill D. Peterson

MONTICELLO

O n April 13, 1782, Thomas Jefferson, lately governor of Virginia, welcomed to his home, Monticello, a distinguished guest, the chevalier de Chastellux. It happened to be Jefferson's thirty-ninth birthday. Chastellux, a member of the French Academy, author of *De la Felicité publique*, had traveled westward from Williamsburg, where he was stationed with General Rochambeau's victorious army. His literary portrait of Jefferson was the first to present him to the world in philosophical colors, and it was only enhanced by placing it in the context of the remarkable house this Virginian had raised on a mountaintop in Albemarle County. Chastellux's *Travels in North America* appeared in Paris in 1786 and the next year in English translation.

"Let me describe to you a man, not yet forty, tall, and with a mild and pleasing countenance, but whose mind and understanding could serve in lieu of all outward graces," the Frenchman wrote. "An American, who, without ever having quitted his own country, is Musician, Draftsman, Surveyor, Astronomer, Natural Philosopher, Jurist, and Statesman . . . , finally, a Philosopher, retired from the world and public business, because he loves the world only insofar as he can feel that he is useful." (Jefferson had recently endured the ordeal of legislative inquiry into his conduct as governor.) Chastellux went on to say "that Mr. Jefferson is the first American who has consulted the Fine Arts to know how he should shelter himself from the weather." The house, being in "an Italian style," was well named. A large square pavilion ornamented with porticoes and columns front and back and with small wings on either side made up the ground floor. The lofty salon, Chastellux noted, was "decorated entirely in the antique style." Above it was the library. He noted as well the cellar with its offices, kitchens, and storerooms, which Jefferson intended to join with a terrace at ground level. The house thus described was essentially the first version, later superseded. The visit extended over four days, as these two philosophers found much to talk about. Chastellux said the time passed like four minutes. He went away convinced that his host was a supremely enlightened man. "It seemed as if from his youth he had placed his mind, as he had done his house, on an elevated situation, from which he might contemplate the universe."

The coupling of Jefferson and Monticello is immensely significant for our understanding of both. Rarely in history has a great man encompassed himself so completely in his domicile. President Franklin D. Roosevelt, a frequent visitor, once wrote admiringly: "More than any historic home in America, Monticello appeals to me as an expression of the personality of its builder. In the design, not of the whole alone, but of every room, of every part of every room, in the very furnishings which Jefferson devised on his own drawing board and made in his own workshop, there speaks ready capacity for detail and, above all, creative genius." Jefferson and Monticello are two sides of the same coin. And anyone who has a five-cent piece in his pocket can verify this literally.

But Monticello was more than a house and home. In Jefferson's lifetime it was a farm, or plantation, more accurately the head farm of a group of five farms comprising five thousand forested acres in Virginia's Southwest Mountains. No more than one fifth of the acres were in cultivation. They were worked by up to 120 slaves, of whom half were children under sixteen. Jefferson also, for a time, had a mill on the Rivanna River that flowed in the valley below, as well as simple household manufactories in small shops along Mulberry Row east of the mansion. Of these, the joinery and the naillery were particularly distinguished. Here the quiet and beauty felt at Monticello today gave way before the babble of workmen and children, the clang of hammers, and belching smoke.

Today's Monticello, restored in pristine elegance, is a museum and a shrine. It is dedicated to the memory of its master, architect, and builder, whose fingerprints may be observed in every last detail of the mansion as well as in the surrounding gardens and landscape. An early visitor, George Ticknor, remarked upon "the strange furniture of the walls" of the spacious entrance hall. "On one side hang the head and horns of an elk, a deer, and a buffalo; another is covered with curiosities which Lewis and Clark found in their wild and perilous expedition. On the third, among other striking matters, was the head of a mammoth.... On the fourth side, in odd union with a fine painting of the Repentance of Saint Peter, is an Indian map on leather, of the southern waters of the Missouri, and an Indian representation of a bloody battle, handed down in their traditions." The house was full of books, of course, over six thousand books, which in 1815 became the nucleus of the Library of Congress. The visitor today misses them and wonders how such a great collection could have been accommodated within the walls of the Monticello library. Some of Jefferson's guests found the house too idiosyncratic for their tastes. All agreed, however, on the magnificence of the panoramic spectacle seen from the mountaintop. Here, too, Monticello expressed the mind and temperament of the builder. In William Wirt's classic description:

> It stands upon an elliptic plain, formed by cutting down the apex of the mountain, and to the west, stretching away to the north and the south, it commands a view of the Blue Ridge for 150 miles, and brings under the eye one of the boldest and most beautiful horizons in the world; while on the east it presents an extent of prospect bounded only by the spherical form of the earth, in which Nature seems to sleep in eternal repose, as if to form one of the finest contrasts with the rude and rolling grandeur of the west.... It is fit to nourish those great and high-souled principles which formed the elements of his [Jefferson's] character, and was a most noble and appropriate post for such a sentinel over the rights and liberties of men.

The master's tomb lies on the westerly slope, and the epitaph from his own hand resonates with the rights of man.

Jefferson called the highlands where he lived—the forested hills and valleys, the orange-red soil, the azure sky—"the Eden of the United States." Monticello was an idyll, a dream place, the idealized expression of his soul. It was the center of his domestic affections, which ran deep, as well as his refuge from the heats and turmoils of the world. The pivotal ambivalence of Jefferson's life lay between his sense of civic duty to state and nation in the founding era and his preference for a retired life of farm, family, and books he thought to find at Monticello. His career exhibits an alternating rhythm of withdrawal and return. Thus, in 1781, as the perils of governing hit him during the British invasion of Virginia, Jefferson took leave of his post, retired to Monticello, and renounced public office forever. Then, when his wife died a year later, he was thrown into a stupor that made even Monticello hateful to him. Fortunately, Congress threw him a lifeline: renewal of the commission, earlier declined, as minister plenipotentiary to negotiate peace in Paris. Before Martha's death, he wrote to Chastellux, his scheme of life had been determined: "I had folded myself in the arms of retirement, and rested all prospects of future happiness on domestic and literary objects. A single event wiped away all my plans and left me a blank which I had not the spirit to fill up." Toward the close of the year 1793, he resigned the post of secretary of state in President Washington's admin-istration with much the same resolution as before, "preferring infinitely to contemplate the tranquil growth of my lucerne and potatoes," as he wrote, to the turbulent seas of politics. Then, as his project to rebuild Monticello dragged on and on, he was overcome with ennui and allowed himself to be drawn back into politics as a candidate for the presidency in 1796. It resulted in his becoming vice president, then president four years later. The ultimate withdrawal came in 1809. Nature had intended him for the tranquil pursuits of science, he declared. "Never did a pris-oner, released from his chains, feel such relief as I shall on shaking off the shackles of power." And so he returned to Monticello for a retirement of seventeen years in which he found much happiness but also much distress and disappointment.

Thomas Jefferson grew up at Shadwell, his father's place, and often roamed the adjacent wooded summit that he named, in Italian fashion Monticello, meaning "little mountain." Here, in a decision that many thought whimsical, he chose to build his country seat. Jefferson had just turned twenty-five when he leveled the mountaintop in 1768. A young lawyer-farmer, with a fair estate, he had, in the same year, been elected to the Albemarle seat in the House of Burgesses in Williamsburg, once held by his father, Peter. The site rose about six hundred feet above the Rivanna River and was approached through a gap in the Southwest Mountains running parallel with the Blue Ridge some twenty miles west. The little town of Charlottesville, the county seat, lay three miles away. To build a house with pretensions of elegance on such a site might seem an act of folly. Jefferson may have been influenced by his reading of ancient authors or by modern ideas of the sublime and the beautiful gleaned from Edmund Burke. At any rate, Jefferson liked the view from his little mountain. The grandeur of the natural spectacle uplifted him. "Where has nature spread so rich a mantle for the eye?" he exulted. "Mountains, forests, rocks, rivers. With what majesty do we ride above the storms! How sublime to look down into the work-house of nature, to see her clouds, hail, snow, thunder, all fabricated at our feet! And the glorious sun when rising as if out of distant water, just gilding the tops of mountains and giving life to nature." Actually, water was the one ingredient missing in the landscape, but, as if compensating for that, Jefferson called the grand vista to the east his "sea view."

For the design of the house Jefferson turned to the sixteenth-century Italian Andrea Palladio, who had gone to Roman antiquity for his models. He learned architecture, as he learned most things, from books. The neoclassicism he got from Palladio's *Four Books of Architecture* appealed to him because in that, rather than in the vernacular of his own time and place, he discovered a definition of beauty as universal, chaste, and orderly as the Newtonian laws of motion. The versatility Jefferson demonstrated in this first "essay in architecture" marked a permanent trait, one that exploded in all directions.

The house Jefferson designed, the one to which he brought his bride in 1772 when it was little more than a shell, and which was essentially complete when Chastellux visited a decade later, was a two-story central block with octagonal bays on three sides. The design called for a double portico, Doric capitals below, Ionic above, but the upper one was apparently omitted. Jefferson's plan also called for L-shaped wings of dependencies sunk into the hillside on either side, terminating in small pavilions and covered by a terraced walkway at the level of the first floor. This radical solution to the problem of utilitarian outbuildings would not be realized until much later. Jefferson had plans, too, for extensive gardens in the new English landscape style; however, these remained but a sketch on his canvas and, indeed, would never be realized as he hoped.

Jefferson set out to rebuild his house in 1794, and it was substantially completed fifteen years later upon his retirement. The two reasons usually offered for this undertaking are first, that he needed more room for his own comfort and for his extended family; and second, that he wished to incorporate in the mansion features of convenience and of beauty he had observed with his own eyes in Europe. Previously he had studied architecture in books; in France he saw the noblest models. And so, in 1785, in association with the architect Clerisseau he designed a new capitol for the Commonwealth of Virginia after the Maison Carrée at Nimes, "the best morsel of ancient architecture now remaining," he said. When it rose in Richmond, the capitol became, in Fiske Kimball's words, "the first monument of the classical revival in America." In Paris he was "violently smitten" by the Hôtel de Salm, a majestic new town house crowned with a dome on the Seine. A dome became the paramount feature of Jefferson's new vision of Monticello. At bottom, what mattered most was the master's exuberant passion for building. "They was a forty years at work upon that house before Mr. Jefferson stopped building," his slave Isaac recalled. Monticello was the work of a lifetime, a continuing act of creation and re-creation, Jefferson himself said, "and so I hope it will remain during my life as architecture is my delight, and putting up and pulling down, one of my favorite amusements."

The new Monticello began with pulling down the walls of the east front and doubling the breadth of the house. The doors from the re-mounted portico led into a large airy hall intended not only as a gathering place but as a museum. To the sides three bedrooms and a book room, or library, were added. The southern breadth of the house was Jefferson's private domain, his "sanctum sanctorum," as an early guest called it, and it adjoined his bedroom. The two octagonal bays were flanked by an arcaded loggia, or piazza, used as a greenhouse. This was duplicated on the north side. The parlor was unchanged structurally. Above it rose the dome in the space earlier given over to the library. A new parquet floor of beech and cherry was a brilliant feature. The Corinthian capitals and rich entablature of the parlor contributed to make it an elegant space. The dining room and tea room remained as before. The second floor was treated as a mezzanine above the entrance hall. Three bedrooms ran off either side. They were reached by ladder-like staircases, two feet wide and steep. Jefferson had an aversion to grand staircases, which he may have thought aristocratic but rejected mainly because they consumed too much space. The same reasoning, however, did not keep him from adding a dome. What use Jefferson intended for the graceful octagonal space below was never known, though fables were told about it. Three additional bedrooms on the top floor had skylights. Those on the second story had single sash windows at floor level, melding on the outside into the long windows below. The treatment contributed to the one-story effect of the house viewed from the east front. It looked much smaller than it was. This trick, in the view of some critics, epitomized the main defect of Jefferson's architecture: it sacrificed the use within to the pleasure of the facade.

The house was filled with the furnishings, the pictures and sculptures, the household goods Jefferson had acquired during his five years in Paris. As has been said, he shopped for a lifetime in Paris. Packed in eighty-six crates, the shipment of goods followed him home. Some of the pieces, considered too formal for a country house, were left behind in Philadelphia, when he retired as secretary of state in the new government, but mostly they furnished Monticello. Other furnishings—bookcases, tables, campeachy chairs—were products of the Monticello joinery. Jefferson's taste in painting approximated the cultivated taste of the time. The subject matter ran to the biblical, the classical, and the biographical. Here, too, his taste was refined in Paris. David was the greatest living painter, he thought, as Houdon was the premier sculptor of the age. Jefferson returned with copies of many fine paintings. Some of them are exhibited in the parlor. The attention of the visitor today is drawn to *Herodias Bearing the Head of Saint John*, after Guido Reni, above the mantel, though a discerning visitor during Jefferson's lifetime, George Ticknor, described the picture in that place as "The Laughing and Weeping Philosophers, dividing the world between them." In the polygonal tea room, Jefferson installed on brackets terra-cotta copies of Houdon's busts of Franklin, John Paul Jones, Lafayette, and Washington. His own bust, after Houdon's original, rests on a pedestal in the parlor. Another likeness in marble, by the Italian Cerrachi, long since disappeared, stood on an ornamented column in one corner of the entrance hall directly opposite another of Alexander Hamilton, of which Jefferson was wont to say, "opposed in death as in life."

Reading Jefferson through his house, Americans have expressed sharply contrasting views of the man. "Monticello is a curiosity!" Richard Rush exclaimed. "Artificial to a high degree; in many respects superb. If it had not been called Monticello, I would call it Olympus, and Jove its occupant." Others thought it personal, warm and charming and comfortable. Jefferson was the Great Democrat, as everyone knew. "But look at this!" protested Thomas R. Reed, speaker of the House of Representatives at the turn of the century. "This is inherent. He was an aristocrat." The writer John Dos Passos thought that Monticello was a corollary of the Declaration of Independence: "a house where a free man could live in a society of equals." The dualities of Jefferson's life, synergistic though they might be, were on display at Monticello. Here, Gerald W. Johnson thought, Hamilton and Jefferson, one the hardheaded realist, the other the visionary dreamer, changed places. Monticello was "an amazing palace of gadgets." The swivel chair in the study, the dumbwaiter in the dining room, the "double-acting street car doors" between the hall and the parlor, the clocks everywhere, the polygraph with which Jefferson anticipated Xerox, the wind-vane on the eastern portico that allowed Jefferson to see which way the wind was blowing without getting his feet wet—where was the poetry of these things? Where indeed? Yet there was much poetry at Monticello. Perhaps the truth lay in the tension between the ideal and the real. Thus May Sarton wrote in a poem to the place:

> All the joys of invention and of craft and wit,
> Are freely granted here, all given rein,
> But taut within the classic form and ruled by it,
> Elegant, various, magnificent—and plain.

Landscape—gardens, orchard, vineyard, grove—had taken a backseat to house-building until Jefferson retired to Monticello in 1809. He was an avid gardener. "No occupation is so delightful to me as the culture of the earth, and no culture comparable to that of the garden," he declared. The grounds he desired to improve in the English fashion were not easily managed, as he wrote to his botanical friend William Hamilton in Philadelphia. Spreading over the whole crown of the mountain, "the unfortunate disposition of the ground takes from me the first beauty in gardening, the variety in hill and dale, and leaves me as an awkward substitute a few hanging hollows and ridges." Moreover, under the "almost vertical sun of Virginia, shade is our Elysium," and this worked against the beauties of gardens. But Jefferson persevered. The winding walk with its flower border was laid out; an eighteen-acre grove containing 160 species of trees rose on the northwestern slope; a huge terraced vegetable garden, a thousand feet long, was laid out below Mulberry Row; and a "fruitery" and vineyard rose nearby. These were all parts of the *ferme ornée* that survives gloriously at Monticello today.

Jefferson never ceased to be an active architect. No sooner was Monticello finished than he began to build an amazing single-story octagonal house at his Bedford County retreat, Poplar Forest, eighty miles south. He was fascinated by the octagon form. It was used in the bays at Monticello, of course. Here the inspiration came from the Englishman Robert Morris, whose *Select Architecture* served Jefferson as a copybook. The virtue of the octagon, as a present-day student observes, is "that it gives the illusion of a circular space while retaining flat surfaces for the carpenter and bricklayer." Or for the housekeeper, as furniture fits better against a straight wall. Jefferson, of course, was the architect of the University of Virginia in all its parts, beginning with the buildings and grounds. Its foremost edifice, the Rotunda, is a one-half scale model of the Pantheon adapted to the service of a library. It is authoritatively rated the greatest historical monument of American architecture.

Jefferson was over a hundred thousand dollars in debt when he died on July 4, 1826, and Monticello, with all his property, was lost to his heirs. Some of the debt traced back to the Revolution and in fact was part of the large inheritance from his father-in-law John Wayles. Jefferson's lifestyle was intolerant of small economies. What Monticello may have cost him was beyond reckoning. As president he ran the White House as "a general tavern" for the arid Washington community. As a result, he left the capital owing ten thousand dollars to local creditors. At Monticello he continued his hospitable ways. It was a curiosity, after all, and its master was identified with the prodigy of the New World. During the summers, when travelers from the low country to the Virginia springs came in gangs, they crowded the stables and occupied every bed in the house. Of course, they had to be fed. "I have killed a fine beef, and it would be eaten in a day or two," said the farm manager. Yet Jefferson might have made out but for the Panic of 1819 and ensuing depression. He had endorsed two bank notes, each of ten thousand dollars, for one of his dearest friends, and when that man collapsed the debt fell upon Jefferson. He never recovered from the blow. Not long before his death, the General Assembly bowed to his request to dispose of much of his property by lottery. But this fell through and all was lost.

In 1832 James T. Barclay, a Charlottesville apothecary, bought the house and 552 acres for approximately seven thousand dollars. He planned to cultivate silkworms on the mountain, but this failed, and Barclay soon tired of the sightseers who had invaded the property. In 1834 he sold the house, outbuildings, and 218 acres for $2,700 to Lieutenant Uriah P. Levy of the U.S. Navy. Levy revered Jefferson for his political principles, above all for the Virginia Statute of Religious Freedom. He commissioned the French sculptor David d'Angers to execute the first statue of Jefferson, and it would finally be placed before the White House. Levy restored some two thousand acres to the domain, took care of the mansion, and sought out original furnishings, paintings, and memorabilia that had been dispersed at auction. He is remembered, justly, as "the Savior of Monticello." But Levy made his life in the North and strove against heavy odds, as a Jew, to advance his naval career. After a time, he mistakenly placed the property under the beggarly custody of an overseer, who installed pigpens on the front lawn and stored grain on the parquet floors of the parlor.

Levy, having risen to the rank of commodore, died in 1862, and Monticello fell to rack and ruin. He willed the property to the nation for use as a school for the orphan children of naval warrant officers. The eccentric bequest was doomed by the Civil War. The Confederacy confiscated the property; it was broken up and sold under decree of a Confederate court in 1864. Before this could be effected, the property reverted to the United States. In the course of prolonged litigation, Levy's executors broke the will. Finally, in 1882, Jefferson M. Levy, the commodore's nephew, became sole owner of Monticello.

Just at this time Congress enacted a law authorizing a new monument over Jefferson's grave and appropriated the money to build it. The original tombstone with its granite obelisk had been chipped away by souvenir hunters, and the tablet bearing the epitaph had disappeared. (By some accounts Uriah Levy had safely secured it to a wall inside the house.) Nor was desecration confined to the grave. A quarter century earlier, the popular historian Benson J. Lossing had written: "In many a private cabinet are 'relics of Monticello,' a fragment from the monument, a splinter from the delicately carved cornice, a brick from the foundation, or a piece of putty from a window-pane." More recently a student at the university, who often hiked up the mountain, described the house as "a total wreck." In May of each year, he wrote, the students along with the town's fair daughters frolicked on the mountaintop and crowned their queen to the tunes of the Charlottesville String Band.

The scandal surrounding the monument evoked the old complaint of the ingratitude of republics, and so suggested other ways of commemorating Jefferson. These included public ownership and operation of Monticello. The first leading citizen to set his heart on this object was William Jennings Bryan, the defeated Democratic presidential candidate, in 1897. Bryan wrote to his fellow Democrat Levy asking what price he placed on Monticello and implored him to sell it to the nation. Levy replied that all the money in the U.S. Treasury could not buy Monticello. He took pride in his custodianship of the property. He had lavished money and affection on the place, where he was usually in residence four to six months of a year. He recovered several hundred acres of the original property, installed central heating and modern plumbing, brought back Jefferson heirlooms, employed a skilled superintendent, and, altogether, put house and grounds in good order again. To be sure, he had taken liberties, the installation of dormers on the top floor, for instance. Times had changed, and Levy's tastes were not Jefferson's, which was a cause of distress in some quarters.

In 1909 Mrs. Martin W. Littleton, the effusive wife of a Democratic congressman from New York, mounted a crusade to make Monticello a national shrine. She, with her husband, visited the place as Levy's guest. "Ever since I was born I have been hearing of Monticello," she wrote. But growing up in far-off Texas, she had never seen it. Now, she discovered, the house was so full of the Levys that Jefferson had virtually disappeared. "My heart sunk. My dream was spoiled." Taking as her motto Jefferson's moving line "All my wishes end where I hope my days will end, at Monticello," she wrote an attractive brochure, *One Wish*, on behalf of her crusade. Her Monticello Memorial Association petitioned

Congress in 1912 to acquire Monticello. But Levy, who was then a New York congressman, was adamant: "My answer to any proposition seeking the property of Monticello is, 'when the White House is for sale, then I will consider an offer for Monticello.'"

Over the years Levy's defenses crumbled, and in 1923 he agreed to sell Monticello—the house and some six hundred acres—for five hundred thousand dollars, half its reputed value, to the Thomas Jefferson Memorial Foundation, a nonprofit corporation in New York. Its mission was twofold: historic preservation and education. In the course of a half a century, or longer, house and grounds were renovated and expertly restored to Jefferson's idealized image of the place. Today it is one of the most familiar sites on the American historic landscape. Over half a million people a year come to visit. And it occupies a distinguished place on the United Nations World Heritage List.

I first visited Monticello in the summer of 1948. Embarked on a doctoral dissertation at Harvard about Jefferson's place in American thought and imagination, I pursued my research to "Jefferson country," particularly the University of Virginia. There I met an older scholar, Nathan Schachner, engaged in writing a biography of Jefferson; and he kindly offered to introduce me to Monticello. Seeing it on that bright afternoon, I was more taken with the grounds and the scenic panorama than with the house itself. Viewed for the first time, the mansion was smaller and simpler than expected; and I was put off by the ladylike sweetness of the guided tour of the interior.

Since that initial encounter, my life as a historian has been entwined with Jefferson's and, *pari passu*, with Monticello. As to both I have come to believe that whatever the fault or blemish, it pales before the magnificence of the achievement. The dissertation later became my first book, *The Jefferson Image in the American Mind*, in 1960. (It also happened to be one of the first manuscripts upon which Sheldon Meyer, at Oxford University Press, cut his editor's teeth.) The book led me into a virtual career of scholarship on Jefferson and to my appointment as the Jefferson Foundation Professor of History at the University of Virginia. Subsequently named to the board of directors of the Thomas Jefferson Memorial Foundation, I became much better acquainted with the house and its possessions, the gardens and grounds, and the scholarship that invests every detail of the foundation's stewardship of Monticello. Now, at seventy-nine years of age, I find myself, remarkably, living but a crow's flight from Monticello and in view of Jefferson's magical dome where, as an early visitor, with scant regard for literal truth, observed, "the fog never rises."

The Musso & Frank Grill, 1928. *California State Library.*

The New Room, built in 1956. *Musso & Frank Grill.*

Kevin Starr

THE MUSSO & FRANK
GRILL IN HOLLYWOOD

I knew it the moment I walked in. This was it: the rich wood paneling, the red leather booths, the equally red-jacketed waiters moving to and fro at their own pace, the long and crowded bar alight with fine-stemmed martini glasses, the steaks and chops on patrons' plates, and, above all else, the joyous reverberations of the room. This was Hollywood, this was Los Angeles in its golden age! This was the Musso & Frank Grill at 6667 Hollywood Boulevard between Las Palmas and Cherokee avenues in the heart of Hollywood: at the center of a dream as well, at the center of my own hopes for an imaginative connection to the City of the Angels and the larger Southern California past. If I could understand this place, first encountered in 1977 when I was working for *trend-meister* Clay Felker on *New West* magazine—understand the way the room seemed alive with memory—then perhaps I could get to the emotional center of Los Angeles itself. Once arrived at such center, once having made this connection, I could better experience the LA/Hollywood dreams of another era. In the matrix of such a fusion of research and emotional/imaginative connection, I could then write a better history for my *book-meister* Sheldon Meyer, *auteur* of my *Americans and the California Dream* series.

Restaurants have by and large not received their full measure of regard in the writing of American history, despite the fact that they are paradigms of place. To enter such establishments as Durgin Park, Jacob

Wirth's, and the Locke-Ober Café in Boston; Keen's Steakhouse, the Old Homestead, and "21" in Manhattan; Gage & Tollner and the Peter Luger Steakhouse in Brooklyn; Bookbinder's 15th Street Seafood House in Philadelphia; John W. Faidley Seafood in Baltimore; Joe's Stone Crab Restaurant in Miami Beach; Ratzsch's in Milwaukee; the Chop House and the Berghoff in Chicago; the St. Elmo in Indianapolis; the Buckhorn Exchange in Denver; Antoine's and Galatoire's in New Orleans; Sam's and the Tadich Grill in San Francisco; the Pacific Dining Car and the Musso & Frank Grill in Los Angeles—this is to encounter a density of ambience and collective memory that is of the essence of history itself.

Writing in *American Heritage* for April 1997, restaurant historian J. M. Fenster described American restaurants as originating from four distinct sources: taverns, oyster stands, market eateries, and the French (and later German and Italian) restaurants which are the first to be considered restaurants proper, beginning with the opening of Delmonico's in New York on December 13, 1827. In the eighteenth century, very few people dined outside their own home, unless they were dining at the home of friends or were staying at a tavern-inn while traveling. Tavern-inns served no-nonsense fare and strong drink. They also provided something akin to a club for locals and in the case of the Committees of Correspondence helped bring about the American Revolution. Today, the direct lineal descendants of these tavern-inns are hotel restaurants (many hotel restaurants are distinguished by their cuisine as well as being convenient to travelers) and those delightful roadhouses which experienced a whole new burst of activity during Prohibition and which even today, bright and sassy in neon, the sound of a jukebox heard from within, bespeak people having more fun than they really should be having.

The oyster stands of the early nineteenth century led to later, more ambitious seafood establishments and help explain why so many venerable restaurants in this country are seafood oriented. Market-originated restaurants offered either seafood or red meat, depending upon the dominant product of nearby markets. Thus Durgin Park grew out of the Quincy Market near the wharves of Boston, and John W. Faidley Seafood in Baltimore, founded in 1886 (home of the all-lump crab cake), began as an oyster stand, while the Old Homestead in Manhattan was founded in 1868 to serve butchers and meatmen working in the old Washington Market. Jack's, the Tadich Grill, and Sam's in San Francisco each has its origins in the city's California Market in the 1860s, with the Tadich Grill going in the direction of seafood, Jack's orienting itself toward grilled meat, and Sam's combining the two.

Fine dining—and the restaurant genre proper—belong to that day in New York City, December 13, 1827, when two Swiss brothers named Delmonico, Peter and John, began serving customers at twelve tables. The brothers provided well-trained waiters and printed menus that listed offerings in English and French. This simple establishment was the first of eleven increasingly luxurious restaurants to bear the Delmonico name, until the last one closed in 1923; and along with other establishments— Sherry's, Louis Martin, Bustanoby's—it bore witness throughout the nineteenth century to both the appetites and the preeminence of the New York oligarchy.

To experience such restaurants today, where they have survived, is to journey into the very historical texture of the cities and regions they serve. Like great hotels, restaurants are stylizations of place, connected to dreams of pleasure and transcendence. As architecture and menu, surviving American restaurants distill, hence carry through time, the memory of high moments in the urban past. From a number of per-spectives, after all—the rooms themselves, most of them of a certain vintage, the photographs or other visual materials on the walls, the dis-tinctive styles of crockery, napery, and silverware, distinctions of menu and wine service (not to mention the bar in which one waits before the meal), the commanding presence of the maître d', the venerability of the waiters—such restaurants present a stylized encapsulization of historical memory, indeed the very physical presence of time itself.

Thus Locke-Ober's evokes the Boston of Harvard, Old South Church, Ticknor & Fields, the *Atlantic Monthly*, William Dean Howells. Here is the Boston of the mid- and late-nineteenth century, secure in its identity, its taste, its scholarship. Keen's Steakhouse, founded in 1885, still serves a gigantic mutton chop similar to the one that English actress Lillie Langtry was hungry for one night in 1901—but was denied because ladies were not allowed in Keen's. Langtry sued in court and won, and Keen's was ordered to admit women (into a separate dining room); and for the rest of twentieth century Keen's continued to exude the Anglo-philic mood of David Belasco's and Victor Herbert's New York. By con-trast, "21," which began as a speakeasy, continued through the 1960s to suggest the sportiness, the sense of being on the town, of the New York of John O'Hara and Walter Winchell. Can anyone enter the busy splendor of the Berghoff in Chicago without recalling how Hurstwood leaned against the bar there in Theodore Dreiser's *Sister Carrie* (1900), florid and amiable, feeling very much a man in control of his own life? To dine on an all-lump crab cake at John W. Faidley Seafood in Baltimore or finish a meal with Indian pudding at Durgin Park or savor eggs Sardou at Antoine's (poached eggs on artichoke hearts with hollandaise sauce) or a mutton chop at Jack's in San Francisco is to participate in a ritual of place that allows one, almost, to dine on time and history.

All this obtains, quite clearly, to the Musso & Frank Grill in Hollywood, founded in 1919, the takeoff year of twentieth-century Los Angeles. Restaurateur Joseph Musso had moved to the city in 1916 from Oregon when that state banished liquor service in restaurants. Three years later, with two other partners, one of them named Frank Toulet, he opened the Musso & Frank Grill. Just as the opening of Delmonico's prefigured the rise of New York to preeminence, so too did the opening of the Musso & Frank Grill coincide with the transformation of Los Angeles from a nice but negligible southwestern town to an important American city that, because of the film industry, had been jump-started into international recognition. These were the years in which Los Angeles absorbed more than a million and a half new residents, when it annexed the San Fernando Valley, San Pedro/Wilmington, Watts, and Venice, opened the Miracle Mile, constructed the Coliseum, the Biltmore Hotel, the City Hall, the Central Library, the Hollywood Bowl, the campuses of USC and UCLA. These were the years in which two formative industries—aviation and motion pictures—centralized themselves in the City of Angels and its immediate suburbs. Within one decade, certainly two decades, after Musso & Frank opened, Los Angeles had become, in *Los Angeles Times* columnist Harry Carr's terms, America's City of Dreams: an urban *tabula rasa* onto which, increasingly, Americans and all moviegoing peoples were projecting their longings and centering their subliminal aspirations for glamour and a better life.

Because the Musso & Frank Grill was in Hollywood, and not in the Downtown, it did not attract politicians and other deal-makers as did the Pacific Dining Car on Sixth Street. It attracted, rather, intellectuals and book men and—because both Paramount Studios and the headquarters of the Writers' Guild were nearby—it especially attracted actors and screenwriters. In the 1920s, the Grill was a favored hangout of the circle that centered on Jake Zeitlin, a poet and bookseller with a gift for friendship. The circle included a literary law student from USC, Carey McWilliams, destined to become the finest nonfiction commentator on California in the twentieth century. Also on hand, and in the booths, could be found Paul Jordan Smith, literary editor of the *Los Angeles Times*, Arthur Millier, art critic of that same newspaper, photographer Will Connell, architect Lloyd Wright (son of Frank Lloyd Wright and designer of the shell at the Hollywood Bowl), impresario Merle Armitage, designer Kem Weber, musicologist and radio commentator José Rodriguez, journalists Herbert Klein and Louis Adamic, architects Richard Neutra, R. W. Schindler, and Harwell Harris, librarian and critic Lawrence Clark Powell, painter S. MacDonald Wright, fine printer Ward Ritchie, and bookseller and Hollywood character Stanley Rose, whose bookstore next door later served as the model for the pornography-selling bookstore in Raymond Chandler's *The Big Sleep* (1939), Rose having once been busted for selling naughty books and pictures.

The Zeitlin circle constituted the creative bohemia of Los Angeles in the 1920s; and although its members frequented the Musso & Frank Grill, they were not as addicted to the place as the screenwriters from the nearby studios were in the late 1930s. Many of these screenwriters gathering at Musso & Frank represented the great names of twentieth-century American literature, but in those Depression days, they were more interested in making a buck than making undergraduate reading lists. And so, to the list of such actor regulars as Tom Mix, Charlie Chaplin (a daily luncher with a preference for martinis), Paulette Goddard, and Humphrey Bogart, together with studio moguls Harry and Jack Warner, must be added the names of such other Musso & Frank regulars as F. Scott Fitzgerald, John O'Hara, Dorothy Parker, Dashiell Hammett, Raymond Chandler, Nathanael West, Budd Schulberg, S. N. Behrman, Lillian Hellman, Horace McCoy, John Fante, A. I. Bezzerides, Frederick Faust (Max Brand), and William Faulkner. So many screenwriters made of the Musso & Frank Grill their club that management provided them the exclusive use of a small back dining room for their Saturday lunches when another week of their servitude at the studios ended. There were other places—Sardi's, the Brown Derby, the Knickerbocker Hotel, the Cocoanut Grove (as it was spelled locally, with an added *a*), Sebastian's Cotton Club, even the Clover Club on Sunset Boulevard in unincorporated West Hollywood, where the syndicate, petty crookdom, and Hollywood met—but the screenwriters preferred the Musso & Frank Grill for their Saturday afternoon get-togethers. "Bill sat drinking with me," Twentieth Century-Fox script girl Meta Carpenter later reminisced in her memoir *A Loving Gentleman* (1976) of those Saturday afternoons with her lover William Faulkner, "smoking his pipe, laughing freely. He did not mingle much with his colleagues, yet he was happy to be among writing men."

Today, sixty, nearly seventy, years later, the Musso & Frank Grill remains a throwback to this earlier era. The decor has changed little, if at all, since the 1920s, especially the great mahogany booths and red leather banquettes in the original dining room, where customers also dine at a long counter, reading *Variety* or the racing form. Red-jacketed waiters are middle-aged or older and are totally devoid, as Southern California restaurant critic Orlando Ramirez points out, of that "Hi-my-name-is-Jason-and-I'll-be-your-server-tonight" greeting, usually uttered by aspiring-actor waiters in other Los Angeles bistros. These gentlemen and their few female counterparts are professional waiters in the old sense of the word (meaning full-time and for real), and they sustain the kind of hauteur one frequently encounters in waiters and waitresses working in historic restaurants, from Sam's in San Francisco to Durgin Park in Boston. The food they serve is equally old-fashioned. J. M. Fenster describes the Musso & Frank Grill as "a veritable safe house in the midst of trendy California cuisine. There is nary a poppy seed in sight or a blade of lemongrass. Instead, there is beef stroganoff. There are also veal scallopine, liver and onions, Welsh rarebit, and other dishes long past mere trends." To this list, one might also add such other Musso & Frank favorites as corned beef and cabbage, oyster stew, lamb kidneys, a three-inch-thick prime rib, broiled squab with bacon, pork and lamb chops, and smoked tongue. The tavern/roadhouse dimension of the Musso & Frank Grill is evident in its long—very long—bar where martinis, Manhattans, Rob Roys, stingers, and other very direct and very alcoholic drinks have remained in fashion since the repeal of Prohibition. Its market origins are evident in its usually adequate offerings of fresh fish as well as red meat. Hollywood's connection to New York can be detected in huge servings of Lindy's-style cheesecake. The spirit of Los Angeles in the 1920s, the Los Angeles of Aimee Semple McPherson and the

Folks, is evident in the fact that Musso & Frank still serves Postum as well as good coffee and Jell-O in many of its seven delicious flavors.

Interestingly enough, Hollywood continues to frequent the Musso & Frank Grill, despite the fact that the film industry has diversified itself elsewhere and that the Hollywood district itself has been a decidedly nontrendy, run-down place since the 1960s. Admittedly, the Grill does not attract name actors in such numbers as it once did; yet the tradition remains. In the 1950s and 1960s Peter Lawford and Jack Webb were regulars; current regular Red Buttons survives from this era. Other recent Musso & Frank sightings include Henry Winkler, Sean Penn, Brad Pitt, Nicholas Cage, Al Pacino, Ben Kingsley, and David Lynch. The Rolling Stones have dropped by. Stones guitarist Keith Richards, in fact, hosted a dinner here for fourteen of his buddies during the Stones' 1997 Los Angeles concert. As recently as the *Los Angeles Times* magazine for February 6, 2000, former child actor turned biographer Tom Nolan testified to the continuing vitality of Musso & Frank as part of the Hollywood legend. Nolan's Musso & Frank's sightings, dating from his child-actor days and edging into the present, included Rita Hayworth, Orson Welles, Tony Perkins, Jason Robards Jr., Alan Hale Jr. (*Gilligan's Island*), director David Butler, pulp-noir writer Jim Thompson, novelist Joseph Heller (picking up some spare change as a writer for *McHale's Navy*), and singer-songwriter Phil Ochs.

And so I found myself dining with Mary and Sheldon Meyer on a rainy late winter/early spring night early in the 1990s at the Musso & Frank Grill in Hollywood. Each spring, Sheldon, accompanied by his wife, a senior translator for the United Nations, would conduct a grand tour of the Far West, spending quality time with his authors. Mary Meyer's presence was not devoid of historical reverberations as far as California was concerned; a member of her family, Michael Maurice O'Shaughnessy (1864–1964), the Irish-born city engineer of San Francisco in the first three decades of the twentieth century, was one of the re-founders of San Francisco, having played a major role in the rebuilding of the city after the Earthquake and Fire of April 1906 and having designed and built San Francisco's Hetch Hetchy water system.

As he does in so many other settings I have seen him in—the Century Association in New York, the Bohemian Club in San Francisco, Patina in the Hancock Park district of Los Angeles—Sheldon fit into the setting almost immediately. Indeed, Sheldon and Musso & Frank seemed made for each other. Sheldon is a native Chicagoan, after all; and Chicago, more than any other city in the United States, was responsible for the re-foundation of Los Angeles in the first twenty-five years of the twentieth century. Time and Princeton, however, have made of Sheldon a polished easterner; and his longtime career at the Oxford University Press and an equally long residence on the Upper West Side of Manhattan (with summers on Fishers Island) have made of him a quintessential New Yorker. How appropriate, then, that Sheldon should be sitting in a recognizably midwestern or East Coast restaurant that continued to express in its ambience and cuisine the fact that Los Angeles in the takeoff year of 1919 was not an eccentric place, or even a Hollywood creation, but a colony of the Midwest and, more remotely, of the eastern United States. Boosters of the era, in fact, were claiming that Los Angeles was perhaps the last major English-speaking city that would be created on the North American continent. They were mistaken, of course; but the very fact that they believed this underscored the inner psychology and ethos of the City of Angels in these Great Gatsby years.

Sheldon and I could have gone to other historic Los Angeles restaurants for discussion of my continuing social and cultural history of California. Chasen's, for example, was still open, albeit in its last years, as was the Brothers Taix on lower Sunset Boulevard, albeit in reduced circumstances. But the Musso & Frank Grill spoke directly to the California that Sheldon Meyer had for the previous decade and a half been encouraging me to pursue: the California that somehow, for all its eccentricities, remained an important instance of American civilization, or at the least a recognizably American place, just as the Musso & Frank Grill, for all its storied movieland history, remained a restaurant that might very well be found in Chicago or Indianapolis.

Over the years, I have been frequently asked why my California series was being published by the Oxford University Press in New York rather than by, say, a California-based publisher. The answer is rather simple, but it will take some explaining. I am a native Californian who discovered the history of California at Harvard within the context of American literary, intellectual, and cultural history; and my work has been guided—no, more than guided, shaped and inspired—by a midwesterner who has become a quintessential easterner with an abiding love for the full range of American cultural achievement, including jazz and popular music. Sheldon Meyer is a big-city guy. Even his love of country-

and-western music has more of Nashville to it than the boondocks. His urbanism, however, is not merely a matter of New York, although New York is his *mise-en-scène*. Pure New York, after all, has a very narrowly defined range of American possibilities. Sheldon Meyer, by contrast, is urban in the sense that all culture in this country is, in the long run, city-centric: flowing into and out of cities, that is, from hardscrabble and out-of-the-way places. Sheldon Meyer is America staying up late at night in cities, as Sheldon likes to do, hearing the velvet voice of one of his authors, Mel Tormé, scatting to a jazz combo late of a foggy San Francisco night, or hearing in the mind a droll take by Bobby Short, recalled amidst the taxicab traffic on Fifth Avenue up from the Century. Sheldon Meyer is about knowing and understanding why Americans love neon lights, city skylines, fish-tailed Cadillacs, watering holes and roadside joints, port and good cigars, late-night jazz joints, Frank Sinatra, the taste of whiskey in the wee hours of the early morning, the memory of Franklin Delano Roosevelt, and cities with such improbable names as Milwaukee, Sheboygan, Chicago, Indianapolis, Mobile, Seattle.

So, too, are the echoes and reverberations one experiences at the Musso & Frank Grill also big-city echoes and reverberations. They suggest Los Angeles as the Chicago of the Pacific, a city with big shoulders of its own sort. The bohemians of the 1920s and the screenwriters of the 1930s who frequented this restaurant had one thing in common: they were big-city colonists, exiles of a sort, spending time in a town which was itself trying to learn how to be big-city, just as Sheldon Meyer was always encouraging me to find how California had been trying to learn, over some 150 years of its American history, just exactly how to evolve for itself a regional culture possessed of the best American possibilities. Let others speak of California, Los Angeles especially, as the erasure of memory. Fascinated by the eccentricities of California, Sheldon was equally interested in the persistence of memory on this far American shore, the way California hungered for history and orthodoxy along with a sense of new beginnings. Sheldon perceived California as new, innovative, eccentric: the California, say, of Aldous Huxley and Evelyn Waugh, lost from traditional history. But he saw it simultaneously, not just in the Bay Area but in Southern California as well, as an instance and reassertion of American civilization as valid and as shaping, in the long run, of our national culture as New England, the Mid-Atlantic, the Midwest, and the South.

The food upon which we were dining at the Musso & Frank Grill was obviously not nouvelle or California cuisine, as it would have been in Chez Panisse at Berkeley or the award-winning Patina in the vicinity. Such restaurants and such food underscored California as innovative, cutting-edge, even slightly precious. The food served at the Musso & Frank Grill, by contrast, was the food that had nourished an earlier (and openly imperialistic) generation of Americans who, sometimes quite ruthlessly, were creating an empire. True, even then, other nourishment was available. Mexican food, for example, had never fallen out of favor in California since its annexation by the United States in 1848. Even the regulars of Musso & Frank in that Anglo-Protestant year of 1919 when the restaurant was founded knew and loved Mexican fare: as if, one is tempted to speculate, they somehow knew, if only subliminally, that the past and the future—if not the present—of California was linked to Mexico. So, too, could they enjoy Asian cuisine, Chinese especially; but here even one's wildest speculations cannot bring about any linkage between the Chinese and Japanese cuisines of Los Angeles in the 1920s and the rise of California as Asia sixty years later.

And so Sheldon and I each enjoyed two martinis, straight up, accompanied by olives and a split order of herring and sour cream, followed by a small shrimp Louis salad, followed by oversize grilled pork chops, creamed spinach, a serviceable Louis Martini Cabernet Sauvignon from early in the previous decade, crusty French bread, and for dessert a wedge of that New York-style cheesecake. It was the food of empire builders: the kind of meal which might have been enjoyed on these very premises sixty years earlier by engineers responsible for the Los Angeles Aqueduct as well as by screen stars and screenwriters down through the decades. Around the room and across it to the bar, we caught glimpses of the screenwriters, techies, and other Hollywood and television types of the present, their hair long, rings in their ears, no neckties, a lot of Hawaiian shirts, and there—over in a far corner—a gray-haired Red Buttons attacking a mound of tuna fish salad.

Ah, Musso & Frank! Ah, humanity! Time and life are fleeting, and of such occasions, such in-gatherings of dreams, are books and cities made. Like the neon lights illuminating Sunset Boulevard to the north, the food and ambience of Musso & Frank were saying something ephemeral yet powerful. I was in Los Angeles. I was in the company of Sheldon Meyer of Oxford University Press. I was haunted by America as I had encountered its culture at Harvard: even more haunted by the California variation thereof. With Sheldon's guidance, I would pursue the story and the meaning of the vast and meretricious beauty that was all around me—to borrow a line from another midwesterner turned easterner who was also a regular at Musso & Frank.

"The Catch": Willie Mays in pursuit of Vic Wertz's 450-foot blast at the Polo Grounds, September 29, 1954. *AP/Wide World Photo.*

Jules Tygiel

THE POLO GROUNDS

I first experienced the Polo Grounds in its afterlife. It was no longer what writers in the 1910s dubbed "the eighth wonder of the world"; nor was it the "opera house and the fighting cockpit of the golden age of Sports" of the 1920s, or even the inspirational site of Bobby Thomson's 1951 "Shot Heard 'Round the World" or Willie Mays's miracle catch in the 1954 World Series. The Polo Grounds in 1962 more resembled, according to a *Sporting News* headline, a "Torpedoed Ship That Refuses to Sink," or, in the words of Roger Angell, a "doomed old stadium." Given up for dead after the Giants had moved to San Francisco in 1958, the Polo Grounds had won a brief reprieve from demolition with the arrival of the New York Mets. While New York City built a new pleasure palace in Flushing Meadows, the fledging Mets would cavort in the well-worn arena on the banks of the Harlem River in upper Manhattan.

For a thirteen-year-old Brooklynite, little more than a month removed from his bar mitzvah, the trek to the Polo Grounds on April 27, 1962, marked yet another rite of passage. I had attended baseball games before—at Ebbets Field, where the Dodgers had celebrated my baseball baptism by hitting three ninth-inning home runs to defeat the Phillies 6–5, and at Yankee Stadium, where Mickey Mantle and Ted Williams had welcomed me with titanic home runs—but on those occasions my father had accompanied me. Now Robert Dorin, one full month my junior, and I were to attend our first ball game unescorted and unsupervised, newly anointed young men unleashed into the urban wilderness. The journey itself tested our adolescent mettle. We boarded the Remsen Avenue bus en route to the Utica Avenue station, where we caught the IRT Seventh Avenue subway. At 42nd Street in Manhattan, we transferred to the D train on the Independent Line and traveled north to 155th Street, where we climbed the stairs to Eighth Avenue in the shadow of the looming stadium.

I have read that during the Met years, the Polo Grounds emanated the familiar signs of urban decay: peeling plaster, loose chunks of masonry, soot-blackened passageways, and cockroach-ridden lavatories. "It was like some 90-year-old person suffering from arteriosclerosis," wrote Harold Rosenthal in *The Sporting News*. I don't remember it that way. The Polo Grounds possessed for me the same magical quality that all ballparks radiate: the silver-plated turnstiles that respond to a brisk forward movement, the vaulting ceilings and wide ramps of the entryways, the dark tunnels leading to the stands, and the sudden, irrationally unexpected, green expanse of outfield.

Robert and I purchased grandstand seats. In a modern arena the grandstand, if it existed at all, would place us in the far reaches of the upper deck. At the Polo Grounds we found ourselves in the front row in right field, less than three hundred feet from home plate, almost touching the players gathered beneath us during batting practice. We saw another schoolmate, Arnie Schurz, nearby. Before we had even settled in, a fly ball came soaring our way, dipped over the fence past Arnie's outstretched hand, caught him flush on the chest, and dropped to the ground. A horde of youngsters scrambled unsympathetically around Arnie's feet until one emerged with the ball, while Arnie rubbed his chest, dismayed more at losing the souvenir than at his discomfort.

The game itself, as re-created from the scorecard that Robert has faithfully kept for thirty-seven years, proved a representative sampling of the Mets' play in 1962. The Mets started their ace pitcher Roger Craig, who would lose twenty-four games that year, two other former Dodgers (Charlie Neal and Don Zimmer), and a couple of onetime major league stars (Richie Ashburn and Gus Bell). By the middle of the second inning, Craig was gone and the Mets trailed the Phillies 5–0. Catcher Hobie Landrith, the Mets' first pick in the expansion draft that had stocked the team ("You've got to start with a catcher or you'll have all passed balls," explained manager Casey Stengel), already had three passed balls. After the top of the sixth, the Phillies led 11–1. Then a remarkable transformation occurred. In the sixth the Mets scored three runs. In the eighth they scored four more. Heading into the bottom of the ninth, the score stood at 11–8. The Phillies hurler quickly retired the first two batters, but rookie pinch hitter Jim Hickman singled and then stole second base. Neal singled to drive in Hickman, making the score 11–9. This brought the potential tying run to the plate.

Although neither Robert nor I realized it, we were witnessing a characteristic Met moment. The trademark of the '62 Mets, writes Leonard Koppett, was "the futile rally. . . . They would fall far behind, rally to close the gap and come within sight of a tie or victory—and fall short." To the plate strode veteran utility infielder Don Zimmer. He had not had a hit that day. Indeed, he had not had a hit all season. He began his career as a Met with no hits in his first thirty-four at-bats. With Neal prancing off first and our youthful hopes high, Zimmer struck out to end the game. Many baseball fans have never forgiven Zimmer, who to date in 2000 has spent five decades in the game, for his mismanagement of the Boston Red Sox in the 1970s. I have never forgiven him for frustrating my naive expectations in 1962. Within three weeks Zimmer would be gone, traded for a left-handed pitcher named Bob Miller (not to be confused with a right-handed pitcher named Bob Miller who also pitched for the Mets that year). Catcher Landrith, who failed to fulfill Stengel's passed-ball prophecy, had also departed, traded for a legend-to-be-named-later, Marvelous Marv Throneberry.

During the next two seasons, I spent many happy days and evenings at the Polo Grounds, blithely impervious to its shortcomings, blissfully suffering through the Mets' misadventures. The ballpark sat in Coogan's Hollow, a narrow expanse of land sandwiched between the Harlem River and a massive outcropping of mica schist (known as Coogan's Bluff) that loomed over the structure. King George I of England had granted the land to John Gardiner in the eighteenth century, and the Gardiner manor house had sat on the bluff. In the late nineteenth century, James J. Coogan, a Bowery upholsterer with Tammany Hall connections, married into the Gardiner family and gave his name to the property. Coogan became Manhattan's second borough president in 1899. His family would own the bluff, hollow, and stadium into the 1960s.

In the 1880s the New York National League baseball franchise had played its games on a tract bordered by Fifth and Sixth Avenues and 110th and 112th streets in Manhattan. Previously the land had hosted polo games, and the area became known as the Polo Grounds. In 1889 the city government announced plans to complete 111th Street and bisect the park. Giants owner John Day looked northward to the outskirts of the city and built a new ballpark at Coogan's Hollow. To avoid confusion and attract the faithful, he carried the name Polo Grounds to the new site. The following year, however, labor troubles rent the National League as most of its stars bolted to form their own Players' League. The New York franchise also leased land at Coogan's Hollow and built Brotherhood Park alongside the new Polo Grounds. So close were the two arenas that fans in one park could watch the game in the other. Hemmed in by Coogan's Bluff on one side and the National League facility on the other, Brotherhood Park adopted an elongated, horseshoe shape with a distant center field and short foul lines. Nonetheless, the Players' League stadium was by far the superior field. When the uprising collapsed after the 1890 season, National League owner Day insisted that as part of the settlement he be allowed to move his Giants from the new Polo Grounds to Brotherhood Park, which, to be consistent, he renamed the Polo Grounds.

The Giants remained in their new home for twenty years. After 1903, behind the leadership of John McGraw and the pitching of Christy Mathewson, they became the dominant franchise in the National League. The Polo Grounds, however, like most stadiums built in the nineteenth century, had been constructed entirely of wood. In the early morning hours of April 14, 1911, a night watchman saw flames engulfing the right center field stands. By the time firemen arrived in their horse-drawn equipment, the fire had consumed all but a small section of the outfield bleachers, destroying the third version of the Polo Grounds.

John T. Brush, who now owned the Giants, vowed to replace the old wooden structure with a modern concrete and steel facility to match those already in place in Pittsburgh, Chicago, and Philadelphia. In the latter two cities team owners Charles Comiskey and Ben Shibe had named their new arenas for themselves. In New York Brush envisioned a magnificent new amphitheater, the largest in the major leagues, to suit the nation's greatest city. He would call it Brush Stadium. The fans, however, from the moment it opened on June 28, 1911, with Christy Mathewson shutting out the Boston Braves, called the new ballpark the Polo Grounds. After 1919, when the Stoneham family bought the team, the Brush imprimatur faded from memory. The Stonehams also renovated the ballpark in 1923, creating the arena of most common memory.

Most people associate the Polo Grounds with baseball (and especially the New York Giants, its primary occupants), but during its half century of existence, the venerable ballpark witnessed a wide, and often improbable, assortment of spectacles. In April 1912 the Giants and the crosstown Highlanders (soon to be renamed the Yankees) held an exhibition game to benefit the survivors of the *Titanic*. George M. Cohan and other celebrities sold programs and newspapers to raise funds. During World War I, Isadora Duncan danced at the Polo Grounds during a war bonds rally.

In the 1920s the Polo Grounds emerged as a primary showcase for the golden age of sports. The Yankees had made the Polo Grounds their home since 1913. Thus, when Babe Ruth arrived in New York in 1920, he alighted not in Yankee Stadium, which would not be built until 1923, but at Coogan's Hollow. Indeed, the Polo Grounds added to Ruth's sensation. The Babe's unprecedented home-run hitting in 1920 and 1921 owed much to the friendly dimensions of his new home. Playing with the Red Sox in 1919, he had hit only nine home runs at Fenway Park. He hit twenty-nine home runs at the Polo Grounds in 1920 and thirty-two in 1921. These totals tailed off when the Yankees moved to the Bronx. "I cried when they took me out of the Polo Grounds," confessed Ruth.

Since the Yankees and Giants dominated baseball in the early 1920s, the Polo Grounds became virtually synonymous with the World Series during those critical years. The arena played host to nineteen out of twenty-six World Series games between 1921 and 1924, including thirteen consecutive games in 1921 and 1922, when the Yankees and Giants both won pennants. The first radio broadcasts of the World Series occurred there in 1922, and pioneer baseball announcer Graham McNamee debuted at the Polo Grounds in 1923.

These years also established the Polo Grounds as a haven for college and professional football. The Army-Navy contest was held in the oddly shaped arena nine times between 1913 and 1927. On October 19, 1924, after sportswriter Grantland Rice watched Notre Dame defeat Army 13–7, he indelibly christened the Irish backfield the "four horsemen." Beginning in 1925, the New York Giants of the National Football League made the Polo Grounds their home. On one memorable 1925 weekend seventy thousand fans turned out to watch Army beat Navy on Saturday. On Sunday an even larger crowd literally stormed the stadium to see Red Grange debut as a professional football player. Fans scaled walls and crashed through locked gates to see "the Galloping Ghost," demonstrating the economic potential of the professional game for the first time. The football Giants would play their home games at the Polo Grounds for more than three decades.

The Polo Grounds also welcomed boxing in the 1920s. Eighty-two thousand fight fans posted the sport's first million-dollar gate to watch Jack Dempsey fight Luis Angel Firpo, "the Wild Bull of the Pampas," for the world's heavyweight championship in 1923. In the first round Dempsey and Firpo exchanged knockdowns. At one point a Firpo blow drove Dempsey through the ropes and into the press row. The referee delayed the count, allowing Dempsey to crawl back into the ring, where he devastated the Argentine challenger, winning in the second round. A second memorable heavyweight championship fight occurred in 1941 when an aging Joe Louis met Billy Conn. When experts predicted that the younger Conn, a deft strategist, might outmaneuver Louis in the ring, the champ responded, "He can run, but he can't hide." After Conn dominated Louis for twelve rounds, Louis finally found him and knocked him out in the thirteenth.

At various times the Polo Grounds featured midget auto races, rodeos, soccer, tennis, rugby, lacrosse, trap shooting, dog shows, and ice-skating and skiing festivals, complete with ski ramps and snow. Religious rallies and opera graced the field. Ironically, no one ever played polo there.

In retrospect, it is hard to believe that the Polo Grounds ever existed in the twentieth century. With its odd configuration, unexpected hiding places, erratic angles, and eccentric nooks and crannies, it evokes more the ethos of a medieval castle or abbey, or perhaps an unexplored corner of Harry Potter's Hogwarts School for Witchcraft and Wizardry, than a modern stadium. The massive clubhouse in center field sometimes served as home to the baseball Giants' owner Horace Stoneham, who often slept there. Stoneham also constructed an apartment under section 35 in the left field grandstand where groundskeeper Matthew Schwab and his family lived during the 1950s.

As Robert Creamer noted, "The Polo Grounds [was] a terrible place to watch a ball game." Although the stands officially seated fifty-five thousand people, half that number, Creamer observed, seemed to fill the park. In the upper decks, people in right field could not see the right fielder and people in the left field could not see the left fielder. Many seats were located behind the stadium's bountiful array of posts and pillars. According to Creamer:

> Some seats in the Polo Grounds are behind several posts simultaneously, particularly those in the rear of the lower stands behind the dugouts. Watching a game from there is like watching it through a picket fence, and the people who sit there sway back and forth continuously during a game, first one way to get a glimpse of the pitcher winding up—as the batter disappears behind a post—and then the other way, abruptly dismissing the pitcher to watch the batter swing.

Even the field managers did not have an unobstructed view. Because the elevation of the playing surface dropped by eight feet between the infield dirt and the most distant fences, a manager seated on the bench could only see his outfielders from the waist up.

The horseshoe-shaped stands opened in center field, creating a unique, absurd, yet unforgettable configuration. The clubhouse loomed at a sixty-foot height in far distant center field, five hundred feet from home plate. Atop the structure sat a giant Longines clock. Along the top level a row of windows overlooked the field. A mammoth advertising billboard covered the bottom half of the clubhouse. In the Giants' heyday the sign advertised Chesterfield cigarettes, and the *H* or the *E* would light up in the brand name to indicate a hit or an error. During the Mets era, the clubhouse wall also functioned as a scoreboard, with a Rheingold beer sign providing the lighted scoring assistance. A wide runway leading to the clubhouse separated the two sections of bleacher seats. In the absence of underground tunnels, pitchers and other players removed from the game had to march the hundred-plus yards across the field, walk between the bleachers, and climb an open flight of steps to reach the clubhouse locker room, exposed to the cheers, or more often taunts, of fans throughout the extended journey.

The center field bleachers, arrayed on both sides of the clubhouse runway, consisted of long, narrow, uncomfortable slats of wood, officially holding 3,900 people. Since there were no specific seats, however, the capacity varied from game to game. The highest rows of the bleachers located people a distant six hundred feet from home plate. Even in the front sections, fans watching an errant play often experienced, as Arnold Hano wrote in *A Day in the Bleachers*, "the same miserable frustration of a man who watches a holdup but is too far away to warn the victim." Two square green screens, designed to provide a dark backdrop for the batters, blocked out the lower centermost seats in each section.

The Polo Grounds also offered unusual vantage points for those who could not or would not pay for a ticket. Since the ballpark sat directly beneath Coogan's Bluff, fans could sit atop the mica escarpment and watch games for free. In the old wooden Polo Grounds, the grandstand only ascended halfway up the escarpment, offering a relatively full panorama of the game from the cliff, a nearby viaduct, or the elevated train. After 1911 the new ballpark yielded a more obstructed view. Fans atop the bluff could hardly see the pitcher, catcher, or batter and rarely saw either the right fielder or first baseman. The shortstop, left fielder, and center fielder, however, were in plain view, as was the second baseman on plays near the base and the third baseman when he cut in front of the shortstop. One could also see the big scoreboard above the center field bleachers.

The view became more cramped after the 1923 renovation when the Giants extended the grandstand, effectively cutting the shortstop and left fielder from the picture, and eliminated the scoreboard. The advent of portable radios in the 1930s somewhat offset this disadvantage. Hano, who as a boy lived across the street from the Polo Grounds, remembered climbing the wooden stairs to the top of Coogan's Bluff. "There, with a scattered hundred other fans enjoying a sun bath, we'd watch the game," he recalled. "All you can see through the open work of the stadium is the rear portion of the pitcher's mound, the area around second base, and a portion of the outfield. But after awhile, you get the hang of it from the noise of the crowd and what the second baseman does." In the 1950s the completion of the Colonial Park Housing Project on the Harlem River Drive eliminated even more of the view. Nonetheless, Roger Angell discovered a crowd of about forty people clustered atop the bluff peering at "a slice of emerald grass in deep center field" and listening to their radios during a Mets-Dodgers game in 1962.

The most peculiar part of the Polo Grounds lay in the dimensions of the playing field itself. Its oblong shape placed the foul line fences dangerously close and center field and the power alleys dauntingly remote. The right field wall stood a scant 257 feet from home plate. The distance to the seventeen-foot-high left field barrier was calculated at 279 feet, but even this minimal measurement exaggerated its depth. Since the upper deck in left field featured a twenty-three-foot overhang, a pop-up hit a mere 250 feet could clip the edge of the stands and become a home run. Polo Grounds regular Hano recalled, "At least a dozen times I have seen this happen—the left fielder pressed against the fence as though he hoped to push back the stands to make room for the lazily dropping fly ball, and then the gentle smiting of the facade and the ball lying innocently at the feet of the left fielder, while the batter runs around the bases, sometimes hesitating at second base as though not sure he had actually hit a home run."

Balls rocketed to center field usually suffered an opposite fate. The power alleys in left and right center field were so deep that they housed the bullpen and warm-up areas for both teams unprotected by any screen or barrier. The center field bleachers languished almost 450 feet away. The runway between the two bleacher sections added another fifty feet of playing area. Even the clubhouse, over five hundred feet distant and sixty feet high, remained in play. No line demarcated the height above which a blast would be deemed a home run, but then again no batter ever reached the clubhouse on a fly.

Few men ever hit a ball into the bleachers. Visiting National Leaguer Spud Davis once hit a ball off the screen, but only legged out a double for his efforts. In 1948 Luke Easter of the Negro League Homestead Grays became the first man to clear the center field fence during a game. Five years later a ball hit into a gale wind by Milwaukee Brave Joe Adcock carried eight rows up into the stands. Easter and Adcock remained the only hitters to reach the bleachers until 1962, when the Mets occupied the premises. In the first inning of a game on June 17, Lou Brock, a slender, left-handed rookie Chicago Cubs outfielder, came to the plate. Brock would play eighteen years in the majors, averaging a scant eight homers a season. Yet on this day he unexpectedly drove a ball into the right-side section of the bleachers. The following day the Braves came to town. Before the game someone pointed out where Brock's shot had landed to Henry Aaron. Aaron stared at the far-off fence as if measuring it in his mind. Several innings into the game he stepped up to bat with the bases loaded and lifted a Jay Hook pitch over the fence into the opposite sector of the bleachers from where Brock's blast had landed. Thus, on consecutive days in their third month of existence, the Mets surrendered more home runs into the Polo Grounds bleachers than the Giants had in over thirty seasons.

Nonetheless, fans better remember the Polo Grounds for its long outs than its mammoth home runs. In the 1922 World Series Babe Ruth hit a ball a reported 480 feet on the fly only to have it caught by Giants center fielder Bill Cunningham. Fourteen years later in the sixth game of the World Series, with the Yankees needing just one out to win the championship, Hank Lieber of the Giants smashed a ball into straight-away center into the gap between the bleachers. Joe DiMaggio glided under the ball and caught it at the base of the clubhouse steps. Without breaking stride he started up the stairs and had ascended to the club-house before many fans had realized that the series had ended.

The most remarkable demonstration of Polo Grounds perversity occurred on an October afternoon in 1954 when the Giants met the Cleveland Indians in the first game of the World Series. In the top of the eighth inning, with the score tied and fleet-footed Indians runner Larry Doby on second base, Vic Wertz drove a high arcing drive into deep right center field. Giants outfielder Willie Mays wheeled and took off in pursuit of the ball. The photographs of the play capture a classic juxtaposition of determined player and expectant fans. Mays has his back to home plate, his arms outstretched toward the fence, his number 24 flashing defiantly. The bleachers host a diverse ensemble of men (but few women). A policeman leans forward next to the stairs leading to the clubhouse. The head of a young boy barely peers over the barrier. Two men desperately grasp the screen at its rightmost extension. A vendor holds a soda frozen in midair, watching the action before finishing his service. A handful of African Americans are seated in the front row; others are sprinkled throughout the crowd. Most white fans are dressed in sport shirts and have bare heads. The blacks, continuing the traditions of Negro League fandom, wear sport jackets and hats. All have their eyes fastened on Mays.

Hano, seated in the bleachers, described the moment: "Mays was turned full around, head down, running as hard as he could ... Mays simply slowed down to avoid running into the wall, put his hands up in cup-like fashion over his left shoulder, and caught the ball much like a football player catching leading passes in the end zone." Equally miraculous, Mays instantaneously whirled and heaved the ball toward second base, falling flat on his stomach from the effort. Doby had tagged at second base after the catch, intent on taking two bases and scoring the go-ahead run. But Mays's Herculean throw arrived in the infield just as Doby reached third, preventing his further advance and preserving the tie.

Two innings later, in the bottom of the tenth, Giants pinch hitter Dusty Rhodes lifted a gentle fly over the head of the Cleveland first baseman. Second baseman Bobby Avila dashed out, thinking that he might have a chance to catch the drifting fly ball. Right fielder Dave Pope eased backward, settling under the ball. Suddenly he felt the intimate right field fence at his back as the ball continued to float. Pope stretched his glove upward and leaped as high as he could, but the ball cleared the wall, bouncing off a front row seat and back onto the field at Pope's feet. Wertz's long, fruitless out had traveled more than 420 feet, Rhodes's game-winning home run less than 300. No other ballpark could have produced so unlikely an outcome. The Giants went on to sweep the World Series in four games.

The Giants had now played in the Polo Grounds for more than forty years. The age of John McGraw, during which the Giants had won eight pennants in their first fourteen seasons there, had drawn to an end in 1932 with the team uncharacteristically languishing in the second division. McGraw's successor, player-manager Bill Terry, revitalized the club into a World Series winner in 1933 and won a pair of pennants in 1936 and 1937. Left-handed slugger Mel Ott, who feasted on the short right field fence, led Terry's Giants. Memorably lifting his right leg high as he swung, Ott hit 323 home runs at home, but only 188 on the road. In the twilight of his career in 1943, he hit eighteen home runs, all of them at the friendly Polo Grounds.

The decade after 1937 was a fallow one for the Giants, but in 1948 owner Horace Stoneham shocked the baseball world by luring longtime

Brooklyn Dodgers manager Leo Durocher to Coogan's Bluff to assume the helm of the Giants. Durocher's arrival ushered the Giants into the golden age of New York City baseball. Between 1947 and 1957, a New York City team appeared in nine of the eleven World Series. Seven times the Series pitted the Yankees against either the Dodgers or Giants. Often the Dodgers and Giants competed bitterly for the National League pennant. The high point of these challenges came in 1951, when Durocher drove his squad from thirteen-and-a-half games back in August to catch the front-running Dodgers at the season's end, forcing a three-game playoff. The Giants narrowly won the first game, 3–1, but the Dodgers roared back to win the second 10–0. The third and final game pitted Dodgers ace Don Newcombe against Giants standout Sal Maglie. The Dodgers took a 1–0 lead into the bottom of the seventh, but the Giants tied the game on a sacrifice fly by third baseman Bobby Thomson. In the top of the eighth, the Dodgers seemingly broke the game open with three runs against Maglie. They led 4–1 going into the bottom of the ninth inning. Three Giants hits, however, made the score 4–2 and drove Newcombe from the mound. Dodgers manager Charlie Dressen brought in pitcher Ralph Branca to face Bobby Thomson with two Giants on base. Thomson drove Branca's second pitch on a line toward the left field fence. The ball was hit so hard and straight it did not need the benefit of the famed overhang. It dropped into the lower left field stands about a dozen feet above the head of left fielder Andy Pafko, who stood forlornly at the wall. The Giants had indeed won the pennant, in perhaps the most famous game in baseball history.

The intense Dodger-Giant rivalries assumed an added significance against the backdrop of the breaking of baseball's color line. Jackie Robinson had joined the Dodgers in 1947. In 1949 the Giants added former Negro League stars Monte Irvin and Hank Thompson to their roster, becoming the second National League team to integrate. In 1951 the two teams between them fielded seven of the league's eight black players, including rookie sensation Willie Mays. The dramatic playoff confrontation posed a compelling argument that even the most hard-line racists among major league owners found difficult to rationalize against or ignore, paving the way for more widespread integration.

This desegregation saga would ultimately offer me a unique opportunity to merge my vocation as a historian with my avocation as a baseball fan. In the 1970s, as a graduate student at UCLA, Jackie Robinson's alma mater, I had chanced upon the 1947 volume of *Time* magazine and avidly searched it for tales of Robinson. I discovered him on the cover of the September 22 issue, his bold, uncompromisingly ebony face high-lighted against a sea of white baseballs. The thought of writing a history of the game's integration occurred to me immediately, but I sublimated this desire for fear that the lords of academe might frown upon baseball as a subject for serious scholarship. Several years later, having completed my doctorate on a more conventional topic and after securing a tenure-track job at San Francisco State University, I resolved to follow my heart and write about baseball's integration. I signed on with an agent, who shopped this idea to numerous publishers. All rejected it, save one. Sheldon Meyer at Oxford University Press, a longtime baseball fan, encouraged my work. Although I had never published anything since my days as the sports editor of my high school newspaper, Sheldon signed me to a contract based on a brief proposal and a sample chapter. Three years later, Oxford published *Baseball's Great Experiment: Jackie Robinson and His Legacy*. Ironically, the book that I had once feared to write established my scholarly credentials.

The 1951 playoffs and 1954 World Series marked the last hurrahs for the Polo Grounds of the Giants. Over a million people came to watch Mays and his teammates in their 1954 championship season. But the ballpark, now four decades old, had begun to atrophy, and the neighborhood around it suffered from crime and decay. Robbers accosted fans, and on one occasion a bullet fired from a nearby rooftop killed a spectator during a game. Built to take advantage of mass transit lines, the Polo Grounds suffered from woefully inadequate parking. As the Giants dropped in the standings, attendance plummeted along with them. In 1956, after thirty-one years of residency, the football Giants announced that they were moving to Yankee Stadium. Rumors floated that when the Giants' lease expired in 1962 the old ballpark would be torn down and replaced by a low-income housing project. On June 18, 1958, Giants owner Horace Stoneham announced, "We can anticipate a decrease in income each year from now on. . . . As a fan and president, I know the Giants must leave the Polo Grounds." Two months later, Stoneham confirmed that the Giants would leave New York and go west to San Francisco.

On September 29, 1957, the Giants played their last game at the aging arena. Eleven thousand fans turned out to watch the veterans of the 1951 and 1954 pennant-winning teams—Mays, Thomson, Rhodes, and others—lose 9–1 to the Pirates. At the game's end souvenir-seeking fans ravaged the field, ripping up bases, pitching rubbers, signs, and telephones. John McGraw's widow, Blanche, disconsolately watched the final game. "I still can't believe I'll never see the Giants in the Polo Grounds again," she exclaimed. "New York can never be the same to me."

"Dispossessed" groundskeeper Matty Schwab and his family moved out of their left field apartment, but the old ballpark retained some vitality. Jay Coogan, whose family still owned the land and stadium, vowed, "The Polo Grounds will not be demolished quickly. I will wait for callers. I am not going to give up." In 1958 the Polo Grounds hosted Israel's tenth anniversary celebration, a rodeo, Gaelic football, and a series of Sunday baseball games featuring the remnants of the Negro Leagues. The next few years also saw professional soccer come to the Polo Grounds. The New York Titans of the new American Football League assumed occupancy in 1960, although owner Harry Wismer called the park a "graveyard" and, according to one sportswriter, most of the fans came disguised as empty seats.

In 1962 the Mets moved into the arena for a planned one-year stay. On the last day of the season, they staged a fond farewell to the Polo Grounds. Television cameras caught septuagenarian manager Casey Stengel, who had played many games at the ballpark in the teens and twenties, slowly walking from home plate to the remote clubhouse as "Auld Lang Syne" filtered through the loudspeakers. Once again, however, the reports of the Polo Grounds' demise had been greatly exaggerated. When problems delayed the opening of Shea Stadium, the Mets found themselves back in their crumbling castle in 1963. "At the end of the season they're gonna tear this place down," Stengel told home run–prone pitcher Tracy Stallard as he removed him from a game. "The way you're pitchin' that right field section is gone already."

But even in New York City construction projects inevitably reach completion. The Mets and the Titans, now renamed the Jets, moved into Shea Stadium in 1964. On April 10 of that year, the long-scheduled destruction of the Polo Grounds began. Employees of the Wrecking Corporation of America, bedecked in Giants shirts, repeatedly slammed a two-ton iron "headache ball," the same ball that had demolished Ebbets Field in Brooklyn, against the superstructure of the Polo Grounds, reducing the once grand sports palace to rubble. Four thirty-story apartment buildings, dubbed Polo Grounds Towers, rose on the site. On the patch of land once occupied by the vast green acreage of center field sits an asphalt playground. They call it Willie Mays Field. To date, no one has played polo there.

Nassau Hall, 1764. Copper engraving by Henry Dawkins. *Princeton University Libraries, Rare Books Division.*

Sean Wilentz

NASSAU HALL, PRINCETON, NEW JERSEY

n June 1956, Edmund Wilson, Class of 1916, returned to Princeton
University to receive an honorary degree, in conjunction with the
fortieth anniversary of his class's graduation and the bicentennial
of Nassau Hall. The occasion was slightly awkward. Wilson had great
affection for his old college, and especially for the memory of his departed teachers Norman Kemp Smith and Christian Gauss. A few years
earlier, when presiding over a set of the prestigious Princeton seminars
named in Gauss's honor—and presenting work that would eventually
wind up as part of his monumental study, *Patriotic Gore*, edited by another Princeton graduate, Sheldon Meyer—Wilson one day took his
friend Leon Edel on a private tour of his former stomping grounds,
enthusiastically showing off the architectural highlights. But Wilson had
never partaken of the rah-rah bonhomie for which Princeton graduates
were, and are, so famous. And more than a few Princetonians regarded
Wilson—the bookish, oft-married ex-radical and (thanks to *Memoirs of
Hecate County*) reputed pornographer—as a disloyal odd duck.

Wilson and his latest (and last) wife, Elena, sensed the underlying
tension. The day before the big event, from their guest quarters, they
could hear the nearby banging of the carpenters who were erecting the
ceremonial graduation stage and dais outside Nassau Hall.

"Come and look, dear," Mrs. Wilson remarked (or words to that effect). "They're building your scaffold."

Of course, Princeton did not hang Wilson, even metaphorically, but honored him. And so, outside Nassau Hall, tension gave way to paradox. Wilson was never shy about showing his disdain for the American academy and for what he regarded as its obscurantist obsessions. He did teach now and again, to help make ends meet (though his monotone lecturing style turned off his audiences in droves). Otherwise, he said, "writers are much better off outside colleges." And yet, there he stood, the supposedly defiant freelance man of letters, happily picking up another Princeton degree in front of the most storied academic building in the United States, two hundred years after its completion.

It was not the first ironic moment, nor would it be the last, in the sometimes unfortunate history of Nassau Hall.

To walk past Nassau Hall, as I do two or three times each workday, gives only the slightest hints of that history. With its massive brown stone outer walls, the place appears to have been there forever. Dominating the university's Front Campus, it looks, to any well-traveled academic, like the quintessential college administrative headquarters: imposing, serene, and official. (Even the bronze tigers that guard the main entrance are at ease.) Apart from small knots of tourists being led around campus by one of the university tour guides, no one ever seems to enter or exit Nassau Hall. The life of the campus is elsewhere, around the classrooms and dormitories, where gaggles of undergraduates, women and men—including, in good weather, the Frisbee players—are perpetually in motion: Nassau Hall is more like a machine that quietly goes of itself. The building is certainly important, especially to a Princeton faculty member, as the Place Where Big Decisions Are Made. But in its tranquil self-assurance, it betrays, at a glance, little of its turbulent—and sometimes paradoxical—past.

While it was still under construction, the place came perilously close to being named Belcher Hall. In 1747, Jonathan Belcher, a devout Massachusetts Congregationalist, was chosen royal governor of New Jersey, and he immediately made a pet project of supporting the fledgling College of New Jersey, then located in Elizabeth. Belcher was shocked at the degraded spiritual condition of Harvard and Yale—where, he said, he had reason to believe that "Arminianism, Arianism and even Socinianism, in destruction of the doctrines of free grace are daily propagated"—and he saw the New Jersey seminary as a potential bulwark of the Lord. Seven years later, when work began on the college's new building in Princeton, the trustees tried to honor the governor for his support by naming it after him. ("And when your Excellency is translated into a house not made with hands, eternal in the Heavens," the trustees entreated him, "let Belcher Hall proclaim your beneficent acts.") Belcher graciously declined, and suggested instead the name Nassau Hall, dedicated "to the immortal memory of the glorious King William III, who was a branch of the illustrious house of Nassau." Thus, thanks to Belcher's modesty, began the tradition that in later decades would lead to the composing of "Old Nassau"—imagine a school song entitled "Old Belcher"—as well as to the adoption of orange and black as Princeton's official colors.

The village of Princeton had been chosen as the college's new home in part because of its proximity to New Light Calvinist Pennsylvania, Delaware, and Maryland, and in part because of its salubrious location on a high ridge, well protected from the then-fearsome New Jersey mosquito. For the new college building, the trustees wanted the finest and most imposing design they could find. A basic plan, offered by the trustee Edward Shippen in 1753, called for a structure 190 feet long and 50 feet deep. Thereafter, Shippen's brother, Dr. William Shippen, in collaboration with the distinguished Philadelphia architect Robert Smith (who had designed Carpenter's Hall, later the meeting place of the First Continental Congress), translated the rough plan into a formal proposal. The cornerstone was laid on September 17, 1754, and for nearly two years workmen raised the walls of local stone and then plastered the interior. In November 1756, as the finishing touches were still being applied, the College of New Jersey officially moved in, claiming an edifice that, though fourteen feet shorter than Edward Shippen's original outline had dictated, still impressed the trustees as "the most spacious on the continent."[1]

A huge, stylistically up-to-date, Georgian pitched-roof building, the original Nassau Hall was gracious as well as spacious, more so than its later remodeled versions. In contrast to the Old World universities, wrote the college's president Aaron Burr Senior, "[w]e do everything in the plainest . . . manner, . . . having no superfluous ornaments." A depiction of the head of Homer did dominate the flat arch above the building's central doorway, and some decorative urns appeared on the central facade, but otherwise the building had a remarkable lightness for all its solidity, topped off by a bell-tower cupola patterned after the upper part of the cupola of the recently built St. Mary-le-Strand in London, much better proportioned than the current structure.

Befitting the college's primary function as a trainer of clergy, the original Nassau Hall was a place of devotion as well as of instruction. After entering the central doorway, one passed into a hallway that led straight to the Prayer Hall, flanked on either side by classrooms. Here, in the unheated north end of what is now the Faculty Room, students would be summoned by the cupola bell at the crack of dawn for morning worship—an exercise (especially during winter) of bone-chilling piety that did not sit well with later, more secular generations of undergraduates. Below, in the basement, were the kitchen, dining room, and steward's quarters. On the second floor, in a single room, was the library, above which were two rooms probably used for recitations. The building's wings consisted of small suites, most of which included a bedroom and two tiny studies. In 1762, an increase in student enrollment necessitated the completion of student chambers in the basement—gloomy, damp rooms that housed the unluckiest of the first-year pupils.

Like an Anglo-American cloister, the early Nassau Hall almost completely enclosed college life. Here, the college's tutors as well as its students slept, ate, prayed, and attended class. (Only the college president was permitted separate quarters, in a Philadelphia Georgian dwelling, also designed by Robert Smith.)[2] Yet no sooner was the all-encompassing edifice completed than bad fortune descended on the college.

In February 1757, President Burr had to step in to fulfill the duties of one of the college's tutors, the Rev. Caleb Smith, who had fallen ill. Six months later, Burr, worn out from overwork, presided extemporaneously at Smith's funeral; then, after a taxing trip to Philadelphia, Burr rode north to Elizabeth to preach a funeral sermon for the suddenly departed Governor Belcher. Finally, himself overtaken by a raging fever, Burr weakened and died on September 24. Five days later, the trustees named Burr's eminent father-in-law, the renowned Massachusetts evangelist and theologian Jonathan Edwards, as Burr's successor.

In January 1758, Edwards arrived at the President's House to great acclaim from the tutors and students. Unfortunately, smallpox was prevalent in Princeton that year, and Edwards, who had never been exposed, decided to submit to an inoculation from the same Dr. William Shippen who had had a hand in designing Nassau Hall. The inoculation did not take, and on March 22, the great Edwards died. His successor, Samuel Davies, was young, eloquent, and learned—but he had also, for years, suffered from tuberculosis, a condition the trustees apparently overlooked. After punishing himself with a dawn-to-midnight work schedule, the dedicated President Davies died after a little more than a year's service. For the third time in the five years since relocating to Princeton, the college solemnly buried its president in the old cemetery down the road from Nassau Hall.

Here, seemingly, was providence ill enough to chill any Calvinist's soul. Supposedly wholesome Princeton had become a president's graveyard. Davies's death, one correspondent reported, "spread a gloom all over the country" and plunged the college into despair.

It was only under the leadership of the eminent Scots emigré and eventual American patriot John Witherspoon, who served as president from 1768 until 1794, that the College of New Jersey truly began to flourish. Witherspoon steadied the institution's finances, increased its endowment, and ventilated its curriculum with the bracing ideas of the Scottish Enlightenment. Before Witherspoon's arrival, the college's scientific equipage was sorely lacking, especially in comparison to Harvard (which boasted numerous stuffed birds and animals, the skull of an Indian warrior, and the tanned skin of an unidentified Negro); but beginning with the purchase of the famed astronomer David Rittenhouse's intricate orrery (a sort of miniature planetarium, installed in Nassau Hall in 1771), Witherspoon quickly closed the gap. Under Witherspoon, the college also generated a hot republican spirit, carried forth into the American Revolution by, among others, three illustrious members of the class of 1771: Hugh Henry Brackenridge, Philip Freneau, and, most auspiciously, James Madison. Witherspoon himself signed the Declaration of Independence in 1776. Under Witherspoon, Nassau Hall even served temporarily, in 1783, as the new nation's capitol. Yet it was also under Witherspoon (and because of the Revolution) that Nassau Hall suffered the first of a succession of devastating physical blows. And for several years, immediately after the Declaration of Independence, it seemed that the new nation's good fortune was the college's bad fortune—and vice versa.

On December 7, 1776, British forces, fresh from their victories over General Washington's troops in New York, occupied Princeton and commenced what one eyewitness called the "twenty days tyranny." Redcoats pillaged and burned the town's great houses; and suspected rebels wound up imprisoned inside an abandoned Nassau Hall, where a regiment of regulars had taken up quarters, ravaged the library, and turned the basement into a horse stable. Even worse was yet to come. Washington's men rallied on the other side of the Delaware River, and on January 3, 1777, after an all-night march from Trenton, they inflicted their famous disastrous defeat on the British about a mile outside Princeton village. Some of the fleeing British regulars took refuge in Nassau Hall, knocked out windows, and prepared to counterattack—but Washington's artillery hit the building with such lethal force that the British were forced to surrender. (Gouges caused by the cannonade can still be seen on the building's south exterior wall.) Toward the end of the fighting, a rebel cannonball flew through one of the Prayer Hall windows and smashed the college's portrait of King George II—the signal, legend has it, that led the redcoats to lay down their arms.

Though returned to patriot hands, Princeton was a wreck. ("You would think it had been desolated with the plague and an earthquake . . . ," Benjamin Rush observed; "the college and church are heaps of ruins, all the inhabitants have been plundered.") And for Nassau Hall, Washington's victory proved a prelude for further depredations. American soldiers took up residence and stayed for five months, turning benches and doors into firewood, stripping the walls of plaster, destroying the college organ, and covering the floors with what one report politely called "an accumulation of . . . filth." Rittenhouse's orrery, which the British had carefully preserved along with the rest of the college's scientific instruments, became a plaything for the idle Americans and wound up so severely damaged that it could not be fully repaired.[3] When the troops departed in October 1777, doctors converted Nassau Hall into a military hospital where, for over a year, ill and wounded men tried to recover amid the squalid debris.

Slowly—and, in view of what had happened, miraculously—the college also recovered. President Witherspoon, who served in the Continental Congress in Philadelphia from 1776 until 1782, returned to Princeton as often as he could, and with the assistance of one tutor and one professor of mathematics, he oversaw the resumption of classes in nearby private homes during the summer of 1777. Witherspoon also handed Congress a bill for the damage inflicted on college property, and by the end of 1779, he had actually managed to collect nearly twenty thousand dollars in Continental currency. Yet by the time the money arrived, it had so depreciated in value that it could barely cover the cost of patching Nassau Hall's roof, replacing the broken windows, and making stopgap repairs to the classrooms and student living quarters. In May 1782, a newly enrolled student remarked that, inside and out, the building remained badly scarred by the war, with two of its four floors "a heap of ruins."

Local spirits revived in 1783, at a perilous moment for the republic. Menaced by a massed body of mutinous, unpaid Continental soldiers, Congress fled Philadelphia and, at the instigation of their president, Elias Boudinot (a College of New Jersey trustee), the members reconvened in Nassau Hall's barely restored library room. During the war, the British had twice forced Congress to leave Philadelphia; but now, two years after the British surrender at Yorktown and with a peace treaty in negotiation, internal discord sent the representatives packing. For four months (until Congress relocated yet again to Annapolis, Maryland), the New Jersey crossroads village and its battered college served as the capital of the United States—an embarrassment that made it difficult to gather a quorum of seven states, let alone the nine states required by the Articles of Confederation to ratify a treaty.

Despite the immense difficulties, for representatives and townsmen alike, the interlude greatly improved Princeton's morale. Once they had settled in, the temporary congressional residents found the place suitable, even attractive. ("With respect to situation, convenience & pleasure, I do not know a more agreeable spot in America," Charles Thompson, the Congress's secretary, wrote to his wife, Hannah.) And tutors, students, and townsmen got to share in the excitement of a rousing official Fourth of July celebration, the arrival of George Washington in August for a two-month stay, and, at the end of October, the receipt of the exultant report that the Treaty of Paris had, at last, been signed. "The face of things inconceivably altered," the young student Ashbel Green later commented, amid "the passing and rattling of wagons, coaches, and chairs, the crying about of pine apples, oranges, lemons and every luxurious article." After attending the college's September commencement ceremony, General Washington presented the trustees with a personal donation of fifty guineas. The trustees, much encouraged, duly commissioned Charles Willson Peale to paint a portrait of Washington, which still hangs in the Faculty Room, surrounded by the same frame that had contained the battle-destroyed picture of George II.

Congress proved much less grateful than Washington and repeatedly rejected Witherspoon's requests for additional appropriations to restore Nassau Hall. In a preview of Princeton strategies to come, Witherspoon instead turned to graduates and friends of the college for support. He raised more than seventeen hundred pounds, a respectable sum considering the hard times (though, once again, currency depreciation sharply curtailed the collected money's actual value by the time it arrived in Princeton). With the return of fee-paying pupils, along with occasional gifts from graduates, Witherspoon was able to lay aside enough cash to commence rebuilding in earnest. In 1794, the year Witherspoon died, the French traveler Moreau de Saint-Mery remarked that the college's courtyard looked "dirty and unkempt," and that the enclosure wall was in "a deplorable state." Still, the third floor of Nassau Hall had been restored, its roof completely replaced, and its floors and windows repaired. Inside the students' chambers there were new bedsteads and tables; and the hall's interior walls, partitions, and stairways were all thoroughly reclaimed. In 1800, student enrollment climbed above one hundred, and the trustees had to refurbish the basement rooms in Nassau Hall's perennially wet west wing, in order to accommodate "the expected additions." There was even talk of enlarging the faculty with new endowed professorships and of erecting additional buildings.

"Every sign pointed to a continued rapid growth," noted the university's later official historian, T. J. Wertenbaker. Then, disaster struck again.

At one o'clock in the afternoon on March 6, 1802, as students were filing into Nassau Hall for their midday meal, a fire broke out in the belfry. A senior named George Strawbridge rushed upstairs and unsuccessfully tried to quench the blaze with a pitcher of water, while other students and teachers grabbed what books, furniture, clothing, and personal effects they could carry away. By evening, all but a hundred of the college library's three thousand volumes had been destroyed, and Nassau Hall stood a blackened hulk. President Witherspoon's successor, the devout Samuel Stanhope Smith, had no doubt that one or more members of the college's small knot of freethinking Jacobinical pupils had been responsible. ("This is the progress of vice and irreligion," Smith exclaimed as the fire was spreading.) In fact, a neglectful chimney sweep appears to have been at fault. But the trustees, goaded by Smith, summarily suspended a group of "undesirable characters" suspected of foul play.[4]

Smith's judgment was just as swift—and much less questionable—about rebuilding Nassau Hall. While the students lived and attended class in local homes and boardinghouses, Smith left the supervision of the college to subordinates and spent more than a year canvassing wealthy graduates for contributions to a rebuilding fund. His efforts, along with those of several trustees, quickly raised considerable cash, and the college commissioned the distinguished Philadelphia architect Benjamin Latrobe to commence reconstruction plans. Latrobe made some minor alterations, enlarging the cupola, installing new pediments over the three front doors, and paving the hallway floors with brick. (Unfortunately, Latrobe's major contribution, a new iron roof, proved so leaky that it had to be replaced completely.) But because the building's massive original walls had survived the destruction, Latrobe decided against completely overhauling the place in his preferred Classical Revival style, and Nassau Hall retained its essentially Georgian character. The fund-raising efforts, meanwhile, proved bounteous enough to break ground for two entirely new structures—the Philosophical Building (on the site of the present Chancellor Green Library), which housed the college kitchen, dining hall, recitation rooms, and the observatory, and the still-extant Stanhope Hall, set aside for study halls, a new college library, and rooms for the college's two literary societies.

A student rebellion five years after the disastrous fire caused temporary damage to Nassau Hall and lasting damage to the college. In March 1807, three students were suspended, one for getting drunk in a local tavern, one for cursing and insulting a tutor, and one for insulting Professor of Chemistry John Maclean, frequenting taverns, and "bringing strong liquor into the college." Convinced that the suspensions were based on partial and prejudiced evidence, the accused students' friends organized a petition drive, which wound up leading to the suspension of 125 additional students—roughly three fourths of the entire student body. The same night that the penalties were announced, the discharged pupils ransacked Nassau Hall, warding off alarmed tutors and townsmen with bludgeons fashioned from the building's banisters.

President Smith immediately canceled the classes that remained before the five-week spring vacation; and in due course, with peace restored, fifty-five of the rebels were readmitted. (One of those who was not, Abel P. Upshur of Virginia, went on to become secretary of state under President John Tyler, only to get blown to pieces in 1844 when a cannon on a great ship he was inspecting—eerily, the USS *Princeton*—unexpectedly exploded). "We will probably have fewer students," one trustee wrote in the aftermath of the riot, "but a few under discipline is better than a mob without any." The first part of this prediction proved true—by 1812, the student body had shrunk to fewer than one hundred, down from the nearly two hundred students enrolled in 1806–7—but the result was penury and stagnation. Pious families feared Nassau Hall was too licentious for their offspring; others feared it was too draconian; and college receipts rapidly dwindled. Thereafter, the college entered nearly two decades of institutional and intellectual decline, a period that Wertenbaker described as "Princeton's nadir."

The turning point—arguably the most important moment in the college's early institutional history—came in 1826, when a group of loyal graduates organized the Alumni Association of Nassau Hall. After electing the aging James Madison as their president, the members dedicated themselves to promoting the interests of the college—including expanding its endowment—and scheduled annual campus reunions at commencement time. The formation of the association was to have a lasting impact on the sum and substance of Princeton life, giving the alumni an unusually close connection to the college's continuing development and originating the annual reunion celebrations that, over the years, have become spectacles of great iconographic (and even anthropological) interest to observers of elite American mores. More immediately, the association raised the money needed for Princeton's first great period of physical and intellectual expansion, including the hiring of new distinguished faculty to endowed professorships (none more celebrated than Joseph Henry, professor of natural philosophy) and, in time, the erection of two new dormitories, dubbed, respectively, East and West College.

Nassau Hall (which gained the nickname North College) was dingy and drafty compared to the newly built dorms, but into the 1850s it kept its reputation as the "swell" residence on campus. Aside from the somewhat larger cupola, it would have seemed little changed to anyone who had seen the original as constructed a century earlier. But in March 1855, yet another fire, this one starting in a student's room on the second floor, reduced the place once again to nothing more than its exterior walls. President John Maclean Jr., in office for less than a year, following his predecessor Stanhope's example, turned to the alumni for rebuilding funds, and looked to Philadelphia for an architect. Unfortunately, Princeton's choice, the fashionable designer John Notman, was far less circumspect than Latrobe had been, and he initiated an architectural vandalizing of Nassau Hall more damaging than anything the redcoats and rebels of 1777 or the hothead students of 1807 could have imagined.

Notman was a champion of the Florentine Italianate Revival style, first made popular by Queen Victoria's Osborne House on the Isle of Wight and imitated thereafter, in the 1850s and 1860s, by mansion owners and church builders all across England and the United States. Notman himself had brought the style to Princeton with his design for the Prospect mansion on the old Morgan estate near the college (later the president's house, and currently the university's faculty and staff club); and when given the commission to remodel Nassau Hall, he tried his best to turn the old Georgian pile into a squat, squared-off, arch-windowed imitation Tuscan villa. He was restrained by the college's demand that he utilize the surviving original walls; otherwise, though, he let his imagination run wild. The old central doorway was replaced by an arched stone entrance, above which Notman built a stone balcony with a large arched window. At either end of the building, he added square Italianate towers, both of them rising a full story's height above the roofline. Atop the entire building he placed a new cupola, much larger than its predecessors, that utterly dominated the building beneath it.

Notman also changed the building's interior. The old staircases flanking the central entrance were replaced by winding red-stone steps in the new towers. Partitions arose across the east and west hallways, in order to discourage student pranksters and rioters; new hallways connected adjacent rooms to create single rooms; a new library room was placed on the building's south end; and the entire place was joisted with galvanized iron as a fireproofing precaution. The improvements, especially in the spacious new library, were obvious; and when workmen hung Peale's portrait of Washington (which had been rescued yet again from the flames) on the library's north wall, a clear connection was made with the old Nassau Hall. But when students finally returned in August 1856, they occupied a very different structure from the one completed exactly one hundred years earlier.

Nassau Hall's second century, from John Notman's restoration to the awarding of Edmund Wilson's honorary degree, was much less turbulent than the first—and, architecturally, much kinder. During the decades after the Civil War, the building of additional dormitories led to the departure of the resident undergraduates, replaced first by museums and laboratories and, after the completion of Palmer Laboratory and Guyot Hall in 1909, by academic administrators. (John Grier Hibben, president from 1912 until 1932, was the first president to have his office in Nassau Hall; and beginning in 1924, the building was devoted completely to offices of the university's central administration.) Notman's most egregious error, the brooding Italianate towers at the building's eastern and western ends, was partially corrected in 1905, when the tops of the towers were cut down to conform with the main building's roofline. (Notman's grandiose cupola had been earlier improved by the installation of a four-faced neo-Georgian clock in 1876, a donation from the Class of 1866 in honor of their tenth reunion.)

The outstanding positive contribution of the 1856 restoration, the new college library, was rendered superfluous when the nearby Chancellor Green Library was completed in 1873. After serving for more than thirty years as the college museum, the room was handed over in 1906 to the firm of Day and Klauder, which designed the impressive Faculty Room. Modeled on the British House of Commons, the room is still used for faculty meetings, debates, and official convocations. Thirteen years later, in the patriotic aftermath of World War I, Day and Klauder also redesigned the entrance hall as a marble memorial to Princeton's war dead, beginning with the names of ten ex-students killed in the American Revolution.

Decorative elements also sprouted up outside Nassau Hall, at odds with President Burr's old admonition against "superfluous ornaments," but not with the building's basic integrity. Beginning some time in the 1860s or 1870s, successive groups of graduating seniors have planted ivy around the building's wall, marked off by discrete inscribed stone tablets.[5] In 1879, the graduating seniors—including one Thomas Woodrow Wilson—presented a pair of sculpted lions (adapted from the House of Nassau's crest) to guard the hall's entryway. Thirty-two years later, when the lions were much the worse for wear—and by which time, worse still, the tiger and not the lion had become Princeton's mascot—the same class donated the two recumbent, placid bronze tigers, designed by the renowned sculptor A. P. Proctor, that continue to adorn the main entryway.

A year after Proctor's tigers appeared, President Hibben, the first president to move his office into Nassau Hall, was inaugurated—and the young Edmund Wilson arrived for his freshman year. A generation later, when Wilson received his honorary degree, Nassau Hall was virtually unchanged. And so, apart from some interior and minor exterior alterations finished in 1967, Nassau Hall remains the same today.[6]

Time has softened most of the old wounds, including the self-inflicted ones. Not that the old spirit of unrest has completely departed. By moving the administration's nerve center to Nassau Hall, the university (so renamed in 1896) ensured that, from time to time, Nassau Hall would be a staging ground for protests, by activist students (most notably over the war in Vietnam in the 1960s and over Princeton's investments in South Africa fifteen years later) and, more decorously, by complaining faculty members (over the entire panoply of university issues).

Still, the prevailing note today is of sturdiness and tranquility. It takes some historical research, and a little historical imagination, to see beyond all that to a deeper appreciation of what the building has been through, and what it stands for. No longer the largest structure in town, dwarfed by the towers of Gothic dormitories and postwar science labs, Nassau Hall is, on close inspection, far more than an administration building: it is a battle-scarred monument to the university's—and the nation's—continuities and changes. As I pass by and see it, artificially illuminated, at workday's end, it glows as an emblem of Princeton's better nature, which is to be (as Woodrow Wilson proclaimed in 1896) a university "in the nation's service."

Inside the truncated unfortunate Italianate towers, countless footfalls have worn down the stone steps into venerable slopes, blending in with the genuine Georgian surroundings. And, from a distance, even Notman's cupola looks more graceful with the passing of years, vaulting above the small forest of the Front Campus, breaking through the modern car-infested clamor of Nassau and Witherspoon streets, beckoning to what Edmund Wilson called the "languid amenities" of a place of great privilege and great learning.

A group about to enter Graceland for the tour. Photo by Bert Sharpe.

Joel Williamson

GRACELAND

I first came to Graceland on a bitterly cold day in the winter of 1984. Elvis Presley had died in 1977, and the house and grounds where he lived the last twenty years of his life had been open to paying visitors for only some eighteen months.

I bought my ticket in a frigid barnlike structure in the staging area across the street from the estate. I recall vividly the squat, early middle-aged man behind the chest-high counter and his condescending manner. He had a proprietary air, as if he were allowing me a privilege rather than selling me a ticket. Dourfaced, colorless, and fish-eyed, he tossed my change on the counter with a gesture of irritation and dismissal as if my money was nothing compared to the value of the ticket he pushed toward me. I suspected from his lordly manner that he was an insider of some sort who had never before had a job he loved so much.

In 1978 Vernon Presley, Elvis's father, had the bodies of Elvis and Elvis's mother, Gladys, removed from nearby Forest Hill Cemetery, their initial resting place, and interred in the "Meditation Garden" at Graceland. The stream of Elvis fans that had previously flowed through Forest Hill then began to flow through Graceland, hundreds of them each day.

In part, Vernon brought Elvis and Gladys home to Graceland as a security measure. Already thieves had attempted to steal Elvis's body from the cemetery. Also, there were people who did not value Elvis or his memory and would desecrate his unprotected tomb. Adequate security at Graceland, however, was expensive, and Elvis's estate, of which Vernon was the administrator, was facing bankruptcy. In the crisis, Vernon vacillated. Possibly the City of Memphis might take over. Or the estate might accept donations, as did the Vatican. They could, of course, simply charge admission, but that might cheapen the memory of Elvis.

Meanwhile, Vernon prepared the Meditation Garden on the south side of the house to receive the bodies. The project included tearing up the masonry and concrete where the swimming pool and the patio had been. Vernon saved money by renting a jackhammer and putting the remnants of the "Memphis Mafia"—Elvis's bodyguards, aides, and hangers-on—to work. It was a task far beneath their already embattled dignity. Dead Elvis was no fun: no more bonuses, no more gifts of cars, no more leftover girls after Elvis had taken his pick.

Vernon buried Elvis and Gladys in the Garden, but he left a space between them for his own remains. With astounding effrontery, he thus arbitrarily determined to separate in death two people who had been absolutely inseparable in life. Moreover, he would separate forever with his own dead body the only two people in all the world who had given him any significant measure of security, love, and happiness. The decision bespoke Vernon's egregious vanity and deep need.

Vernon died in 1979. The probate court then named Priscilla Presley, Elvis's ex-wife, to succeed him as one of three trustees of the estate. It was Priscilla who turned the finances of the estate around. She did it for her daughter, Lisa Marie, Elvis's only heir. Priscilla had a talent for seeking out good advice and taking it. One adviser was John "Jack" Soden, an able and very ambitious young businessman out of the Midwest. Priscilla and Jack decided to develop a dozen acres that the estate owned across the street from Graceland as a staging area from which to shuttle people over to visit not only the Meditation Garden but the house itself. They would charge visitors a fee calculated to maintain Graceland and produce a profit. It was a brilliant idea, and it was superbly executed. Within a month of its opening, Graceland repaid the $560,000 invested in starting up the project. The Graceland tour became the core business for the estate, which operated under the name Elvis Presley Enterprises.

On that first visit I went through the house at Graceland with two friends and a very pleasant young woman guide. We talked with her and among ourselves about what we saw. Our comments, I confess, were sometimes snide. Nowadays, the visitor is tethered to a portable audiotape machine by a sort of harness and earplugs. Both sound and sight are carefully orchestrated to encourage awe and reverence. Graceland becomes a palace in a fairy tale, a Camelot, earthly yet somehow suffused with spirituality, a cathedral without sacraments. Snide comments would not get through the earplugs, and even if they did would mark the speaker as insensitive, rude, and unworthy in the temple.

The decor of the house was, I thought in 1984, "Redneck Eclectic." There was, overall, no plan. Each room seemed inspired by its own genius, and the house as a whole jarred my sensibilities.

I saw a very spacious foyer with a plain and elegantly turned staircase, overhung by a bright, glitzy chandelier. To my left, I saw a glossy hard-surfaced dining room with a run-on table and another bright chandelier. To my right, in the living room, I saw a mind-boggling, impossibly long couch—absurdly long like a stretch limousine. If Elvis had a number of visitors in his parlor at the same time, almost all would sit facing the same way like a whole row of people miraculously plucked out of a theater audience and plumped down again at Graceland. They would look at a fireplace tastefully faced in white marble and topped by rectangular mirrors reaching up to a line of perfectly spaced guttae beneath the molding around the ceiling. Beyond the living room, a sunroom housed Elvis's white and gold Knabe grand piano.

Passing to the rear of the house, I saw what everyone called, with an open wink and sly humor, "the Jungle Room." With animal skins, large dark green plants ponderous with moisture, chunky driftwood furniture, and a stiff-armed tribal throne for the King, it seemed a set for a bad Hollywood movie. The hero would be an American sailor, perhaps played by Elvis himself, shipwrecked on a South Sea island. The primitive native king would sit in the chair while commanding that the beautiful sailor, Elvis, and the beautiful petite native girl who loves him be thrown into the burning cauldron of the volcano. He is barechested, and she wears a sarong that opens well up her thigh as she struggles against her captors. In the background of all this is a noisily splashing waterfall and pool, suggestive of a toilet endlessly flushing.

The Jungle Room was a joke such as a fifteen-year-old boy with money would contrive. The same kid would think it hilarious to throw lighted firecrackers at friends and acquaintances or shoot colored fireballs propelled from Roman candles at them. Elvis and his guys, the Memphis Mafia, played such games well after they had achieved their full physical growth.

In the basement were two more exceedingly disjunctive rooms. The TV room had three television sets built into the wall side by side so that Elvis could watch CBS, NBC, and ABC all at the same time. One story was that he got this idea from a practice President Lyndon Johnson brought to the White House. The president watched the news. Elvis watched football. The furniture in the TV room seemed hard, sharp-edged, and relentlessly angular. It was anxious and irritating. Mirrors all around produced unconvincing illusions of space and reflected endless images of ugliness—large bright-yellow and black ceramic tiles grinding against each other. It seemed an unwitting attempt at Bauhaus and one that failed: chemicals and metals mixed, melted, and molded into hard shapes that hated human flesh. It was loud, and it was shallow.

The poolroom across the hall was the opposite—soft and warm, quiet and contained, like a womb. The walls and ceiling were completely covered with silk-like cloth pleated in narrow, delicate rows sometimes arranged in fanlike shapes. The finely woven cloth lined the room in rich dark shades, with quick random flashes of bright colors, a womb with myriad tiny stars. The pool table, velvety swath boxed in by heavy dark wood, footed the chamber solidly to earth. Low-hanging lamps, with broad, multicolored, cut-glass shades lighted the table and suffused the room with a comfortable, slightly reddish glow like light seen through flesh. If the TV room across the hall said "cut and wound," the poolroom said "heal."

In a curious way these two rooms tell the story of Elvis's life—the mother who gave him birth, the deep cut he suffered when she died in 1958 at the age of forty-six, and the resulting wound that never healed. Elvis's death was long in coming, but the trajectory became increasingly, appallingly clear in the last years and months of his life as his addiction to prescription drugs rapidly escalated. Vernon did practically nothing to combat his son's illness. "Elvis needs them drugs," he said. And in the last weeks, members of the Memphis Mafia vied with each other to predict the exact date of his death.

On Tuesday morning, August 16, 1977, Ricky Stanley, a Mafia veteran, was in the poolroom guarding Elvis's life while Elvis died of a drug overdose two floors above his head. He was Elvis's "brother" only by dint of Vernon's second marriage. Ricky was zonked out on Demerol. At noon, Ricky was relieved of his duties by his brother David Stanley, who locked himself in the poolroom with a friend whom he never identified. He later told conflicting stories about what he did there instead of checking on Elvis.

Meanwhile, at about 9:00 A.M. Elvis in distress had risen from the toilet in his bathroom, either crawled or walked a few feet forward, his pajama bottoms hanging about his knees, and collapsed, kneeling and face straight down in the deep pile rug. Elvis expired, and David only came out of the poolroom that afternoon, perhaps when he heard Lisa Marie crying. Lisa Marie, age nine, was home for a rare visit in Graceland with her father. At ten days, it was her longest visit since Priscilla had taken her to live permanently in California in 1972.

Interestingly, the decor of the poolroom was conceived and executed by Bill Eubanks, a Memphis decorator well known for exquisite taste and daring ventures. Paradoxically, he also did the TV room. Tradition says the Jungle Room was a window display in a store that Elvis saw, bought, and brought in toto to Graceland. One elaboration says that Vernon saw it first and expressed his revulsion in Elvis's hearing, whereupon Elvis quickly installed it permanently in Graceland, in his father's face, as it were.

Elvis bought Graceland for his mother, and before her death in 1958 the two of them had a good year's run at decorating "the mansion," as the Presleys always called the house. Gladys and Elvis discussed the decor for the remarkably continuous sweep of dining room, foyer, living room, and sunroom that ran across the entire front of the first floor. Elvis decided upon wall-to-wall red carpeting for all the seventy-five-foot length. The walls would be painted purple and trimmed in gold. White corduroy drapes would cover the ceiling-to-floor windows. "That's the way they're doing it in Hollywood," Gladys explained to a reporter.

The Presleys also intended to take down and sell a large imported French chandelier hanging in the dining room and replace it with one that was new. Furthermore, Elvis wanted to brighten up the entranceway with sky effects—clouds painted on the ceiling for day and tiny electric lights like stars for night. Elvis had been much impressed with comedian Red Skelton's house in Hollywood, and he wanted to outdo him at Graceland.

Gladys and Elvis brought to Graceland the possessions they had gathered at their previous home on Audubon Drive, a modest three-bedroom ranch-style house in upscale east Memphis. They had filled up that house and yard rapidly—including teddy bears for Elvis in his room and chickens for Gladys in the less-than-spacious backyard. Things got really tight on Audubon when the Presleys put in a swimming pool and a basic incompatibility developed between the pool and the chickens.

Elvis fans on Audubon Drive in 1956 and 1957 increased in numbers and boldness. Privacy quickly diminished. Neighbors complained and threatened to raise a fund to buy the Presleys out. Most disturbing to Gladys was the hate mail that came to her and Vernon along with the large sacks of fan mail that came to Elvis. Hundreds of letters a day, she complained, accused them of spawning a monster bent on destroying the purity of the young women of America. She began to fear for the safety of her family.

Elvis bought Graceland, then, for his mother's protection as well as her comfort. He built a six-foot stone wall in front of the house and around the sides. The rest he closed in with a high wooden fence. He installed his diminutive, lively, and loquacious uncle Vester Presley as the chief guard in the gatehouse out front and hired as many guards as needed to achieve around-the-clock security.

In the end, however, Graceland security worked hard, not to secure the estate against those who would kill a Presley, but against those who would—unbidden—kiss Elvis's feet. The most glaring breach of security of all came when two girls crawled into a box and mailed themselves to Graceland. They got there, but when they got out of the box they were too battered to do much good.

Gladys brought her chickens to Graceland along with her other possessions. She populated the backyard with, perhaps, Rhode Island Reds, and they littered it with the residue of their living. If chickens in the backyard of the mansion were incongruous, the Presleys in time heightened the incongruity by installing mobile homes there. Three of these were on the grounds on the day of Elvis's death. Two were occupied by members of the extended family; the third, by a nurse hired to control Elvis's drug intake.

All but lost to the presentation of Graceland to the world by the managers of Elvis Presley Enterprises is its true provenance. In view of what it became, it is ironic that it was conceived, built, and furnished in 1939 and 1940 by a lady of impeccable breeding and taste upon land that had been in her family for nearly a century.

Ruth Frazer Brown was born into the very pinnacle of turn-of-the-century southern culture. She was the granddaughter of Stephen C. Toof, a French Canadian who came to Memphis to work as a printer in 1852 while still in his teens. He rose quickly to become foreman of the crew that printed the *Memphis Daily Appeal* and in 1864, as the Civil War neared an end, began his own printery. By 1913, S. C. Toof and Company supplied businesses in nine states with account books, forms, and other printed matter. Moreover, any occasion properly conceived always required a Toof printing. For example, Toof printed material for the June 1887 graduation exercises at Ole Miss. The Toof Press performed again in 1986, almost a century later, to announce a reception in Memphis celebrating my marriage in North Carolina to a native Memphian.

S. C. Toof's daughter Ruth married Battle Manassas Brown, so named because news of that great Confederate victory came to Memphis on the day of his birth in July 1861. The Browns were Confederate generals, businessmen, and, after the war, exceedingly wealthy cotton merchants. Ruth and Battle Brown had two sons and a daughter, also named Ruth.

When another S. C. Toof daughter, Grace, married, Toof gave her his five-hundred-acre farm several miles south of Memphis. Grace loved her farm, and it came to be called Graceland after her. When she died, Grace, who had no children, left her farm to her two nephews and her niece, Ruth Frazer Brown.

Ruth married Dr. Thomas D. Moore, born in 1894 in Hopkinsville, Kentucky, the son of a Methodist minister. Like Elvis, he was a small-town boy who came to the big city and did well. He, however, had a head start, having finished Vanderbilt in 1916 with an M.D. and matriculated at the famous Mayo Institute in Minnesota after service in World War I. In 1923, he came to Memphis and flourished in the practice of his specialty, urology.

Dr. Moore's marriage to Ruth Brown brought him instant acceptance into the highest order of social life in the city. No doubt it was her name and the eminence of her family that caused the young couple to be included in *The Social Register of Memphis* in 1925 with one of the more lengthy and laudatory entries. This discreetly plain, blue-backed volume declared itself to be "the nearest approach to a complete record of the socially elite that has appeared in recent times." Dr. Moore got eight lines in the *Register*, mostly detailing his professional accomplishments. Ruth got three lines indicating her ancestry and education, including attendance at Dana Hall in Wellesley, Massachusetts, and Smith College in Northampton. The couple's good fortune continued the next year when their baby daughter, Ruth Marie, arrived.

Ruth Marie was a child prodigy. At four, she played the piano and the harp. When the Moores built their thirteen-room house at Graceland, it was with Ruth Marie's talent very much in mind. "Our entire house is centered around music," Mrs. Moore proudly told a reporter preparing a large spread on the new house for the October 27, 1940, society page of the *Commercial Appeal*. "We planned it for our daughter," she explained. Ruth Marie was then fourteen and a student at Miss Hutchison's School in Memphis, probably the most prestigious school for girls in the Mid-South. "The rooms have been designed with an eye for future musicales and space was essential," she went on, "not only for seating purposes, but for tone volume." The rooms along the entire front of the house, which Mrs. Moore called "the dining room, reception hall, drawing room, and solarium," could be opened up to seat five hundred people for a musical event.

Ironically, Elvis made his final personal appearance in the very space that was specially created for, in effect, the musical debut of a young woman. It was the scene of his funeral. On the day after Elvis's death, Vernon had his body brought home and placed in the drawing room, aligned east-west across the entrance to the music room. That afternoon they moved the open casket into the entrance hall, opened wide the front door, and allowed thousands of mournful fans to file by for one last look. It was risky business. Overwrought fans might attempt to throw themselves over the body. Another danger was that Elvis might literally melt in the August afternoon heat. He had lost a lot of his parts during the autopsy, and morticians made up for the loss by adding artificial materials to the remains.

Vernon also permitted private viewings of Elvis's body. That evening Caroline Kennedy appeared at Graceland's crowded gates and sent a message up to the house. The Presleys were touched. They thought that the daughter of the slain president had come to pay the respects of the Kennedy family and allowed Caroline a private viewing of Elvis in his casket, now returned to the drawing room. Vernon and Priscilla talked with Caroline briefly, and Priscilla walked with her to the casket. The Presleys were surprised that she missed the funeral the next day and even more surprised when her write-up of her visit appeared in *Rolling Stone*. She was, after all, a journalist as well as a Kennedy, and she had a story that no other journalist could match.

In the end, when Elvis died, Graceland was an aberration in the southern social order, undeniably bizarre, a silk purse turned into a sow's ear. In the beginning, however, the Graceland of the Toofs, Browns, and Moores cohered and fit smoothly into the larger cultural community. The original Graceland was Twelve Oaks—not Tara. It was the home of the genteel Wilkes family who well knew their place in the world—not that of the parvenu Irish immigrant Gerald O'Hara.

Sophisticated visitors to the Graceland of the Moores perceived immediately that these people were of the elite. The furnishings almost shouted wealth and antiquity. The reception hall was lighted by a magnificent chandelier in gold supporting arrays of crystal prisms. It had hung in the old S. C. Toof mansion at the corner of Linden and Lauderdale in downtown Memphis. The front rooms were paneled, painted a quiet oyster white, and filled with treasures gathered by Toofs and Browns over the generations: Oriental and Persian rugs, Dresden china, French blue damask draperies, a six-foot Chinese vase transported from the Chicago Columbian Exposition in 1893, in the dining room a massive century-old gold and crystal chandelier brought up from a French château in New Orleans, and in the drawing room over the fireplace, pier mirrors carried over from England by Mrs. Moore's grandfather.

Dr. Moore himself made a weighty contribution to Graceland's manorial image. Using a portion of the estate's farmland, he developed a widely known herd of purebred "polled" (meaning hornless) Hereford cattle and thus rose into the elite ranks of gentleman farmers—the gentry. At Graceland in 1940 he organized a meeting of well-to-do cattle breeders and led in the founding of the Mid-South Hereford Breeding Association. The association elected the good doctor its inaugural president.

Driving south from Memphis toward the Delta on Highway 51 in the fall of 1940, you would have seen Graceland rising among spreading oaks a few hundred feet to your left atop a low hill. It was a large house, carefully crafted in colonial Georgian style out of distinctive and costly white Tishomingo limestone, Mississippi's best. There was no wall to arrest your eye as it followed the smooth sweep of the grounds up along the curving drive and focused on the four white Corinthian columns rising two stories from the portico to support the low triangle of the pediment. For the Toofs, the Browns, and Dr. Moore, the social barrier was wall enough.

Driving farther along you might see the doctor's Hereford cattle, red bodies with white faces, peacefully grazing behind well-kept fences. Beyond the pasture were more of Graceland Farm's five hundred acres, including parts of where the Memphis airport and FedEx's headquarters now are, and where Elvis's big jet with a bed in the back, the *Lisa Marie*, would sit and wait his bidding.

Among those who called upon Mrs. Moore in Graceland in the early 1940s was Betty Carter Woodson, my wife's mother. Her husband, Dr. Howell D. Woodson, was then serving as a surgeon in the U.S. Army in the front lines in Europe. As a medical student and young doctor, he had become a protégé of Dr. Moore. Mrs. Woodson brought along her infant son, born while his father was away in the army. It was a proper occasion, and charming: the young wife calling, with her child, upon the older wife of her husband's mentor, sitting and talking quietly in the oyster-white drawing room with the French blue damask draperies.

By the early 1950s, the Moores had divorced. Dr. Moore sold his prime herd of cattle to Memphis's premier Ford dealer. The doctor became president of the American Urological Association and held important positions in the American Medical Association. He married again and moved into a house near Overton Park. In 1958 at age sixty-three he died of a heart attack while hunting wild turkey across the river near Marianna, Arkansas.

Ruth Marie, the daughter for whom Graceland had been built, became a harpist in the Memphis Symphony Orchestra, concertized in Europe, married, and had children. Mrs. Moore moved into town and in March 1957 sold Graceland to Elvis Presley. Elvis did not quibble. He paid the asking price, a bit over one hundred thousand dollars.

Graceland, in one sense, was made for Elvis. It was a classically beautiful house waiting to be taken by him, worthy of being taken and made by him into an internationally famous and lasting landmark.

Elvis himself was classically beautiful. He was gifted with the kind of body that the Greeks and Romans in antiquity taught Western civilization to idolize. He was also gifted with a uniquely rich and versatile singing voice that ranged comfortably through three octaves. Further, he had an amazing sense, a sixth sense, for music. He *felt* music, and he knew it all, from grand opera through Delta blues. Elvis had gifts, but he himself worked at and perfected his art. Music became his life, and he developed a feel for the music that masses of people wanted to hear and the performances they wanted to see. Finally, he was compulsive about giving his audiences what they desired.

Elvis took from its original setting whatever he wanted. He was ruthless in taking for his performances music originally created by other artists. One might argue plausibly that Elvis stole everything and created nothing. In truth, in all his years in music he never wrote or even conceived a single song. Apparently, he never had the slightest desire to do so. Always he canvassed the current options exhaustively. The options were vast because his interests were catholic and his talents were broad. Finally, he chose what he wanted to use and made it totally his own.

All that Elvis knew, really knew, with a depth that anyone need care about, was music. Even when he talked seriously with someone, he would borrow thoughts and lines from songs. Occasionally, when he ad-libbed lyrics—silly at best, irredeemably vulgar at worst—it became very clear that it was good that he eschewed composition.

Nine years into studying Elvis Presley, I prefer to think that he had a genius for appropriation, not theft. His great genius was precisely his capacity for recognizing in objects already made (for example, in "Love

Me Tender," a ballad already generations old when he found it) essences
that he could put with other elements—his voice, his body, his feel for
music, and certain chosen musicians—and create performances that really did move millions. Elvis plucked out of his culture and put mar-
velously into music and performance what masses of people were already
thinking, feeling, and yearning to express. He was intelligent, but his
passion was for entertainment, not philosophy, and he had no profound
personal message to convey. Hence, he was totally and uniquely free.
His performances were so compelling precisely because he was so shallow, so thoughtless, so careless.

Elvis appropriated girls and women much as he appropriated music.
He loved women, and he loved sex with women. He was uninhibited
in his sexual performance and practiced consciously to improve his mas-
tery of the art. He found his women as he found his songs, canvassing
the field thoroughly and taking whomever he pleased. During his
twenty-three years as a star, Elvis had sex with hundreds of girls and
women, many of them recruited and almost literally lined up by his
Memphis Mafia and other hangers-on. "Would you like to meet Elvis?"
they would ask attractive girls and women as casually as other people
would talk to strangers about the weather. Indeed, that was how he met
Priscilla, then only fourteen years old and barely a ninth grader in school.
Within weeks, she was sharing his bed. Yet just as Elvis himself created
no great song, he created no great and lasting love. He serviced his
lovers—performed for them—and sooner or later they all left him. All.
In the deepest way, after Gladys died, Elvis lived alone, and he died
alone.

Graceland, too, was an Elvis appropriation. It was English mirrors,
French chandeliers, Dresden china, Smith College, Miss Hutchison's
School for girls, the Memphis Symphony Orchestra, and a plantation
mansion. It was purebred polled Hereford cattle grazing quietly in the
pasture and Gladys Presley's chickens clucking and scratching in the
backyard. Graceland was the Jungle Room appropriated whole from a
store window in Memphis and a womblike poolroom created by Bill
Eubanks turned loose and running wild. It was a coat of oyster-white
paint beneath the layer of purple paint on the panels in the drawing
room and a wall-to-wall red rug in an upstairs bathroom with three-
inch pile in which Elvis died face down, having risen from his reputedly
wall-hung black ceramic toilet with a seat padded in imitation black

leather and having collapsed in the proximity of teddy bears, empty syringes, and an illustrated book of Asian derivation that coordinated the birth dates of men and women with certain cosmically optimal sexual positions.

In 1957, Elvis appropriated the Graceland that the Toofs, the Browns, and Dr. Moore had made. When he died twenty years later, seven years before I first saw it, Elvis was Graceland and Graceland was Elvis. To-day, that mutuality of identity continues, institutionalized, privatized, made profitable and perpetual by Elvis Presley Enterprises. Graceland materializes with marvelous fidelity an idea—"Elvis"—and it shows no sign of dying.

In Montgomery for the inauguration of Jefferson Davis at the Alabama State Capitol, February 18, 1861. *Alabama Department of Archives and History.*

C. Vann Woodward

MONTGOMERY

Montgomery is a memorable place, to be sure, but there is a particular place within the place that first captured my imagination. That place is a broad thoroughfare that runs up through the city to the elevation overlooking the Alabama River where the state capitol has stood for more than a century and a half. This approach was named Dexter Avenue in honor of one of the city's founders. The founding father so honored could hardly have imagined the street becoming the scene of as many historic events as it has. Marching up Dexter Avenue as a participant in one of them, the enormous demonstration in 1965 against the state's assault upon Martin Luther King's supporters in Selma, it suddenly dawned upon me that we were actors upon a stage where numerous scenes had been acted out before our time by players in many roles, with different ends in mind and different scripts to follow.

At first there were two towns, or rather rival town sites, both laid out in 1817 near the high banks of the Alabama River by speculators to attract immigrant settlers. One was named New Philadelphia by Andrew Dexter, a transplanted northerner, its leading promoter. His bitter rivals from Georgia named their adjacent site Alabama Town and called the Dexter venture "Yankee Town." Prospects for both were blighted by the national panic of 1819, and the rivals agreed to merge under the new name Montgomery. It was then a frontier village of a few hundred, half of whom lived in log houses. A malaria epidemic wiped out many of them, but survivors carried on and increased with their faith in the future of the village.

Their hopes were not without reasonable foundations. Montgomery lay at the juncture of the Federal Road from the East and the highest navigable point on the Alabama River. For human traffic as well as for cotton bales it marked the welcome transfer from land to water transportation—steamboats to Mobile and thence to any market or port in the world. Around Montgomery lay rich cotton land, vast stretches of it within the territory of Creek Indians, who were promised protection by treaty with the federal government. Squatters and thieves nevertheless crowded in to rob the natives of their land, demoralize them with alcohol, and reduce them to beggary and despair. The government's solution was to send in troops, not to remove the squatters and thieves but to remove the Indians. Manacled and chained, thousands of them were loaded into steamboats at Montgomery for Mobile and thence to the West and out of mind. With rich land in abundance, labor was supplied by black slaves brought in by owners or traders to raise the cotton. By 1840 Montgomery had earned the distinction of being the largest slave market in the state. About half of its three thousand residents were black, nearly all slaves, and on slave-sale days the number was increased by those brought in for the market and seated in groups on public benches placed there for inspection and purchase in what came to be called the "Queen City of the Black Belt."

In 1845 the city, still a small town, gained added attraction by being named capital of the state. In flush times by then, the citizens rallied to erect the new "statehouse" on an elevation known as "Goat Hill," so called because it was the place where the Yankee founder, Andrew Dexter, kept his flock of goats. The structure was built in the current style for capitols, with dome and columns, and the legislature met there from 1847 to 1849, when the building caught fire while the lawmakers were in session and was destroyed. A new statehouse of the same style was immediately begun on the same site. Completed in 1851, it still stands, serving the same purpose—though in the meantime it has served other purposes.

Only a decade after the new statehouse was completed, it became not just the capitol of the state but also for three months the capitol of the newly formed Confederate States. On February 4, 1861, delegations from the six states of the Lower South that had seceded by that time met in Montgomery. Sitting in the senate chamber of the statehouse to establish a provisional government for the new nation, they quickly adopted as its constitution a slightly altered version of the old one and established a congress of one house. Speed and unanimity were all-important under the circumstances. By a unanimous vote they also elected Jefferson Davis of Mississippi provisional president and Alexander Stephens of Georgia provisional vice president.

Davis set forth from his Mississippi plantation for the inauguration with mixed feelings and rather poor health. He made twenty-five speeches to excited crowds on the long route he took to Montgomery and arrived exhausted. But the thousands awaiting the ceremony that followed on February 18 hungered for display, and they got it. The London *Times* reporter declared, "The inaugural ceremonies today were the grandest pageant ever witnessed in the South," and the paper published the entire text of the inaugural address. Davis was driven in an open barouche drawn by six white horses through a street lined with wildly cheering crowds, some on rooftops, and up the hill to the capitol. There he took his stand between columns of the front portico (a spot now identified by a metal plaque) to deliver his address.

President-elect Davis's speech was brief by prevailing standards, but he knew he was addressing a world audience and had to offer a justification and defense of the South's cause. After admitting that he approached the duties assigned him "with humble distrust of my abilities," he proceeded to justify secession in the terms the Founding Fathers used to justify independence from Britain: "the American idea that governments rest on the consent of the governed" and that "it is the right of the people to alter or abolish them at will whenever they become destructive of the ends for which they were established." Secessionists were motivated "solely by the desire to preserve our own rights," and he hoped the North would peacefully recognize their independence, "but, if the contrary should prove true, a terrible responsibility will rest upon it, and the suffering of millions will bear testimony to the folly and wickedness of our aggressors." He closed with the promise that "we may hopefully look forward to success, to peace, and to prosperity." Not long after taking the oath of office, however, he privately admitted that as he looked out beyond the great sea of smiling faces, "I saw troubles and thorns innumerable."

The Alabama statehouse continued to serve as capitol of the Confederacy while the less impulsive states of the Upper South awaited the outcome of events. The seceded states, joined by Texas, started arming for defense and seized federal forts, and Lincoln hesitated. The shooting war began April 12 with the firing on Fort Sumter, one of the few southern forts left in Union hands, and its capture the next day without bloodshed. During the following month four states of the Upper South joined the secession, putting a total of eleven stars in the flag of the Confederacy. On May 12 its Congress in Montgomery decided for both political and military reasons to move the capital to Richmond. Four years and 620,000 fatal military casualties later the Confederacy might be said to have ended where it started. Although Montgomery's Confederate commanding general promised "full defense" of the city, its people had no heart for it. After burning more than eighty thousand bales of cotton behind ragged retreating Confederates, the mayor of Montgomery surrendered the city to Union troops in handsome uniforms and bright buttons to end the fighting at the first capital of the rebellion—three days after General Lee had surrendered at Appomattox.

My Montgomery acquaintances and friendships began in 1938, when I met the Durrs, Virginia and Clifford, living at that time in a lovely old farmhouse at Seminary Hill, a few miles out of Washington in Virginia. Cliff, a lawyer, came from five generations of Montgomery Durrs, and Virginia from the old Alabama planter family of Fosters from Union Springs, "right in the heart of the black belt," as she put it. In April 1933, Cliff became a member of the New Deal's Reconstruction Finance Corporation. Preceded to Washington by Virginia's father, a passionate supporter and friend of Franklin Roosevelt in 1932, and by her brother-in-law Hugo Black, then a U.S. senator from Alabama and destined to become a justice of the Supreme Court, the Durrs arrived with strong connections in New Deal Washington. In the summer of 1938 I was doing research in Washington. Virginia had just read my first book and invited me and my wife out to their Seminary Hill home for dinner. She had made it into a gathering place for kindred spirits from the South, mainly from her native state and Montgomery.

My frequent use of the Library of Congress, then years of naval duty in Washington during the war, followed by a professorship at Johns Hopkins kept us in touch with the Durrs during the 1940s. My admiration for Cliff as a man of principle grew in those years. He had shifted from the RFC to the FCC (Federal Communications Commission) for a time until President Truman asked him to become the head of the commission. Cliff declined, on the ground that this would oblige him to enforce the president's new loyalty program inspired by the anti-Communist hysteria and to fire anyone accused of being a spy by faceless informants of J. Edgar Hoover's FBI. He resigned instead in 1948 and opened a law office of his own. But his clients turned out to be victims of red-baiting and the loyalty policy, which scared away wealthier clients and left the Durrs financially strapped. Cliff finally returned to Montgomery and opened a law office in 1952, with Virginia as his secretary.

Our common views and occasional visits kept me in touch with the Durrs during their vicissitudes. Cliff loved Montgomery, and we were relieved to know that he was back with friends and family and kin where everybody knew him and trusted him—that is, before the civil rights struggle set in during the mid-fifties. The trouble then was race instead of red-baiting, and in Montgomery race was deep trouble indeed.

Virginia had been active and outspoken for some time in movements to abolish the poll tax statute and other state laws designed to disfranchise blacks and poor whites. That was enough to break some old friendships, lose clients and law business, and be threatened with ostracism. Then in May 1954 came the Supreme Court's *Brown* decision declaring segregation unconstitutional. At first there was no violence in Montgomery. Then the Ku Klux Klan went into action and the White Citizens Council was organized. Bitterness, threats of violence, and acts of violence broke out along with defiance of the law and contempt for anyone who sought to enforce desegregation.

Cliff was plunged into the turmoil by his defense of black people involved in the Montgomery bus boycott called in December 1954 to end Jim Crow in public transportation. That event might be said to have marked the beginning of the civil rights movement. The person who unwittingly touched off the boycott was Rosa Parks, a friend and sometimes seamstress and nurse for the Durrs. Her offense was silently refusing to give up her bus seat to a white passenger and stand after a hard day's work. When the driver ordered, "Nigger, move back," she remained seated and he called a cop, who arrested her and took her to jail.

E. D. Nixon, a prominent black leader in Montgomery, called Cliff Durr for help. Cliff went with Virginia, bailed Rosa Parks out, and met with her and her friends to discuss legal strategy. Cliff told her he thought he could get her case dropped on a technicality, but he asked, after warning that it would be a long ordeal, if she would like to use her case to test the constitutionality of the Jim Crow law. While her husband repeated incessantly, "Rosa, the white folks will kill you," Mrs. Parks calmly decided to make her case a constitutional test of segregation. Fred Gray, lawyer for the Montgomery NAACP, would represent her, and Cliff would do all he could to help without being a lawyer of record.

The response of the city's black community to Rosa Park's challenge to Jim Crow was enthusiastic, massive, and determined. At her trial she was found guilty and fined, whereupon Gray announced they would appeal the case. E. D. Nixon declared a bus boycott the very day of the trial and called a mass meeting that night, though he could not attend. Instead a brilliant new leader took over. At that crucial point the Reverend Martin Luther King, age twenty-six, stepped into the scene—and into history. He had only recently arrived to become pastor of the Dexter Avenue Baptist Church and was persuaded to let the mass meeting be held there and to speak himself. The Durrs had already met the Kings, and Virginia attended the mass meeting without, she wrote, "the slightest feeling of fear being the only white person present," because of her many friends in the black community. She estimated that there "must have been ten or fifteen thousand black people crowding in and around that church. King made a magnificent speech that electrified the black people. He became their undoubted leader that night."*

The solid support of the black people for the bus boycott amazed the whites of the city. In the morning a tide of people emerged from the outlying black section, walking to their jobs in town, and in the evening it flowed back again, still afoot. Some found car pools. The boycott lasted more than a year. Meantime, the Rosa Parks case dragged on and on until Cliff Durr persuaded attorney Gray to transfer the case to a federal court.

---

* Here and elsewhere I have quoted or depended upon Virginia Durr's autobiography, *Outside the Magic Circle* (1986), when she was present at events recounted.

That brought to the front two white heroes of the movement: Judge Richard T. Rives Jr. and Judge Frank M. Johnson Jr., both members of the three-judge U.S. District Court. Judge Rives, the older of the two by a generation and member of a prominent Montgomery family, was gentle of voice, gracious in manner, and firm as a rock in matters of principle and law. Quite as firm was Judge Johnson, whom I was privileged to know better through the Durrs, and who later invited me to his home for a good talk about the racial scene and its history. Despite legislative efforts to reinforce segregation, the two judges did not give an inch. Nor did they yield to violence when in a two-to-one decision they declared bus segregation unconstitutional and brought victory to the boycott. After that, the house of Judge Johnson's mother, mistaken for his, was bombed, and a cross was later burned in front of his own home.

The black leaders suffered even worse violence. The house of Martin Luther King was bombed, and King spoke to a crowd that was calling for revenge. The Durrs, who were present, thought he could have set fire to the city with a word, but instead he sought to persuade them not to "respond to this hatred with hatred." Next, both the home and the church of King's friend and ally, the Reverend Ralph Abernathy, were bombed. So were two more churches. In addition, the home of the white Lutheran minister of a black congregation was twice bombed, the second time completely wrecked in the family's absence. Asked why his house escaped the bombers the night of the King's bombing, E. D. Nixon explained that he sat all night on his porch with his shotgun conspicuously displayed in his lap, and the bombers passed on by his house. The bombers of Abernathy's church (completely destroyed) were identified by police and brought to trial, but none was convicted.

After local segregation was held unconstitutional, Montgomery officials closed the city zoo and public park, removed all chairs from the public library, and threatened to close the public schools rather than integrate. Local defiance of law was part of a region-wide movement, some at high levels. After Senator Harry F. Byrd Sr. of Virginia called for "massive resistance," 101 of the 128 senators and representatives from the South signed a "Southern Manifesto" calling for "lawful" state resistance to integration. At lower levels, bombing, lynching, and defiance of law equaled or exceeded that of the First Reconstruction.

Montgomery black people showed no signs of giving up their struggle in the face of violence. Martin Luther King had been convicted in 1956 by a court in the city of violating the state's antiboycotting law and was sentenced to a fine of five hundred dollars or 386 days in jail. When the sentence was suspended on appeal, King walked out of the courthouse and spoke to his followers in terms that echoed the message of Mohandas Gandhi. "We will continue to protest in the same spirit of nonviolence and passive resistance," he told them. And so they did, without violence but with peaceful marches and demonstrations. They persisted with such help as they could get from the NAACP and such white friends as they had in Montgomery.

It was during those years that I first met Martin Luther King and got to know him personally. He had read my book *The Strange Career of Jim Crow* (1955) and expressed warm appreciation of it. With him often was John Lewis, later congressman from a district in Georgia. In and out of jail and under constant legal harassment, King was doing all he could to keep his civil rights movement in vigorous action and prevent his followers from resorting to violence. The main leaders in agreement with his strategy were members of the Southern Christian Leadership Conference, a few of whom I met. An independent group, the Congress of Racial Equality, organized the "Freedom Rides" in 1961, two buses with passengers of both races that set out from Washington to ride to New Orleans in order to put to the test the Supreme Court's decision of 1960 prohibiting segregation of interstate bus passengers. The trip was relatively uneventful until the buses entered Alabama. There they met with extreme violence. One of the buses was destroyed by fire, but the other one made it to Montgomery on May 16.

By that time, "living in Montgomery was like living in the midst of a storm," according to Virginia Durr. "You never knew what was going to happen." They found themselves barred from the old Presbyterian church where five generations of Durrs had occupied the same pew. They were virtually ostracized, even by old friends, and witnessed visiting northern friends being locked up or roughed up. The worst of it was inflicted on the white and black Freedom Riders in the streets of the city. I saw all I could on TV. Virginia watched in horror from Cliff's office window. With a huge crowd yelling, "Go get the niggers! Go get the niggers!" the beatings continued while the white policemen and city officials looked on.

Virginia later wrote of her feelings: "These were my people and all they needed was the right leadership. But all of a sudden I was terrified. These were the people I was living among and they were really crazy.

They were full of hatred and they were full of bigotry and meanness." Several, however, including three local white ministers, were forced to leave Montgomery because of their views on race. Among those who stuck it out and never wavered were the two federal district judges, Richard Rives and Frank Johnson.

Confronted with outright rebellion in Montgomery and other Alabama cities, Attorney General Robert F. Kennedy had dispatched John Siegenthaler as the personal representative of the president to meet Governor John Patterson and his cabinet at the state capitol. There the governor dramatically declared, "If troops come into Alabama, our National Guard will declare war!" When Siegenthaler then called President Kennedy in his presence, Patterson appeared to back down. Even as they spoke, however, a state injunction was issued forbidding Freedom Rider buses from entering the state. The next day the one that did arrive at Montgomery set off the savage mob scene that Virginia Durr witnessed. FBI cameramen, unknown to her, recorded the whole bloody affair. When Siegenthaler intervened to save a woman student from assault, he was knocked unconscious and lay in his blood. John Lewis, one of the Freedom Riders, was also knocked out. That night Martin Luther King called President Kennedy from the basement of a church where he was speaking to report that a Klan mob outside was trying to burn it down.

Attorney General Kennedy had previously decided to file an injunction forbidding interference with the rights of interstate travelers in the state. He was urged to file it in Montgomery "if possible," because there, his advisers assured him, he would find "a very strong judge"—District Judge Frank Johnson. That did prove possible, and their expectations were not disappointed. Judge Johnson called his court to order in a courthouse surrounded by federal marshals to protect the judge and witnesses from a mob that threatened them. First he heard and denied in rapid succession eighteen motions to change the venue or otherwise delay the hearings. Before him sat the Klan chief and other Klan leaders as well as police officials charged with failure to provide protection—all with their lawyers. Also before him sat Dr. King, who represented four black ministers of Montgomery charged by the state with inciting the riots. The hearings that followed revealed strong evidence of Ku Klux Klan conspiracy to attack Freedom Riders.

On June 2, Judge Johnson was ready to read his order. A menacing crowd again surrounded the courthouse, and the courtroom was packed with observers. After calmly surveying the defendants and the crowd, the judge warned that anyone who disturbed the peace of his court would soon find himself in the federal penitentiary. He then firmly enjoined the Klan and its followers from all acts of violence and interference with interstate travelers and their rights. He also enjoined the Montgomery police from "willfully and deliberately" failing to provide protection for King and the Freedom Riders. He then delivered a stern rebuke to the state attorney general for his efforts "to enforce segregation contrary to the federal law, a law he was bound to uphold." While granting that Freedom Rides were "within the law of the United States," he forbade King and others from continuing the Freedom Rides locally in order to avoid further disorder. After the ruling, Judge Johnson was assigned federal marshals to protect his life.

Federal marshals might enforce Judge Johnson's injunction locally, but their very presence enhanced the appeal of racist demagogues and states' rights politicians. They were at work all over the South, but none of them equaled George C. Wallace of Alabama in vehemence. Wallace had suffered defeat in a race for governor in 1958 when he accused his opponent of being a Klansman. But in his next race, in 1962, he *employed* a Klansman, a notoriously racist radio performer, to write his campaign speeches, and easily won election.

His inauguration on January 14, 1963, brings us back to the spot under the front portico of the old capitol in Montgomery where the new president of the Confederacy had taken his oath of office a century before. Like him, the new governor then addressed thousands of cheering listeners packed below on Dexter Avenue. Wallace began:

> Today I have stood where Jefferson Davis stood and took an oath to my people. It is very appropriate that from the Cradle of the Confederacy, this very heart of the great Anglo-Saxon Southland, that today we sound the drum for freedom . . . and send an answer to the tyranny that clanks its chains upon the South. In the name of the greatest people that ever trod this earth, I draw the line in the dust and toss the gauntlet before the feet of tyranny, and I say: segregation now, segregation tomorrow, segregation forever.

He concluded with a dire threat, warning "those of any group who would follow the false doctrines of communistic amalgamation that we will not surrender our government" and adding menacingly that Alabama's "freedom of race and religion" had been "won at a hard price, and if it requires a hard price to retain it, we are able—and quite willing—to pay it."

Next, Governor Wallace launched a national campaign for the presidential nomination in 1964 that won cheers as far away as Oregon for his promise that "the Confederate Flag will fly again." He also proved a conspicuous candidate in two later races for the nomination.

In the meantime, Dr. King won national and international fame for his persistent nonviolent crusade for equality. In 1964 *Time* chose him Man of the Year, the pope received him in Rome, and he was awarded the Nobel Peace Prize—all at the age of thirty-five. In the same year, youthful members of his staff chose Selma, Alabama, as the site for demonstrations for the voting rights bill to provoke racist retaliation and thus arouse national support. They got more retaliation than they asked for—some fifteen hundred jailed by the sheriff, one murdered, and others beaten by thugs. King then announced a march from Selma to Montgomery and petitioned the governor for protection. Wallace outlawed the march, and when the marchers attempted it anyway he ordered in two hundred deputy sheriffs and the state militia. They attacked the unarmed marchers, including women and children, with tear gas, cattle prods, and nightsticks. This savage "Bloody Sunday" outraged TV watchers everywhere.

King appealed to Judge Frank Johnson in Montgomery for relief. At the hearing, edited footage from the TV film of "Bloody Sunday" was displayed. John Lewis watched the judge's face closely and found it as immobile as usual in court, but later wrote, "From his demeanor, I just knew he was going to rule for us." And so he did. But before issuing the order he called Washington to ask if it would be enforced by the federal government in case Wallace, who had already shown such inclinations, attempted defiance. His question was referred to President Lyndon Johnson, who assured him it would and followed up by federalizing the Alabama National Guard and ordering them to protect the marchers. He also sent federal marshals to see that they did so.

Judge Johnson's order rang with the moral authority of an ancient prophet:

It seems basic to our constitutional principles that the extent of the right to assemble, demonstrate and march peaceably along the highways and streets in an orderly manner should be commensurate with the enormity of the wrongs that are being protested and petitioned against. In this case, the wrongs are enormous. The extent of the right to demonstrate against them should be determined accordingly.

The number of marchers would be unlimited where the highway from Selma to Montgomery had four lanes and limited to three hundred where it had only two lanes. After the order was issued, his elderly friend Judge Rives paid him a rare visit in his chambers to congratulate him.

It took some time to arrange for overnight accommodations and provisions for hundreds of people to be engaged in the five-day march from Selma. That gave thousands of sympathizers time to arrive from all parts of the country to attend the concluding ceremonies at Montgomery on April 26. Virginia Durr knew very well she could expect urgent calls from out-of-town friends. "The first call," she wrote, "was from C. Vann Woodward. . . . He and Lou Pollak, dean of Yale Law School, were coming down and wanted to know if they could get a bed at our house." And there were many more calls. "The house was just full of people, absolutely full." Our evening there was a spirited reunion with old friends and allies full of exciting expectations.

The next morning we were off to join the weary marchers from Selma at a religious establishment a few miles out of town that had put them up on their last night. There, with other latecomers, we joined the march into the city. We entered through the muddy streets of the large black section of town, lined with cheering supporters, and proceeded to the paved streets of the white section, lined with sullen and jeering opponents. Finally, we turned into Dexter Avenue and headed up toward the frowning portico of the old capitol. It was then that the idea struck me that this time I was onstage for another of Montgomery's historic encounters with history.

Martin Luther King was the speaker this time—but not on the "sacred spot." That had been sealed off by Governor Wallace, and King mounted a platform built at the foot of the steps. Judge Rives joined Judge Johnson to watch, and from a window of the capitol the governor watched also. The crowd, estimated to be some twenty-five thousand, parted for the marchers, permitting me to gain a place up close to the platform. King looked exhausted from his week of strenuous efforts and not at his best. But the cheers and soaring songs of the crowd must have helped him rise to the occasion, for he delivered one of his memorable speeches. This, he said, was "a shining moment in the conscience of man," a moment that proved "we are on the move now," headed to "the land of freedom." He warned that "a season of suffering" still lay ahead, but beyond that lay "a society at peace with itself, a society that can live with its conscience." "How long will it take?" he asked, and answered, "However difficult the moment, however frustrating the hour, it will not be long." Repeating his question "How long? How long?" he soared to a climactic "Not long," and bowed before a thundering ovation.

That evening we gathered for another party at the home of the Durrs, this time to celebrate feelings of fulfillment and triumph over old fears and apprehensions. I confess personal cause for elation: hearing Martin Luther King read a quotation from my Jim Crow book in his speech. The festivities grew livelier, but hours later they were suddenly brought to a cruel and ironic end. A phone call informed the Durrs that a white woman from Detroit driving black marchers back to Selma had been shot and killed in her car by Klansmen. The news seemed tragic confirmation of King's warning just a few hours earlier of "a season of suffering" ahead and his apprehensions of violence to come.

It would be unfair and misleading to break off my account of Montgomery with such a grim ending. It took time to happen, but change for the better has come over the years since the events of 1965. Not all problems have been solved, but views have changed, passions have cooled, laws against segregation are observed, and respect has grown for those once despised who helped bring about the new order. A memorial to civil rights leaders has even been established to honor their courage.

I offer the best illustration of the change I know by a brief account of the memorial service in Montgomery at the funeral of Virginia Durr, who died February 24, 1999, at the age of ninety-five. Clifford had died in 1975. Both of them had endured hatred and ostracism for what they believed. Yet at the memorial service in 1999, attended by hundreds of mourners, the governor of Alabama ordered that the flag over the old state capitol fly at half mast, and he spoke in eloquent tribute and praise of his fellow citizen and friend. In a joint note to those who loved their mother, her daughters wrote: "We laughed, we cried, and we clapped, as we celebrated her life with reverence and irreverence. The memorial service captured all of the contradictory, complex, and magnificent things about a woman who had hot rage inside of her about the injustices and inequities in this world that God created."

Storm clouds pass over the "Vishnu Temple" formation. Taken from the Hole in the Rim, Grand Canyon. *Grand Canyon Museum and Library.*

Donald Worster

THE GRAND CANYON

C rossing a dry plateau covered by a wearisome labyrinth of pinyon and juniper, the Spanish conquistador García López de Cárdenas and his small band of men came suddenly to the edge of the greatest natural wonder in the world. What those tired and thirsty travelers actually said to each other at first sight of the Grand Canyon in A.D. 1540 is skimpily recorded. Regrettably, they did not bring along a Cervantes or El Greco, who might have risen to the occasion and produced an extraordinary work of art. The soldiers did not need writers or artists to tell them how to react to the scene, but we can wish they had them to record the moment and leave us an account.

Since that "discovery" (the Spaniards were led by Hopis), the Canyon has been an overwhelming experience for a host of visitors who have come abruptly to its edge. I have myself arrived here several times—yet on each occasion my senses grope for a bearing, my tongue seeks words and finds them inadequate, and I, too, have usually come away with no written report. Strangely, bare statistics seem the best language to express the first impact of the place: it is more than two hundred miles long, eighteen miles across at the widest spot, over a mile deep, and filled with billions upon billions of finely chiseled facets of rock and light and with thousands of plant and animal species. At the bottom is the great river of the West, the Colorado.

Plenty of words, pictures, and stories of the Canyon have accumulated since that first *entrada* four and a half centuries ago. By now the shock of encounter has become anticipated and ritualized. The place has acquired complicated meanings that we turn over and over in analysis. Secretary of the Interior Bruce Babbitt, a descendant of early Arizona pioneers, has correctly pointed out that "this canyon has come, more than any other national park, to symbolize the West, the out-of-doors, the national park system, what it is the United States is about." A massive fact of nature has been transformed into the symbols of cultural history, until sometimes the symbols seem more important than the physical reality.

More than that, the place itself has changed considerably since Cárdenas was here. A historian of the cultural landscape could write a fascinating story about how humanized this environment seems to have become. Before it was established as a national park in 1919, the Canyon had seen a scattering of private buildings—hotels for railroad tourists, mining shacks, toll gates barring the trails. Eventually it grew into what the Park Service now calls a "village," populated by nearly a thousand man-made structures on the North and South Rims, including train depots, churches, schools, barns, banks, gift shops, and employee housing. Most of those buildings have something to sell: a gourmet meal, a hot shower, a helicopter ride over the Canyon, a Navajo blanket. You can curl up on a sofa and read Marguerite Henry's juvenile novel about a charming little feral burro, *Brighty of the Grand Canyon*, or plod through more sobering accounts of clashes between itchy-fingered entrepreneurs and the ever-sluggish Park Service. You can watch spectacular videos of whitewater rafting and never get wet.

Five million people visit the Grand Canyon Village in a single year, most of them staying only a short while. On a peak day they may number thirty thousand. They choke the asphalted roads with their automobiles and tour buses and pollute the desert air with oxides of sulphur and nitrogen. To satisfy those tourists the village annually buys thirty-seven thousand megawatt hours of electricity, generates over four thousand tons of solid waste, and uses 160 million gallons of water, taken from a spring across the chasm and pumped uphill to the South Rim. America's consumer habits and urban problems have been brought even to this remote location.

In myth and reality the Canyon has come to represent for the late twentieth century the encounter between Civilization and Nature, those powerful polarities in our national experience. It offers what remains to

354

us of "the edge"—the frontier experience that we continue to seek and need. Along the rim, civilization now seems in full command, improving the accommodations and interpreting the scene. Below the rim, on the other hand, nature continues to stretch away at the tourist's feet, wild and dangerous, an unmarred and beguiling other world. Standing at the rim, the modern man or woman can feel the cusp that separates the ordering energies of culture from the disordering forces of nature. Or the chaos of contemporary life from the clean, rational order of nature. Both views of the encounter exist, and both can be heard expressed by hikers on the path that runs along the South Rim.

Not only Americans find such a place of elemental confrontation a thrill to visit; so do other nationalities. Forty percent of the tourists come these days from foreign countries; the strollers along the rim are almost as likely to speak German, French, or Japanese as English, and they bring diverse feelings to the place. Whatever their cultural differences, they manage to agree that this place offers a perspective that is no longer available in most parts of the world. America is fortunate to have such natural grandeur left; we have been wise to preserve it, and perhaps even wise to make it so accessible to all the mechanized multitudes of the world.

Coming here as a historian, I am tempted to concentrate on those diverse, multicultural readings of the Canyon, the abstractions and symbols that have developed from Cárdenas's day to our own, or to trace the human impact on this landscape. My academic training tells me to emphasize how much nature has been "constructed" even here—arranged, protected, and packaged. If I stayed up on the rim very long, undoubtedly that is what I would do: find a seat in the small library that the Park Service maintains, with no distracting windows, and focus on what people have been writing and recording here.

The truth is that I find such indoor and inward-looking history hard to write in this place. Usually, the historian seeks a story of humans making changes, but in this place the most dramatic changes lie beyond any human experience; they occurred before our species appeared on the earth. The Canyon beckons us to put aside for a while our tendency to measure everything in human terms, to reduce the world to a succession of cultural ideas, to frame everything as a confrontation between rival abstractions, or to insist on the triumph of the human imagination over the natural world.

Take, for example, the rock that defines the rim: a long, creamy-white ledge intricately carved by rain and sun, where Utah junipers and Gambel oaks thrust their roots into narrow cracks. This Kaibab limestone, named for the high plateau on the north side of the Canyon, speaks of a past that is older than North America. It dates back 225 million years and more. Limestone is made of sediments from shells and fine-grained calcium carbonate derived from plants and animals that lived in tropical waters. It indicates that once there was no canyon here; this was a shallow lake. Fossilized brachiopods and crinoids, found abundantly in this formátion, testify to that past. Grand Canyon Village sits directly—and often unwittingly—on those chalky fossils, on the hard, solidified remains of that ancient lakebed.

But when this place was a large lake, it was not exactly here—near the thirty-sixth latitude north. It was located much closer to the Equator and was part of a small continent (or large island) that was drifting toward collision with other land masses to form, eventually, the supercontinent Pangea. Think on that fact for a few moments and the mind begins to reel and boggle, not over today's dizzying vista but over a past that nearly defies our imagination.

Where are the missing 225 million years that have transpired since the Kaibab limestone was laid down—the natural archives that might link the present to that pre–North American past? They have been washed away by the rain, deposited by the Colorado River at its delta, now in the possession of Mexico. Gone from this place are some of the most amazing stories ever "written": chapters entitled Triassic, Jurassic, and Cretaceous. Gone is the entire Mesozoic era when reptiles became dinosaurs and dinosaurs may have become birds, when mammals first appeared in the underbrush. Gone, too, the whole sixty-five million years of the most recent Cenozoic era. Those stories, to be sure, can still be found in the Vermilion Cliffs that run along the northern Arizona border, for example, or higher up on the great staircase of plateaus that constitute southern Utah. But they are no longer in this place.

I watch a small rock squirrel venture out on an outcropping of the Kaibab rock to wash its face in a shaft of sunlight, only a few fatal inches from a five-hundred-foot precipice. It lives indifferent to the dangers of its perch and ignorant of how it evolved and got here. Humans point and smile, as though they know something the squirrel does not. Perhaps so, but much of what they call "history" is as indifferent to the deep chasm of time as the brown little rodent, and they stand on a tiny mental outcropping that is not much larger than hers.

Cárdenas and his troop had a great deal of trouble getting down the steep face of the Kaibab limestone; it was a cause of their discouragement and departure. The modern tourist is more fortunate. In the 1930s the Park Service put dynamite and pickaxe to work carving improved trails down the rock face, making easier gradients, tunnels, downslopes, retaining walls, and water breaks all the way to the river. Henceforth the hiker or mule rider enjoyed a wide path through even older layers of the past—a highly instructive trail if one looked at the towering rock walls and not at the yawning abyss.

No Industrial Revolution is recorded here, nor High Middle Ages, nor Ming Dynasty. This history has other names: Toroweap Formation, Cocinino Sandstone, Hermit Shale. Then one enters into the Pennsylvanian period—which has nothing to do with the politics or settlement of Pennsylvania—and the Supai Group, a thousand-foot-thick series of reddish cliffs and slopes dating back 270 to 320 million years ago. Then appears the Redwall Limestone, whose pale white rock has been stained rusty red by the overlying sediments seeping over its sharply vertical face. We are now trailing through a time of marine, not fresh, waters, thickly inhabited by small aquatic animals, a condition that also created the Temple Butte Formation with its marine sediments. Then one descends across the broad, gradual slopes of the Tonto Platform before plunging down its serrated sides, marked off in greenish layers of Muav Limestone, Bright Angel Shale, Tapeats Sandstone. The names speak of long-lasting periods when this place was the slowly receding shoreline of a continent; sand beaches gave way to mud flats, which gave way to a shallow sea invading the land from the west. Picture the Pacific Ocean covering all of California and much of Arizona. But realize that there was no Pacific Ocean four to five hundred million years ago. We are hiking through a period when this place lay over in the Eastern Hemisphere close to where the center of Africa now sprawls.

Scholars have termed all those thick sedimentary layers, from the Kaibab down to the Tapeats, including the remnants of hot deserts and warm seas, the Paleozoic era—the time of ancient life. Mainly what one sees from high on the canyon rims is the Paleozoic on display. Spectacularly carved and richly colored, it was formerly populated by invertebrate organisms (trilobites and dragonflies) or strange green forests or powerfully toothed sharks. Then, three hundred million years down, it abruptly ends at the Great Unconformity, where the rocks change drastically. Put more accurately, the Paleozoic begins there, and the phenomenon we call life begins to acquire momentum.

At this point twelve thousand linear feet of records, the Grand Canyon Supergroup, are nearly all missing from the center of the park. A huge gap in the files, and then we are into the Precambrian rocks, the oldest archives on earth, dating back 1.75 billion years and more. Exposed to sunlight, they look like well-aged slabs of beef marbled with fat. They bear the name Vishnu Schist, and the pale streaks across their grain are granite—one rock metamorphic, the other igneous. Like all the superseding layers the schist began as sediments, but in this case they were bent, folded, and compressed into immense mountain ranges, soaring higher than the Rockies, as crustal plates collided. Incredibly, all those peaks of schist were worn down to a low peneplain before the Paleozoic commenced and covered them over.

I have journeyed back in time nearly to the point where life itself first emerged on this planet, to the dark brown of the inner Granite Gorge. The rock in the walls looks fully its age, but the Canyon is actually a young river valley, only some three to five million years old. The entire chasm, with its side-canyons, buttes, towers, and buttresses, is a comparatively recent feature on the face of the earth. It was created by the Colorado River, which at last can be heard rumbling through its narrow channel. Once the river followed a different course than it does today, up the channel of the Little Colorado into a closed basin in what is now eastern Arizona. But one momentous day it broke across the divide and, with astonishing speed, began to slice through the land like a razor-sharp knife cutting through layers of soft and then more resistant cake.

The distance from the South Rim down to the river's banks by the popular Bright Angel Trail is about eight miles. In that distance the trail passes through one and a half billion years of earth history. Each dusty mile down the trail, a simple calculation shows, covers 187,500,000 years. A single foot of twelve inches covers thirty-five thousand years. A mere fraction of that foot covers more time than railroads, nation-states, the printing press, Catholicism, Taoism, written languages, cities, iron tools, and agriculture have existed. A vigorous walker can, in a single stride, pass through a hundred thousand years—more time than transpired during the last glacial period, which saw the rise and fall of Neanderthal man. In less than a minute even a plodder can pass more years than any kind of hominid or proto-hominid has existed on earth.

Have we headed down a path that leaves history behind? Certainly, we soon leave behind the history of our own kind of creature, one that has a penchant for crafting legislation and holy scriptures, that invents alphabets and domesticates livestock. But we have not left behind the history of the millions of other species that have inhabited this earth nor the history of tectonic plates, falling and receding seas, uplifting plateaus, tumultuous orogenies, lava flows, fissures and faults, climate, or erosion. Scientists call this stuff history, too, and themselves earth historians. I see no reason to deny that they are my colleagues in the study of change over time. A full sense of history, the Canyon teaches, must include more than the literate human civilizations, which have occupied only a couple of inches in the record books of nature. It must reach back to the pre-literate societies that once lived near and within the Canyon, and on all the continents except Antarctica. It must extend before humans emerged as a branch on the primate tree, and before animals with backbones or the flowering plants or blue-green algae emerged.

To the dismay of the creationists (and the more anthropocentric historians, whose unwillingness to see humans as part of the natural world is akin to creationism), this broader view of history has been gathering force for more than a century. It offers a well-established, though constantly revised, narrative. Charles Lyell, the British geologist, and his contemporary Charles Darwin were the first great historians in the broadest sense. The sciences they founded—historical geology, evolutionary biology, ecology, and biogeography—have furnished the intellectual base on which modern thought stands.

The names of those scientific historians are attached to prominent features in the Grand Canyon, fittingly, for the Canyon may be the single best place anywhere to take in the earth's history that they told. Unfortunately, those features are not easily accessible to the casual visitor. Darwin Plateau, along with the adjoining Evolutionary Amphitheater and Spencer and Huxley Terraces, is located along the south side of the Canyon far from the hotels and shuttlebuses. Likewise, LeConte Plateau, Shaler Plateau, Geikie Peak, Marsh Butte, and Cope Butte (all named after prominent British and American geologists and paleontologists of the late nineteenth century) take more than ordinary effort to see. Lyell Butte is situated midway between the parking lots at Yaki and Grandview Points, but it is too far from either to get much notice.

The most famous figure in Canyon exploration was John Wesley

Powell, who in 1869 led the first expedition down the Colorado River, from its tributary waters in Wyoming through the Canyon and beyond. It was he who named this place, as he named many of its prominent features. Although celebrated as a heroic feat of adventure, the Powell expedition was conceived as a scientific exploration, a journey into unknown time as well as unknown space. Powell's government report of 1875, *Exploration of the Colorado River of the West and Its Tributaries*, has become a classic work in popular scientific and outdoor nature writing. Directly across the river from the Darwin Plateau stands the Powell Plateau—and this is fitting, too, for it was Powell who first brought the full force of the new earth history to bear on this place.

Extending from the Powell Plateau is a small appendage, Dutton Point, named after the man whom Powell encouraged to write a more complete narrative of the place, Capt. Clarence Dutton of the U.S. Army. He too was a historian, as testified in the title of the magnificent book he published in 1882, *The Tertiary History of the Grand Canyon District*. Never mind that much of the science in that document has since been revised; Dutton, like Powell and his other teachers, understood the essential fact that one could see deeper into time here than anywhere else. One needed an entirely new sense of the past, with more years in it than either oldtime religion or oldtime science had allowed, in order to create what Dutton called "the sublimest thing on earth."

It is late afternoon when I sit down to rest on the sandbar where Bright Angel Creek meets the Colorado River. Powell encamped here on August 15, 1869. A few things have changed since then. I can see two small footbridges nearby, the only ones within the length of the Canyon. Behind me are a campground and the rustic cabins of Phantom Ranch where hikers may stay overnight. It is not difficult to find even here the handiwork of humans or the ironies of a civilization seeking comforts in the wild. The great river, light brown and smoothly rippling at my feet, seems to flow unchanged. But since Powell's expedition it has been altered by modern engineering: where once it carried four hundred thousand tons of sediment a day, it now carries only forty thousand tons; the rest are left behind Glen Canyon Dam, which sits less than a hundred miles upstream.

Yet it is not man's triumph that seems most obvious at this bottom of the world but rather the transience of what we have done. Almost none of the structures put here by humankind is older than a century, and the dam has been standing for a mere thirty-six years. The oldest structure in this place is an Indian ruin consisting of the bare floorplan of a rock-walled house, indicating that a few hundred years ago people tried to live and raise a garden here. They have left only the barest trace of their existence. Humans have come and they have gone from this place. So have other organisms—the giant Shasta ground sloth, the early horse, the camel, a mountain goat. The impermanence of any achievement is the insistent, humbling message.

With a historical narrative so big and complex, historians clearly have to arrange a division of labor. Some must focus on telling the Precambrian, others the Tertiary, still others that little sliver of events labeled American. But division of labor should not bring isolation or ignorance of what other historians are finding. Even those who choose to write about twentieth-century politics should be aware that, in the end, the earth has only one history—a history in which humans have played a sometimes significant, but more often an insignificant, role or none at all.

Even from an incorrigibly anthropocentric view, this place suggests that what humans have done to the earth may be less important than what the earth has done to humans. Powerful forces have long been setting the terms of our existence; they have influenced what we have done and what we have been able to do. If we acknowledge that nature is not a permanent, unchanging fixture in our lives that we can take for granted, that it is ever-active and filled with extraordinary change, we may better grasp that lesson of the Canyon. Shift the environment ever so slightly this way or that, and there must be immense consequences ramifying throughout all forms of life. Prolong a drought, move a shoreline, change the soil, stir up a storm, eliminate a key species, drop a rock on an unsuspecting victim, and the fate of individuals and societies may be profoundly affected.

What if the Colorado Plateau still happened to be under water, as it so often has been? What if this place remained a coastal beach facing a wide ocean? What difference would that have made in the westward movement of Americans across the continent? In the construction of railroads, the development of mineral wealth, the placement of industry and towns, the appeal of tourism, the power relations between nations?

What if this place were better favored by rainfall so that it supported a lush green forest or grassland, preventing erosion on anything like the scale that has occurred? What if the Colorado River coursed through a broad, gentle valley like that of the Ohio or Missouri, rich in agricultural possibilities? Or what if, on the contrary, this place was a veritable Sahara swept by unrelenting winds, heaping up dunes to the horizon and covering over the roads and hotels with sand? Or what if imposing mountains still stood here, deflecting the flow of the prevailing wind currents, creating a rain shadow to the east? How might those alternative environments affect the lives of humans in this place, on this continent, and over the whole planet?

Those are not the fantasies of science fiction but real possibilities derived from the real history of the earth. They point us toward asking not only what might have been different in human terms had the earth been different, but why societies have taken the paths they have. Culture alone can never account for all historical changes, perhaps not even the largest changes. Nature also must be reckoned with, and human history must share the vision and insight that has animated all those other historians—geologists, evolutionists, geographers, geneticists—who have come to this place and tried to fathom the past. A human history of Arizona or the United States that is not animated by that vision, or is scientifically illiterate, is no longer defensible.

I came to that realization long before ever visiting the Grand Canyon or hiking its trails. Years ago, while sitting in graduate seminars offered by one of the world's finest universities, something important seemed to be missing from the conventional historian's view of the world: a sense of soil, of the vulnerable ecosystems on which societies depend, of the still-powerful cycles of nature that can disrupt and destroy, of the visceral pleasures of the outdoors. History was as myopic, and as arrogant, as humanism in general.

In those days I had to read a great deal about the significance of New England theology, but nothing about the significance of the glaciated landscape where the Puritans tried to make a new home. In my seminars I learned much about oppressive labor conditions in the South, but nothing about the boll weevil or malaria or hurricanes or the Mississippi River in flood season. And few of my distinguished mentors seemed aware that the defining fact of life for Americans living west of the hundredth meridian, particularly those engaged in agriculture, was aridity. Few of them, I suspect, had ever read John Wesley Powell's *Report on the Arid Lands*, or had read even Charles Darwin or Othniel C. Marsh.

Down the street from my seminar rooms, in the institution that Marsh established, the Peabody Museum of Natural History, there were displayed large dark bones of ancient reptiles dug out of the loess beds of Kansas and Nebraska, but the Department of History seemed unaware that those fossils were also part of the history we must write, that those bones came from a past that is still setting the terms of human life.

Growing up as I did on the banks of the lower Colorado River and on the Great Plains, where nature is always an immediate and obvious agent in human affairs, I must have been unconsciously prepared to see the deficiencies of the academic imagination. Seminar rooms are not good places to gain a feeling for the shifting earth; no more are temperature- and humidity-controlled libraries. They can distort judgment and obscure vital ecological dependency.

My first project as a different kind of historian was to teach myself ecology, which I did by writing its history. From there I went west, back to revisit the Plains in their most tragic modern moment, the Dust Bowl thirties, and then back to the Colorado River and its canyons to learn how Americans had tried to escape aridity by building dams and irrigation canals. In both cases I discovered strategies that have produced as much failure as success. Most recently I have taken up the life of Powell, the Canyon's first great interpreter, because in his driving quest to understand scientifically and aesthetically the infinitely variable American land, I believe, lay the possibilities of a new, broader history as well as a more careful settlement and use. We can find in Powell and, indeed, in our whole wonderful panoply of explorers, scientists, writers, artists, and conservationists a tradition of thinkers who were alert to the significance of nature and who stand ready to help us recover a deeper sense of the past.

The way back to the Canyon rim, where civilization so overwhelms the senses and imagination, is long and arduous, always harder on the body than the way down. I would rather sit by the river for a while and reflect with Powell on the formidable power of nature demonstrated in the historical record here. It is no denigration to say that civilization is neither sufficient nor omnipotent unto itself. Civilization is a late, often glorious, but highly precarious and ephemeral moment in earth history. We will never fully understand our little moment in time until we acknowledge all that has come before.

Lucas Myers as Prospero in William Shakespeare's *The Tempest,* with other members of the cast, Spring 1941.

The Rev. George Boggan Myers and Margaret Jefferys Hobart Myers in front of Saint Luke's Chapel, Sewanee, on their motor-scooter, c. 1941.

Bishop Hunter Wyatt-Brown (*left*) and Bishop Frank Juhan (*right*), Sewanee, c. 1948.

Bertram Wyatt-Brown

SEWANEE—HOW TO MAKE A YANKEE SOUTHERN

Memories of the 1940s

Honore invicem praevenientes.

—Romans 12:10

A dead mule was lying in the middle of the two-lane road. The trip in the late summer of 1940 to reach the University of the South on the Cumberland plateau had been scary enough for an eight-year-old from Pennsylvania Dutch country. Although Harrisburg, my birthplace, was not at the center of that culture, I had had two teenage Amish girls for nannies. The new territory was something really different. I had no experience at all with mountains or country life, much less farm animals, alive or dead. Hairpin turns on a narrow highway, yawning vistas into the deep coves below—these motions and sights had me slightly dizzy. We were riding in my much older brother Charles's "Blue Flash," as he had christened his 1936 four-door Ford convertible.

I wish to thank Lucas Myers, Elizabeth Winton, and John Gass Bratton of Sewanee, Tennessee; Anne Wyatt-Brown and Susan Lewis of Gainesville, Florida; Charles and Mary Shepherd Quintard Wyatt-Brown of Port Royal, South Carolina; Laura James of Barnes, London; and Werner Honig of Halifax, Nova Scotia, for their indispensable assistance.

The mule remains in my mind more than the ride up from Chattanooga sixty meandering miles behind us. Where I was going was one of the choicest, most beautiful parts of the Appalachian range. Even the names of the most prominent sights were almost poetic: Morgan's Steep, so named (no doubt mythically) for a Rebel general officer who had fled pursuing Federals by leaping with his horse over a high bluff and escaped; Lost Cove Cave, situated below poet and memoirist William Alexander Percy's summer place, Brinkwood; Point Disappointment; and, my favorite, Fiery Gizzard, with its waterfall and swimming hole. Wonderful names for the scattered settlements near Sewanee abounded: Sherwood, presumably named for Robin Hood's hangout, and nearby, Garnertown, perched on the side of the mountain and famous locally as the moonshine capital of Franklin County.[1]

Similarly poetic, for white southerners at least, were the Confederate deities who stood watch over the place. The Episcopal college had been founded a few years before the Civil War as a refuge from lowland summer heat and malaria. In those early days, the school year began in May and closed at Christmastide. Politics also determined the choice of location. By situating the school on so isolated a Parnassian height, the founders hoped to quarantine planters' sons from those dangerous abolitionist ideas and city ways that prevailed at northern institutions of higher learning. After the Civil War, penurious Rebel officers sheathed their swords to enter a quiet, academic life. Josiah Gorgas, the former Confederate chief of ordnance, had served for a time as vice chancellor, though not very happily. Football was played on Hardee Field, dedicated to the memory of Confederate General William J. Hardee. The papers of Leonidas L. Polk, a university founder, bishop of Louisiana, and general under Joe Johnston, were deposited in the library. The descendants of Edmund Kirby Smith, the last Confederate general to surrender in 1865, headed local society. His son, the town's physician, occupied a Tara-like mansion opposite Hardee Field. The oldest house in Sewanee, a spacious, sturdy log cabin still in use, called "Rebel's Rest," was owned by the heirs of Major George Rainsford Fairbanks, another Civil War hero. In the college's St. Augustine's Chapel, fading Confederate battle flags filled casements along the side aisles.

On this first encounter, I cared little about any of such attractions, not even the Rebel ghosts. Nor had I yet had the experience of reading the Barsetshire series to notice any resemblance between Sewanee's enclosed Anglican domain and Anthony Trollope's imagined cathedral close. As at Oxford or Cambridge, all professors and upper-class students had to wear black gowns to class and church. The university's buildings—classrooms, chapels, dormitories, and even the fraternity houses, designed for parties and meetings and not student living—were chiefly in the English gothic style. They were constructed, however, with skillfully cut sandstone that Sewanee village workmen had quarried. Moreover, many of the residences had so mid-Victorian an appearance that a visitor might expect to see emerging from one of them a figure resembling Archdeacon Theophilus Grantly or some other Trollopian clergyman resplendent in gates-ajar collar, gaiters, and black frock coat.

We swerved around the mulish impediment. The Tennessee legislature may have passed fencing laws by then, but mountain folk—covites, the university people called them—were not likely to pay much mind even when their cows and mules wandered into unlucky circumstances. I felt that I had been wrenched from Pennsylvania in order to live on a desolate mountaintop. To be sure, I was glad to be reunited with my grandmother, as we were old companions. Then in her seventies, Eliza Matthews Little was my mother's mother. Yet, though things turned out better than I anticipated, that mule struck me at the time as a very inauspicious sign of the new life I was about to lead.

It was a matter of perplexity why I was taking this journey in the first place. I had loved Harrisburg. To me it seemed a great metropolis, although fairly small to more experienced city-dwellers. Streetcars cheerily clanged bells; streetlights blinked on when it turned dark; sidewalks teemed with all sorts of people, some well dressed, some in ragged cast-offs. A few years before, a strolling prostitute was furious when I accidentally tore her stocking while pedaling my velocipede (i.e., tricycle). Sitting on the stoop in front of the house, my grandmother had shooed her off, but I recall the woman's angry, garishly red-lipped face as if it were yesterday. Those were Depression times. Across from our house at 321 North Front Street, I remember seeing men, clearly out of work, settling themselves under the trees and on the park benches overlooking the Susquehanna. They sometimes shared whiskey hidden in brown paper bags, much to the consternation of the high-toned residents on our block.

Riverfront Harrisburg had its dramatic moments. In March 1936, one of the most exciting events in my early years had occurred. The memory is still fresh. Swollen by melting snow and rain, the Susquehanna had become almost level with Front Street and had cut off the flooded north end of the city from our section, which was on higher ground. The angry waters rushed underneath the Walnut Street bridge with no more than a foot or two of clearance. Fascinated, I watched the water rise within a few feet of the bank across the street. Every day I would tug the skirts or pants legs of somebody to take me out to see if the bridge were still upright. Over it traveled a seemingly endless parade of oil trucks, filled with fresh water from Philadelphia since flood water had polluted the city reservoir. Without the benefit of electricity and natural gas, a small birthday cake, with four candles, had magically appeared on March 19 with the help of a tiny kerosene stove.

No less wonderful than the vagaries of that river were the Saturday afternoon children's concerts of the Harrisburg Symphony Orchestra under the direction of a Dr. Rauschenbush. The auditorium had a sky-blue ceiling covered with gold stars. Looking upward had often set my imagination flying into the cerulean heavens, especially if the orchestra was playing "The Ride of the Valkyries" or some other galloping music.

Apart from such experiences as sliding on waiters' metal trays down wintry slopes at the Harrisburg Country Club or throwing rocks at debris floating in the river, I missed roaming the oversized mansion we occupied but did not own. My father's predecessor, the elegant Episcopal Bishop James Henry Darlington, had called it "Bishopscourt." Darlington arranged for this palace, so to speak, to be used as his diocesan office and residence. (He had married into Pittsburgh oil.) At his death in 1930, the bishop willed it to the Diocese of Harrisburg for the comfort and grandeur of his apostolic successors. In 1931, the year before I was born, Father had become the second bishop of this recently created episcopacy, which extended through central Pennsylvania from the Maryland to the New York border—some seventeen-thousand square miles in the midst of a predominantly Lutheran and Mennonite-Amish population. At Bishopscourt, I remember measuring the distance from the front door to the end of the laundry room—120 feet. Though narrow in width, the house ran the length of a city block. The front parlor was furnished with Persians, uncomfortable cherry-wood Victorian furniture, pictures of sailing ships mounted in gilt frames, and an ebony Steinway.

On the second floor was "the baronial hall," as it was called. It seated at least a hundred people, with a low platform at one end and a balcony at the other. My mother used to give an elaborate Christmas reception there and sing for the guests. (She had studied in Berlin before World War I under "Signor Lamperti," as she used to sigh nostalgically, and had an apprenticeship appointment with the Bremen Opera Company before accepting my father's offer of marriage in 1911.) The hall was perfect for roller-skating—that is, until I was caught ruining the wooden floor. On the first floor, Father held early Sunday morning family services in a small chapel called "the Chapel of the Holy Spirit," with tile floor, marble altar, and a stained glass window with a dove of peace descending. Most often he was not home Sundays because episcopal duties sent him on trips to such struggling parishes as the mission at Shamokin in the coal-mining district, the railroad town of Altoona, or Hershey. I fondly remember that I once visited there with my parents and at the famous factory watched the churning of chocolate liquid in the steel vats. Before her departure to Sewanee early in the summer of 1940, my grandmother and I had lived snugly on the fourth floor. At that elevation it was possible through a window to see the glow from the lights illuminating the state capitol not far behind the house.

What had induced my parents to exile me from such grand surroundings? Until about five years ago, I did not know. What I recall, however, is an incident at our summer house, Blue Ridge Summit, Pennsylvania. It stood within walking distance of the Mason-Dixon line, which ran through the woods nearby. I had sobbed one summer evening in 1940 when it was still fairly light. Downstairs everyone else was engaged in animated conversation. Meantime, I had been consigned to early bed for what I thought was no good reason. Mother came up to investigate the noise. She offered a guess: "You miss Grandma, don't you?" At once, I agreed. No doubt it seemed a better justification than a whine about exclusion from the goings-on below. "Well," she said, "your father and I have decided that she needs you, too. Grandma would be so lonely down there in Tennessee, and so we are going to send you to her." I was stunned into silence, I am sure. And so a few weeks later began the trip to that Episcopalian stronghold in the midst of the Cumberland Mountains.

Initially Sewanee failed to excite me. Yet, by comparison with much of the South, the place was—and is—gently urbane. Its sophistication lay chiefly in the realm of learning but obviously not in the appointments of a city. Sewaneeans—a population of less than a thousand—were justly proud, though, that University Avenue, the main street, had been recently widened and concreted. Many of the tributary lanes, however, were still unpaved. Handsome sidewalks of local brownish pebbles set in concrete flanked University Avenue. Yet, unlike Harrisburg, there were scarcely any people—well dressed or otherwise—to watch as they made use of them. The college town always looked forlorn and abandoned when the students were away on vacation. No marquees of movie houses announced the shows inside; no storefront windows could be inspected. One or two places sold ice cream cones, chiefly the University Supply Store, but in Harrisburg my teenage sister Laura used to take me with her friend Mary Herman to a variety of places for sodas. Instead of city noises at nighttime, I heard few reassuring sounds in the vast silence of Sewanee.

After I was gradually introduced to things southern, some compensations emerged. Grandmother had taken up temporary quarters in Powhatan, the home of Confederate General Edmund Kirby Smith's two daughters, Mrs. Ruth Hale and Miss Carrie Kirby Smith. The former general, who had led the Rebel forces in the southwestern theater, had learned to survive on old memories and the meager salary that a professor of mathematics could draw. The widow and her sister were famous on the mountain for the astonishing range of their profanity. They had a very self-possessed black servant who had charge of their wagon and horse. As a treat to the newcomer, he let me hold the reins when we clopped down University Avenue to Preston Brooks's general store on some errand for the landladies. Preston Brooks, the proprietor, it should be added, was the grandson of the famous South Carolinian assailant of the fiercely antislavery Charles Sumner, senator from Massachusetts, in May 1856. Delivered with a gutta-percha cane, the attack aroused the fury of northern voters and helped to prompt the great conflict. In the South, Brooks was hailed as a hero for vindicating the honor of his state and a senatorial kinsman, whom the passionate Sumner had denounced on the Senate floor in a two-day harangue about "the Crime against Kansas." Congressman Brooks's Sewanee grandson liked to tell the story of how Yankee soldiers had ransacked the house in Edgefield during William Tecumseh Sherman's savage advance through the state. They seized the many canes they found on the premises. Years after the war, a looter returned one of them to the family, explaining how he had long regretted stealing the instrument that had felled Sumner in the Senate chamber. Brooks's family had been amused: the original cane, of course, had been shattered to smithereens over the luckless senator's head. The Union veteran had simply sent back one of the scores of canes that Brooks had received as replacements from sympathetic admirers of his praiseworthy deed, as fellow fire-eaters saw it. I was to waste many hours avidly reading the ten-cent comic books that Brooks's emporium had in stock and bought just enough of them to prevent being chased out for making the remainder shopworn and unsaleable.

We spent only a week or two at Powhatan boardinghouse before moving to the university's guest house, Tuckaway Inn, run by the outspoken, very wide-beamed, and half-blind Miss Johnnie Tucker. She had a gruff manner and a gravelly voice, but you could not help liking her. Along with the various Kirby Smith women, she was one of the many old ladies who governed the morals and social life of the inhabitants. Miss Johnnie and another Kirby Smith—known as Miss Amy, though widowed—could almost outyell the undergraduates at the football games. Usually, however, the results between the opposing goalposts were disappointing. After a week or two at Tuckaway, we finally moved into the house on University Avenue that Mrs. Little, as Grandmother was generally called, was renovating. It had been built shortly after the Civil War. It had a two-story porch on the front, floors made of wide plank boards, and a huge coal furnace with a red metal hopper. Grandmother had the building encased in asbestos shingling (to save future paint jobs), and she ordered the porches to be removed to give the front rooms more light. It was a mistake, I thought at the time. No doubt I had planned to roller-skate on the upper veranda, even if the space could not match the old baronial hall.

My resentment about the transfer south was inevitable. From the perspective of family history, however, my presence in Sewanee had its rationale. Both region and locale were deeply embedded in the very devout Episcopal, patriarchal household into which I was born. Father never let his children call him Dad, only Father. To catch his attention in the Harrisburg days, I sometimes burst out with the forbidden word and for my temerity was tickled in the ribs, causing nearly painful spasms.

Born in 1884, Wyatt Hunter Brown, as his name then was, came from a somewhat financially straitened family of eight children in Eufaula, Alabama. His father, Eugene, had been postmaster during the two Grover Cleveland administrations but was demoted to assistant post-master under a Republican placeman. The latter, who was the assistant in the Cleveland days, was illiterate. So Eugene had to perform the same work for less money during the succession of Republican regimes—at least if family legend can be trusted. In any event, it's hard to imagine that either one of them was overtaxed in sorting mail for the sleepy little cotton village on the Chattahoochee. At age fourteen, Grandfather Eugene had served in the Civil War. As the family tale goes, he and a brother, still younger, had arrived at the Virginia front only to get home-sick after a few days. Some generous-minded officer put the pair on a train heading toward home. Notwithstanding, Eugene liked to tell the story on himself, a not so conscientious veteran of the momentous war.

My father and his favorite elder brother, Bertram, somehow scraped up enough money to attend both the college and St. Luke's Seminary at distant Sewanee. Father was an excellent pool player. If family legend is reliable, he financed his studies by his bank-shot skills at eight-ball, de-spite a nearsightedness that bordered on blindness. Mother, formerly Laura Hibbler Little of Montgomery, Alabama, had attended a girls' finishing school in Monteagle, a mountain hamlet close to Sewanee. In the mid-1930s my two older brothers, Wyatt and Charles, also took their degrees at the university. Deciding to follow in our father's footsteps, Charles was still enrolled at the theological seminary when I arrived in 1940.

Another early source of southern-ness for me was Bishop Wyatt Brown's dedication to the Democratic party and the Lost Cause. Al-though among the more conservative southern politicians Franklin D. Roosevelt's standing had diminished by 1940, his stature in our house was matched only by that of Robert E. Lee and Jefferson Davis. They formed a kind of secular trinity for the family to worship. In the ves-tibule of Bishopscourt, Wyatt Brown proudly hung a steel engraving of the solemn, white-bearded general, with a Confederate flag tastefully draped over a corner. For him, as opposed to its usage today, the Rebel banner did not signify racial antipathies but did mark his sense of alien identity in the land of the Union victors. No doubt, he took pleasure in gently affronting Yankee guests in Harrisburg with the display. Had he lived to see such a sight, Simon Cameron, whose town house was next to ours, would have been displeased. Cameron, unsavory boss of Pennsylvania politics, had been Abraham Lincoln's first and fairly incompetent secretary of war. As for Jefferson Davis, family lore has it that he had taken tea at Eugene Brown's house in Eufaula on a nostalgic post–Civil War tour of the Lower South.

Father liked to remind Governor George Earle, a one-term state executive of Pennsylvania and author of the state's "Little New Deal," that they were the only Democrats on Front Street. The governor's residence was down the block. As if to prepare me for my coming years in the South, at bedtime Father often read aloud from the Rev. Abram Ryan's collection of melancholy post-Confederate poems. The Catholic priest's lugubrious "The Conquered Banner" was a favorite and closed with the immortal lines:

> Furl that Banner, softly, slowly!
>   Treat it gently—it is holy—
> For it droops above the dead.
>   Touch it not—unfold it never,
> Let it droop there, furled forever,
>   For its people's hopes are dead!

I used to read it to myself when that become possible. At one time I could recite it complete.

Those first weeks in Sewanee before school began were easy neither for me nor for Grandmother. I had little to do but fidget, driving her to distraction. A stranger herself, she had no idea with whom I could get together, and the famous southern hospitality had not materialized to our benefit. At wit's end, she told me to run out and ask that "nice colored boy walking down the street to come over to play." Although he was much bigger and older than I was, I took the chance. In those days, a black kid had little choice but to do what white people commanded. But Grandmother's gesture failed to work. He only wanted to roughhouse. Worse, from my point of view, he had six fingers on each hand. The vestigial double thumb could have been surgically removed if there had been money for an operation, but I found the genetic anomaly pretty alarming.

My parents and grandmother had fortunately enrolled me in a little grammar school called Bairnwick. As the day for starting school approached, I thought here at last would be salvation from boredom. Housed in the airy ground floor of a great stone mansion, Bairnwick— Scottish for "home of the children"—was a fitting place for me. Margaret Myers, the headmistress, a Yankee through and through, had brought a touch of the reforming spirit from that region into a conservative society. The South had changed her outlook very little. For that reason, she was not well liked by the more reactionary keepers of the old Confederate flame, who were still powerful in community life. In later years she was very active in promoting the civil rights cause and public school integration on the mountain. She and Scott Bates, a professor of French at the university, ran a summer remedial program to prepare African-American pupils for entering the public school system.

Margaret Myers had to have been one of the most intellectual, dynamic, and large-hearted women on the mountain, or indeed in the South as a whole. As her son Lucas puts it, she was "a force of nature" with an air of command that one dared not cross.[2] In 1920, she had married the Rev. George Boggan Myers, professor of pastoral care, ethics, and philosophy of religion at St. Luke's Seminary. He had two children—Alice and Alexander—by Verna, his first wife, who had died in 1919, in the devastating flu epidemic. There were six more by Margaret: George Clifton, killed in action in World War II, Henry Lee, Rosamond, Elizabeth, Lucas, and Hobart, who also has died. The highly learned professor's new bride, Margaret Jefferys Hobart, had attended Brearley School in New York City and had graduated in classics from Bryn Mawr in 1911. Her father, Henry Lee Hobart of New York, a transplanted New England financier of note, had served as senior warden of Trinity Church at the end of Wall Street. Before her marriage, she had once marched in a mid-Manhattan suffragist parade. Hoisting her own banner in the front rank, she had boldly passed the windows of the Union League Club where her father, a deep-dyed McKinley-style Republican, stood transfixed in horror at the sight.

Placing the highest priority on education, Margaret Myers had determined to instruct her four sons and two daughters in their early years. The local public school, a typically underfunded school for the white villagers and surrounding covites, was not up to the mark. At Bairnwick, other children, chiefly sons and daughters of parents connected with the university, attended too. Their inclusion helped to create a lively environment. The tuition received doubtless assisted in paying for three of the Myerses' four boys to attend Groton. They were supposed to gain a northern experience, a curious parallel to my assignment for immersion in a southern one. After Bairnwick, the Myerses' two girls, Rosamond and Elizabeth, went to St. Catherine's Episcopal School in Richmond, then on to Ole Miss and Bryn Mawr respectively.

Margaret Myers adopted the Calvert School educational system. It had been designed for children of foreign service officers and the like, stationed in remote places without sufficient means to educate the English-speaking young. If a more exciting educational program then existed in this country than the one that Margaret Myers and Helen Buck, her assistant and teacher of French, fashioned with the help of Robert Hillyer's Calvert method, I cannot guess where it was. Looking back, it is clear that without Bairnwick, my parents would have been hard put to know what else to do about me at a time when the storm clouds of war were thickly gathering.

Caught up in schoolwork and the new life, I gradually forgot Seiler School in Harrisburg and got used to the absence of my parents. The curriculum that Hillyer had devised in Baltimore was especially strong in history. The happiest moments in the course of the Calvert regimen were the half hours when my brother Charles's new wife, Mary Shepherd Quintard, read me Greek myths before lunch. The class studied Hillyer's *A Child's History of the World* and Mary Tappan's illustrated books on the ancient Greeks and Romans. Along with Mrs. Buck's French instruction, we had lessons from Mrs. Myers in Latin.

On the first day of classes, the headmistress advanced me to the fourth grade. It must have been hard going at first. I had special trouble with arithmetic. The teacher was retired Bishop Morris's daughter Edith, whose face would flush purple and her knuckles turn white around her clutched pencil at my inability to understand the mysteries of the multiplication tables. Her impatience did little to shore up a feeble mathematical confidence. But Mrs. Myers had no students in third grade, so it had been necessary to promote me, ready or not.

When answering questions in class, I would in ignorance say "Yes" and "No" straight out. I learned the proper lingo the hard way. Having lined themselves up on either side of the school door and armed with switches, the children, yelling in glee, attacked me as I ran the gauntlet.

The stings were not that painful, but the humiliation of a small-scale charivari was. (In later years I would analyze that form of public shaming and punishment in a work on southern ethics.) What had I done to deserve such treatment? They promptly told me. "You must say 'Yes'm' and 'No'm', or 'Yes, Miss Morris.' And you must say 'Yes, sir' and 'No, sir' to men, and to us, it's 'y'all.'" That was fairly easy to master. My Pennsylvania Dutch hard *r*, though, never did soften into the southern style. After being away from the Deep South in later years, I unconsciously lost any regional lilt and reverted to Pennsylvania dialect.

Fellow Bairnwickians Frank Smith, Barbara Ware, and some others had a further prank to play. I had been assigned to write my first term paper, a history of the Trojan War. They told me this requirement, which every pupil had to meet, could be no briefer than twenty pages. Given the limited sources available, I manfully did my best, but I think I fell about ten pages short. Complicating the assignment was the stipulation that the first letter in each paragraph had to be in Old English style—to improve penmanship and, I suppose, reenact the tedium of a medieval scriptorium. With an almost illegible handwriting that drove Mrs. Myers to urge me simply to print, I nonetheless managed the illuminated lettering. It turned out that I had written the longest—and most repetitive and boring—Trojan War account in the annals of the little school. That was appropriate, my classmates agreed. They often called me "V" for vague, a problem of absentmindedness from which burden I have never, unfortunately, found release.

Bairnwick had a rich supply of ritual and activities, beginning each morning with worship in a little, cramped chapel on the top floor of the house. It customarily began with the Bairnwick grace, "Benedictus, benedicat; / Benedictum, benedicamus, / Per Iesum Christum Dominum Nostrum. Amen." The school motto from Romans was also in Latin, as it appears in the epigraph. Loosely, it means "Honor one another above yourselves" (New Revised Standard Version).[3] Every Wednesday afternoon at Bairnwick an elaborate tea took place with special cakes we children relished. It was held for the benefit of college and seminary students and faculty and their guests. These affairs brought the pupils into the presence of such dignitaries as William Alexander Percy, whose romantic classic *Lanterns on the Levee: Recollections of a Planter's Son* was published in 1941; young Walker Percy, his adopted son, medical student, and later novelist; Allen Tate, poet and editor of the literary quarterly

Sewanee Review; his wife, Caroline Gordon, also a prominent future writer; and Father and Mrs. Flye of nearby St. Andrew's School, mentors of the writer James Agee. I remember seeing some of these notables on the campus but do not recall any particular exchange with them. Especially unforgettable were the Flyes. They were brilliant intellectuals, but when they walked to St. Luke's Chapel or St. Augustine's, their black cloaks and hats and small, pinched faces made them resemble a pair of underfed crows.

Some years later, though, when in college at Sewanee, I listened to a memorable conversation at one of the Myerses' weekly teas, a tradition outlasting Bairnwick School itself. Stephen Spender, the English poet and guest of honor, John Palmer, then editor of the *Sewanee Review*, Allen Tate, Monroe Spears, and Robert Penn Warren were discussing how to boost the circulation of the *Review*. The gist of it was to get T. S. Eliot into a controversy with Tate over the merits or harmful influence of John Milton's poetry. Whether the subsequent articles did much for circulation I do not know.

The Bairnwick school year had three climaxes. The first was a New Year's Eve party in the White Room, handsome and well designed for entertaining. After a brief service and just before the stroke of midnight, in her inimitable, New England way, Mrs. Myers would intone Alfred Lord Tennyson's poem with passionate gesture and thrilling emotion: "RRRing out, wild bells, RRRing out the old, RRRring in the new!" Then we would return to the punch bowl and the dancing, the Virginia Reel being a popular number.

The second annual rite was the presentation of a play on the Bairnwick lawn in the spring, an occasion that drew a sizable audience. I was the jester, Trinculo, and my good friend, John Gass Bratton, played opposite as the drunken butler, Stefano, in Shakespeare's *Tempest*. Lucas Myers, two years my senior, had the chief part, Prospero.[4] With flashing dark eyes, fierce expression, and a shock of black hair, he really looked more like the wizardly character than one might have expected of an early teen. Or at least so it seemed to me at the time. How many elementary schools could have mounted such a production? It was fun, but I preferred playing Friar Tuck in *Robin Hood*, with pillows stuffed under my brown monk's habit. On a less ambitious scale, on Christmas Eves, we also performed a mystery play, composed by Margaret Myers's mother, in the spacious but uncompleted St. Augustine's on the campus.

Nervously I processed down the main aisle with the other two costumed potentates and sang in tremulous soprano the verse appropriate for Balthazar's gift: "Myrrh is mine; its bitter perfume/ breathes a life of gathering gloom." Honors, however, went to a little Bairnwickian who was dressed as a long-eared donkey in a stable stall. He brayed quite raucously—"OOObie, OOObie" [Latin *Ubi,* for "where?"].

The third event, which truly outmatched all others, was the annual May Day celebration at Fiery Gizzard. Werner Honig, professor of psychology at the University of Dalhousie, Halifax, and Bairnwick alumnus, recalls his first May Day outing, in 1942, with remarkable precision. Werner was the son of a distinguished professor of jurisprudence at the University of Berlin until in 1933 Hitler had all those of Jewish descent ousted from all universities, even scholars whose ancestors, like the Honigs, had been Christians as far back as the eighteenth century. The Honigs had fled first to Turkey and then to America, where Dr. Honig obtained a teaching position at St. Luke's Seminary. Highly cultivated and musically gifted, the family gave Sewanee a touch of Old World sophistication sorely needed. And so we gathered sleepily in front of Bairnwick at five o'clock on the morning of May 1. Mrs. Myers handed us Books of Common Prayer, ordered picnic baskets to be stowed in the cars, and dispatched couriers to roust the laggards. According to Werner's account, we were uncomfortably stuffed into the least number of automobiles possible. Gas rationing was in full, patriotic force. The procession of five or six vehicles headed for Fiery Gizzard in neighboring Grundy County, twelve miles away. Their car having died early in the war period, George and Margaret Myers used a motorcycle with sidecar, gift of a sympathetic friend. In full academic attire for some college ceremony, Dr. Myers could drive only with stately progress or risk entanglement. The motorcycle never ventured, however, as far as Grundy County. For the May Day outing, the pair piled in with someone lucky enough to have a functioning sedan.

Werner remembers that on the way to the falls his father "wanted to listen to the news of the war from a station in Chattanooga." When the most sensational developments were about to be announced, the frequency disappeared as the road snaked through the mountain passes. "However, the signal was perfect during the ads for laundry soap and breakfast cereal," Werner recollects. Whenever the newscaster returned to his task, the children at once raised their chatter to a pitch that drowned him out. Yet they were seemingly mesmerized into silence during the commercials. Dr. Honig fretted with growing impatience, "but Mother pointed out that he would get an excellent summary" that evening from the sepulchral, "authoritative voice of H. V. Kaltenborn."

After what seemed an endless trek through brambles and past unpainted farm cabins, we lugged the hampers of food and other heavy paraphernalia to the picnic site, hoping to set upon breakfast right away. But, no. Instead, we had to face the stern visage of white-haired, black-browed Dr. Myers, in full regalia of billowing vestments, chanting such verses as "O all ye Green Things upon the earth, bless ye the Lord; praise him and magnify him forever." Werner wondered how "Green Things," beasts, cattle, "and all things that move in the waters" were supposed to manage that exemplary feat. Birds and "the Fowls of the air" could sing and crow his praises, but whales, hills, and wells in the earth? Mrs. Myers, he recalls, then set the pitch for "All Things Bright and Beautiful." She was slightly tone-deaf, so the male voices had to screech into falsetto while the women and girls found the low notes unsingable. "The Lord may have been honored," Werner muses, "but he probably turned down the volume."[5]

I remember that we howled with the unmerciful laughter of children while Werner, thoroughly embarrassed, had to submit to his mother's holding a towel around his middle so that he could get into his bathing suit. The rest of us had worn ours underneath our regular clothing, but Mrs. Honig had not permitted it. She thought it indecent to substitute trunks for underpants. The water spilling over the falls was just short of freezing. The Spartan spirit of the occasion—not inappropriate for a once pagan ritual—required us all to get thoroughly wet. That unpleasant condition accompanied us homeward through our redonned clothing and onto the cars' upholstery. These were the Bairnwick highlights—scarcely typical of southern life, and yet events to be located neither in Harrisburg nor anywhere else in the world.

Warming to the task of making me a true southern gentleman, my grandmother, Mrs. Little, was wholly sympathetic to the Bairnwick curriculum and activities. She was herself a very intellectual woman. She had firm opinions about everything. Yet, steeped in southern traditions of womanhood, she had not combined her Victorianism with a feminist outlook in the manner of Margaret Myers. Born in 1869, Eliza Scott Matthews of Montgomery had been educated at Miss French's school in

Baltimore and in 1890 had married James Hibbler Little of Livingston, Alabama. In his brief life, her husband had been a highly successful municipal solicitor for that raw iron and coal city, Birmingham. Handsome and dashing, he was reported to have commonly worn a black cape, lined with white silk, top hat, and gold-headed walking stick. They had had two daughters, my mother and a toddler who died very early. Then, in 1895, James Little fell fatally ill with what a Birmingham newspaper's obituary column bluntly called paresis—advanced syphilis. The family insists he had died of a rapidly advancing brain tumor, and that account may well be right. The term *paresis*, as then used, had not fully taken on its venereal meaning. But if not, the less convenient possibility might help to explain Grandmother's antipathy toward other women, at least young and attractive ones. Seldom did she blame men who had fallen from grace. They were readily excused for their many failings on the grounds that they were hapless victims of some woman's evil wiles.

Early rendered a widow, Eliza Little was much attracted to my father, then a young, ambitious curate at St. John's Episcopal Church in Montgomery, to which city she and her young daughter had returned from Birmingham. Edgar Gardner Murphy, an Episcopal leader of the Social Gospel movement, had been rector of St. John's. Under his influence, Grandmother and other ladies of the parish had sat in the galleries of the state capitol to glower at the country politicians who were loath to pass child labor laws. On his first day in town, Father and a fellow assistant at the big city church were strolling down the sidewalk, when his companion pushed him quickly into an alleyway. "What's the matter?" asked father. "Why, Mrs. Little is passing in her carriage," his colleague whispered. She would soon have the freshman clergy polishing brass candlesticks or passing out tracts on the street corner for some noble cause or another. Father ended up as a boarder in her house and fell for her beautiful daughter, whom he married after a long courtship when she reached age eighteen.

Father used to say that his mother-in-law was the only person, male or female, he knew who read the philosopher Herbert Spencer for pleasure. He had ample opportunity to observe her. In a fashion familiar to small-town southerners, she lived with and, indeed, *through* her daughter and son-in-law and their four offspring—Wyatt, Charles, Laura Serena, and me. I came along some ten years after Laura. The arrangement offered financial advantages. Grandmother usually bought the automobiles, furnishings, and houses that the family used. Parsons made little money. After Father had served St. Phillip's Church in Asheville, North Carolina, for several years, he received a phone call from one of the Pittsburgh Mellons. The owners of Gulf Oil had attended the church when guests at the Vanderbilt's Biltmore estate nearby, I suppose. In any case, the vestry of Ascension urged him to accept the rectorship. Father, however, was reluctant to leave his beloved Southland for the steel city and wondered if God had called him to so rich and powerful a post. Grandmother, it was said, declared, "I hope the good Lord will decide the matter soon because I have already sold the house." Off they went to Pittsburgh.

Grandmother was both formidable (a quality not so rare in Sewanee women) and eccentric (equally common). She had piercing gray-green eyes and a ramrod posture a grenadier would have envied. "Bertram, don't slouch so, do sit up straight" was a command heeded only temporarily. She held strong convictions about things political and sexual. Over the next five years I was accustomed to her putting down the Chattanooga *Times* and exclaiming, "Oh, Bertram, you must read this splendid column by Walter Lippmann." Seated in full view from the street at the front window, she fanned herself in the stifling heat of late spring and summer, wearing only her corset and slip, with steel curlers in her white hair. Riffling through a magazine, she would bemoan the impending fall of civilization while scanning photographs of scantily clad models advertising women's underwear. The irony escaped her.

On a more positive side, Grandmother's teaching abilities were considerable. She had missed a calling she might have profitably entered, had it been considered acceptable for southern women of her social status to do so. She taught me how to remember historical information. I had to repeat to her paragraph by paragraph the contents of a text, and she guided me in how to decide what was important and what was not, how to make an educated guess about the next exam questions. Not that the lesson was fully mastered, then or later.

After two years at Bairnwick, I had become so used to life in Sewanee that it did not occur to me to fuss about separation from my parents during the school years. But, then, early in 1942, they suddenly arrived to live temporarily with Grandmother and me. Father had had a physical and nervous collapse. He preached with an unusual fervor and specificity, especially if his forceful style were compared with the customary

Anglican hemming-and-hawing. Yet underneath his robes he would be drenched in perspiration as he stepped from the pulpit. He had long had heart trouble—ventricular fibrillation—and there were dangers of another attack like the one experienced in his forties from overwork. The diocesan trustees had given him a half year's sabbatical to recover. Where else to go but Mrs. Little's? I was happy about their arrival, but Father's health was a constant subject of conversation. No one thought it necessary to go over old ground about why I had been sent southward. At the end of six months, Father returned to run the diocese and visit parishes by trains filled with jostling soldiers or, if gas and tire rations allowed, by car. In June 1944, about the time of the Normandy invasion, when I was still in Sewanee he suffered a nearly fatal attack and had to relinquish work altogether. Again, my parents brought themselves to the accommodating house in Sewanee. In 1947 at age seventy-eight Grandmother died peacefully. We were summering at Blue Ridge Summit when the news arrived that her heart had stopped as she slept. By then I had left Sewanee to attend St. James Episcopal School near the Antietam battle site in western Maryland.

To be frank, leaving Sewanee for a more northern environment suited me fine. After grammar school at Bairnwick, I had attended the Sewanee Military Academy as a reluctant day student. Missing out on dormitory life, I could not get the hang of it, disliked military science, and never got over a C+ in that unstimulating subject. Moreover, my shoes never seemed polished enough to suit the drill sergeant. I left Sewanee of the 1940s behind with no regrets at all. Three years later, I eagerly returned, though, for four rewarding collegiate years in which I enjoyed both school and the last years of my father's life. But once again, while the reunion was welcome, Father's medical situation dominated the atmosphere.

No one liked retirement better than Father. Living in the college town had its rewards. He renewed friendships with his old Sewanee and St. Luke's classmates, including George Myers and retired bishops Bland Mitchell of Arkansas and Frank Juhan of Florida, all three men of unusual dignity. Father was accustomed to march down University Avenue with his walking stick in hand and greet old Poss Trigg, who sat waiting for him by the Supply Store. Poss would ask after Father's health and was duly rewarded with the expected tip. They had known each other since Poss had waited on tables when Father was an undergraduate. No doubt, the gratuity was repayment for past extra helpings. Never seen in public without his clericals, Father sometimes even wore old-fashioned gaiters to Sunday services.

"The Bishop," as Mother always called him, faithfully attended the interfraternity and college athletic events. On some midwinter evenings, Father would have to leave the college basketball games when the action grew too exciting for his arhythmia. After I entered the University of the South as a day student in 1949, he taught me pool at the Phi Delta Theta house. All the Sewanee Wyatt-Browns had belonged to that society. Yet Father took special interest in those who could not afford the dues for any fraternity or were otherwise rejected for membership. He harried the university authorities until a clubroom for the small nonfraternity minority was provided. In addition, he insisted that the Panhellenic Athletic Council no longer officially stigmatize them with the label of "Outlaws" but dub them respectably as the "Independents."

Still, Father was loyal to the Phi Delts. He used to challenge the members at pool and beat them regularly. Deep in the game, Father was an almost comical sight—bending over the cue and wearing his clerical vest and a black hat marked by a bishop's rosette on the band. It sheltered his eyes from the glare of the overhead lamp as he stared with the intensity of the half-blind at the ball and signaled that it would fall in the far corner pocket. He died in 1952 during my junior year. I have missed his infectious humor, intellectual intensity, and companionship ever since.

For the Thanksgiving holiday in 1995, my wife, Anne, and I invited my two brothers and sister and their families to visit us in Gainesville, Florida. It was the first such gathering in which all four of our generation of Wyatt-Browns had been assembled in fifty-five years. The previous occasion had taken place in July 1940 when U.S. Army Colonel Alexander Shepherd Quintard gave his daughter in marriage to my brother Charles at Fort Sill, Oklahoma. We all had driven out in Grandmother's 1940 Lincoln Zephyr. The ride in a wedding procession of army caissons was more memorable to me than the ceremony. Some months later Colonel Quintard, aide to General Jonathan Wainwright, endured the Bataan Death March in the Philippines and spent the war in a Japanese prisoner-of-war camp in China.

By 1995 it was time for another get-together, and eighteen members of the family came. In the course of that celebration, my sister, Laura, asked me, "Why have you complained that Mother and Father sent you to Sewanee?" I replied, "I never understood why they did. It made no sense." Laura was surprised that no one had bothered to inform me. But that was perhaps understandable. Children of my generation were seldom told important, adult things. By 1940 Laura herself had reached the age to participate in family confidences, and she was the only sibling at that time living in Harrisburg. To set the background for my parents' decision on that Thanksgiving weekend, she reminded me about the international events so many years before. Great Britain was fighting for its life against Germany. Outraged that Adolf Hitler was threatening Western civilization and Christianity itself, Father had been preaching boldly since the fall of Poland in 1939 that the time for another crusade had arrived. As far as he was concerned, Hitler was the Anti-Christ. It was the moral and divinely inspired duty of the United States, he thundered on every occasion he could find, to come to Britain's aid and enter the war. Clerical pacifists righteously called for his resignation as a warmonger. When he received honorary degrees from the Philadelphia Divinity School and from Dickinson College in Carlisle, young seminarians and clergymen were there to picket and protest.

The views of these Episcopal pacifists were unpleasant reminders of how blind some were to the horrors of the Nazi regime. Father, on the other hand, had long believed that America had cavalierly rejected its obligations by failing to join the League of Nations in the first place. I remember listening with my parents to a shortwave broadcast on the old Philco in the Harrisburg parlor. Mother, who knew German from her days studying opera in Berlin, translated one of Hitler's impassioned speeches, which to me sounded like guttural poison. The peace-loving clerics were no threat, but the Pennsylvania Nazi Bundists were. Father began to receive anonymous, menacing letters and phone calls. At first, he apparently dismissed them. But there seemed to be an escalation as he continued his denunciations of the Jew-hating Nazis. After all, if the brutality of Kristallnacht in 1938 was any indication, Hitler's American supporters might become equally terroristic. Harrisburg was not far from the German-speaking counties to the east of the capital. Whereas most of the Pennsylvania Dutch had no use for dictatorship in any form, a small minority were loud and increasingly aggressive.

To escape the truculent phone calls, Father reached an unusual but unfortunate decision. He would change his patronym, at least enough so that those unfamiliar with Bishop Brown would have difficulty locating him and his family. I vividly recall the day that I and the rest of us went before Judge Fox at the Dauphin County Courthouse in downtown Harrisburg. We could not, however, as someone must have suggested, take Mother's maiden name to hitch to the Brown. She was a Little, and we had no connection with any publishing house. Father and my eldest brother, Wyatt, had to dance a curious step. Both would have become Wyatt Wyatt-Browns, a confusion to be avoided. Instead, they were recast as Hunter Wyatt-Brown (Sr. and Jr.). Father had resurrected his long-unused middle name and made it his Christian name. Son Wyatt obligingly did the same. My case was simpler but perplexing, at least to me. By judicial decree I was no longer Bertram Brown III, for no ostensible reason that I could fathom. (I had been named for Uncle Bertram, Episcopal minister of Tarboro, North Carolina.)[6] I had been rebaptized in the judicial procedure as Bertram Wyatt-Brown. The change suited me very little. A letter to Mother from Sewanee (May 11, 1941) was signed Bertram Wyatt-Brown III, when, of course, there's only one person by that name in all the world. Unregrettably, there never will be more.

Whether this name-changing maneuver did any good with the Nazi cranks, I cannot say, but it has been thereafter a source of vexation for all of us. For instance, I graduated from a U.S. Navy training program in the Korean War period as Brown B. Wyatt. At least three times a year, every other sort of garbling crops up on room reservations, tax forms, airline tickets, or whatever.

The other decision, to send me south, was more successful though less permanent. Father had received notification from the zealots that they knew when and how I went to school down North Front Street to Seiler. If Father did not stop his warmongering against the Führer, they rumbled, his son might be kidnapped and harmed. The Lindbergh case, it should be added, was still the event of the decade. At that Thanksgiving gathering in 1995, sister Laura recalled the night when I had complained about going to bed fifty-five years before. The family had been discussing what to do about my safety. Father had reached the decision that the best plan would be to pack me off, at least for the time being, to Grandmother in Sewanee.

I would guess that the Bundist threat was much more bluff than reality. The FBI was then actively curious about the fanatical doings of Nazi cells. Nevertheless, the times were certainly fraught with peril everywhere. If it had not turned out as well as it did, I could boast of being one of the first American refugees of World War II, exiled to the fastness of Tennessee. I make no such claim, however. The fate of so many other real victims of Nazism was much too tragic for me to belong anywhere near their company. But at least a mystery had been cleared up, thanks to my sister.

Many years later, I gradually learned that a Yankee, properly southernized, may contemplate with a degree of intellectual profit the strange and honorable behavior of that perplexing tribe of Anglo-Saxons who reside below the Potomac. For helping me to bring some insights to bear in two books, I heartily thank Sheldon Meyer of Oxford University Press, along with his indispensable colleague Leona Capeless.

Although later intellectual and editorial influence played their part, the early experience of being an immigrant from another region infused my understanding of the South. It had set me on a course that I did not fully recognize until many years later. Without that sojourn in Sewanee, I could have composed neither *Southern Honor* nor *The House of Percy*.[7] In fact, *Southern Honor* was very consciously derived from the perspective that those years had engendered. The classical references and examples in the work, the use of literary and sometimes biblical sources, the quest to understand the cavalier mentality, the character of honor, as both internal and external to its claimants, and the functions of such public shaming rituals as the gauntlet I had had to run in the first week at Bairnwick were partially derived from those formative years. Perhaps it all started with that overly ambitious history of war and honor on the plains of Troy. Dealing with such emotional fundamentals in my own background did not make the writing of *Southern Honor* a pleasure. Rather, the effort oddly involved an introspection that I only discovered after the heat of composition subsided.

The Percy book also had Sewanee roots. Mary Shepherd Quintard, my brother Charles's wife, had once been pinned by Walker Percy (an SAE from the University of North Carolina). Although they were separated by hundreds of miles, their friendship continued after both were married to other partners.[8] When I asked Walker for a comment on *Southern Honor*, he kindly obliged with a few sentences for the dust jacket. More important, Sewaneeans had long found the Percys a subject of curiosity, especially Walker's "Uncle Will" of Brinkwood, a memorable and much admired eccentric. Exploring the Percys' family history was perhaps a substitute for delving into our own.

An alien in the midst of a strange culture—as I then was in the 1940s—may adopt a new country but never wholly forget the first homeland. The viewpoint that emerges from initiation into two worlds could well permit a degree of detachment that the native resident has less reason and perhaps less inclination to seek. But that objectivity may not be as deep as the historian, usually reticent about influences beyond the studied documents, would care to admit. Despite its outward tranquility, Sewanee had at first held little appeal for that eight-year-old, unaccustomed to dead mules, country solitude, and loneliness away from parents and familiar things. Only in retrospect have I fully come to appreciate its immense impact upon me. At this point, though, I can express enormous gratitude for the richness of the experiences, both intellectual and personal, which that extraordinary place and those gentle people generously and unwittingly provided me.

Notes

FINDING HISTORY IN WOODSIDE, CALIFORNIA

1. For a much more complete examination of the Charley Ross kidnapping and its role in kidnap history, see my *Kidnapped: Child Abduction in America* (New York: Oxford University Press, 1997), 21–56. All quotes about the case are taken from that source.

2. Douglas E. Kyle, ed., *Historic Spots in California*, 4th ed. (Stanford, Calif.: Stanford University Press, 1990), 376–77; Frank Merriam Stanger, *Sawmills in the Redwoods: Logging in the San Francisco Peninsula, 1849–1967* (San Mateo, Calif.: San Mateo County Historical Assn., 1967), 42–43.

3. Kyle, ed., *Historic Spots in California*, 376.

4. See David A. Kaplan, "Silicon Heaven," *Newsweek*, June 14, 1999, 48–51.

BOSTON COMMON

1. Robert Means Lawrence, *Old Park Street and Its Vicinity* (Boston, 1922); Joseph Henry Curtis, *Life of Campestris Ulm, the Oldest Inhabitant of Boston Common* (Boston, 1910). Other works on the Common include Nathaniel Shurtleff, *Topographical and Historical Description of Boston* (Boston, 1871, 1891); Mary Farwell Ayer, *Early Days on Boston Common* (Boston, 1910); Mark De Wolfe Howe, *Boston Common: Scenes from Four Centuries* (1910, enlarged 1921); David McCord, *About Boston: Sight, Sound, Flavor, and Inflection* (Boston, 1973); Walter Muir Whitehill, *Boston: A Topographical History* (Cambridge, 1959; 2d ed. enlarged, 1975). The most valuable primary materials are the reports of the Boston Records Commission, which include many of the town's records.

2. The Common has been much misunderstood in academic historiography. An example is an academic monograph by Professor Joseph Wood, a geographer who believes that New England's town commons are an "invented tradition" that "emerged only in the nineteenth century" as a material result of commercial growth and urban development. Professor Wood's bibliography and notes list none of the major histories and primary sources on Boston Common, and few

primary materials on other towns. He missed the first two centuries of the history of common lands in New England, and the ideas and experiences that led to their creation. In these errors he is not alone. Similar interpretations became an academic orthodoxy in the 1980s and 1990s, when relativist models of "invented traditions" and materialist models of "market revolutions" were much in fashion. When employed with restraint (and research) these ideas have their uses. But as historical interpretations of New England commons they are far off the mark. Cf. Joseph Wood, *The New England Village* (Baltimore, 1997); Eric Hobsbawm and Terence Ranger, eds., *The Invention of Tradition* (Cambridge, 1983).

3. J. Franklin Jameson, ed., *Johnson's Wonder-working Providence, 1628–1651*, (New York, 1910), 46, 64; Thomas C. Amory, "William Blaxton, 1595–1675," *Bostonian Society Publications* 1 (1886): 3–25; John L. Motley, *Morton's Hope* (Boston, 1839); Charles Francis Adams, *Three Episodes in Massachusetts History* (Boston, 1892), 1: 322–38.

4. Deposition of John Odlin et al., 10 June 1684, reproduced in Shurtleff, *Topographical and Historical Description*, 295–97.

5. *Oxford English Dictionary*, s.v. "Common," 5. For many examples of commons in this sense see A.R.H. Butler and R. A. Butlin, eds., *Studies of Field Systems in the British Isles* (Cambridge, 1973), 314, 317, 319, passim. For their deep roots in the east of England see K. C. Newton, *The Manor of Writtle: The Development of a Royal Manor in Essex, c. 1086–c. 1500* (London, 1970), 8–10, 30–31.

6. An example was Berkhamsted in Hertfordshire, where there was much strife and even violence over this question. The manorial lord in Berkhamsted was the Prince of Wales; his tenants included a good many Puritans who came to Massachusetts. That story was repeated in many parts of England during the era of the Puritan Migration. On the importance of the contested question of the commons in the era of New England's Great Migration and the English Civil War see B. Manning, *The English People and the English Revolution* (London, 1976). For the violent struggle at Berkhamsted see Joan Thirsk, ed., *The Agrarian History of England and Wales,* volume 5.1, *Regional Farming Systems* (Cambridge, 1984), 240. For migration from Berkhamsted to Massachusetts see Sumner Chilton Powell, *Puritan Village* (Middletown, 1964).

7. John Winthrop, *The Journal of John Winthrop, 1630–1649*, ed. Richard Dunn (Cambridge, 1996), 138–39.

8. *Boston Town Records* 2:30. For helpful discussion see Darrett Rutman, *Winthrop's Boston: A Portrait of a Puritan Town, 1630–1649* (Chapel Hill, 1965), 68–97, which overstates the decline of community, and John Frederick Martin, *Profits in the Wilderness* (Chapel Hill, 1991), 249–50, an excellent and balanced work.

9. John Winthrop, "A Model of Christian Charity," *Winthrop Papers* 2: 282–95, 294.

10. Paul J. Lindholdt, ed., *John Josselyn, Colonial Traveller: A Critical Edition of Two Voyages to New-England* (Hanover, 1988), 114; this account was first published in London, 1674.

11. Garrett Hardin, "The Tragedy of the Commons," *Science* 162 (1968): 1243–48; idem, *Living within Limits* (New York, 1993).

12. *Boston Town Records* 2: 18, 27, 29; John Cotton, *Exposition on the 13th Chapter of the Revelation* (London, 1656), 72, 77.

13. Further, it decided that nobody had a right to sell his commonage, and "no common marsh or pasture ground" could be alienated by gift or sale or exchange or otherwise without the consent of the "major part of the inhabitants." *Boston Town Records* 2: 18, 88; for discussion see Roy Akagi, *The Town Proprietors of the New England Colonies* (Philadelphia, 1924), 71–72; Shurtleff, *Topographical and Historical Description*, 302–3.

14. John Putnam Demos, *Entertaining Satan; Witchcraft and the Culture of Early New England* (Oxford, 1982) 64, 75, 87–88, 91, 286; also idem, "Proceedings of Excommunication against Mistress Anne Hibbens of Boston" (1640), *Remarkable Providences* (New York, 1972), 222–39.

15. Edwin Powers, *Crime and Punishment in Early Massachusetts, 1620–1692: A Documentary History* (Boston, 1966), 461; the Common was used as a place of execution as early as 1638, when Dorothy Talbye was hanged for murdering her child, named Difficult Talbye.

16. John Winthrop, *Journal*, ed. Richard S. Dunn et al. (Cambridge Mass., 1996), 27 March 1638.

17. Shurtleff, *Topographical and Historical Description*, 338, thought the tradition that she was hanged from an elm on the Common was "extremely doubtful." Others have wondered if it happened somewhere else in Boston. Howe, *Boston Common* (1921 ed.), 12–15, reviews the evidence at length and concludes that the Common was probably the place of execution.

18. Perry Miller, *The New England Mind from Colony to Province* (Cambridge, 1953, 1962), 206.

19. Samuel Sewall, *Diary*, ed. Milton Halsey Thomas, 2 vols. (New York, 1973), 22 June 1716.

20. Sewall, *Diary* 1: 440–41; the Thomas edition reproduces the poem in its original broadside, "Wednesday, January 1, 1701, A little before Break-a-Day."

21. John Murrin, "Anglicizing an American Colony: The Transformation of Provincial Massachusetts" Ph.D. diss., Yale University, 1978.

22. Ayer, *Early Days on Boston Common*, 57.

23. Shurtleff, *Topographical and Historical Description*, 310.

24. Sewall, *Diary* 2: 715, 20 May 1713.

25. Sewall, *Diary* 2: 692 18 June 1712; Ayer, *Early Days on Boston Common*, 6, 10.

26. Massachusetts Historical Society *Proceedings*, ser. 1, vol. 5.

27. William M. Fowler Jr., *The Baron of Beacon Hill: A Biography of John Hancock* (Boston, 1980), 34–35.

28. Ayer, *Early Days on Boston Common*, 14; Sewall, *Diary* 1: 147, 19 August 1687.

29. *Boston Gazette*, 11 February 1788.

30. Harold Kirker and James Kirker, *Bulfinch's Boston, 1787–1817* (New York, 1964), 76–100.

31. Ayer, *Early Days on Boston Common*, 40.

32. The best biographies are Edmund Quincy, *Life of Josiah Quincy of Massachusetts* (Boston, 1868); and Robert A. McCaughey, *Josiah Quincy, 1772–1864: The Last Federalist* (Cambridge, 1974).

33. Shurtleff, *Topographical and Historical Description*, 341.

34. Whitehill, *Boston* (1975 ed.), 98.

35. *Boston Daily Journal*, 30 May 1846.

36. Harris, 5; Ayer, 52–57.

37. Shurtleff, 344

38. Boston Selectmen's Minutes, 38, 120.

39. Shurtleff, *Topographical and Historical Description*, 325.

40. Ibid., 318, 326, 334.

41. Ibid., 320, 324, 326, 332.

42. Nathaniel Shurtleff commented, "The old name, homely perhaps, but sufficiently good, has continued in use until the present day. May it never be recorded in our city annals, that such a folly as that then contemplated has been perpetrated." *Topographical and Historical Description*, 328.

43. *The Public Rights in Boston Common, Being the Report of a Committee of Citizens* (Boston, 1877).

44. Howe, *Boston Common* (1921 ed.), 68; *Boston Globe*, 1 September 1897.

45. Howe, *Boston Common* 1921 ed.), 79.

NASSAU HALL, PRINCETON, NEW JERSEY

1. It was, in fact, the largest stone building, and the largest academic building, in the colonies.

2. The house still stands. Known today as Maclean House, after the mid-nineteenth-century president John Maclean Jr., it contains the offices of the university's Alumni Council.

3. Exhibited at the Columbian Exposition in Chicago in 1893, the orrery

disappeared until it was discovered, still in its packing crate, in the basement of McCosh Hall in 1948. Thanks to the generosity of Bernard Peyton, Class of 1917, the contraption was then fully restored, though with a modern electric motor. The restored orrery is on permanent display in the lobby of Peyton Hall.

4. It is unclear from the surviving records whether five or six students were suspended.

5. The oldest tablet reads "1870," although University records state that ivy was planted at the Gymnasium that year. The first reference to any ivy planting occurs in 1864, though where on campus this took place is unclear. The graduating class of 1865 planted woodbine at Nassau Hall. My thanks to Ann Halliday and John S. Weeren for this information.

6. The 1967 renovations involved flooring over the two-story well in the east wing to provide additional office space, as well as the removal of an unsightly skylight above the east wing. Alexander Leitch, *A Princeton Companion* (Princeton: Princeton University Press, 1978), 331.

SEWANEE—HOW TO MAKE A YANKEE SOUTHERN

1. Lost Cove Cave and Sherwood appear in Walker Percy, *Love in the Ruins* (New York: Farrar Straus Giroux, 1971). The novelist, who knew these places well, has Dr. Thomas More, his hero, identify his home as "Sherwood, Tennessee. It's a village in a cove of the Cumberland Plateau. My farm is called Lost Cove" (221). According to Lucas Myers, Ralph Garner of Garnertown, who died in July 1999, had the reputation for being the last of the great moonshiners, though others claim that he was not really the last. His body was found in a pond near Sherwood, but the lungs held no water, a circumstance which has thrown up questions about his demise. In those parts, most moonshiners have disappeared, but crank production seems to be catching on, and the old traditions, alas, are dying.

2. Lucas Myers, "George and Margaret Myers of Bairnwick," (1992), unpublished paper kindly lent by the author, 3.

3. A colleague, Gareth Schmeling, in classics at the University of Florida, tells me that the English translation used here is actually closer to the Greek original than St. Jerome's Latin version. Literally the Latin means, he says, "anticipating (*praevenientes*) each other (*invicem* is really an adverb meaning 'mutually') with or in or by means of honor." The Roman tongue apparently does poorly with such abstractions as honor, whereas the Greeks had a better grasp of the many textures of that ethical construction.

4. It may be worth mentioning that Lucas Myers, a poet and writer in his own right in later years, was perhaps the English poet laureate Ted Hughes's

best friend. He saw Hughes through the incredible tragedies in his life. See Lucas Myers, Appendix I in Anne Stevenson, *Bitter Fame: A Life of Sylvia Plath* (New York: Houghton Mifflin, 1989), 307–21. For my own limited role in the poetic circle at Cambridge University in the 1950s in which Lucas, Ted, and Sylvia moved, see Bertram Wyatt-Brown, "Reuben Davis, Sylvia Plath, and Emotional Struggle," in Peter Stearns and Jan Lewis, eds., *An Emotional History of the United States* (New York: New York University Press, 1998), 431–59, and idem, "Sylvia Plath, Depression and Suicide: A New Interpretation," in Frederico Pereira, ed., *Eleventh International Conference on Literature and Psychoanalysis* (Lisbon: Instituto Superior de Psicologia Aplicada, 1997), 177–97.

5. Werner Honig, "May Day at Fiery Gizzard," (1995), unpublished paper, kindly lent to John Gass Bratton and passed along to me.

6. Uncle Bertram's saintliness reaches the mythological. The Rev. Bertram Brown was supposed to have visited an old parishioner on the edge of death and politely asked if there was anything he could do. The old man gasped that he longed for a quail dinner before he died. After a few minutes of silent prayer for the dying, Uncle Bertram was startled to see a plump and healthy quail fly through the window of the sickroom and fittingly die at his feet. Uncle Bertram's name honored *his* uncle Bertram Hoole, a depressed, bookish recluse of Eufaula. He survived into the 1880s by selling off his dwindling acres, until the unrepaired house alone was left. Its sale paid for the funeral. Yet he had known more sociable days. His portrait (c. 1850), hanging in our house, bears its origins in a horse-racing gambling debt owed by one or another Ravenel from South Carolina. The Ravenels, however, thought the victory highly suspicious. They gave Bertram Hoole a choice: he could demand the thousand-dollar prize and fight a duel to get it or have his portrait painted. He took the sensible course. One of the later Ravenels told this story to my brother Hunter when they were classmates at Sewanee in the 1930s.

7. Bertram Wyatt-Brown, *Southern Honor: Ethics and Behavior in the Old South* (New York: Oxford University Press, 1982) and *The House of Percy: Honor, Melancholy, and Imagination in a Southern Family* (New York: Oxford University Press, 1994).

8. See esp. Wyatt-Brown, *House of Percy*, 294–95, 305–6.

Contributors

Edward L. Ayers Jr. is the Hugh P. Kelly Professor of History at the University of Virginia. His books include *Vengeance and Justice*, on crime in the nineteenth-century American South; *The Promise of the New South: Life after Reconstruction;* and *The Oxford Book of the American South*, edited with Bradley Mittendorf. He created the Valley of the Shadow project, a Web site studying the Civil War in two communities on either side of the Mason-Dixon line.

Paul F. Boller Jr. is Professor of History Emeritus at Texas Christian University. Among his many books on American history are *Freedom and Fate in American Thought, Presidential Anecdotes, Presidential Campaigns, They Never Said It*, and *Not So!: Popular Myths about America from Columbus to Clinton.*

T. H. Breen is William Wrath Mason Professor of American History at North-western University. His publications include *Tobacco Culture: The Mentality of the Great Tidewater Planters on the Eve of Revolution; Puritans and Adventurers: Change and Persistence in Early America;* and *Imagining the Past: East Hampton Histories*, winner of the Historical Preservation Book Prize.

William H. Chafe is Alice Mary Baldwin Distinguished Professor of History and Dean, Faculty of Arts and Sciences, Duke University. He received the Robert F. Kennedy Book Award for *Civilities and Civil Rights: Greensboro, North Carolina, and the Black Struggle for Freedom* and the Sidney Hillman book award for *Never Stop Running: Allard Lowenstein and the Struggle to Save American Liberalism*. His other titles include *The Unfinished Journey: America since World War II.*

James C. Cobb is B. Phinizy Spalding Distinguished Professor of History at the University of Georgia. His books include *The Most Southern Place on Earth: The Mississippi Delta and the Roots of Regional Identity* and the forthcoming *From New South to No South: The Great Struggle with Southern Identity.*

Robert Dallek is Professor of History at Boston University and Professor Emeritus at UCLA. The author of several books, including *FDR and American Foreign Policy,* and a life of Lyndon B. Johnson in two volumes, *Lone Star Rising* and *Flawed Giant,* he is currently writing a biography of John F. Kennedy.

CONTRIBUTORS

David Brion Davis is Sterling Professor of History at Yale University and Director of Yale's Gilder Lehrman Center for the Study of Slavery, Resistance, and Abolition. Professor Davis has won the Pulitzer Prize, the National Book Award, and the Bancroft Prize, among many other awards. His books include *The Problem of Slavery in Western Culture, The Problem of Slavery in the Age of Revolution*, and *Slavery and Human Progress*. He is now working on a book for general readers on the rise and fall of New World slavery.

Carl N. Degler is Margaret Byrne Professor of American History Emeritus at Stanford University. His books include *Neither Black nor White*, which won the Pulitzer Prize; *At Odds: Women and the Family in America from the Revolution to the Present; Out of Our Past: The Forces that Shaped Modern America;* and *The Other South*.

John Demos is Samuel Knight Professor of History at Yale University. He is the author of *Entertaining Satan*, winner of the Bancroft Prize, and *The Unredeemed Captive: A Family Story from Early America*, which was nominated for the 1994 National Book Award, as well as several volumes of colonial history.

Paula S. Fass is Chancellor's Professor and Professor of History at the University of California at Berkeley and has written on many aspects of American social and cultural history. She is the author of *The Damned and the Beautiful: American Youth in the 1920s, Outside In: Minorities and the Transformation of American Education,* and *Kidnapped: Child Abduction in America* and co-editor of *Childhood in America*.

David Hackett Fischer is Warren Professor of History at Brandeis University. His books include *Albion's Seed: Four British Folkways in America, Paul Revere's Ride, The Great Wave: Price Revolutions and the Rhythms of History*, and *Bound Away: Virginia and the Westward Movement*.

William W. Freehling is co-holder of the Singletary Endowed Chair in the Humanities at the University of Kentucky. His books include *Prelude to Civil War: The Nullification Controversy in South Carolina*, which won both an Allan Nevins and a Bancroft Prize; *The Road to Disunion; The Reintegration of American History;* and the forthcoming *The South vs. the South: How Anti-Confederate Southerners Shaped the Course of the Civil War*.

Louis R. Harlan is Professor Emeritus of History at the University of Maryland, College Park. His publications include a two-volume biography of Booker T. Washington. Vol. I, *The Making of a Black Leader,* won the Bancroft Prize; Vol. II, *The Wizard of Tuskegee,* won the Pulitzer Prize for History and the Bancroft Prize.

Kenneth T. Jackson is the Jacques Barzun Professor of History and the Social Sciences at Columbia University, where he has taught since 1968. His many books include *The Ku Klux Klan in the City, 1915–1930* and *Crabgrass Frontier: The Sub-*

urbanization of the United States. He edited the *Encyclopedia of New York City.* He has won both the Francis Parkman and the Bancroft Prizes.

Robert W. Johannsen is J. G. Randall Distinguished Professor of History at the University of Illinois at Urbana-Champaign. His books include *Stephen A. Douglas, To the Halls of the Montezumas: The Mexican War in the American Imagination,* and *Lincoln, the South, and Slavery: The Political Dimension.*

Michael Kammen is the Newton C. Farr Professor of American History and Culture at Cornell University. He is the author of *People of Paradox: An Inquiry Concerning the Origins of American Civilization,* which received the Pulitzer Prize for History; *A Machine That Would Go of Itself: The Constitution in American Culture,* awarded the Francis Parkman and Henry Adams prizes; *Mystic Chords of Memory: The Transformation of Tradition in American Culture;* and *In the Past Lane: Historical Perspectives on American Culture.*

David M. Kennedy is Donald J. McLachlan Professor of History at Stanford University. He is the author of *Over Here: The First World War and American Society; Birth Control in America: The Career of Margaret Sanger,* which won the Bancroft Prize; and *Freedom from Fear: The American People in Depression and War, 1929– 1945,* which received the Pulitzer Prize.

Alice Kessler-Harris is the author of *Women Have Always Worked: A Historical Overview, Out to Work: A History of Wage-Earning Women in the United States,* and *A Woman's Wage: Historical Meanings and Social Consequences,* among other books. She teaches in the Department of History and the Institute for Research on Women and Gender at Columbia University.

William E. Leuchtenburg is William J. Kenan, Jr. Professor of History at the University of North Carolina, Chapel Hill. His many books include *The Perils of Prosperity; Franklin D. Roosevelt and the New Deal, 1932–1940,* winner of the Bancroft and Francis Parkman Prizes; and *The Supreme Court Reborn.*

James M. McPherson has taught at Princeton since 1962. His many books include *The Struggle for Equality: Abolitionists and the Negro in the Civil War and Reconstruction; Battle Cry of Freedom: The Civil War Era,* which won the Pulitzer Prize in History; and *For Cause and Comrades: Why Men Fought in the Civil War,* winner of the Lincoln Prize.

Merrill D. Peterson is Professor of History Emeritus at the University of Virginia. His books include *The Jefferson Image in the American Mind,* which won the Bancroft Prize; *Lincoln in American Memory; The Great Triumvirate: Webster, Clay, and Calhoun;* and *Thomas Jefferson and the New Nation.*

Kevin Starr is the State Librarian of California and a University Professor at the University of Southern California. Since 1973, his multi-volume history of California, *Americans and the California Dream*, has been appearing from Oxford University Press. He also serves as contributing editor to the *Los Angeles Times*.

Jules Tygiel is Professor of History at San Francisco State University. Editor of *The Jackie Robinson Reader*, he is author *of Baseball's Great Experiment: Jackie Robinson and His Legacy*, winner of the Robert F. Kennedy Book Award; *The Great Los Angeles Swindle: Oil, Stocks and Scandal in the Roaring Twenties; Workingmen in San Francisco, 1880–1901;* and *Past Time: Baseball as History*.

Sean Wilentz is Dayton-Stockton Professor of History and Director of the Program in American Studies at Princeton University. His books include *Chants Democratic: New York City and the Rise of the American Working Class, 1788–1850* and, with Paul E. Johnson, *The Kingdom of Matthias*.

Joel Williamson is Lineberger Professor in the Humanities at the University of North Carolina, Chapel Hill. His books include *William Faulkner and Southern History; The Crucible of Race: Black-White Relations in the American South since Emancipation*, winner of the Parkman Prize and the Robert F. Kennedy Book Award, among others; *New People: Miscegenation and Mulattoes in the United States*, and *After Slavery: The Negro in South Carolina during Reconstruction, 1861–1877*.

The late **C. Vann Woodward** was Sterling Professor of History at Yale University and the author of, among many distinguished and award-winning books, *Origins of the New South; The Burden of Southern History; The Future of the Past;* and *The Strange Career of Jim Crow*, one of the most influential works ever published on the history of race in America. He edited the Pulitzer Prize–winning *Mary Chesnut's Civil War* and served as president of the American Historical Association.

Donald Worster is Hall Distinguished Professor of American History at the University of Kansas. His *Dust Bowl: The Southern Plains in the 1930s* won the Bancroft Prize; his other works include *The Wealth of Nature, Under Western Skies*, and *A River Running West: The Life of John Wesley Powell*.

Bertram Wyatt-Brown is Richard J. Milbauer Professor of History at the University of Florida. He edited *The American People in the Antebellum South*, which won the Ramsdell prize. His publications include *Southern Honor: Ethics and Behavior in the Old South*, which won the Phi Alpha Theta History Book Prize; *Yankee Saints and Southern Sinners;* and *The House of Percy: Honor, Melancholy, and Imagination in a Southern Family*.